EVOLUTION OF THE HIGH PERFORMANCE DATABASE

▬ Prentice Hall Informix Press Series ▬

EVOLUTION OF THE HIGH PERFORMANCE DATABASE
Informix Software, Inc.

OPTIMIZING INFORMIX APPLICATIONS
Robert D. Schneider

ADVANCED INFORMIX-4GL PROGRAMMING
Art Taylor

PROGRAMMING INFORMIX-SQL/4GL: A Step-By-Step Approach
Cathy Kipp

INFORMIX PERFORMANCE TUNING
Elizabeth Suto

INFORMIX DATABASE ADMINISTRATOR'S SURVIVAL GUIDE
Joe Lumbley

INFORMIX-NewEra: A Guide for Application Developers
Art Taylor & Tony Lacy-Thompson

INFORMIX STORED PROCEDURE PROGRAMMING
Michael L. Gonzales

EVOLUTION OF THE HIGH PERFORMANCE DATABASE

Informix Software, Inc.

To join a Prentice Hall PTR Internet
mailing list, point to
http://www.prenhall.com/register

Prentice Hall PTR
Upper Saddle River, New Jersey 07452
http://www.prenhall.com

Library of Congress Cataloging-in-Publication Data

Evolution of the high performance database/Informix Software, Inc.
     p.   cm.
   Includes index.
   ISBN 0-13-594730-8
   1. Database management. 2. Databases. 3. World Wide Web
(Information retrieval system) I. Informix Software, Inc.
QA76.9.D3E943   1997
005.74—dc20

96-27620
CIP

Production Editor: *Kerry Reardon*
Acquisitions Editor: *Mark Taub*
Cover Designer: *Jeannette Jacobs*
Cover Design Director: *Jerry Votta*
Marketing Manager: *Dan Rush*
Manufacturing Manager: *Alexis R. Heydt*
Informix Tech Notes Editor: *Angela Vargas Sanchez*

©1997 Informix Press, Informix Software, Inc.
4100 Bohannon Drive Menlo Park, CA 94025

Published by Prentice Hall PTR
Prentice-Hall, Inc.
A Simon & Schuster Company
Upper Saddle River, New Jersey 07458

The publisher offers discounts on this book when ordered in bulk quantities. For more information contact:
Corporate Sales Department, Prentice Hall PTR, One Lake Street, Upper Saddle River, N.J. 07458.
Phone: 800-382-3419, FAX: 201-236-7141, E-mail: corpsales@prenhall.com

The following are worldwide trademarks of Informix Software, Inc., or its subsidiaries, registered in the United States of America as indicated by ®, and in numerous other countries worldwide: Illustra™, Illustra™ Server; INFORMIX™; INFORMIX-4GL; INFORMIX-ESQL; INFORMIX-NewEra™; INFORMIX-OnLine; INFORMIX-OnLine Dynamic Server; INFORMIX-OnLine Extended Parallel Server; INFORMIX-SQL; INFORMIX-SuperView™; INFORMIX-Universal Server. Other product names mentioned herein are the registered trademarks or trademarks of their respective owners.

Printed in the United States of America

10 9 8 7 6 5 4 3 2 1

ISBN 0-13-594730-8

Prentice-Hall International (UK) Limited, *London*
Prentice-Hall of Australia Pty. Limited, *Sydney*
Prentice-Hall Canada Inc., *Toronto*
Prentice-Hall Hispanoamericana, S.A., *Mexico*
Prentice Hall of India Private Limited, *New Delhi*
Prentice-Hall of Japan, *Tokyo*
Simon & Schuster Asia Pte. Ltd., *Singapore*
Editora Prentice-Hall do Brasil, Ltda., *Rio de Janeiro*

CONTENTS

5   World Wide Web Application Development   53

6   Using the INFORMIX-4GL CGI Interface Kit   59

7   Tools for Internet Development   85

SECTION II THE OBJECT-RELATIONAL DBMS

SECTION III THE DATA WAREHOUSE

SECTION IV THE HIGH PERFORMANCE DATABASE

SECTION V GUI DESIGN IN A DATABASE ENVIRONMENT

27 GUI Design Considerations   387

28 Good Design Concepts for Informix Applications   397

29   Exploring the Functionality of INFORMIX-NewEra   419

30   Comparing and Contrasting User Interaction in INFORMIX-4GL and INFORMIX-NewEra   435

31   An Overview of the VCL   443

32   An Overview of SuperTables

447

Index   451

Preface

This book is a compilation of the best articles from Informix Software, Inc.'s award-winning technical journal *Informix Tech Notes* which is normally available only to Informix support customers. Written by leading information technologists such as Michael Stonebraker and William (Bill) H. Inmon, the articles describe the evolution of Relational Database Management System (RDBMS) and also discuss the new technologies which are rapidly revolutionizing the traditional RDBMS model. This book is intended both for a technical audience of developers and designers, and for general readers who are interested in acquiring an in-depth knowledge of the Information Technology (IT) market.

Section One, The Database Revolution on the World Wide Web (web), provides articles which describe the implications of the web on DBMS development. The articles also explore the complimentary use of DBMS technology and the medium of the web. This section contains the article "Notes from the World Wide Web Frontier" by Netscape co-founder Marc Andreessen. Andreessen discusses the developing Internet infrastructure, and its impact on enterprisewide networks and systems.

Section Two, The Object Relational DBMS (ORDBMS), features Michael Stonebraker's article, "Object Relational DBMS—The Next Wave." Stonebraker examines the unique features of ORDBMS technology which contribute to its increased prominence in the IT industry and its growing acceptance as the new paradigm for the DBMS model.

Section Three, The Data Warehouse, contains articles on data warehouse concepts, applications, and strategies. A distinguished expert on the data warehouse, Bill H. Inmon, focuses on the design and deployment of decision-support systems in the parallel environment.

The following sections feature articles by premier technologists at Informix and Informix Solution Alliance Partners whose technical expertise and methodologies provide competitive and strategic advantages in the fast-paced IT environment.

Section Four, The High-Performance Database, explores issues of performance related to the RBDMS model, including factors such as scaleability, extensibility, mirgration, optimization, and tuning.

Section Five, Graphical User Interface (GUI) Design in a Database Environment, offers articles on GUI criterion, design, usability, requirements, and tools.

While this book is a useful resource for Informix products, it also explores the evolving IT trends and technologies presented by the best and brightest minds of the industry. We hope that you enjoy reading this book.

Angela Vargas Sanchez
Editor, Informix Tech Notes

Section I

The Database Revolution on the World Wide Web

1

NOTES FROM THE WEB FRONTIER

by Marc Andreessen

Introduction

Informix and Netscape signed a premier value-added partner agreement in July 1995 to jointly develop solutions based on the use of the World Wide Web (WWW, or web) technology and relational databases. Such solutions build on the information systems companies already have, allowing for the wholesale retrieval and mining of information.

This article describes the capabilities of the Internet to serve the needs of enterprises, encompassing both internal, enterprisewide requirements and external demands to connect to the world, to customers, suppliers, and the potential market.

This article is based on the keynote address to the Informix Worldwide User Conference, held in July of 1995 in San Jose, California.

The Global Network

A PC that is not connected to a local area network (LAN) is just another piece of metal sitting on a desk. The biggest LAN of all is the Internet in that it's the global interconnection of some 50,000 independent networks—each run by a business or company, or run by a service for its own purpose—whose individual contribution is increased by its connection to all other networks.

The Human Dimension

Many companies are deploying enterprisewide networks and systems which allow employees to draw on the data that is resident throughout the entire corporation, to communicate with branch offices, and to link to the outside world. In many cases, companies become tighter and leaner organizations since this technology provides direct feedback from customers.

The transparent access in linking to the world is a key concept. It is no longer extremely difficult or extremely complex to reach out and access necessary information across the network. Increasingly, it is simple to link to the world, take advantage of the world resources, and also present yourself to the world over the network. John Netherly, formerly of Lotus, calls this an entirely new computing model based on Intranet computing on the one hand, and Internet computing on the other.

Intranet Computing

Intranet computing—rather than data processing—is providing a means to build teams and to share information throughout the company. What is really significant is how Intranet computing can improve the performance and efficiency of a company. Companies are also using networks to enhance customer service and product development.

Internet Computing

Internet computing makes it possible to reach the market and customer base, communicate with suppliers and partners, and to watch what competitors are doing, while crossing boundaries on platforms securely.

The Common Denominator

A standard technology platform is emerging. This platform will provide a foundation on which to build applications, with hardware operating systems and network platforms becoming relatively homogeneous and rapidly converging in functionality. For software developers, it will be easier to span development across different platforms and to present the same application.

A Universal Networking Protocol

The universal way to tie computers together on LANs and WANs, and to inter-connect them to the world is the Internet Protocol Suite. This protocol is being endorsed and proliferated throughout the world by virtually every vendor of computer hardware and software, including Microsoft, Novell, IBM, Apple, among others. Soon, commonality will be available across different environments, whether on private, internal, public or open networks.

The Internet is a universal open network to which anyone can connect. Under the control of no one, it gives the benefit of inter-connection with 50,000 networks. Major consumer online services—such as CompuServe, Prodigy, America Online, Delphi, and others, including the Microsoft Network—are rapidly shifting to the Internet model and technologies. Users and customers rely on the on-line service providers for access to the richness of the Internet. In turn, the on-line service providers improve the content of the Internet by working with their content partners.

Telecommunications companies, such as MCI and Pacific Bell, leaders among long distance carriers, are increasingly adopting the Internet. To date, every other major telecommunications company, including cable companies such as TCI, are rapidly becoming involved in the Internet revolution.

Businesses are increasingly linking into the Internet. In addition, there is a very big stronghold in both education and government to build on top of the WWW. On a lesser scale, this trend is bringing the Internet rapidly into homes. A recent survey suggests that perhaps as many as 11 million people in homes today have Web access. Regardless of whether there is an actual interconnection between these seemingly diverse networks, they are being built on the same standard technologies, the same off-the-shelf hardware and software that everyone else uses.

The Opportunity

Another way to look at the Internet phenomenon is that there are three exponentials or drivers of growth in the industry:

- Moore's Law dictates that the density of transistors on chips, thus the price/performance of computers, doubles every 18 months. The PC is being driven into the commodity range and powers everything else in the computer industry.

- Metcalfe's Law states that connecting any number of "n" machines—computers, phones, etc.—returns an "n" squared performance and value. In other words, the network itself becomes a more valuable resource for everyone on the network. The value of the network grows exponentially.

- Finally, the more widely available the platform is, the more people write applications for it.

The results of these trends are converging. Moore's Law drives the power of the network. Metcalfe's Law drives the value of the network. Lastly, the new emerging software platform makes it possible for people to deploy broadly distributed applications over the Internet.

The growth of the Internet follows the exponential curve predicted by all three growth factors. It is reasonable to assume that this growth will continue, since all three of the drivers also continue. This rate of innovation will ultimately drive the computer industry, and the types of software and hardware and systems deployed in these network environments will change and evolve radically over the next several years.

The result of these trends is new value and usefulness to people and businesses. The Internet software revolution takes all of these trends—the standard networking platform, the mix and leverage of both private and public networks—and generates a need and motivation to create a new class of software for the Internet.

Internet Software and the Hypermedia Model

Internet software concentrates on transparent access to information, making it easy and seamless to traverse information across an entire broad network. The experience of information access is generally user-friendly and flexible.

Hypermedia is a simple concept: any piece of information can be linked to any other piece of information. Where the information resides is not important, what matters is that there is a means to reach it. More importantly, this software handles different protocols, formats, and other associated tasks, enabling people to simply access the information. Hypermedia expands the scope and reach of individuals and enterprises.

Viewed as one immense system, the Internet is scaleable and global, and facilitates the wide distribution of information, minimizing replication and providing immediate access to information. Information on the Internet is generally rich in multimedia content (i.e., formatted to contain dynamic or graphical elements). The Internet can also supply real-time information, material which is periodically updated, or legacy information which can be 20 or even a 100 years old.

One of the reasons that the Internet environment is so rich is its distributed nature. Many companies are integrating the back-end of the WWW with information-handling technologies, such as relational databases, to allow for access of information which resides in other repositories. The addition of Web browsers provides for a common user interface and easy access to information.

Significantly, the Internet has three very important characteristics in today's world—it is secure, open, and cross platform. A key part of the software that Netscape builds, as Internet software, incorporates security. The software can be encrypted, encoded, and authenticated to provide protection against those who shouldn't have access to the software. Open standards and interoperability are extremely important, especially as companies plan systems with a long shelf life. Companies are also interested in access to a wide range of vendors who can provide to plug-and-play components to add value to existing systems.

The Internet plumbing is everywhere—it's on the on-line services, the enterprise network, and the public networks provided by telecasts through cable companies. The fact that it's everywhere means that it is possible to leverage across enterprise users and external users, then tie the two together. It is possible to tie the enterprise network with the outside world, without completely connecting the two.

Completely integrated, top-to-bottom systems do not omit any of the fundamental pieces. Two years ago, such systems would have been found in a proprietary on-line service with its own infrastructure. Companies are finding it increasingly easy to establish a presence on the Internet to do business, interact with customers, or provide services. Vendors provide components, and Web developers provide system integration and customization capability.

The technology designed into Internet software products makes them simple to use and relatively turn-key. Netscape is working with Informix to use INFORMIX-OnLine Dynamic Server, an ideal compliment to Netscape's products.

The Future

Innovation in the Internet is happening. First of all, the underlying infrastructure is improved and enhanced continually. Internet products and technologies continue to evolve quickly, including their uses and applications. From those uses and applications, value is created for businesses and people.

It's becoming even more imperative that everyone is able to network inside and outside of an organization. Therefore, the Internet, driven by this demand for interconnectivity, continues to explode. Also continuing is the integration of public and private networks: private networks run for specific organizational needs, and public networks provide broad connection for many people. It is no longer an issue that an organization be fully connected to the Internet or not; there are many ways to take advantage of broader networks without sacrificing the benefits of a contained environment. Corporate networks are now being personally linked to the outside world because interconnection and communication is important and valuable.

Consumer on-line services are moving to the Internet as fast as possible. A notable example is Microsoft, which will reposition MSN as an Internet-based product—including all the tools, and the software. This repositioning will finally remove the Windows operating system barriers which made it so difficult for users to go on-line in the past.

The new direction in the design of products and technology built on the Internet infrastructure is to provide more functionality and power to users. Internet software vendors aim to guide customers to extension languages such as Sun Microsystems' *Java™*, to enriched media types like Macromedia's Director and *Adobe™ Acrobat™*, to *VRML* for 3D presentation of information—in short, making the customer more capable in the presentation of enriched information.

Server software provides the back-end to build new platform capabilities and an enhanced ability to deal with documents and information. Back-end systems and critical relational databases provide a lot of value and are the necessary components to easily and seamlessly piece together applications to meet specific needs. Performance, scalability, and reliability are key.

Tools which are being created will make it easy for people to create content and build applications to showcase that content. Soon, content that is static and relatively flat will be increasingly live and interactive. Databases will be essential in providing this interactivity.

Conclusion

Making existing systems more powerful is the goal of the Internet revolution. This infrastructure allows for the leveraging of existing systems, that you can build upon the incorporation of new systems. It is no longer necessary to discard the investment in existing systems. Companies can layer applications on top of the Internet and improve access to information almost immediately.

This infrastructure also makes it easy to communicate with customers and establish feedback loops. Constant interaction with customers on a minute-by-minute basis allows companies to learn more, and better leverage knowledge as a result of that level of interaction.

Publishing information, as a role of offering services to the world, will become an increasingly common way for businesses to extend their offerings to new audiences and to new markets. There are opportunities for new business models on the Internet, emerging from the concept of networks, rather than the traditional structures.

About the Author

Marc Andreessen is a vice president of technology and co-founder of Netscape Communications Corporation.

About Netscape Communications Corporation

Netscape™ Communications Corporation is a premier provider of open software for linking people and information over enterprise networks and the Internet. The company offers a full line of Netscape Navigator™ clients, Netscape servers, development tools, and Netscape Internet applications to create a complete platform for next-generation, live on-line applications. Traded on Nasdaq under the symbol "NSCP," Netscape Communications Corporation is based in Mountain View, California.

≡ 2   The Web/Database Revolution

THE WEB/DATABASE REVOLUTION

by Diana Jovin

Introduction

The integration of relational databases with the World Wide Web (Web) technology is a powerful way for organizations to fully leverage the Web as a business environment and as an enterprisewide information system. The Web, as a powerful distribution mechanism, adds value to the vast stores of information already residing in an organization's relational databases. Relational databases serve as a means for collecting and distributing information on high-traffic, interactive Web sites. The convergence of the two technologies serves as a means to lower costs, reach new customers, and explore new business opportunities.

A New Applications Paradigm

The development of content for the Web can be split into two phases. In the first phase, organizations develop media-rich content for the Web that takes advantage of the ability to move from page to page via Hyperlinks. In most cases, this content contains basic marketing information about companies' products and services.

In the second phase, companies explore the business potential of the Web as an interactive environment. Web developers, in an effort to increase the value and traffic of the Web site, implement Web applications—ranging from forms that request customer information to electronic malls in which visitors can select and store items in "electronic shopping carts." Within organizations, MIS managers in search of new ways of distributing information have found the Web to be a compelling alternative to traditional client/server applications.

Both groups face similar challenges. The challenge for Web developers is to manage the vast amounts of information that are collected and distributed through interactive sites. The challenge for MIS managers is to take information stored in relational databases and use the information to develop Web-based applications. It is here that we see the convergence of the World Wide Web with the relational database market, and the emergence of the "Web/database application."

The Web/database revolution is taking place on two fronts. Organizations are deploying internal applications as a way to realize cost savings and improve organizational effectiveness. Companies are also deploying external applications as a way to find new customers, seize new business opportunities, and re-engineer current business practices.

Regardless of whether an organization develops applications for internal or external use, the Web/database application revolutionizes how companies view the role of applications in their enterprisewide information systems. The Web/database applications paradigm is:

■ *Platform independent.* The Web, as an application graphic user interface (GUI), allows companies to seamlessly integrate a heterogeneous platform environment—protecting a company's investment in hardware and software.

■ *Flexible.* The application, because it resides on the server, can be modified as often as necessary. This allows companies to rapidly respond, whether internally or externally, to changing competitive and market environments.

■ *Cost-effective.* Web/database applications, using the Web browser as a common front-end GUI, significantly reduce the cost and time of client-side software installation and the training associated with deploying traditional client/server applications.

Enabling Applications Development

Until now, Web/database connectivity required significant effort, both in development and in maintenance. Web/database applications were written in C++ or Perl code, and required the skills of software engineers familiar with both Web and database technology. Few companies were eager to develop custom solutions for an environment known for rapid change in both content requirements and in the underlying technology.

The emergence of enabling technologies for Web/database applications development is eliminating many of the barriers to implementing Web/database solutions. These technologies speed up the transformation of the Web from a network of static files to a network of interactive applications. Developers require applications tools that are:

- *Intuitive.* Developers are under pressure to bring their applications to market as soon as possible—to take advantage of short-lived market opportunities as well as to protect against the loss of a competitive advantage. Once an application is developed, it must be easy to modify and maintain. Intuitive, easy-to-use tools eliminate the bulk of the effort required to create a custom solution.

  Intuitive tools also extend basic development capability to non-technical personnel in the organization. Tools that lower the barrier to development for people who lack familiarity with SQL and/or HTML give the organization more flexibility in the assignment of development work.

- *Powerful.* Application builders require powerful functionality, giving programmers ease of use without sacrificing functionality.

- *Open.* Companies need an open solution which provides the flexibility to choose the right Web servers, Web authoring tools, platforms, and relational databases.

- *Portable.* Companies also require solutions that can adapt to tomorrow's requirements. Since the Web is a rapidly changing environment, developers prefer to create applications which can migrate to tomorrow's environment.

The Spider Solution

Spider Technologies, Inc. developed its application builder, NetDynamics, around the requirements of customers who use the Web for business purposes. NetDynamics integrates visual development, a high performance application server, and scalable database access into a robust architecture that is optimized for the rapid delivery of commercial grade Web/database applications. NetDynamics provides corporate developers with a fast, automated environment to leverage the power of Java into innovative business applications.

NetDynamics works with any Web server or HTML editor, on Windows NT and major UNIX platforms, and on any database. NetDynamics works with multiple databases, allowing companies to standardize on one technology to create Web/database applications and to easily integrate a heterogeneous computing environment into a common application.

NetDynamics's object-oriented architecture facilitates the support of new technologies for both the Web and databases. NetDynamics easily supports new user interfaces, such as JAVA or PDF, and new innovations in database technology. NetDynamics provides customers with a migration path from the applications developed today to the applications which will be required tomorrow.

Finally, NetDynamics is a secure solution. NetDynamics serves as a bridge between industry standard Web server and database security mechanisms. Using NetDynamics, developers can link database security to the security provided through the Web infrastructure. In addition, NetDynamics provides application-level security that complements existing security mechanisms by offering developers the ability to control navigation flow and user privileges within the application.

NetDynamics Studio

The NetDynamics solution integrates a development tool with an application server for Web/database applications. NetDynamics Studio is the visual environment in which developers create Web applications. NetDynamics Studio incorporates the following elements:

Project Window that displays all application components: data sources, pages, and SQL objects; Wizards that automate application development; Editors for the editing of application objects; Property and Events Sheets which can be associated with each object; Design palette of application objects; and Java event code editor

Within NetDynamics Studio, developers use wizards to automate the process of building the application and to generate server-side Java code directly from the graphical interface. The wizards also generate page templates which make use of reusable objects. The objects include databound and non-databound page display controls, such as text, list, radio buttons, database access objects, and security objects. The tool incorporates a palette which can be used to add HTML elements and databound controls directly to the application.

NetDynamics Studio automatically generates server-side Java and incorporates Java class libraries for database access, input and output objects, and security. NetDynamics developers can use Java to integrate business rules and application logic using pre-built Java events or by integrating custom Java, C++, or other code. Java applications which are compiled by the tool are then deployed on the NetDynamics application server.

Spider Technologies' approach allows developers to rapidly construct prototype applications, and then iteratively refine the applications from within the visual environment. This approach is familiar to most corporate database application developers and has proven successful in client/server application development.

NetDynamics Application Server

The NetDynamics application server delivers the high performance and scalability required for robust Web/database applications. The NetDynamics server(which communicates with the Web server through an optimized interface to NSAPI, ISAPI or CGI(runs over ten times faster than CGI-based applications. The application server caches applications objects, and maintains and reuses persistent connections to the database which virtually eliminates the overhead associated with the CGI start-up process, or the opening and the closing of database connections.

Based on a distributed architecture, the NetDynamics application server is easily scaled across multiple platforms. When distributed over several systems, the NetDynamics applications server's request brokers manage automatic load balancing in order to maximize performance. Application services may also be partitioned(allowing the separation of Java processing and database access.

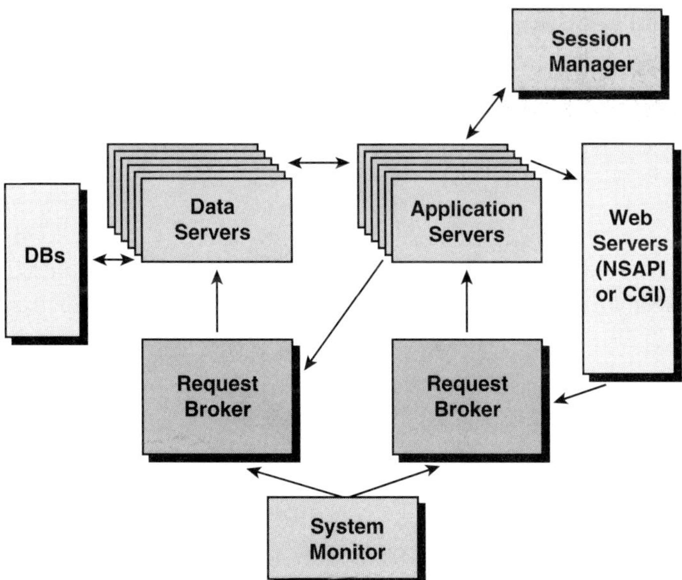

Figure 1: NetDynamics applications server's request brokers manage automatic load balancing in order to maximize performance.

Looking Forward

The Web, although rapidly becoming a powerful business environment, is still a developing technology with some limitations. Developers recognize that there are some limitations in HTML as a user interface, and that CGI scripts or code written for the Common Gateway Interface (CGI) are limited in their capability to support complex transaction processing or scaleability. Spider's twofold vision is to:

- Enhance functionality while maintaining an easy-to-use, intuitive interface for applications development; and

- Deliver high-performance and scalable solutions.

About the Author

Diana Jovin is a marketing manager at Spider Technologies, and can be reached via e-mail at diana@w3spider.com, or by phone at 415 944 7403.

About Spider Technologies, Inc.

Spider Technologies, Inc., based in Palo Alto, California, is dedicated to providing leading-edge Web/database applications software and solutions. The first company to bring visual development to the Web/database applications market, Spider has forged partnerships with Informix Software, Silicon Graphics, *Sun*™ *Microsystems*™, *Hewlett Packard*®, and Netscape.

Spider Technologies, Inc. is located at 1054 Elwell Court, Palo Alto, California, 94303 (phone: 415 944 7400; e-mail: info@w3spider.com; and URL: http://www.w3spider.com).

= 3

THE WORLD WIDE WEB: THE INTERNET UNLEASHED

by William H. Grant

Introduction

No innovation in recent history has been so well received and widely implemented as the World Wide Web (Web). A framework of previous and new innovations, the Web is quickly redefining the way business, research, and communications are conducted. On a par with the telephone, radio, and television, the Web is a communications evolution of revolutionary proportions.

For a number of years, the Internet has enhanced global educational and scientific interests through the use of *e-mail, usenet news, ftp, telnet, WAIS,* and virtual libraries complete with search engines. Use of these facilities was left to the technically elite. However, with the introduction of the Web, the Internet has become a global communication system.

With the explosive growth of Web sites on the Internet, there is a growing number of on-line newspapers and magazines. They allow users to manage checking and credit card accounts; preview and buy products; perform self-directed study; instantaneously research virtual libraries and archives; and communicate with business associates, peers, relatives, and friends. In the future, the Web will allow even greater flexibility with the "virtual desktop."

Of even more importance, the Web is transforming how organizations conduct business. Information is more free-flowing and efficient, allowing faster and better responses to customer and employee needs. External Web uses include customer support, advertising, electronic shopping, and on-line publishing. As the security issues of electronic commerce improve, demands on Web functionality and infrastructure will increase dramatically.

There are many things which can be done today to improve communications and market positions using the Internet and the World Wide Web. This article describes how this evolution happened, how it works, and how to use its benefits.

Largest Client/Server System Ever Devised

The Internet is the largest cooperative client/server system ever devised. Users are able to communicate on a virtually real-time basis with other users anywhere on the globe.

Statistically, the Internet is growing at a rate of over 100 percent per year based on the number of hosts connected to the Internet. According to Mark Lotter's Domain Survey, which counts the number of registered Internet addresses, there were 6.6 million hosts in July of 1995 as compared to 3.2 million just a year before, with more than half in the United States. The Internet Society projects that there will be an estimated 120-million hosts worldwide by the turn of the century.

In the U.S., there are approximately 4.5 million hosts, up from 2.1 million hosts a year earlier. Of these, there are 70,000 private networks. There are 76,000 businesses on the Internet, growing at a rate of just under 300 percent per year.

According to Nicholas Negroponte, director of the Massachusetts Institute of Technology Media Lab, if the Internet is growing at a geometric rate, the Web is growing at an exponential rate. The number of Web sites doubles every 55 days.

It is nearly impossible to determine how many actual users are on the Internet. Estimates range from three to ten users per host. According to a recent survey completed by *CommerceNet*™ and the A.C. Nielson Co., there are 37 million Americans (17 percent of the nation's population) with access to the Internet. An estimated two-million users worldwide are added every month. A conservative estimate places 200-million users on the Internet by the end of the century.

E-mail is the primary use of the Internet. It is the equivalent of postal mail with the exception that it is much faster and cheaper. This year, 95-billion e-mail messages will be sent in the U.S. alone, exceeding the total mail sent by the U.S. Postal Service by ten-billion pieces. Approximately 10 percent of these messages are sent by households.

Usenet is the second most popular application of the Internet. Usenet is a worldwide, distributed conferencing and discussion conduit that allows the exchange of information using universally recognized headings called newsgroups. It consists of a collection of thousands of computers that work cooperatively to post and distribute articles. Currently, there are over ten-thousand external newsgroups. Many organizations also utilize newsgroups to facilitate internal communications.

Internet tools, such as *telnet, ftp, gopher* and its permutations, *archie, veronica* and *jughead,* are standard tools that allow technically oriented users to perform work on the Internet. The cryptic character user interface and the influence of the hard-to-use *UNIX*[®] operating systems has prevented these tools from gaining wide acceptance in the business and home consumer markets.

Internet Relay Chat (IRC) is a multi-user chat system, where people convene on "channels" to talk in groups, or privately. Originally written by Jarkko Oikarinen in 1988, it is constantly evolving as a global, interactive communication system for the exchange of news and ideas. It gained international fame during the Persian Gulf War in 1991 when updates were posted in real-time.

On the other hand, Web browers are designed to be open in nature, supporting these tools with a much friendlier graphical user interface. Also, browsers are available in almost all popular platforms, often at little or no cost, contributing to their wide acceptance. Add to this the "fun" elements of the Web —the ability to handle any type of data including graphics, sound and video— and suddenly the Internet becomes useful to everyone.

A Historical Perspective

Although the misconception persists that the Internet and the Web are new, the Internet has existed officially for 26 years. The Web, on the other hand, has been available for over two years, and constantly changes the way we conduct our daily lives. Like a toddler learning to crawl and master its environment, the Web continues to grow and mature at an alarming rate. A large part of this growth is due to the number of very talented people from all walks of life who explore and chart this new medium.

To fully comprehend this phenomenon, it is important to understand that the Web is not a single technology hatched in a vacuum, but rather a continuation of an evolution.

Definition of Internet

The word "Internet" is an abstract phrase that literally means "network of networks." It describes the massive collection of computers throughout the world which are connected by linking together the smaller regional networks that are scattered throughout the world. The composition of the Internet is changing over time. First employed for military purposes, it grew into a seamless, global network of federal, regional, campus, private, and foreign networks. Today, the

Internet is a global backbone for the transfer of digital information. It is now an entirely new form of common carrier.

Birth of the Internet

Thirty years ago, the U.S. Department of Defense created a decentralized computer network, a hub without a single "point of failure" in case of nuclear attack. This experiment was administered by the Defense Advanced Research Projects Agency (DARPA) and became known as the "ARPANet." Early versions of what are now known as "routers" were installed in 1969. A router is a device that forwards traffic between networks.

This experiment is generally considered the birth of the Internet, and makes it already 26 years old. Ironically, this Cold War experiment became the foundation of what is considered by many to be a communication medium as important as the telephone, radio, and television.

TCP/IP—Reliable Transmission

The next four years saw the introduction of lower-level protocols, Transmission Control Protocol (TCP) and Internet Protocol (IP), which are still in use today. TCP adds reliable communication, flow control, multiplexing, and connection-oriented communication. It essentially provides full-duplex process-to-process connections. Today, the TCP protocol is built on top of IP, and both work in concert as a single protocol. IP is a network layer that provides a connectionless, best-effort packet-switching protocol for packet routing, fragmentation, and the re-assembly of data streams.

Ethernet—A New Architecture

Dr. Robert M. Metcalfe, working for the Xerox Palo Alto Research Center (PARC), first proposed a type of network cabling and signaling specifications called Ethernet in 1976. The specifications were based on the Open Systems Interconnect (OSI) reference model which is the International Standards Organization (ISO) structure for the "ideal" network architecture.

Information passes between clients and servers in packets with the highest reliability. Data is broken into packets, transmitted over a coaxial network, and re-assembled on the other side.

Domain Name System—Virtual Addressing

ARPANet split into ARPANet and MILNET in 1983. Desktop workstations came into being, most of which utilized the University of California at Berkeley

UNIX™ and TCP/IP versions. TCP/IP became the official standard for ARPANet and, by default, the international standard. The Internet began experiencing rapid growth.

The Domain Name System (DNS) provides for the translation between hostnames and addresses. Within the Internet, this means translating a name, such as "www.informix.com," to an IP address such as "192.216.240.4." The DNS is, then, simply a set of protocols and databases.

DNS also provides for registering DNS-style names for other hosts reachable (via e-mail) through gateways or mail relays. The records for such name registrations point to an Internet host (one with an IP address) that acts as a mail forwarder for the registered host. This allows e-mail users a transparent, uniform mail addressing scheme.

In 1986, the U.S. National Science Foundation (NSF) initiated the development of the NSFNET to interconnect high-speed computers. This experiment became the first high-speed backbone for the Internet, providing the model for regional service providers throughout the world.

Hypertext Vision

In spite of its role as an integral and fundamental part of the Web, the idea of Hypertext actually originated in 1945 by an engineer named Vannevar Bush. He proposed a sort of database machine called a "memix" which would allow users to follow "trails" of information. In 1981, computing visionary Ted Nelson coined the term "Hypertext" in a book called *Literary Machines*. He described a system called "Xanadu" which allowed the user to create a Hypertext that consisted of linked nodes. The first practical application for this was the HyperCard for the Macintosh in 1987. It linked textual material and multimedia, and became known as "hypermedia."

Birth of the World Wide Web

Tim Berners-Lee, probably the person most responsible for the commercialization of the Internet, is considered the father of the World Wide Web. He joined CERN in 1989 and developed his vision of how the world of physics could be dramatically improved with Hypertext tools. In 1990, collaborating with Robert Cailliau, he published his first paper, "World Wide Web: Proposal for a Hypertext Project", which included proposals for its languages, consisting of URL, HTML, and HTTP. In the proposal, Berners-Lee and Cailliau stated, "Hypertext is a way to link and access information of various kinds as a Web of nodes in which the user can browse at will. Potentially, Hypertext provides a single user interface to many large classes of stored information, such as reports, notes, databases, computer documentation, and on-line systems help. The texts are linked together in a way that one can go from one concept to another to find the information one wants. The network of links is called a 'Web.'"

By 1992, the first Web server was released on the Internet. Shortly thereafter, he released a line-oriented browser capable of making use of Web server technology. Today, Tim is the director of the W3 Consortium, affiliated with MIT's Laboratory for Computer Science. He has devoted his life to the Web, and concentrates today on making the Web interactive and secure for electronic commerce, while simplifying access to Web resources.

Web Browsers—Friendly Windows to the World

Since the introduction of the Web browser, the Web has grown at a phenomenal rate. Today, the Web browser is the most extensively used client/server application ever invented.

As word spread around the world about a working Hypertext model, several versions of line-oriented browsers were devised and became available. The most popular one, Lynx, is still in use today where networks are too slow to display images.

In February 1993, Mark Andreessen, a student at the University of Illinois at Urbana-Champaign, introduced the alpha version of a Web browser called "Mosaic for X." A research prototype for the National Center for Supercomputing Applications (NCSA), *Mosaic*™ was the first GUI-based Web browser and provides a seamless browser interface obscuring the Internet's complexity. A number of browsers, including those from *Spyglass*™ and *Microsoft*®, are based on this prototype.

Mark later joined forces with James Clark, former Chairman of *Silicon Graphics*™, and founded Netscape Communications Corporation. The Netscape Navigator now accounts for 73 percent of the browser market. The company also markets a variety of Web servers and is a partner of Informix Software.

Definition of the World Wide Web

For the past half-century people have dreamed of the possibility of a universal communication and database system—accessible to everyone in the world. This system would allow users to easily link together pieces of disparate information logically—electronically putting together parts of a large jigsaw puzzle in order to see the whole picture. With the birth of the Internet and the Web, this dream is now a reality.

According to the proposal by Tim Berners-Lee in 1990, the World Wide Web is defined as a "wide-area hypermedia information-retrieval initiative aiming to give universal access to a large universe of documents." Berners-Lee commented, "Hypertext is a way to link and access information of various types as a Web of nodes in which the user can browse at will." His solution was to build a server capable of openly supporting a number of protocols and Internet tools.

Purpose

The Web's initial goal is to provide a single, uniform means of accessing hypermedia documents from anywhere on the Internet using client/server protocols. The development of graphical user interface (GUI) based client browsers, such as Netscape's Navigator or NCSA's Mosaic, provide a seamless browser interface that hides most of the complexity of the Internet.

Protocols

The Web primarily consists of three standards: Uniform Resource Locator (URL), Hypertext Transfer Protocol (HTTP), and Hypertext Markup Language (HTML). These standards are used by all Web browsers and servers to provide a simple mechanism for locating, retrieving, and displaying information. Web browsers also understand other common Internet protocols including ftp, gopher, and telnet. However, HTTP serves as the primary communication medium between client and server.

Uniform Resource Locators (URLs)

A URL is a simple addressing scheme that uniquely identifies a document or file regardless of the protocol. URLs can also identify newsgroups, Gopher menus, and e-mail addresses. There are three elements of a URL: the protocol to be used, the server and port to which it connects, and the file path.

The "protocol://server-name[:port]/path" format is typical. The protocol must be in lowercase. The server name is case insensitive. If no port is designated, port 80 is assumed. A URL may also include other specific information, including arguments to be passed to an application or shell scripts. Special, or "meta," characters, are represented by a percent (%) sign followed by the character's hexadecimal equivalent. A Web browser breaks down each URL link request into its constituent components and uses the protocol section to determine how to proceed.

Since it is an "open" standard, a URL can use any number of protocols. Over time, the number of protocols is likely to increase.

file

The file command is designed to return a text document from the local file system. If the URL includes a hostname, the ftp protocol is substituted.

HTTP

Hypertext Transfer Protocol (HTTP) is a very simple language that facilitates the transfer of files between Internet sites. HTTP requires a client (browser) and an HTTP server. HTTP is the most important protocol of Web.

HTTPS

The https is a special version of an HTTP server which has built-in security features. Unlike its counterpart, the HTTPS server has a default port of 443, and provides additional ports for security and administrative functions.

news

Several Web browsers now incorporate the ability to view and manage usenet news.

mailto

Electronic mail has long been a staple of the Internet. Web browsers usually have a protocol called "mailto" to send messages to another user. New Web browsers now incorporate a "mail" protocol with extensive mail services to manage e-mail.

telnet

Telnet is a protocol that allows a user to *login* from one Internet site to another and performs work on that host. Web browsers will usually open another window for the telnet session.

ftp

File transfer protocol (FTP) is a standard method for sending and receiving files between two Internet sites. There are two methods to *login* to a remote site. A user may *login* as himself/herself if he/she is known on that host. The other method is to perform an anonymous *login* to a remote site. Sites that allow an anonymous *login* run special services to accommodate this and are known as "anonymous ftp servers." Web servers (http) are also capable of easily returning files to the user, although not as efficiently.

gopher

Gopher is a widely used client/server application. Data is either a menu, a document, an index, or a telnet connection. As the name implies, the user is able to burrow into the Internet and pop up at another server to list and retrieve documents. It is quickly being replaced by the Web as the preferred medium to retrieve files of all types.

wais

A commercial software package, Wide Area Information Servers (WAIS) is a client/server application that indexes numerous documents and returns the results of queries to the user. Everything is an index and everything that is returned from the index is a document. WAIS introduced the concept of "scoring," which ranks document Hyperlinks according to the relevance of the request.

Hypertext Transfer Protocol

HTTP is the primary and most important protocol to distribute information on the Web. It is highly flexible and defines simple transactions between the client, the Web browser, and the HTTP server. The main goal of HTTP is to provide a simple algorithm to enable fast response times. To achieve this, HTTP was defined as a "stateless" protocol, one that does not retain any information about a connection after a request is complete. States may be maintained, however, apart from the server through Common Gateway Interface (CGI) programs or databases.

With the addition of in-line images, HTTP server performance suffers due to the increased number of separate and individual connections established to return the images. Newer Web browsers maintain an open connection until the entire transaction is complete. Netscape, revision 1.1, added multithreaded connections and cached in-line images to improve performance.

Hypertext Markup Language

HTML is derived from the Standard Generalized Markup Language (SGML) and is considered the final major innovation associated with the Web. Unlike typical programming languages, markup languages define areas of textual information by tagging them with a specific format. Tags are defined functionally rather than visually. Each Web browser interprets the tags according to their configuration settings, supported fonts, and windowing environment.

HTML also provides the ability to create Hypertext links between documents and parts of documents using the URL. Links provide relationships between documents. A user can follow links from one topic to another regardless of their locations on the Web. Link threads are the foundation of the organizational structure of the Web.

There are several levels of support for HTML. Current releases include versions 0.9 and greater. HTML is backward compatible. If the Web browser does not understand the newer extensions, it ignores them. Netscape Navigator, version 2.0, supports the highest level of HTML extensions.

Client/Server Communications

Each transaction consists of four parts:

1.   The client establishes a connection with the server;
2.   The client issues an HTTP request to the server;
3.   The server sends a response (i.e., a page or a file) and a status code; and
4.   Either the client or server disconnects.

Each request consists basically of a URL and a Request-Method. Each Request-Method communicates a different class of messages to the server. This allows servers to be small, simple programs. Based upon the URL and Request-Method, the server may return a document or execute a CGI program. When executing a program, the server spawns a new process, sets a number of external variables, and passes the standard arguments and standard input, and calls the requested script. Information is returned to the standard output.

The Request-Method is sent as an environmental variable called REQUEST_METHOD. There are five REQUEST_METHOD arguments used by the server to determine how to process a request. In reality, only three are currently in use. The other two methods, PUT and DELETE, are generally considered unsafe for public use and, by default, are turned off in the configuration file.

HEAD

This command returns information about a particular document rather than the document itself. It is used primarily by browsers that use caching to retrieve the Last-Modified-Date. If the date is newer than the document in the cache, the newer document is returned.

GET

The GET method is used to return a specific document or run a simple program, and is the most widely used method. It is capable of accepting a simple command line argument. The HTTP server automatically populates the QUERY_STRING environmental variable and also sends arguments to the standard arguments. The simplest form method, ISINDEX, uses GET. The argument is restricted to about 200 characters before overflowing the buffer.

POST

The POST method is used to transfer data from the client to the server. The server transmits the arguments as a single, continuous string to the standard input stream. It uses an ampersand (&) and the end-of-line marker as argument dividers. It replaces spaces with a plus sign (+) and separates the field name and argument with an equal sign. Finally, special characters are preceded with a percent (%) key and are then converted to hexadecimal.

The standard input can consist of one to many arguments. A large form can contain as many arguments. Each argument consists of a field name, an equal sign, and a field value. Meta characters are received in hexadecimal form and converted to ASCII. A custom set of routines is required to read from the standard input and parse it into usable arguments. Each argument is then allocated room on the memory heap as a linked list.

MIME Types

File types are defined by their extension, which defines their MIME type. MIME is an acronym for "Multipurpose Internet Mail Extensions." It is the standard for sending multi-part, multimedia, and binary data using the worldwide Internet e-mail system.

Web servers can return any type of file. The file type is important since it allows the Web browser to correctly display the file. Web browsers and servers natively recognize over eighty kinds of files. Based on the file type, Web browsers either display the information, ask the user to configure a viewer, or prompt the user to save the file on the local host.

Both the Web server and browser can be trained to understand virtually any kind of file, whether textual in nature, multimedia, or one of many kinds of files associated with proprietary applications.

Typical uses of MIME include the sending of images, audio, word processing documents, programs, or even plain text files so that the mail system does not modify any part of the file. MIME also allows for labeling message parts so that a recipient, or mail program, can determine what to do with them.

When a file is retrieved from a Web server, the server looks at the file extension and compares it with a list of known file types. If found, it returns its MIME type and then the file. If unknown, the server sends a MIME type of "Web/unknown" and then the file. The browser uses the MIME type to correctly display information to the browser or to launch an appropriate application.

Common Gateway Interface (CGI)

When pointing to a file in the "cgi-bin" directory, every file in the directory is recognized by the Web server as an executable. Information is passed to the program through a combination of standard input, standard arguments, and environmental variables. Information is returned to the Web server from the program via the standard output. Virtually any form of work can be performed by these executables as long as they follow the Common Gateway Interface (CGI) protocol.

Gateway programs, or scripts, are external executable programs which can be run by the HTTP server. They are external to the server to offer maximum flexibility in providing information to the user. Gateways conforming to the specification can be written in any language that produces an executable file. Some of the languages include the C shell, bourne shell (sh), korn shell (ksh), PERL, C/C++, TCL, and most 4GL or object-oriented languages.

Interface kits for INFORMIX-4GL and INFORMIX-ESQL/C are available on the World Wide Web at http://www.informix.com. The user must include these libraries with any INFORMIX-4GL or INFORMIX-ESQL/C programs that are to be used for Web documents.

Advanced Parameter Passing

Every program should check to determine the proper method for processing. This is accomplished by checking the environmental variable REQUEST_METHOD. It should return either GET, HEAD, or POST, depending upon the method used to access the program.

For GET programs, earlier HTTP servers used the first command line argument (argv[1]) to present the path information, and the second argument (argv[2]) to return the query string. This information is found in the environmental variables PATH_INFO and QUERY_STRING, respectively. For non-form GET requests, the query string is decoded and placed on the command line.

For POST programs, the first argument (argv[1]) is used to contain the content length. This information has been moved to the environment variable CONTENT_LENGTH. The query string is not automatically populated. It can be populated by using the cgiutils program provided with the HTTP server, but security may be compromised by using shell-scripting languages. It is generally safer and more efficient to parse the information from the standard input.

Potentials for INFORMIX-OnLine Dynamic Server and the Web

The Web is used in many ways, either to enhance internal or external company communications, or customer interactions. The uses of the Web are only limited by the user's imagination.

Many of the current applications on the Web are adequately served by flat-file information systems. As the sophistication and complexity of Web applications increase, access to relational databases will be essential. Any transactional systems, such as order processing, or complex search engines, will need the power and flexibility provided by RDBMS connectivity. Tracking orders, customer account information, product specifications, and many other forms of data will be immediately accessible to those who need the information.

Browsers like Netscape's Navigator or Mosaic's NCSA can be considered as other front ends to the database. All of the advantages of RDBMS over flat files—increased speed of inquiries, flexibility of queries, ability to store many terabytes of data, inclusion of complex data types, etc.—will be available to users from the Web site. All information which is provided to employees and customers is available from one source, without having to change the structure or format of the existing database.

A Web site is actually a collection of flat files. An indexing scheme may also be incorporated to help locate key information. Any active Web site must be carefully managed, and this task consumes considerable resources. Most commercial Web sites are relatively large and, in spite of the best efforts, are difficult to manage and navigate.

The Informix Web site, "http://www.informix.com/," although relatively small, contains over 8,000 static pages and images. The internal Web site holds as many pages, as well as numerous programs and multimedia for worldwide dissemination.

INFORMIX-OnLine Dynamic Server has the unique ability to efficiently manage textual and binary information through its BLOB data types. With the use of the INFORMIX-4GL CGI interface kits, a Web site administrator is provided an easy way to manage and distribute Web pages and graphics, images, sounds and movies, and reports from Informix databases. The use of the kits can be extended to develop an interface for data warehousing. Backing up a Web site is as easy as backing up a database server.

Challenges of Connecting Databases to the Web

Security

The benefits of connecting databases to the Web are extraordinary. There are issues, however, which must be addressed before launching a Web/database project. The strength of the Web project is also its greatest weakness. To promote transfer speed, data integrity checking is minimal; packet switching is used to move data, making it difficult to provide for secure transactions; and data transfer is asynchronous, making it difficult for the client and server to keep track of each other's state.

A trade-off was made between reliability and security, as well as speed and near-universal, no-hassle access. The architecture and application programming interface (API) of modern databases are diametrically opposed to the methods used on the Internet. Access is relatively unrestricted, error checking non-existent, the server is unaware of the client (secure servers excepted), and the client knows the server only through numerous unguarded anonymous connections.

A great number of advances have been made to ensure secure transactions. Although unlikely, it is possible to intercept credit card and other secret information through numerous devious means. To this end, the major credit card companies have been very active in developing solutions that may be used in an "open" atmosphere. Netscape has been instrumental in creating "secure" servers, but with today's computing power, it is possible to break security algorithms in a short period of time. Such shortcomings of security may be addressed by products in the near future.

Stateless Transactions

The Web is stateless and asynchronous: the server and client are unaware of each other regardless of the state of either. This is a complex challenge, as today's database technology makes extensive use of the state of both client and server. For instance, clients are "smart" in that they qualify and test information which is fed to them. In some cases, a lookup of table data provides additional information to the user. With Web technology, these familiar elements of the transactional model disappear, and the developer is left to address any deficiencies.

Given the state of current tools, the Web is not an end-all solution to information systems. It will not replace the efficiency of proprietary applications. Online transaction processing can not be efficiently handled with Web tools. However, given careful planning, the Web can enhance the dissemination of timely data to users in a relatively efficient and friendly way.

The type of transaction is also very important in determining whether it is a good candidate for the Web. When selling products or services where availability is not a problem, it is a good candidate. For instance, if too many copies of a book or software package are sold, more can be ordered. The customer may not be concerned about a short delay.

On the other hand, sales of inelastic demand items may create major headaches if, for instance, a hotel room is double-booked. Each time a reservation is taken, it needs to be immediately reserved. A user can make changes to a reservation during a booking cycle. Since the Web does not offer the ability to maintain a persistent connection and thereby allow the locking of records in progress, it is possible that a room may not be reserved correctly.

Performance Problems with Queries

Users are generally aware that some reports take a considerable length of time to prepare and execute. In these cases, the process usually runs as a background task, and the user is notified at completion time. Users on the Web, however, will hardly wait for the results of the report. Users will suspect that there is something wrong, and break the connection. Unfortunately, this may also leave zombie processes on the server, and leaves the user and administrator disheartened. Another problem is that the user may request a considerable number of records to be returned, consuming additional resources both at the client and server.

Few Web servers use enhanced multithreading and no Web server uses shared memory to improve performance. Nor do they allow persistent connections to a database. Although there are no fool-proof workarounds, careful planning on the part of project developers yields dramatic results. Be sure to plan the types of queries available to the user, and plan the database access in such a way as to provide near-instantaneous results. Also, be sure to limit the quantity of results which are available to the user.

Reasons for Connecting Databases to the Web

External Web Sites

An external Web site is an excellent way to communicate a company's story to an educated public. It is unique in that it can be updated constantly to present the most current information to investors, customers, vendors and employees, both present and potential. It is a very important extension of marketing efforts. Customer Services personnel greatly appreciate the efficiency of publicly available upgrade information and files, and this can dramatically reduce costs and improve communications and performance.

INFORMIX-OnLine Dynamic Server databases can vastly improve navigation, management, and performance by allowing administrators to create a Web site in a database. Combining queried, variable content with template information allows a Web site to become a free-flowing, friendly source of information.

Internal Web Sites

Most of the discussion in journals, magazines, and newspapers deals with the external or public uses of the Web. However, the best results can be achieved by using an internal Web server, or intranet. Besides providing a friendlier window into the vast information stores of the Internet, the tools of the Web can radically change a corporation's internal information systems.

Many businesses are beginning to experiment with internal Web sites as an easy way to publish information once for use by thousands of employees. It is a powerful communication tool that crosses disparate geographic boundaries. The Web can move corporations one step closer to the "paperless office," reducing the required resources to empower employees with the necessary information to stay competitive.

Uses for internal Web sites include employee databases, human resource documents, employee handbooks, standards documents, project management tools, case and bug tracking, and various information centers. The Web can also be used to distribute site license programs and other useful textual and binary files. Using the multimedia aspects of the Web, applications can be developed and tracked for self-paced instruction and examinations.

An internal Web server is also an excellent window into the vast storehouse of information in databases. Applications can be developed that allow sales personnel to track inventory, orders and invoices. Using a data warehouse database scheme, simple applications allow management to track the overall company sales performance.

As a Web site grows, it is more difficult to maintain static HTML pages and other files for dissemination to employees. An INFORMIX-OnLine Dynamic Server database is extremely useful since it provides administrators with a fast and easy way to store and save massive amounts of information. Informix text and byte BLOB types allow for the easy storage and retrieval of various information from a database in a transparent and efficient manner.

Deploying a Database Across the Web

One of the first decisions to make in connecting a database to a Web site is whether the connection should be visible to the user. This not only determines the appearance and content of the Web page, it also influences the choice of database access technology.

If the user is looking for specific information (i.e., searching on a single field), it is not necessary to display any of the database. Web searchers, such as *Yahoo*™, *Lycos*™, *InfoSeek*™ and *Webcrawler*™, are good examples. Obviously, there is some form of database behind the scenes, but it is completely invisible to the user.

At other times, it can be useful to display portions of the database, for example, to create the illusion that a user is accessing data from a graphical front end. Frequently, this is the case for database interfaces that are deployed internally to organizations using local Web sites as company-wide servers.

Examples of Web Applications

Programs in "cgi-bin" can range from the simple to the complex. There are a number of standard programs available on the Internet to assist in returning documents and behaviors to the Web browser. Below are some simple examples of how to return information through a Web server. These examples can be improved by the use of additional formatting.

To provide a basis for the creation of the Web site, note the following examples of simple applications which can be used to provide more than static HTML pages.

Uptime.sh

This is a shell script which returns information on the standard output after issuing the uptime command from the hardware on which the HTTP server resides.

```
#!/bin/sh
####################################################################
### uptime.sh
####################################################################
UPTIME=`which uptime`
echo Content-type: text/html
echo

### Test for executable
if [ -x $UPTIME ]; then
  cat << EOM
    <TITLE>Uptime</TITLE>
    <BODY>
    <H3>Uptime</H3>
    <PRE>
EOM
  $UPTIME
  cat << EOM
    </PRE>
EOM
else
  echo Cannot find uptime command on this system.
fi
```

Database.sh

This example uses the sysmaster database to return information about databases on a selected server. The HTML command ISINDEX is used to create a form entry field.

```
#!/bin/sh
################################################################
### database.sh
################################################################
echo Content-type: text/html
echo
### Test for incoming arguments
if [ $# -ne 1 ]; then
  cat << EOM
    <TITLE>Database List</TITLE>
    <H1>Database List</H1>
    <P>
    Enter the server name
    <ISINDEX>
EOM
  exit 0
fi

### Test for the INFORMIXDIR directory
IDIR=${INFORMIXDIR-/usr/informix}
if [ ! -d "$IDIR" ]; then
  echo The directory INFORMIXDIR is invalid
  exit 2
fi

### Test for dbaccess
if [ ! -x "$IDIR"/bin/dbaccess ]; then
  exit 3 echo The tool dbaccess is unavailable
fi

### return the information
echo \<PRE\>
SERVERNAME=$1
```

```
$IDIR/bin/dbaccess - - 2>/dev/null <<EOM
  DATABASE sysmaster@$SERVERNAME;
  SELECT name, owner, created
   FROM sysdatabases
   ORDER BY name;
EOM
echo \</PRE\>
### database.sh ###
```

INFORMIX-4GL CGI Interface Kits

Another issue to consider is whether you need a database. For some applications, it is faster and easier to use a product like Informix Software's "C-ISAM" combined with a flexible Perl, Awk, or SED script. Obviously, this will only go so far. Complex problems, such as multiple joins across multiple tables, require the power of INFORMIX-ESQL/C or a fourth-generation language like INFORMIX-4GL.

The INFORMIX-4GL CGI interface kits were developed in response to the limitations of commonly available tools to interface with Informix servers and databases. They support all Informix data types, and allow all forms of transactions. The requirements for the CGI protocol were incorporated into libraries which can be added at compile time.

These kits allow the developer to supply database information, whether a report, data warehouse application, hypermedia, multimedia, or generic files. These kits are available by linking to "http://www.informix.com/" on the World Wide Web.

Future Directions

In the next few years, the personal computer as we know it today, will evolve into a network-centric machine capable of elementary spoken communication, and will perform common, everyday tasks. It will become the business and social interface of the future, slowly replacing telephone, radio, and television. What final form these revolutionary appliances may evolve to is unclear. However, hardware, communications and entertainment giants are quickly emerging and positioning themselves to become active players in this new era.

Another important area for internal business communications is the use of the Web for group communications (groupware). Web browsers and servers are a natural base for this kind of endeavor because they are able to manage and display many types of files effectively. Expect combinations of interactive hyper-media and multimedia to provide new solutions for businesses. INFORMIX-OnLine Dynamic Server is an excellent extension of this burgeoning market because it is capable of organizing massive amounts of data efficiently and effectively.

Future commercial publishing will be temporarily limited by several technical challenges. Eventually, these limitations will be overcome by keen competition as more businesses and households connect to the Internet.

Capacity

Current technology limits home use to a maximum of 28.8 kilobaud modems. Although the telephone companies are pushing ISDN as a potential solution, the cost of the equipment, training and connection time is prohibitive for widespread home use. Even with the plummeting cost of access, the long-range solution will be a combination of telephone, television and computer into a single home connection, probably by the same vendors who deliver cable television. Cable is the only medium at this time with the bandwidth necessary to allow rapid expansion.

Businesses have a clear advantage in embracing this technology. Larger businesses already have digital communications in one form or another, so the cost of attaching to the Internet will be minimal. Smaller businesses will find that the cost of connectivity is offset by the advantages.

Demand is forcing backbone providers to provide the necessary expanded capacity. Current legislative and regulatory issues hamper innovation. Businesses currently utilize dedicated lines for most data transmission but are hampered by capacity. Several solutions such as FDDI and ATM are utilized to improve capacity. Fundamental changes in the design of the Internet itself, including its TCP/IP protocol, must be made within the next few years to prevent a total breakdown of the infrastructure.

Security

As noted earlier, full-fledged commerce on the Internet is hampered by security issues. Although seemingly risky, the security provided by current Web servers and browsers is more secure than voice and facsimile transmission, and especially, cellular transmission. The risk of financial transactions being intercepted by unknown individuals, although low, is real. And unlike telephone or facsimile, if a hacker breaks security for a commercial site, the loss could be devastating.

With Netscape taking the lead, Web browser and server providers are taking a proactive approach to security. Initiatives, such as the alliance between *Microsoft*®️ and *Visa*™️, the alliance between *Mastercard*®️, *IBM*®️, and Netscape, promise to vastly improve the prospects for the commercialization of the Internet.

Standardization of Markup Language

HTML is a subset of the ASCII-based Standard Generalized Markup Language (SGML) which was adopted in 1986 as an international standard. Recently, Netscape enhanced the language with its extensions and is pursuing the standardization of its enhancements. Netscape also partners with a number of companies, allowing the growth of hypermedia by merging Sun's Java and Silicon Graphics' Virtual Reality Markup Language (VRML). Java is a simple, object-oriented portable language based on C++ that allows the Netscape Navigator and the Java browsers to become interactive with the user.

Netscape now faces serious competition from Microsoft, who has recently declared twenty new extensions for its browser, "Internet Explorer," which are a dramatic departure from the SGML standards. The Microsoft solution is primarily intended for its Web site "http://www.msn.com/" but also allows access to other Web sites.

SGML is also facing stiff competition from newer solutions such as Adobe Acrobat which has many of the Hyperlink features of HTML but allows an improved visual display of documents. If a standard for the World Wide Web is to continue, parties must agree on some composite solution that enhances the standardization of the Internet and World Wide Web.

Development, Deployment and Maintenance Tools

Many vendors have already built a number of new and innovative Web development tools. Some of these tools are now starting to mature. But the cost of building and maintaining Web pages and images is still expensive. Web sites require the skills of a number of disciplines, many of which are in short supply. What is needed now are tools that provide the developer with an integration of text, media and database information.

Conclusion

The World Wide Web is only a few years old. In spite of the technical challenges, the Web empowers businesses and individuals in significant ways. There are many opportunities to grow and profit both internally, externally and individually. Hopefully, this article has provided some insight into the use of World Wide Web technology and INFORMIX-OnLine Dynamic Server to more effectively manage business information and communications.

About the Author

William H. Grant is a principal programmer/analyst in the Advanced Technology Group (ATG) of Informix MIS, Menlo Park, California. He can be reached at wgrant@informix.com.

4

USING THE DATABASE TO MANAGE THE WEB SITE

by Scott Fraass

Introduction

The Informix MIS Advanced Technology Group (ATG) has actively worked with the World Wide Web to develop concepts and ideas into working prototypes and pilot applications. The development of the "Web-in-a-Database" prototype was an outgrowth of the creation of the INFORMIX-4GL Common Gateway Interface (CGI) interface kits. Initially, the group's concept was to use the database as a tool for the management of the Web site, to keep track of the many files and links found within the Web site. Shortly thereafter, the idea for this prototype was posed: Why not put all the contents of the Web site into an Informix database and manage it exclusively with Informix tools such as INFORMIX-NewEra and INFORMIX-4GL. This article describes the implementation of the prototype project called "WebDB."

Why Use a Database?

The use of a database to contain and manage the contents of a Web site makes sense for a number of reasons. Many of the issues faced in Web site management are similar to those which were faced by developers when the first database management systems were created. This section will discuss the issues surrounding Web site administration, the management of links, the definition and support of standards, and locating or developing tools and security. The typical Web site is a massive collection of files which are contained within a defined directory structure on a UNIX or NT™ server. Any given directory contains index files, HTML document files, Perl and/or shell scripts, executable programs, various types of images, and more. Depending on who created or last updated the HTML pages, most have a different look and feel. Some of the HTML pages will be 'informational' in nature; however, there are also Web forms, used to collect data from visitors of the Web site. These forms may use UNIX scripts to append the collected information to existing flat files or to create new files. It is clear that the administration of a Web site is a difficult and time-consuming task for the individuals assigned.

Administration

Administration of the Web site is a manual process. For example, the Informix external Web site (www.informix.com) is actually one of three versions of that site. Alpha and Beta sites are maintained internally to allow changes to be implemented and tested prior to being rolled out to production. Files on the Alpha server may be managed and manipulated by a relatively large number of individuals. The adjustment of UNIX file permissions is sometimes an issue, depending on who is required to update a particular file. Placing new and/or updated files or pages in the proper directory requires a knowledge of the layout of the site which is undocumented. In order to roll the contents forward from Alpha to Beta or from Beta to production, a system administrator must make a tar file of all changes to the Alpha/Beta site, FTP the tar file to the production Web server, and untar the file into the proper directory.

Links

Links or anchors to other sites, pages, or positions in the current document are hard coded into each document. Testing to verify the validity of all the links within a Web site is extremely tedious. The removal of a single Web page may cause a tremendous amount of reconstructive work to be performed on other pages in the site.

Standards for Web sites may be defined and documented, but there are few tools available to support defined standards. Each HTML editor behaves differently, and the author is given a great degree of flexibility. The reality is that the conformance to standards is left up to the developers and administrators to manually support. The security of the Web site is limited to what is available in the server's operating system, unless a customized solution has been implemented.

Within the UNIX file system, files may be accessed at three levels: by a single user, by a group of users, or by the general public. Development of a system to track and/or audit Web site usage under UNIX or NT is reasonably challenging and often precludes a site's movement to a different server or operating system.

Automation

Obviously, the automation of the manual tasks is missing from the Web development and administration environment. As the growth of the Web continues to outpace our ability to keep up, companies will seek the advantage of tools to automate rudimentary and repetitive tasks.

As changes are made to Web pages, there is a need for a way to handle the same multi-user access issues observed in order entry or accounting systems. The locking of Web pages while updates occur is a critical issue; the need to handle groups of updates as a single logical transaction is virtually impossible to support with a Web site comprised of UNIX or NT flat files.

Implementation

Based on the problems defined earlier, ATG designed a prototype that provides a resolution using Informix databases and tools. The broad goals defined for the WebDB project are as follows:

- Simplify the administration of a Web site;

- Provide tools for the management of the site's content and structure;

- Define and enforce a standard look and feel for the site;

- Provide reliable, fault-tolerant, secure Web service;

- Support any file, document, or image format;

- Exploit the capabilities of Informix tools (INFORMIX–NewEra, INFORMIX-4GL, and INFORMIX-ESQL/C); and

- Exploit the power and functionality of Informix Databases.

The implementation of this prototype Web site has a document-centric focus. The reader should be aware that the possibilities of development in this area of databases and the Web appear to be endless at this time. Many, if not all of the concepts described can be modified or customized to achieve other interesting and significant results.

Architecture

At the highest level, the WebDB project employs an open architecture consisting of four major components. A great degree of flexibility is available for physical implementation due to Informix network connectivity tools. Each of the following major components can be physically separated on the network easily (note the illustration of WebDB's architecture):

1. The database underpins the entire system. It was determined that 100 percent of the Web's content would be stored in the database, leaving only a few executable programs to be managed in the filesystem.

2. A presentation component was created to dynamically build the pages as they are requested from the browser (client).

3. A content and structure maintenance component was created to support the definition of the site's structure and the management of its contents.

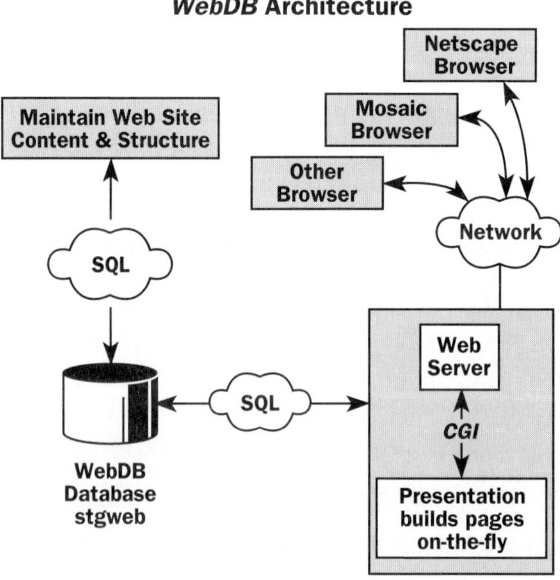

Figure 1: The architecture of WebDB.

4.   The INFORMIX-CGI Interface Kits provided the "Web-to-Database" connectivity necessary to allow the presentation component(s) to connect from the browser through to the database and back.

The Database Holds All

The INFORMIX-OnLine Dynamic Server, version 7.1, database server was the choice for the development of the WebDB prototype. It provides all the required functionality, including support for text and byte BLOBs, and is robust enough to handle a large number of processes at any given time. The database, called stgweb, was created on a Hewlett-Packard G30 with 128 MB of memory.

The design of the stgweb database was modeled with Cadre's (formerly Westmount) *I-CASE*™—a Yourdon-based, structured analysis and design tool. The two key entities which emerged in the design phase were folder and object. The folder entity is logically similar to the 'folder' which is well known in the Microsoft Windows and MacIntosh environments. A folder is logically able to 'hold' objects as well as other folders. The other key entity is the object. In the implementation, an object is a 'thing;' it could be an HTML page, a Microsoft Word document, a PowerPoint presentation, an Excel spreadsheet, an image (.gif, .bmp, .jpg, etc.), or any other sort of file.

Both folders and objects have several attributes which allow the Web site to be customized and standardized. Foldername and objectname are fields which contain a text name (up to 30 characters). Folder description and object description are text BLOBs which allow the user to maintain as large a description as is appropriate. These descriptions and names are 'presented' on the dynamically constructed Web pages in the WebDB project.

A folder/folder cross-reference table realizes a many-to-many relationship which forms the linkage between 'parent' and 'child' folders. Similarly, a many-to-many relationship between object and folder is supported by the object/folder cross-reference table. This allows a single object or document to be linked to many folders—saving disk space and simplifying the management of objects.

In the design of the stgweb database for the WebDB project, the database was implemented with referential integrity—allowing for the implementation of ON CASCADE DELETE procedures to maintain data integrity. The schema was generated directly from the Cadre modeling tool. Figure 2 is a top-level entity relationship diagram (ERD) of the stgWeb database.

Content and Structure Management

INFORMIX-NewEra release 2.0 was the tool of choice for the development of the Folder Maintenance application. It proved to be a good tool for the rapid development of this application—providing good support for BLOBs, applica-

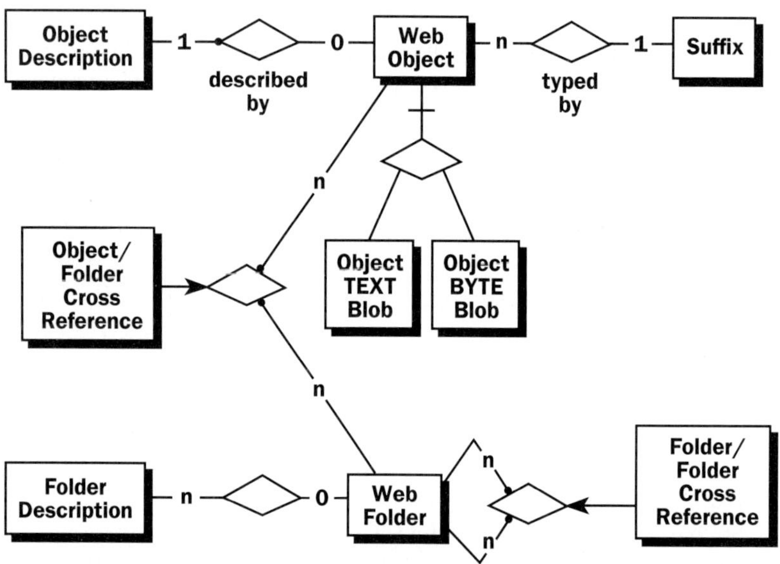

Figure 2: The basic entity relationship diagram of the stgweb database.

tion partitioning, and integration with standard Microsoft objects such as the Windows file picker.

The application was developed in four views: folder maintenance, object maintenance, folder/folder cross reference, and object/folder cross reference. Each view provides the ability to manage a particular portion of either the Web site's structure (via folder maintenance and cross-references) or content (object maintenance).

Folder Maintenance

The folder maintenance program allows users to create a new folder, as well as to update or delete existing folders. The folder title is displayed at the top of the dynamically generated Web page in the implementation. Folder description is defined as a text BLOB which allows users great flexibility in what can be placed in the description (and therefore onto the Web page). The description may be as simple as ASCII text, but it is also possible to embed HTML code or calls to display images or other objects within the BLOB.

The folder header and trailer are also defined as BLOBs, and allow the user to create custom header and trailer sections for each 'folder' page. Other information found on the folder maintenance window includes DATE, TIME, UPDATED BY, and other lesser attributes. Figure 3 is a screenshot of the Web Folder Maintenance window.

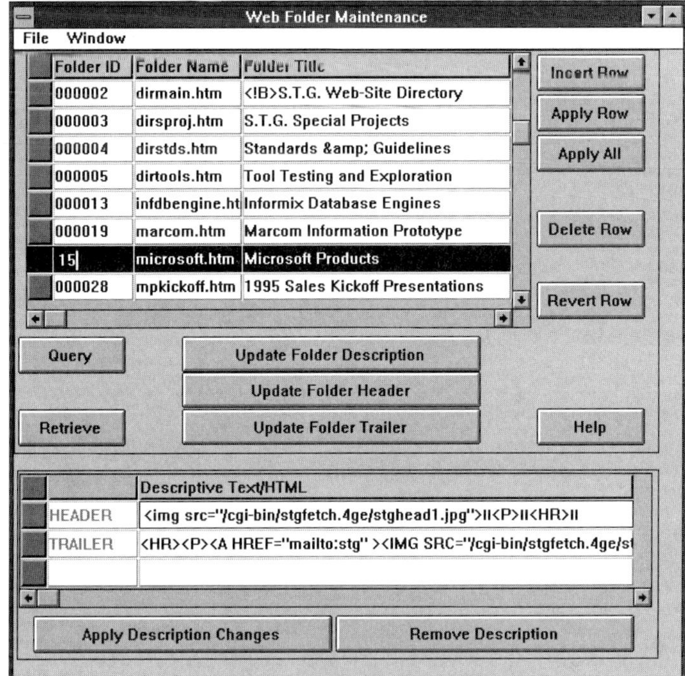

Figure 3: The Web Folder Maintenance window.

Object Maintenance

Object maintenance allows users to load and describe the various files, documents, or images that are placed into the database as Web content. A click of a button inserts a new object row and allows the user to enter a long object name which appears on dynamically built pages. Object description is a text BLOB that allows users to enter as lengthy a description as is appropriate. While describing the object, a user can use a file picker to locate and load the actual document or image file into the database. For local files, the Windows file picker is implemented.

For remote files, a partitioned INFORMIX-NewEra process locates and loads files into the database directly from a UNIX server without using NFS. As the files are loaded, some simple statistics are captured by the INFORMIX-NewEra program. File size and location are two of these attributes. Following is a screenshot of the Web Object Maintenance window.

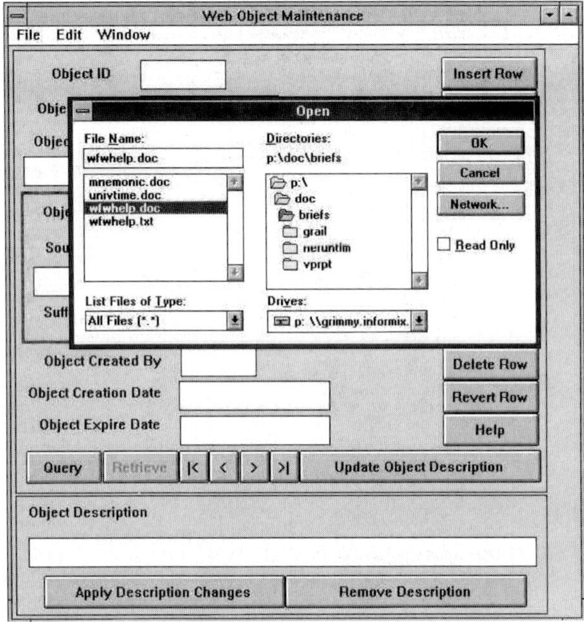

Figure 4: The Web Object Maintenance window.

The Folder/Folder Cross Reference

The folder/folder cross reference allows the actual structure of the Web site to take shape. This is accomplished through the linking of folders, one to another, within the Web Folder/Folder Cross Reference table.

For example, in the ATG prototype Web site, a folder exists to organize documents and information regarding various tools that ATG tests. The folder title is called "Tool Testing and Exploration," although the folder name is actually "dirtools.htm." Within this folder are a number of other folders, including one which holds information regarding Microsoft Tools. This folder is named "microsoft.htm" and is described more completely in the description.

The folder/folder cross reference allows the user to link these two folders together. The result is seen when the folder page is dynamically built and displayed. Any two folders can be linked, so a Web site need not adhere to a purely hierarchical structure. This lends a great deal of flexibility in managing the structure of a Web site. For an example of the dynamic display of a Web page incorporating the folders "MarCom Presentations" and "MarCom Literature," see Figure 7. The following screenshot illustrates the Web Folder/Folder Cross Reference window.

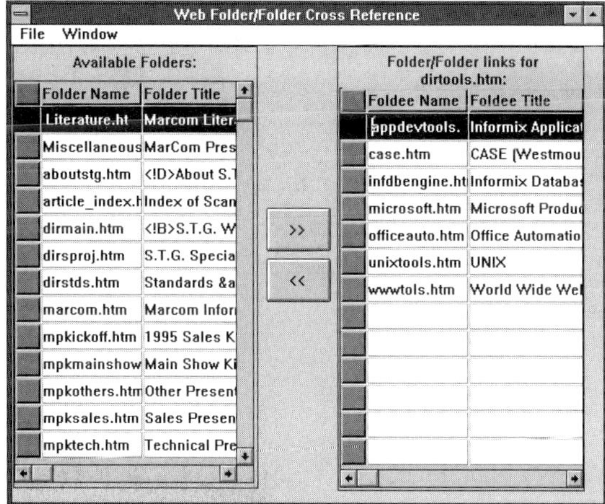

Figure 5: The Web Folder/Folder Cross Reference window.

Object/Folder Cross Reference

The fourth view of the Folder Maintenance program is the Object/Folder cross reference. This window provides the user with the capability of linking an object (i.e., file, image, document, etc.) to a particular folder. The linking is accomplished in two steps. First, the user must query and select the desired object in the Object Maintenance window. Next, the user must open the Object/Folder cross reference window, select a folder and use the arrow button to move the target folder into the list of folders linked to the particular object. This action updates the object/folder cross reference table, virtually placing the object "into" that folder, as illustrated in the following figure.

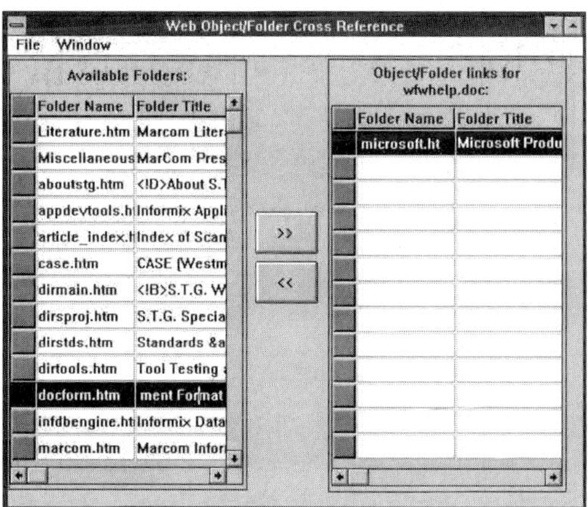

Figure 6: Web Object/Folder Cross Reference window.

Management Benefits

Among the numerous benefits to the document management system demonstrated in this pilot application is the ability to provide instant access to the object when the link is made in the database. While the pilot Folder Maintenance program is presented here with limited functionality, all the rules of traditional on-line transaction processing (OLTP) apply.

Relatively simple modifications to the programs could provide functionality to manage the active/inactive status of folders and documents, and user or role based security for folders and documents. In addition, data integrity can be supported by the use of SQL transactions which insure that all updates complete successfully prior to the presentation of a folder or object.

Presentation

The presentation of the WebDB site is provided by two executable programs which were developed in INFORMIX-4GL (4GL). As was stated above, all information presented to the user by the browser is constructed on-the-fly by these 4GL programs. The following section will discuss the approach taken for this pilot WebDB application. Please note that this is by no means the ultimate solution. In a fully-developed WebDB environment, one might find a number of different applications providing the specialized handling of folders and objects based on unique requirements. Informix development tools have provided a method for the rapid development of these specialized applications.

Two key 4GL applications allow for the delivery of all Web pages to the client's browser. Both programs must be located in the Web site's cgi-bin directory and therefore must be run by anyone who passes the appropriate URL to this particular Web server. Lister and Fetcher were developed on HP-UX 10.0 and INFORMIX-4GL, version 6.0. Both utilize the INFORMIX-CGI Interface Kit libraries for INFORMIX-4GL.

Lister

The lister program was designed simply to process a sequence of five logical steps as it constructs each Web page. It is a simple top-down process flow, with each of these processing steps passing text or images to UNIX standard-out. For an illustration of a lister-generated page, see Figure 7.

The logical steps defined for this pilot application are as follows:

1. Display Title. The title displayed at the top of each page is defined at the folder level. A 60-character column in the "folder" table supports the entry of ASCII text. Some special formatting may be accomplished by entering HTML tags into the column; however, in this implementation space is limited.

2.   Display Header Section. The page "header" is assembled directly below the Title as the page is built. The header is defined as a text BLOB and is physically located in the folderdescr table. By using the text BLOB, it is possible to embed virtually any kind of text, including HTML tags and executable "links" to other objects.

For example, the standard header section developed for the WebDB pilot site first displays a jpeg image, which is then followed by some HTML text and a gif image. The images are actually built into the page through the use of a second 4GL program called "fetcher." This program was specifically developed for the purpose of fetching BLOBs from the database and providing them for display to the Web browser. Called from within the lister program, fetcher is built in such a way that it may be called directly as a URL or from some other process. It requires only a single argument (a valid object name).

3.   List Folder(s). The third section of each lister-generated page presents each of the folders associated with the particular (folder) page under construction. The lister program turns the folder name into an active link by adding HTML tags. If a description associated with the current folder has been entered and stored in the database, it is fetched at this time. In the event that a description has not been entered, only the folder name is built onto the page (as a link). Folders are sorted by alphabetical order in the WebDB lister program, although sorting may easily be adjusted in the 4GL source code.

4.   List Object(s). After all folders are built into the page under construction, the program generates a listing of all objects associated with the page. A query returns to the lister program a set of objects (object name and description) which have been linked to the folder in the object/folder cross reference table.

Each object name is formatted as a link using HTML tags by the lister program. If a description exists, lister is coded to present it. In the event that no description is provided, only the object name is provided. Objects are sorted alphabetically in the lister example.

5.   Display Trailer Section. The final block to be created by the lister program is the page trailer section. This section is fetched from the folderdescr table where it is stored as a text BLOB. For the WebDB pilot, the standard trailer included plain text, some HTML formatting, and images. Note the following example trailer section which was unloaded from the pilot database:

```
<HR><P><A HREF="mailto:stg><IMG SRC="/cgi-bin/stgfetch.4ge/stgrobo.gif" ALIGN="MIDDLE" > </A>
Correspond with <A HREF="mailto:stg">Systems Technology Group (stg)</A> <UL><LI>Go to
Newsgroup <A HREF="news:informix.mis" >informix.mis </A>
<LI>Post to Newsgroup <A HREF="newspost:informix.mis">informix.mis </A>
</UL><P><A HREF="http://fox"><IMG SRC="/cgi-bin/stgfetch.4ge/s_logo-l.gif" ALIGN="MIDDLE" > </A>
Return to <A HREF="http://fox" >Informix Internal WebServer </A>
```

In the example above, HTML tags have been added to format the text displayed in the trailer. In addition, external links have been used (see <A HREF). Finally, the HTML code to display gif images has been included (see <IMG SRC>).

Fetcher

The fetcher program is specifically designed to retrieve BLOB data from the database. Coded in INFORMIX-4GL, fetcher expects a single argument and uses that argument to locate and retrieve a BLOB from the database. The pilot application uses the object name as the argument, although it would be simple to modify the application to suit different requirements.

The WebDB pilot uses the fetcher program in a number of different ways. It can be called from within a 4GL program, as is accomplished within the Lister program as it constructs a page. Calls to fetcher can be embedded into any HTML code (see the trailer example above). Finally, fetcher can be directly called as a URL ('open' from the Web browser) as in the following example:

http://fox/cgi-bin/fetcher.4ge/myimage.gif

Figure 7 is an example of a page generated by the lister program.

Summary

This article has provided a high-level view of a project whose purpose was to implement a Web site entirely within an Informix database. While this goal has been attained, the WebDB project has clearly shown that it is just one of a seemingly endless list of possibilities. The database management of Web data can provide tremendous benefits for administrators, content managers, and users alike. The use of tools such as INFORMIX-NewEra, INFORMIX-4GL, and INFORMIX-ESQL/C allows developers to quickly and effectively develop

Lister-Generated Sample Page

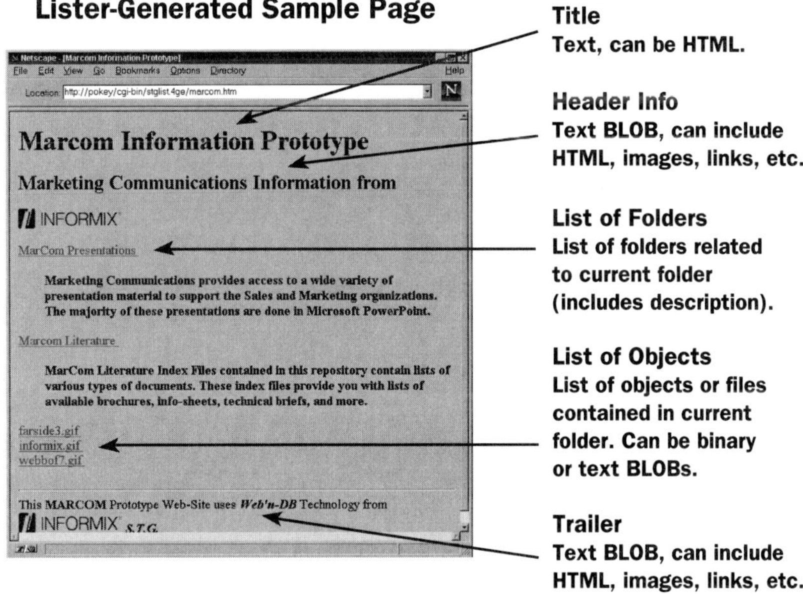

Figure 7: An example of a lister-generated page.

sophisticated Web management systems. As the growth of the Web continues at an accelerated pace, developers can expect to see an ever increasing development of systems and applications that utilize this new technology to meet the enhanced requirements of users.

About the Author

Scott Fraass is the manager of the Informix MIS Advanced Technology Group (ATG). He oversees projects involving the evaluation and adoption of new technology and tools into the MIS organization, while showcasing Informix and partner products.

## 5

WORLD WIDE WEB APPLICATION DEVELOPMENT

by Mel Baiada

Introduction

This article discusses application development, one of the newly emerging uses of the Web. It also explains how organizations can use Web technology to disseminate information more easily, efficiently, and cost-effectively. It is hoped that this paper illustrates how companies can leverage Web technology to give their organizations the competitive advantage needed to succeed in the marketplace.

Succeeding in the Nineties

What will application developers need to succeed in the 1990's? Today and more so in coming years, organizations must respond quickly to changes regarding the business/political environment, customer demand, competition, and internal needs.

In terms of information systems, organizations need certain characteristics to survive or flourish. They need the ability to:

- Develop and deploy software quickly—in response to shifts in customer demands, new products, regulations, etc.;

- Create highly reliable applications;

- Create applications which are easily maintained, modified, or upgraded;

- Develop robust applications which can properly respond to user errors (e.g., formulating queries) or other anomalies;

- Integrate an organization's existing applications and databases with new applications;

- Support an organization's current operational applications, such as very large databases and data warehouses; and

- Implement these applications with the appropriate levels of security.

Any tool which allows an organization to incorporate these characteristics into its application development efforts will be a long-term strategic asset.

The Web as a Tool

In order to explore the Web's appropriateness for application development, it is useful to look at the Web's attributes:

- *Independent of computer architecture.* It is independent of any specific computer architecture, language, or operating system. As John Patrick, VP of Internet Business at IBM™ has said, "It is the GUI of the 90's."

- *Place-independent.* The Web is place-independent. It can be accessed from anywhere in the world, and attached computers can be located anywhere in the world. Thus, a user who uses the Web doesn't need to know the physical location of the computer or home page. This also means that information can be distributed easily, quickly, and inexpensively over the Web.

- *Multi-tiered computing architecture.* The Web is a multi-tiered computing architecture. The Graphical User Interface (GUI) can be on one computer, the application on a second, and the database on a third. The Internet allows for a mix of multiple application and database servers—providing flexibility through modularity.

- *Accommodates incremental updating.* The structure of the Web allows information or applications to be changed incrementally, instead of all at once. On the Web, any individual page can be changed as often as is necessary, without affecting other pages.

Together, these characteristics make the Web an extremely powerful facility. They are the characteristics needed to develop applications for organizations which operate in multiple locations using a widely differing assortment of computer architectures to access, exchange, or distribute information that changes rapidly. Old-style application development—developing software in one place, for one central machine, using expensive talent—is now recognized as a dead issue. What will replace it?

Some Issues and Requirements

The Importance of Standards

Hardware and software standards are a critical issue in information systems. Standards not only create a market for software, but without standards, only a few hardy pioneers will commit corporate resources to projects.

Standards are a way to insure against the sudden obsolescence of an organization's systems. Using a product that meets an established set of standards helps to assure the long-term viability of a project.

Examples of Standards

Some familiar examples of standards are high-level languages such as C or C++, or the use of standard interfaces and links to other software, such as off-the-shelf APIs, or software which supports and uses standard networking tools and practices. In general, standards-compliant software products remove a source of anxiety for buyers and provides the assurance that a purchased product is maintainable and usable.

Conformance to industry standards also assures users that a piece of software is extensible, maintainable, and reliable. For example, such software can be easily integrated with software from other vendors. Similarly, software which conforms to standards allows buyers to upgrade individual components in their systems with confidence and minimal disruption.

Sapphire/Web®

Bluestone, Inc.® has developed a tool, Sapphire/Web, which meets these standards, and makes it possible to develop and deploy enterprisewide applications on the Web in an easy, cost-effective manner.

The cross-platform accessibility of Web technology is the most powerful feature of Sapphire/Web. While an Internet-based solution has quietly evolved, companies have expended resources for years trying to solve cross-platform problems. Sapphire/Web is the first product to take full advantage of this evolution, allowing software developers to bind any HTML element to the following reusable objects:

- *Any Stored Procedure in Informix.* Stored procedures are the building blocks used to build large client/server applications. The beauty of Sapphire/Web is that users can easily bind HTML elements to any stored procedure. Stored procedures can be viewed as "business rules." They are popular for client/server applications for several reasons. First, stored procedures are actually SQL code, compiled into the database for increased performance. Second, they are reusable by many applications. Third, they have referential integrity—if a database table is changed, the database notifies the Database Administrator that there is a change which could affect the stored procedure. This is important in large projects where there are many tables and stored procedures.

- *Any Dynamic SQL (DSQL).* SQL code can be stored in a Dynamic SQL repository. HTML elements can be bound to Dynamic SQL in the same way that a Stored Procedure is bound.

- *Any Executable Program.* Sapphire/Web also adds support for binding to any executable program. For example, a directory-listing command (ls in UNIX, dir in DOS/Windows/NT) is bound to a hot list of directory names. The results are a listing of subdirectories and files that can be placed into a resulting HTML template—perhaps in the form of a hot list. This example shows an easy way to create an HTML file manager; in general practice, the use of an executable program puts a great deal of power behind HTML.

- *Functions.* Legacy systems are typically written as a collection of functions. Sapphire/Web also includes easy binding between HTML documents and functions. This provides a simplified mechanism to put new HTML front ends on existing applications. It also allows the developer to make use of the full power of existing applications. Functions and executables can be distributed with Sapphire/Web, so they need not run on the Web server, but can run on other application servers on the network.

- *Any Flat File.* Flat files can be used as a database. All that is needed is to inform Sapphire/Web of the file name and the column location. An example of this feature is a Lotus spreadsheet, saved in an ASCII format: the user can add and subtract from the file from within the Web browser.

- *Any CGI Script.* The concept of reusable code applies to Web programming, as well. Sapphire/Web permits starting any CGI script, and pre-processing and post-processing the data. A CGI script is just another object which can be bound.

Support for Informix Products

Sapphire/Web offers many advantages which support the use of Informix products, including:

- Direct, native support for INFORMIX-OnLine Dynamic Server—enabling powerful Web client/server applications to take full advantage of Informix databases.

- Full support for the Stored Procedure Language (SPL). This enables organizations to leverage their existing SPL investment, while significantly reducing the need to embed and maintain SQL within the CGIs; and

- The ability to generate complete insert, update, and delete applications which are fully accessible via the Web with just a single line of code.

Additionally, Sapphire/Web compliments and supports Informix's ability to generate high-performance applications. Sapphire/Web's ability to support large development teams and generate robust, portable C and C++ code fully compliments and leverages Informix's position as a leading provider of high-performance databases.

How Sapphire/Web Addresses Standards

Sapphire/Web complies with industry and WWW standards, such as HTML, http, shttp, and CGI, as well as languages like C and C++. It also complies with the native implementations of database vendors.

About the Author

Mel Baiada is the president and founder of Bluestone, Inc. He can be reached at mel@bluestone.com.

About Bluestone, Inc.

Bluestone, Inc. transfers advanced development technology via its software products, training, support and professional services. Its core competency is in object technology, GUI, and database and client/server technologies.

Bluestone, Inc. is located at 1000 Briggs Road, Mountain Laurel, New Jersey. Bluestone can be contacted via phone at 609 727 4600, e-mail at webmaster@bluestone.com, or the WWW at http://www.bluestone.com.

## 6

USING THE INFORMIX-4GL CGI INTERFACE KIT

by Matthew Eichler

Overview

The objective of this article is to provide an example of a Web application. The Web's client/server "connection-less" environment is drastically different from traditional Online Transaction Processing (OLTP) or Decision Support System (DSS) applications environments. The Common Gateway Interface (CGI) environment requires several Web components to be in place and configured properly. This article assumes a familiarity with the INFORMIX-4GL language, and limited or no experience with Web servers and CGI.

The following sections provide a step-by-step example of a successful INFORMIX-4GL Web application using the third example (fgl_catalog.4ge) from the INFORMIX-4GL CGI interface kit:

- Web Components Checklist;

- Configuration;

- Anatomy of an INFORMIX-4GL CGI Program;

- fgl_catalog.4gl Functions;

- Using fgl_catpic.4gl: BLOBs as Web Images;

- Conclusion; and

- Some Helpful Links.

Web Components Checklist

The Web database interface requires the following key components to successfully run and test an INFORMIX-4GL program:

Informix Database Server

An Informix database server must be installed, on-line and accessible by the
UNIX INFORMIX-4GL development machine. The server may be either
INFORMIX-SE or INFORMIX-OnLine Dynamic Server. It may be local or
remote to the INFORMIX-4GL development machine. If remote, any platform
may be used.

If using INFORMIX-SE, it is not possible to store BLOBs for use with CGI
applications. Therefore, the BLOB printing function icgi_print_blob() will not
be useful. Example two illustrates how BLOBs can be used to store images for
display with CGI.

INFORMIX-4GL CGI Interface Kit

The INFORMIX-4GL CGI Interface Kit is available from the Informix Web site
at http://www.informix.com. When accessing the kit, provide some information
about yourself and your Web applications. This information allows Informix to
improve the support for Web applications and to notify you of newly released
software. After completing the questionaire and reading the license agreement,
the kit file (4glcgi.tar) will be downloaded using HTTP. Transfer this file to the
UNIX host used for your INFORMIX-4GL development.

The documentation for the kit, including installation, is on the Web page
called "INFORMIX-4GL CGI Interface Kit Documentation." To prepare for
building the examples and your own CGI programs, complete the following steps:

- Install the Interface Kit Source Code;

- Generate Make Files;

- Make the Library lib4glcgi.a; and

- Make Customized Runners (only if using the INFORMIX-4GL Rapid
  Development System and/or the INFORMIX-4GL Interactive Debugger).

INFORMIX-4GL

If using the INFORMIX-4GL Rapid Development System or the INFORMIX-4GL Interactive Debugger, debug and test p-code versions of INFORMIX-4GL programs before installing them into cgi-bin. However, the installation of machine-code versions (built with compiled INFORMIX-4GL) into cgi-bin provides better performance with the multi-layer Web architecture.

To use p-code INFORMIX-4GL programs with the interface kit, create customized runners (refer to the Making Customized Runners section of the kit's documentation).

Web Browser

Use a Web Browser to test and debug the INFORMIX-4GL application. Any browser that uses HTTP and interprets HTML on any platform is compatible with the INFORMIX-4GL CGI programs. The browser can be on any computer on your TCP/IP network, as long as that machine can access the Web server where the INFORMIX-4GL CGI programs are installed.

Configuration

There are a few parameters in the Web server/CGI environment which contribute to the success of INFORMIX-4GL CGI applications:

Location of CGI Executables (cgi-bin)

The cgi-bin parameter in the Web server (httpd) configuration must be a valid directory and location where compiled INFORMIX-4GL executables can be installed. This parameter is found in the configuration file for httpd and instructs the server process that files in this directory must be executed; for example:

```
Exec  /cgi-bin/*  /usr/local/www/cgi-bin/*
```

This parameter also affects how URLs must be formulated at the browser to run CGI executables. For example, assume httpd is running on a host named grimmy. The third example fgl_catalog.4ge has been installed in /usr/local/www/cgi-bin on grimmy. The user wants to run the third example from the browser. Enter the following URL:

```
http://grimmy/cgi-bin/fgl_catalog.4ge
```

Refer to the Web server documentation for more information on setting these parameters.

Web Server Account

Web servers are configured to control the user and group IDs by which the httpd process will run. Administrators often set a special user ID (e.g., http) and a special group ID (e.g., www) for security/control. The httpd configuration parameters might look as follows:

```
UserId  http
GroupId www
```

This user/group ID provides the identity by which all CGI executables will run. As a CGI developer, make INFORMIX-4GL programs executable by this user and grant the appropriate database permissions so that the processes spawned by httpd can access your database. Refer to the Web server documentation for more information on setting these parameters.

Informix Environment for Web Server Account

The Informix environment must be set correctly for the httpd process to run an INFORMIX-4GL CGI program and access a database. The specific environment variables that must be set depend on:

- The version of the database engine;

- The version of INFORMIX-4GL; and

- Whether the database is local or remote to the Web server.

The INFORMIXDIR variable must be set before an INFORMIX-4GL executable can start. Once started, other environment variables can be set within the INFORMIX-4GL program using a utility function from the kit—i4gl_setenv(). Depending on the above conditions, use this function to set other required variables, such as INFORMIXSERVER, SQLEXEC, DBPATH, SQLRM, DBNLS, etc. If unsure about setting the Informix environment, refer to the Environment Variables appendix of the INFORMIX-4GL Reference Manual.

Some versions of the Web server reset the environment (for instance, the NSCA server resets the environment, while the CERN server does not). For developers who use a server that resets the environment, this is a problem since the INFORMIXDIR variable must be set before a INFORMIX-4GL executable is started (it would be futile to set INFORMIXDIR in the httpd environment). There are two possible solutions:

- Provide a shell script "wrapper" for each INFORMIX-4GL program that sets the INFORMIXDIR variable and runs the INFORMIX-4GL executable. This might slow the performance of CGI executables somewhat because the wrapper script is an additional process. Depending on the resources of the host machine, this performance loss may not impact Web applications. A sample wrapper script might look as follows:

```
#!/bin/sh
# set Informix environment
INFORMIXDIR=/usr/infmx7.10
export INFORMIXDIR
# execute CGI application
/usr/local/www/cgi-bin/fgl_cust.4ge
```

■ Install the Informix products in the /usr/informix directory. INFORMIX-4GL programs will try to use /usr/informix if INFORMIXDIR is not set. If the Informix products are already installed in another directory, this can be accomplished by creating a symbolic link to /usr/informix:

```
ln -s /usr/infmx7.10 /usr/informix
```

Database Permissions

The user ID that httpd assumes must have all the required database permissions in order for an INFORMIX-4GL program to execute properly. For example, if an INFORMIX-4GL program inserts rows into a table questionnaire and the httpd process runs as user http, then the developer must grant permissions with the following SQL statement:

```
GRANT INSERT ON questionnaire TO http;
```

Examples and the Stores Database

Refer to the "Building the Examples Yourself" section of the INFORMIX-4GL CGI Interface Kit Web pages. (If using INFORMIX-SE, the loadgif.sh and the second example fgl_catpic.4gl will not work.)

Anatomy of an INFORMIX-4GL CGI Program

CGI is a Different Animal

The main difference between the structure of a CGI application and a traditional OLTP or DSS application is that with each interaction with the user, the connection is opened and then completely closed. Therefore, an entire INFORMIX-4GL CGI executable is run once, then exited—closing any database connections

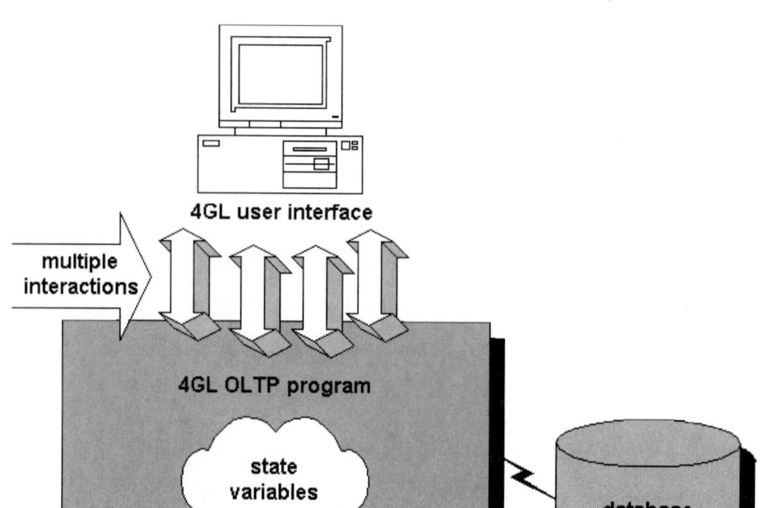

Figure 1: An INFORMIX-4GL OLTP Program.

with it—before the user can interact with the Web server again. Unlike more complex INFORMIX-4GL programs that interact with the user while maintaining an open database connection, INFORMIX-4GL CGI executables only perform a given set of tasks for a single interaction with the user. While an OLTP INFORMIX-4GL program might maintain a set of variables with information about the state of the user's interactions, an INFORMIX-4GL CGI program will rely on values passed at the command line, from the CGI environment or from HTML form entries, to determine the user's state after the latest interaction. Figure 1 illustrates how the single execution of an INFORMIX-4GL program might handle many user interactions in an OLTP application while maintaining state information internally.

In the architecture of an INFORMIX-4GL program within the Web/CGI environment, a single interaction with the browser is handled by a single execution of the program. Notice in Figure 2 that the application's state is communicated through CGI.

An entire INFORMIX-4GL CGI application might therefore consist of many small programs—each handling a single type of user interaction—or a larger program which determines the last user interaction by examining the state passed by CGI. The fgl_catalog.4gl example was designed using the latter technique. The first piece of state information examined in this example is the REQUEST_METHOD environment variable.

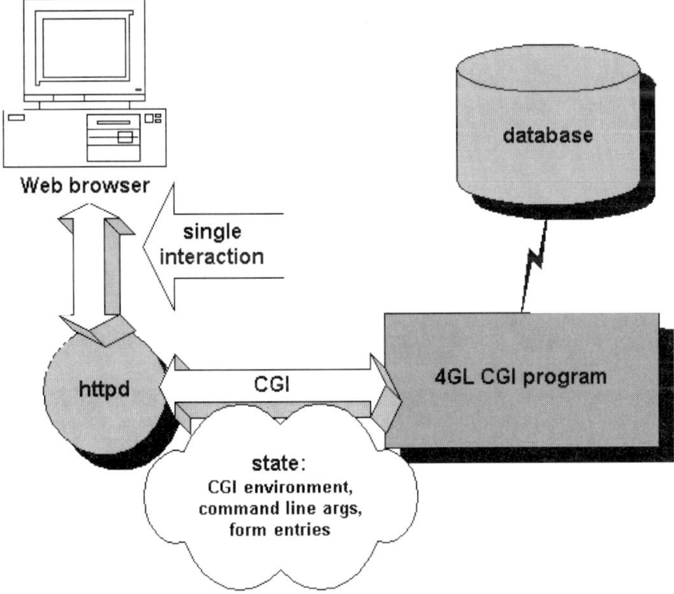

Figure 2: An INFORMIX-4GL CGI Program.

REQUEST_METHOD

The user first executes fgl_catalog.4ge by opening a URL as follows:

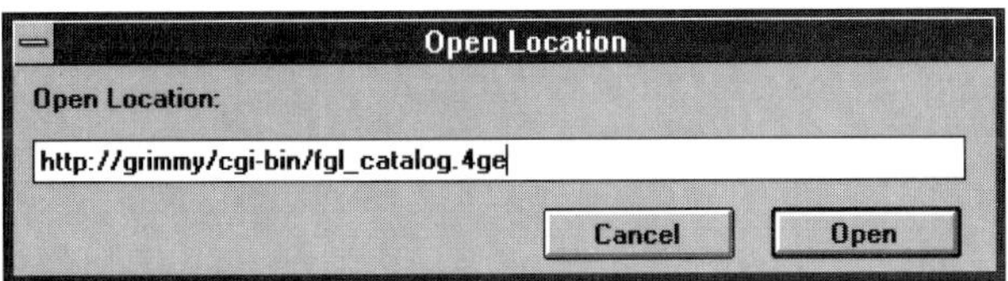

Figure 3: Opening a URL.

In this first interaction, when no entries are passed from an HTML form, the REQUEST_METHOD is set to GET. The program sends a page title and a "Stores Catalog Browser" HTML form so that the user can select the first item to view. The program then exits. After this first interaction, a complete HTML form is displayed in the browser (see Figure 4).

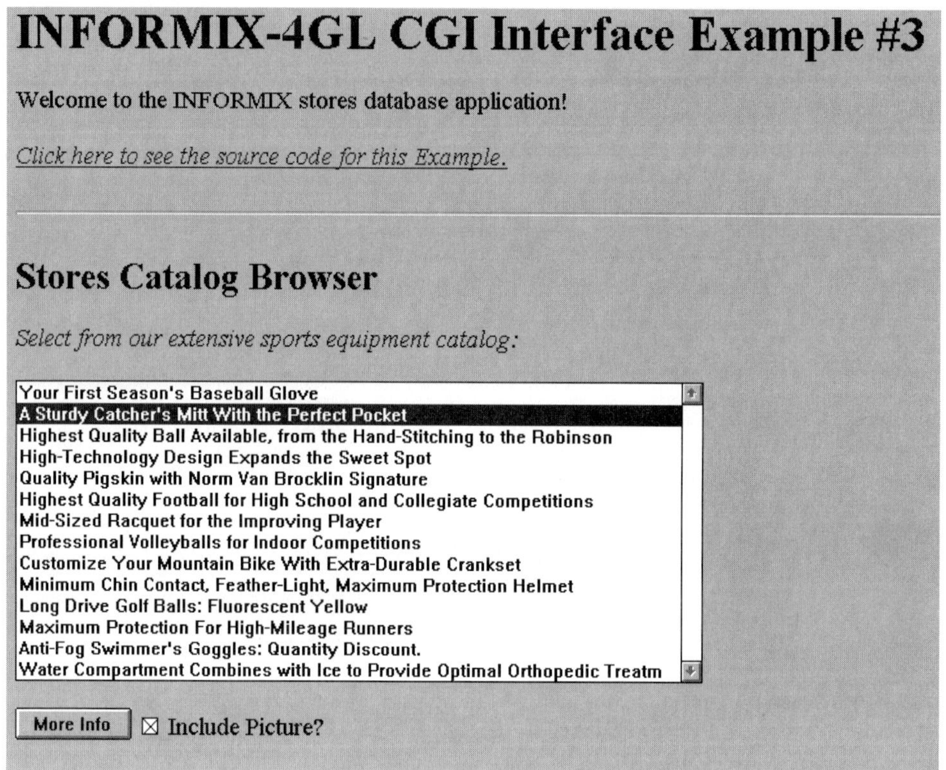

Figure 4: Stores Catalog browser.

For the second and subsequent interactions, the user selects a sports item from the list and clicks the "More Info" button. This button is an HTML INPUT_TYPE form field of the "Submit" type which causes the CGI program to execute again; this time, the REQUEST_METHOD is set to POST. The catalog item number that the user selected is passed from an HTML SELECT listbox field named "catalog_list." When the program executes again, it knows which item's details to display (graphic and textual) from the OPTION value of the "catalog_list" form entry. Also, the "Stores Catalog Browser" is repeated at the end of the page, so that the user may continue to select additional items.

From the browser, the top of the page with the item's details is depicted in Figure 5.

For a sense of the interaction between the browser and CGI, try fgl_catalog.4ge. Use the "backward" and "forward" functions of the browser to review the result of each individual interaction.

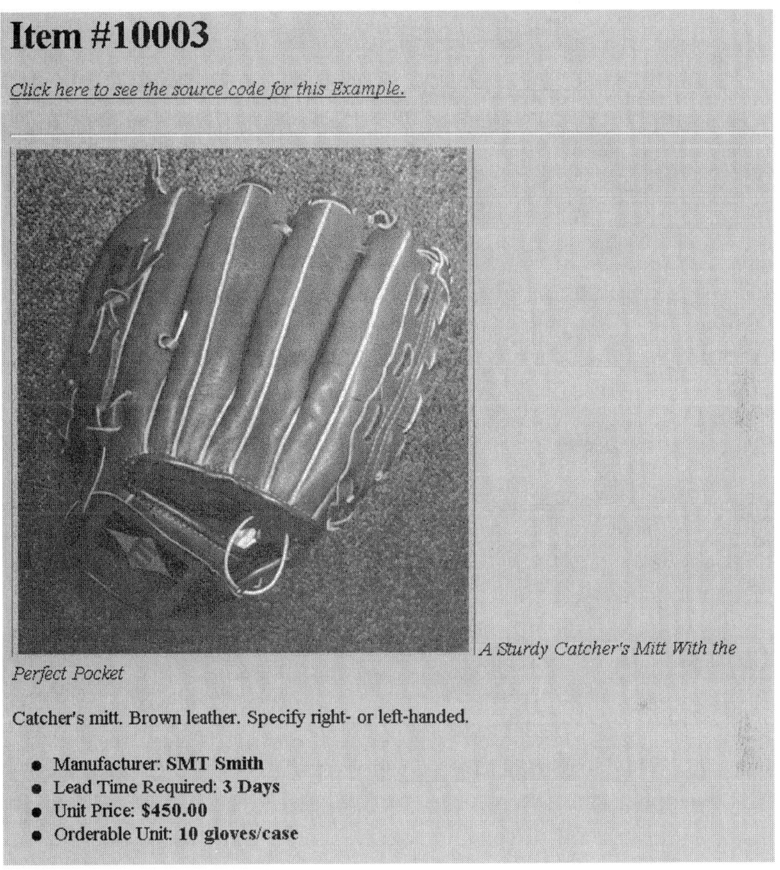

Figure 5: Item Details.

fgl_catalog.4gl Functions

Globals

Global variables are defined to store the values received from CGI and the record data that will be fetched from the database. The array g_form_entry will store the three possible form entries passed from the form. Each form entry has a name and a value. The two record variables g_catalog_list and g_catalog_info will store the data fetched for the "Catalog Browser" listbox and the item detail display.

```
GLOBALS

DEFINE
  g_quote CHAR(1),
  g_request_method CHAR(12),
  g_script_name CHAR(60),
  g_source_url CHAR(255),
  g_catpic_url CHAR(255)

DEFINE
  g_form_entry ARRAY[3] OF RECORD
      name      CHAR(256),
      value     CHAR(2048)
    END RECORD,

  g_catalog_list RECORD
      catalog_num INTEGER,
      cat_advert  VARCHAR(255)
    END RECORD,

  g_catalog_info RECORD
      catalog_num INTEGER,
      stock_num   SMALLINT,
      manu_code   CHAR(3),
      cat_descr   TEXT,
      cat_advert  VARCHAR(255),
      manu_name   CHAR(15),
      lead_time   INTERVAL DAY(3) TO DAY,
      unit_price  MONEY(6,2),
      unit_descr  CHAR(15)
    END RECORD

END GLOBALS
```

MAIN

The MAIN function of fgl_catalog.4gl accomplishes the following:

1. It sends the MIME-type—the browser requires that the MIME-type is sent
    first to instruct it to display what comes next. In this case, the MIME-type
    is "text/html;"

2. It reads the CGI environment and form entries with the kit function icgi_start(). Once this function has been called, the CGI environment variables and form entries can be read using icgi_getvalue();

3. It sets the Informix environment (by calling informix_env()). This is only required when the environment is not set from a wrapper shell script;

4. It opens the database;

5. It reads the value of REQUEST_METHOD using the kit function icgi_getvalue();

    - If the REQUEST_METHOD is GET, the user has called this executable for the first time, as well as a page title (the function html_page_title()) and the "Stores Catalog Browser" form (the function html_catalog_form()) are printed.

    - If the REQUEST_METHOD is POST, the user has requested "More Info" on a particular item, thus query_item_info() is called; and

6. It cleans up and exits. The kit function icgi_free() is called for good housekeeping; it frees the memory used to store CGI environment and form entry information.

```
MAIN

   DEFINE p_retval INTEGER

 WHENEVER ERROR CALL html_error_msg

 ####
 #### always send the MIME-type first, otherwise results
 #### can be unpredictable
 ####
 CALL icgi_mimetype("text/html")

 IF ( icgi_start() != 0 ) THEN
    CALL html_error_msg()
 END IF


 ####
 #### set the Informix environment
 ####
 CALL informix_env()
```

```
DATABASE stores7


####
#### get the request method, the scriptname
####
LET g_quote = "\""
LET g_request_method = icgi_getvalue("REQUEST_METHOD")
LET g_script_name = icgi_getvalue("SCRIPT_NAME")
LET g_script_name = g_quote,
           g_script_name CLIPPED,
           g_quote


####
#### set the URLs for this source code and the CGI function
#### that fetches the picture BLOBS
####
LET g_source_url = g_quote,
          "/grail/examples/source/fgl_catalog.4gl",
           g_quote
LET g_catpic_url = "/cgi-bin/fgl_catpic.4ge"



####
#### set the names of the fields involved in the form
#### we only have 2 fields
####
LET g_form_entry[1].name = "form_name"
LET g_form_entry[1].value = NULL
LET g_form_entry[2].name = "catalog_list"
LET g_form_entry[2].value = NULL
LET g_form_entry[3].name = "include_pic"
LET g_form_entry[3].value = NULL


CASE g_request_method

   WHEN "GET"
      #### get method assumes the executable has been called
      #### without a form, so simply output the query form
      CALL html_page_title()
```

```
     CALL html_catalog_form()

   WHEN "POST"
     #### the post method means a form has been submitted,
     #### so attempt to do the full query
     CALL query_item_info()

   OTHERWISE
     CALL html_error_msg()

 END CASE
 LABEL main_exit:
   CALL icgi_free()


END MAIN
```


FUNCTION *informix_env()*

The function informix_env() sets the Informix environment, if not set within a shell wrapper. For version 7.10 of INFORMIX-OnLine Dynamic Server, the INFORMIXSERVER variable must be set as follows:

```
FUNCTION informix_env()

  IF ( i4gl_setenv("INFORMIXSERVER=pokey_ol2") != 0 ) THEN
    CALL html_error_msg()
  END IF

END FUNCTION
```


FUNCTION *html_page_title()*

The function html_page_title() simply prints the header information for the page in HTML. Notice that the kit function icgi_print_text() is always used to print a character string to CGI:

```
FUNCTION html_page_title()
```

```
DEFINE p_string CHAR(2048)

IF ( LENGTH(g_form_entry[2].value) = 0 ) THEN

   CALL icgi_print_text(
     "<TITLE>INFORMIX-4GL CGI Interface Example #3</TITLE>")
   CALL icgi_print_text(
     "<H1>INFORMIX-4GL CGI Interface Example #3</H1>")
   CALL icgi_print_text(
     "Welcome to the INFORMIX stores database application! <P>")
ELSE

   LET p_string = "<TITLE>Stores Catalog Browser: Item #",
           g_form_entry[2].value CLIPPED,
             "</TITLE>\n"
   CALL icgi_print_text(p_string);

   LET p_string = "<H1>Item #",
           g_form_entry[2].value CLIPPED,
             "</H1>"
   CALL icgi_print_text(p_string);

END IF

####
#### print a hyperlink to this source code
####
LET p_string = "<A HREF=", g_source_url,
       "><I>Click here to see the source code for this Example.",
         "</I></A> <P><HR>"
CALL icgi_print_text(p_string)

END FUNCTION
```

FUNCTION html_catalog_form()

The function html_catalog_form() performs the work, if selecting the catalog_num and cat_advert column data from the catalog table for the purpose of listing it in the "catalog_list" SELECT HTML field. The work of formatting the list into proper HTML is accomplished by the report rpt_selection_list(). The html_catalog_form() function is called from MAIN when the REQUEST_METHOD is GET or from the function query_item_info() when the REQUEST_METHOD is POST:

```
FUNCTION html_catalog_form()

  DEFINE p_counter INTEGER

  ####
  #### this selects the entire list of descriptions from the
  #### catalog table—inadvisable if you had a table with lots of
rows!
  ####
  DECLARE sel_list_curs CURSOR FOR
    SELECT catalog_num,
        cat_advert
      FROM catalog
      WHERE cat_picture IS NOT NULL
      ORDER BY catalog_num

  START REPORT rpt_selection_list
  LET p_counter = 0

  FOREACH sel_list_curs INTO g_catalog_list.*
    LET p_counter = p_counter + 1
    OUTPUT TO REPORT rpt_selection_list(g_catalog_list.*)
  END FOREACH

  FINISH REPORT rpt_selection_list

  IF ( p_counter = 0 ) THEN
    CALL html_error_msg()
  END IF

  RETURN
```

```
END FUNCTION
```

REPORT rpt_selection_list()

The report rpt_selection_list() formats the two columns from the catalog table into an HTML form:

1. The FIRST PAGE HEADER section sets up the form, and defines the FORM METHOD (POST) and the ACTION to be executed when the form is submitted. This section also starts the SELECT form field;

2. The ON EVERY ROW section prints each OPTION VALUE as the catalog_num; and

3. The ON LAST ROW section completes the SELECT box and sets up the "submit" INPUT button.

While it is still possible to take advantage of the conveniences of the INFORMIX-4GL report structure, the PRINT and COLUMN commands have no meaning in the CGI environment. Instead, use the kit functions icgi_print_text() and icgi_print_blob().

```
REPORT rpt_selection_list(p_catalog_list)

  DEFINE
    p_catalog_list RECORD
        catalog_num  INTEGER,
        cat_advert   VARCHAR(255)
      END RECORD,
    p_counter INTEGER,
    p_string CHAR(2048),
    p_value INTEGER

  OUTPUT
    TOP MARGIN 0
    BOTTOM MARGIN 0
    LEFT MARGIN 0
    PAGE LENGTH 2

  ORDER EXTERNAL BY p_catalog_list.catalog_num
  FORMAT
```

```
FIRST PAGE HEADER
   ####
   #### Form Title and Greeting
   ####
   CALL icgi_print_text("<H2>Stores Catalog Browser</H2>")
   CALL icgi_print_text(
     "<I>Select from our extensive sports equipment catalog:</I> <P>")
   CALL icgi_print_text("<FORM METHOD=\"POST\"")

   LET p_string = "ACTION=", g_script_name CLIPPED, ">"
   CALL icgi_print_text(p_string)

   CALL icgi_print_text("<SELECT NAME=\"catalog_list\" SIZE=15>")
   LET p_counter = 0

ON EVERY ROW
   LET p_counter = p_counter + 1
   LET p_value = g_form_entry[2].value

   LET p_string = "<OPTION VALUE=", g_quote,
          p_catalog_list.catalog_num USING "<<<<<<<<<<",
          g_quote
   ####
   #### set the item that is selected
   #### if form was called before, select the previous choice
   #### otherwise the first one in the list is selected
   ####
   IF ( ( LENGTH(g_form_entry[2].value) > 0 AND
          p_value = p_catalog_list.catalog_num ) OR
     ( LENGTH(g_form_entry[2].value) = 0 AND p_counter = 1 ) ) THEN
     LET p_string = p_string CLIPPED, " SELECTED"
   END IF
   LET p_string = p_string CLIPPED, ">",
            p_catalog_list.cat_advert[1,72]

   CALL icgi_print_text(p_string)

ON LAST ROW
   ####
```

```
#### End of List Box
####
CALL icgi_print_text("</SELECT> <P>")


####
#### Action Buttons
####
CALL icgi_print_text(
"<INPUT TYPE=\"submit\" VALUE=\"More Info\">")
CALL icgi_print_text(
"<INPUT TYPE=\"checkbox\" NAME=\"include_pic\" VALUE=\"YES\" CHECKED>")
CALL icgi_print_text("Include Picture? <P>")


####
#### End of form
####
CALL icgi_print_text(
"<INPUT TYPE=\"hidden\" NAME=\"form_name\" VALUE=\"catalog\">")
CALL icgi_print_text("</FORM> <HR>")



END REPORT
```

FUNCTION query_item_info()

The function query_item_info() fetches all the detail data from the catalog table for a specific item that the user has selected (the REQUEST_METHOD is POST). The function uses any valid HTML to format the data to the requirements of the application.

The TEXT BLOB column cat_descr is located in memory before the row is fetched. The kit function icgi_print_blob() is used to print the BLOB to CGI. The MIME-type can be passed as the first parameter of this function. Since this text BLOB is embedded within other HTML text and the MIME-type was already sent back in MAIN, a NULL is passed. A second INFORMIX-4GL CGI executable is used as the image reference to display the cat_picture BYTE BLOB (GIF image). This is explained further in the next section.

When all item details have been printed, the "Browser List" is called again, the function html_catalog_form(), to allow the user to select additional items for display.

```
FUNCTION query_item_info()

  DEFINE i SMALLINT,
      p_sql_stmt CHAR(2048),
      p_string CHAR(2048)

  ####
  #### get the values from the 3 form entry fields
  ####
  FOR i = 1 TO 3
    LET g_form_entry[i].value = icgi_getvalue(g_form_entry[i].name)
  END FOR

  IF ( g_form_entry[1].value != "catalog" ) THEN
    ### called from the wrong form!!
    CALL html_error_msg()
  END IF

  IF ( LENGTH(g_form_entry[2].value) = 0 ) THEN
    ### no catalog item selected
    CALL html_error_msg()
  END IF

  ####
  #### try using MEMORY or temporary FILE here
  #### for TEXT BLOB field
  ####
  LOCATE g_catalog_info.cat_descr IN MEMORY

  LET p_sql_stmt = "SELECT c.catalog_num, c.stock_num, c.manu_code,",
          " c.cat_descr, c.cat_advert, m.manu_name, m.lead_time,",
          " s.unit_price, s.unit_descr",
          " FROM catalog c, manufact m, stock s",
          " WHERE c.catalog_num = ?",
          " AND c.manu_code = m.manu_code",
```

```
       " AND c.manu_code = s.manu_code",
       " AND c.stock_num = s.stock_num;"


####
#### FETCH the catalog row from the table
####
PREPARE pre_item_info FROM p_sql_stmt
DECLARE item_info_curs
  CURSOR FOR pre_item_info
OPEN item_info_curs
  USING g_form_entry[2].value
FETCH item_info_curs
  INTO g_catalog_info.*

IF ( status = NOTFOUND ) THEN
  CALL html_error_msg()
END IF


####
#### output info as HTML
####


####
#### Page Title
####
CALL html_page_title()


####
#### Catalog Picture Field
#### only if "include_pic" field is set to "YES"
####
IF ( g_form_entry[3].value = ìYESî ) THEN
  LET p_string = "<IMG SRC = ", g_quote,
          g_catpic_url CLIPPED, "?",
          g_catalog_info.catalog_num USING "<<<<<<<<<",
          g_quote, " ALIGN = \"BOTTOM\" >"
  CALL icgi_print_text(p_string)
END IF
```

```
####
#### Advertisement Copy Field
####
LET p_string = "<I> ", g_catalog_info.cat_advert CLIPPED,
        "</I> <P>"
CALL icgi_print_text(p_string)


####
#### Description (TEXT BLOB) Field
#### send the MIME-type as an empty string, we don't want it here
####
LET p_string = NULL
CALL icgi_print_blob(p_string, g_catalog_info.cat_descr)
CALL icgi_print_text(" <P>")


CALL icgi_print_text("<UL>")


####
#### Manufacturer Fields
####
LET p_string = "<LI>Manufacturer: <B>",
        g_catalog_info.manu_code, " ",
        g_catalog_info.manu_name, "</B>"
CALL icgi_print_text(p_string)


####
#### Lead Time Field
####
LET p_string = g_catalog_info.lead_time
LET p_string = "<LI>Lead Time Required: <B>",
        p_string CLIPPED, " Days</B>"
CALL icgi_print_text(p_string)


####
#### Unit Price Field
####
LET p_string = "<LI>Unit Price: <B>",
        g_catalog_info.unit_price USING "$,$$$,$$$.##",
        "</B>"
```

```
    CALL icgi_print_text(p_string)


    ####
    #### Orderable Unit Field
    ####
    LET p_string = "<LI>Orderable Unit: <B>",
             g_catalog_info.unit_descr CLIPPED, "</B>"
    CALL icgi_print_text(p_string)


    CALL icgi_print_text("</UL> <HR>")


    ####
    #### Selection List Form
    ####
    CALL html_catalog_form()


    FREE g_catalog_info.cat_descr
    RETURN


END FUNCTION
```


FUNCTION html_error_msg()

The function html_error_msg() is used to display a consistent error message to
the user. The SQL and ISAM error codes, as well as text messages, are displayed
to debug any problems.

```
FUNCTION html_error_msg()
  DEFINE p_sqlcode    INTEGER,
       p_isamcode   INTEGER,
       p_sqlcodestr CHAR(11),
       p_isamcodestr CHAR(11),
       p_sqlmsg    CHAR(2048)


  LET p_sqlcode = SQLCA.SQLCODE
  LET p_isamcode = SQLCA.SQLERRD[2]
  LET p_sqlcodestr = p_sqlcode USING "-<<<<<<<<<&"
  LET p_isamcodestr = p_isamcode USING "-<<<<<<<<<&"
```

```
WHENEVER ERROR CONTINUE

CALL icgi_print_text("<TITLE>")
CALL icgi_print_text(g_script_name)
CALL icgi_print_text(" Error</TITLE>")
CALL icgi_print_text("<H1>")
CALL icgi_print_text(g_script_name)
CALL icgi_print_text(": Error, contact Webmaster.</H1>")


IF ( p_sqlcode != 0 ) THEN
  CALL icgi_print_text("<B>SQL ERROR =")
  CALL icgi_print_text(p_sqlcodestr)
  CALL icgi_print_text("</B><BLOCKQUOTE>")
  LET p_sqlmsg = err_get(p_sqlcode)
  CALL icgi_print_text(p_sqlmsg)
  CALL icgi_print_text("</BLOCKQUOTE>")
END IF


IF ( p_isamcode != 0 ) THEN
  CALL icgi_print_text("<B>ISAM ERROR =")
  CALL icgi_print_text(p_isamcodestr)
  CALL icgi_print_text("</B><BLOCKQUOTE>")
  LET p_sqlmsg = err_get(p_isamcode)
  CALL icgi_print_text(p_sqlmsg)
  CALL icgi_print_text("</BLOCKQUOTE>")
END IF


CALL icgi_free()
EXIT PROGRAM

END FUNCTION
```

Using fgl_catpic.4gl: BLOBs as Web Images

The second example, fgl_catpic.4gl, is of special note for two reasons:

- It illustrates how an INFORMIX-4GL CGI program can fetch images, stored as BYTE BLOBs, from the database and output the images to CGI using the kit function icgi_print_blob(); and

- It illustrates how an INFORMIX-4GL CGI program can receive parameters from command line arguments.

Example two is a simple INFORMIX-4GL program designed as a "BLOB fetcher" so that the catalog.cat_picture column can use in-line images within other HTML pages. Once fgl_catpic.4ge is compiled and installed correctly in cgi-bin, it may be used as an image link. Following is an example of the HTML code to set up the image link:

```
<IMG SRC="/cgi-bin/fgl_catpic.4ge?10001" ALIGN = "MIDDLE">
```

The question mark after the executable name is a delimiter that instructs CGI that the data in the URL is to be passed as command line arguments—as many arguments are passed as there are question marks. The BLOB fetcher is designed to expect that the key value for the catalog.catalog_num column will be passed as the first argument. Since the program uses command line arguments instead of CGI environment variables or HTML form entries, the icgi_start() and icgi_free() kit functions are not needed—instead, the INFORMIX-4GL utility functions num_args() and arg_val() are used.

The fgl_catpic.4gl program uses only two global variables to store values for the primary key and BYTE BLOB column. An informix_env() function, similar to the one used in the other examples, was written to set the correct Informix environment. Once the image is fetched from the database, the kit function icgi_print_blob() is called once with the correct MIME-type ("image/gif") as the first parameter and the BYTE variable as the second.

```
GLOBALS
DEFINE
    g_catalog_num INTEGER,
    g_cat_picture BYTE
END GLOBALS

MAIN
    DEFINE p_stat SMALLINT
    IF ( num_args() != 1 ) THEN
```

```
    EXIT PROGRAM
END IF

CALL informix_env()

LET g_catalog_num = arg_val(1)

LOCATE g_cat_picture IN MEMORY

DATABASE stores7
IF ( status != 0 ) THEN
    EXIT PROGRAM
END IF

SELECT cat_picture
 INTO g_cat_picture
 FROM catalog
 WHERE @catalog_num = g_catalog_num

IF ( status = 0 ) THEN
    # pass the MIME-type and the blob
    CALL icgi_print_blob("image/gif", g_cat_picture)
END IF

FREE g_cat_picture # this is really optional, blob is freed on exit

END MAIN
```

The fgl_catpic.4gl program does not produce any error messages if an argument is not passed correctly or the key value is not found. Instead, the program simply exits, without sending data to CGI. In this case, the Web browser shows the "broken image" icon—indicating the image was not found (assuming that the executable was used in an IMG reference).

Conclusion

The Web/CGI environment may be foreign to experienced INFORMIX-4GL programmers and presents a formidable number of issues. At the same time, the Web provides an exciting new array of solutions for information systems, using a robust client/server architecture. The INFORMIX-4GL CGI Interface Kit is one method that allows the developer to easily combine a familiar development environment with advanced database technology.

Some Helpful Links

The following links provide additional information on Informix products, and the use of Informix databases with the Web and the INFORMIX-4GL CGI Interface Kit:

Informix WWW Home Page:

```
http://www.informix.com
```

Informix Databases on the WWW:

```
http://www.informix.com/informix/dbweb/dbweb.htm
```

Concepts:

```
http://www.informix.com/informix/dbweb/grail/concepts.htm
```

Solutions:

```
http://www.informix.com/informix/dbweb/grail/solution.htm
```

Informix WWW Interface Freeware:

```
http://www.informix.com/informix/dbweb/grail/freeware.htm
```

INFORMIX-4GL CGI Interface Kit Documentation:

```
http://www.informix.com/informix/dbweb/grail/4gldoc.htm
```

INFORMIX-4GL CGI Interface Kit Examples:

```
http://www.informix.com/informix/dbweb/grail/4gl_ex.htm
```

Entire Source File:

```
fgl_catpic.4gl:
http://www.informix.com/informix/dbweb/grail/4glcgi/examples/example2/fgl_catpic.4gl
```

Entire Source File:

```
fgl_catalog.4gl:
http://www.informix.com/informix/dbweb/grail/4glcgi/examples/example3/fgl_catalog.4gl
```

About the Author

Matthew Eichler is a project manager in the Advanced Technology Group (ATG) of Informix MIS, Menlo Park, California. He can be contacted at matthew@informix.com.

=7 TOOLS FOR INTERNET DEVELOPMENT

by Carole Peeler

Introduction

Internet products and standards have made it possible to rapidly and inexpensively access and publish information. In numerous cases, the Internet is provided as an extension to the already familiar commercial on-line service. Due to increasing media attention and the growing audience of Internet users, companies are moving quickly to establish a presence on the Internet.

Pushing the Web Beyond Its Design Limits

Initially, organizations which entered the Internet and the World Wide Web (WWW) published little more than electronic brochures. Organizations are now beginning to explore ways to utilize this ubiquitous technology to interact with data that is already stored in corporate databases. However, the organizations want access to this data to be secure and controlled; after spending a considerable amount of time to collect and secure this data, organizations are very protective of the data. Secure access to information by customers, prospects, and/or employees is a key requirement.

The Internet also includes several major limitations. The Web—an interactive Hypertext information system—is the environment on the Internet where full-screen, multimedia presentations can be delivered. The Web browser display is similar to the full-screen presentation of the personal computer. While this technology is relatively easy to access and use from the end-user perspective, it is a major step backwards in functionality. An interactive Web page that gathers and returns information to the user operates on a submit and return, one transaction at a time. This old technology does not maintain state.

We are now entering the stage where commercial organizations seek to utilize the extensive and easily accessed Internet to deploy robust commercial-grade applications. Applications that are taken for granted in a standard client/server environment generally cannot be accommodated by the Web, particularly those applications which combine multi-step transaction logic with database access. These applications are the heart of commercial processes and are exactly what many businesses want to implement on the Web.

The Problems of Web Application Development

The WWW architecture is not designed for complex multi-step transaction-oriented applications. There are few tools for the development of these kinds of applications, and connecting to databases using only HyperText Markup Language (HTML) can be very complex. Following are specific problems which can be encountered by application developers on the Web:

- Interactivity with a Web application is controlled by a Common Gateway Interface (CGI) script. A CGI script can be cumbersome, difficult to program, and must be rewritten for each application. There is no general purpose interface.

- There is no state or context maintenance. The Web and HTML environment is very different from the client/server environment. An application cannot easily detect individual user interactions, as the application moves from screen to screen. The programmer can be burdened by programming around this problem—resulting in either very simple applications or complex programming to perform relatively simple multi-step processes.

- The data passing between the Web browser and server has been secured using facilities from companies such as Netscape. However, security between the application and the database is poor. Customers wishing to deploy applications—which run on servers dedicated to Internet access and connect to databases which run on a production server—expose the data and the internal network to compromise. Firewalls are installed to protect against unauthorized access to production data through the Internet. However, the data that passes over the Internet between the application server and the database server are at risk.

■ Tools to help developers overcome these limitations have been limited in scope. Many tools which are available are unsupported and not of commercial grade. The development of applications which require programming logic can only be performed by developers who are familiar with multiple low-level tools. Such applications can be difficult to modify and maintain.

Rapid Application Development

VPE®, Inc. began to encounter these problems among its customers in 1994. To assist the Internet developer, VPE created *WebBUILDER*®, a product which provides a rapid application development environment for the Internet. It is comprised of tools that are modular, yet integrated. WebBUILDER's architecture facilitates concurrent development, resulting in applications which are reliable, quickly integrated, deployed, and easily maintained. The separation of the presentation component (HTML) from the logic component (WebBUILDER's programming language) provides a development environment which is conducive to rapid application development.

WebBUILDER is built upon VPE's standard rule-based language; this language has been commercially available for more than seven years. This provides the Internet application developer with the first commercially proven development tool for the rapid building of sophisticated Internet applications. For the first time, businesses have a tool for building Web applications which incorporate transaction processing, ad-hoc query and retrieval, forms-based data processing, data security through encryption, and the manipulation of multiple concurrent relational databases.

WebBUILDER provides a unique networking capability which allows Internet applications to securely access existing databases anywhere on the Internet. Databases can be safely located in a company's data center—behind a firewall—while the Internet applications run at an Internet host provider. This configuration protects databases from unauthorized access. WebBUILDER also provides an additional layer of security for databases; a secure handshake protocol and data encryption are provided as an option. This added security, combined with the normal database and Web browser security, provides maximum end-to-end protection for sensitive data.

WebBUILDER's Database Interface

When a remote database server is used, the application acts as a client in a client/server configuration. This mechanism allows WebBUILDER to accommodate single and multiple database server configurations. Applications may down-load and cross-load database tables, allowing database data on different database servers to be joined programmatically.

Database communication is accomplished through the use of embedded, dynamic Structured Query Language (SQL) statements within the Rules language (see Figure 1). WebBUILDER supports the standard SQL commands, such as INSERT, SELECT, and UPDATE, and all Informix extensions. The database server will accept any command from the event-driven rule engine that Informix is capable of executing.

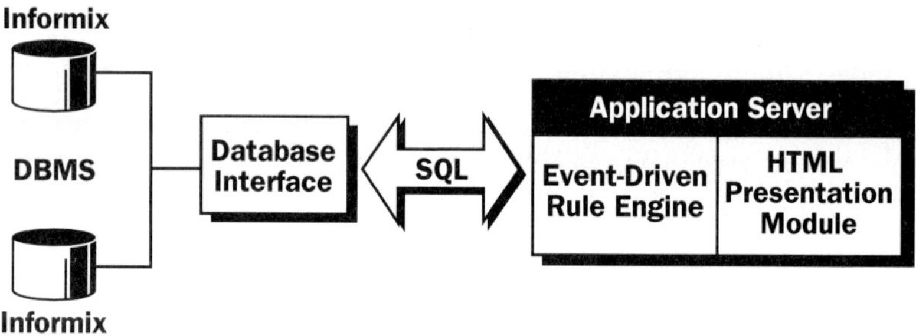

Figure 1: Database interface with the WebBUILDER application server.

WebBUILDER Rules uses the OPEN_DATABASE command to connect to a database:

```
dbid_1 = OPEN_DATABASE("m1", "INFORMIX:stores5", "john:passwd")
```

In this example, a connection is established with the database host called "m1," accessing the Informix "stores5" sample database with the login "john" and password "passwd." The parameters to the OPEN_DATABASE function may be literal strings or variables.

Using OPEN_DATABASE commands, the WebBUILDER Rules developer can open multiple heterogeneous databases on local or remote database hosts. The database servers may reside anywhere on the local network or the Web.

Specifying the database with the USING command allows access to any one of a number of concurrently active databases. The OPEN_DATABASE command returns a database identifier "dbid_1", which is subsequently referenced with the USING command, as shown in thc following example:

```
USING dbid_1 EXEC SQL select company from customer \
    where state = `NJ' \
    into :east_cust[ ]
```

This SQL statement will return the rows from the query into the global array "east_cust." The ":" is used to identify application variables within an embedded SQL statement; the "\" is the WebBUILDER Rules line continuation delimiter.

An SQL command may contain variable strings. This allows the application to dynamically build an SQL statement at runtime that will be expanded when the SQL command is executed. A more sophisticated example of the USING command illustrates this capability. A local variable "where_clause" is dynamically assigned a value at runtime:

```
where_clause = "where state = " + state_name
USING dbid_1 EXEC SQL select company from customer \
        :where_clause \
        into :east_cust[ ]
```

The list of East Coast company (east_cust) names is stored in the dynamically allocated array "east_cust." The entire SQL command, following the WebBUILDER Rules "EXEC SQL" command, is transmitted to the database server—where it is processed as a dynamic SQL statement. Like the "where_clause" portion, any SQL command may be created dynamically at runtime—based on user input, Rules calculation, or external process.

Remote Database Support

WebBUILDER incorporates database connection software so that a WebBUILDER application can connect to a remote database. This capability allows an Internet application to run on a server in one location and easily connect to a production database in another location. Thus, the database can be located inside a firewall and the Internet application outside the firewall. This capability also makes it possible for the WebBUILDER application to reside at an Internet hosting service, but connect to a company's production database located within its internal computer infrastructure.

Figure 2 shows a typical configuration of a WebBUILDER application in a distributed network environment:

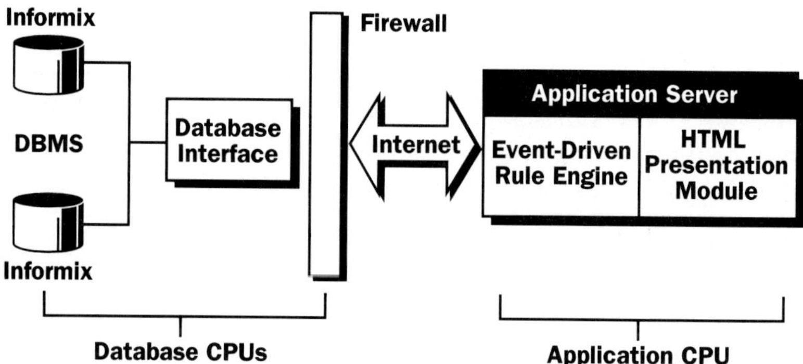

Figure 2: A WebBUILDER application in a distributed environment.

WebBUILDER supports all proprietary database password security schemes and other security capabilities provided by World Wide Web servers. WebBUILDER also allows an organization to establish a sophisticated security environment using the WebBUILDER Security Module, see Figure 3. The WebBUILDER Security Module is an advanced feature of the Database Interface. These security provisions are optional and can be used in conjunction with the password security provided by most relational databases. These security options:

■ Allow connections only from known Internet IDs;

■ Allow connections only from the known machines which route the connection;

■ Allow connections only to an identified machine;

■ Allow connections only to an identified database provider and, where applicable, database name;

■ Allow connections only for named users with identified passwords;

■ Allow only specified users to run the WebBUILDER database Security Module; and

■ Allow connections that have the proper encryption and de-encryption keys.

Users of the WebBUILDER Security Module can define their own encryption/de-encryption security.

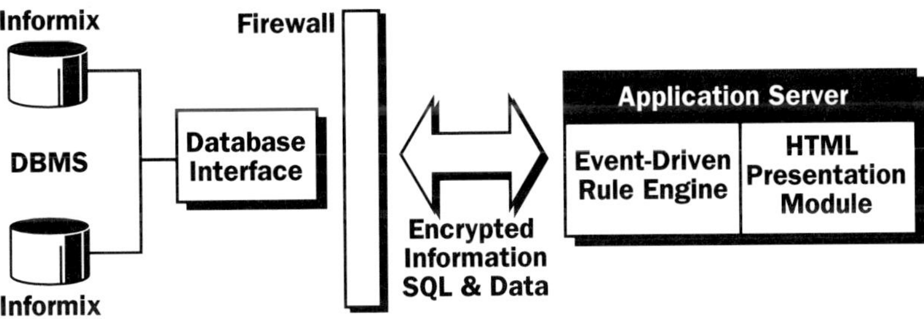

Figure 3: WebBUILDER encryption capability.

Conclusion

The information which companies use to manage their business is valuable and typically takes years to gather and place in centralized databases. This information has value, however, only when it can be readily obtained by those who need it. The current business need is to report the necessary and appropriate information on an "as-needed" basis—independent of location or computer equipment. Along with the newly emerging development tools, the Internet provides a solution to this problem.

About the Author

Carole Peeler is the vice president of total quality service at VPE, Inc., Alexandria, Virginia. Carole has extensive experience in the areas of RDBMS, text retrieval systems, and application development tools.

About VPE, Inc.

VPE, Inc. is a leading provider of Rapid Application Development (RAD) tools which leverage the power of graphical event-driven, rules-based development. VPE, Inc.'s mission is to help customers to develop and deploy information systems that combine text and graphical information for distribution across a range of platforms, operating systems, and databases.

VPE, Inc. is located at 601 Madison Street, Alexandria, Virginia 22314. Contact VPE via phone at 703 684 3700, facsimile at 703 684 3727, e-mail at vpe@worldweb.net, or the Web at http://www.vpe.com.

The Object-Relational DBMS

## 8

Object-Relational DBMS—The Next Wave

by Michael Stonebraker

Introduction

This article presents a classification of the applications that require DBMS technology and indicates where relational DBMSs, object-oriented DBMSs and object-relational DBMSs fit. The purpose of this article is to indicate the kinds of problems that each kind of DBMS solves. As will be seen, there is no DBMS that solves the needs of all applications. Finally, the article indicates why the problems addressed by object-relational DBMSs are expected to become increasingly important. As such, the object-relational DBMS represents "the next wave."

The classification scheme, as represented in Table 1, makes use of the two-by-two matrix.

Table 1 shows a horizontal axis with very simple data to the left and very complex data to the right. In general, the complexity of the data that an application must contend with varies between these two extremes in a continuous fashion. This article assumes that there are only two discrete possibilities—namely, simple data and complex data. Similarly, the vertical axis helps to differentiate whether an application requires a query capability. Such a determination can vary between "never" and "always." Again, there is a continuum between the two extremes. However, for simplicity, this article again assumes that there are only two discrete possibilities: "query" and "no query."

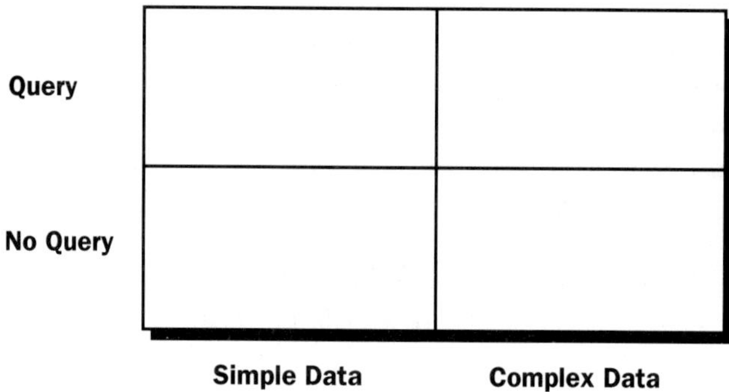

Table 1: Classification of DBMS applications.

A user can examine an application and then place it in one of the four boxes in Table 1, depending on the application's characteristics. To illustrate this classification process, it is helpful to explore an application in each of these four boxes and to address each application's DBMS requirements. Subsequently, this article will recommend a data manager for each of the four applications.

Lower Left-Hand Corner

Consider a standard text editing package, such as Microsoft Word™ for Windows, FrameMaker™, Word Perfect™, vi, or emacs. All text editors allow the user to open a file by name, which results in the reading into virtual memory of the file's contents. The user can then make editing gestures to update the virtual memory object. At intervals, the object is saved to disk storage. Finally, the user can close the file, thereby causing the virtual memory copy to be stored back to the filesystem.

The only query made by a text editor is "get file" and the only update is "put file." As such, a text editor qualifies as a "no query" application and does not require the use of SQL. In addition, a text editor is satisfied with the data model presented by the filesystem, namely, as an arbitrary length sequence of characters. As such, this is a no query, simple data application which fits in the lower left-hand corner of the two-by-two matrix.

Two points should be made before proceeding. First, this article discusses text editors and not more sophisticated groupware products, such as Lotus Notes™. In addition, this article does not discuss document management systems, such as is offered by Documentum. For more information on Documentum, refer to the article "Raising the Standard for Enterprise Document Management in Informix Environments."

The obvious DBMS for applications in the lower left-hand corner of our matrix is the filesystem which is provided by the operating system vendor for a given hardware platform. In fact, most text editors use this primitive level of DBMS service, and there is no plan to move to anything more sophisticated. The reason is simple: if there is no need for queries or complex data, then the service provided by the filesystem is adequate. Moreover, filesystems invariably provide higher performance than more sophisticated systems.

The bottom line is simple. An application in the lower left-hand corner of Table 1 can be deployed on the filesystem provided by a computer. As such, the lower left-hand corner can be labeled as "filesystem." Thus, the article's discussion moves to another box—the upper left-hand corner.

Upper Left-Hand Corner

Suppose it is necessary to store information about a hypothetical company's employees, for example, each employee's name, age, salary, and department. In addition, it is also necessary to record information about this company's departments, such as each department's name, budget, and floor location. The schema for this information can be captured by the following standard SQL statements:

```
create table emp (
  name   varchar(30),
  age    int,
  salary float,
  dept   varchar(20));
create table dept (
  dname  varchar(20),
  budget float,
  floor  int);
```

Notice that the user wishes to store a collection of structured records—each of which has attributes that are simple integers, floats, and character strings. Hence, the records utilize the standard data types found in SQL-92. As such, this data can be classified as "simple." Users can issue a collection of queries against this data, such as:

■   The names of employees who are under 40 and earn more than $40,000.

```
select name
from emp
where age < 40 and salary > 40000;
```

■   The names of employees who work on the first floor.

```
select name
from emp
where dept in
  select dname
  from dept
  where floor - 1;
```

■   The average salary of employees in the shoe department.

```
select avg(salary)
from emp
where dept = 'shoe';
```

Hence, the inquiries that the user wishes to make are queries, and can be expressed in standard SQL-92. As such, this application can be assigned to the simple data, query box. Applications in the upper left-hand corner which have this characteristic tend to be identified as "business data processing" applications and have the following requirements:

Query Language

Query language is a requirement for SQL-89. It is also desirable to adhere to the newer SQL-92 standard.

Client Tools

Client tools are a requirement for a tool kit that allows programmers to set up forms for data entry and display. The tool kit must also allow sequencing between forms through control flow logic. Such tool kits are called fourth-generation languages (4GLs); an example is INFORMIX-4GL. In addition, client tools must include a report writer, database design tool, performance monitor, and the ability to call DBMS services from a variety of third-generation languages—for example, C, COBOL, and FORTRAN.

Performance

Much of the business data processing marketplace entails so-called transaction processing, where many simultaneous users submit requests for DBMS services from client terminals or PCs. The user interactions tend to be fairly simple SQL statements. In addition, many are updates. The user requires a predictable outcome when parallel conflicting updates are processed by a DBMS. This predicament has led to the notion of two-phase locking which ensures so-called serializiability. The user who is unfamiliar with this concept is advised to consult a standard textbook on DBMSs, by either Date, Bradley, or Ullman.

In addition, there is an absolute requirement to never lose the user's data, regardless of what kind of failure might occur. Such failures include disk crashes, as well as operating system failures. Providing recovery from crashes is typically provided by utilizing write-ahead log (WAL) technology. The user who is interested in this topic is also advised to consult standard reference books. Together, two-phase locking and a write-ahead log provide transaction management, that is, a user's queries and updates are grouped into units of work called transactions. Each transaction is atomic (i.e., it either happens completely or not at all), serializable (i.e., it appears to have happened before or after all other parallel transactions), and durable (i.e., once committed, its effect can never be lost).

Security

Since users put sensitive data, such as salaries, into business data processing databases, there is a stringent requirement for DBMS security. As a result, the DBMS must run in a separate address space from the client application, so that an address space crossing occurs whenever a DBMS service request is executed. In this way, the DBMS can run with a different user identifier from that of any application. Moreover, the actual data files—utilized in the database—are specified as readable and writeable only by the DBMS. This client-server architecture, shown in Figure 1, is a requirement of upper left-hand corner applications.

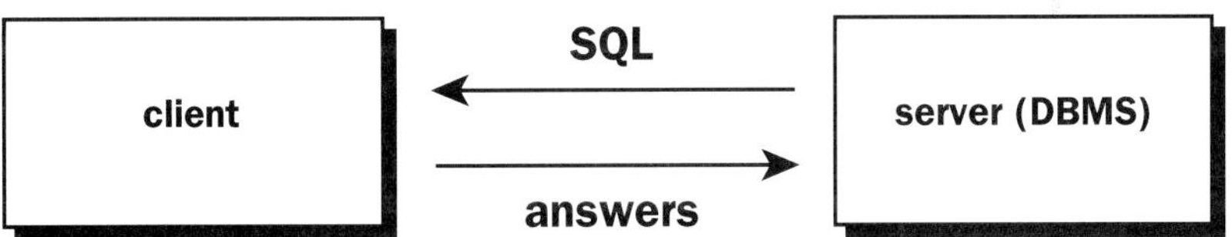

Figure 1: Standard client/server architecture.

In any case, the user requires an SQL DBMS optimized for transaction processing and entailing many simultaneous users. A standard benchmark that typifies this sort of interaction is TPC-A from the Transaction Processing Council. TPC-A is discussed at length in the "The Benchmark Handbook" by Jim Gray. There is a movement, over time, toward more complex transactions, and TPC has responded with a series of "heavier" transaction standards, called TPC-C and TPC-D, respectively.

This set of requirements for an SQL DBMS—with 4GL client tools optimized for transaction processing—is answered by the current relational DBMS model. For the purposes of this article, the decision is quite simple: if you have an application in the upper left-hand corner, use a relational DBMS.

We now turn to the right-hand side of our two-by-two matrix, and discuss the lower right-hand corner.

Lower Right-Hand Corner

In a hypothetical case, one user is the facilities planner for a company that has an "open floor plan"—whereby all employees are arranged into cubicles, with partitions to separate them. Over time, departments grow and shrink, and the arrangement of employees on the physical real estate of the building is suboptimal. Therefore, a global rearrangement of space is warranted. This collection of free space and the concurrent rearrangement of employees is a target application.

The database for this application can be expressed by the following SQL commands:

```
create table employee (
  name   varchar(30),
  space  polygon,
  adjacency  set-of (employee));

create table floors (
  number  int,
  asf    swiss-cheese-polygon);
```

It is necessary to record the name and currently occupied location (space) of each employee, as well as the collection of employees who share a common wall (adjacency). For each floor, it is necessary to record the floor number and the assignable square feet (asf). This quantity is the outline of the building, minus the rest rooms, elevator shafts, and fire exits. As such, it is a polygon with "holes" in it, which can be termed a "swiss cheese polygon." Likewise, space is a polygon and adjacency is a set. Obviously, this data is more complex than the **emp** and **dept** data previously discussed. As such, this application is on the right-hand side of Table 1.

The collection application can be pseudo-coded as follows:

```
main ()
{
read all employees;
read all floors;
compact();
write all employees;
}
```

The program must read all employee records to ascertain their current space, as well as all the floors from which to obtain the asf. The program will build a virtual memory structure for the next step of the program. This compaction routine then measures this structure to generate a revised allocation of employees into the asf on each floor. When compaction is complete, each employee record must be rewritten with a new space allocation.

Obviously, this program reads the entirety of both data collections, computes on this collection, and writes one collection. Hence, it is analogous to the text editor which read, computed, and then wrote a single file. Like the text editor, not one query is involved. Unlike the text editor, the data involved in the application is rather complex. As such, this is a lower right-hand corner application.

The reader might complain that this application seems quite artificial. However, it is representative of most electronic CAD (ECAD) applications. For example, a chip design is stored on disk as a complex object, read into main memory, compacted by an optimization program, and then written back to persistent storage. As such, ECAD applications are similar, although simpler than the cubicle collection application.

Using a traditional filesystem for this application is fairly time consuming. The application must manually read the employee and floor location information. However, the requirement of converting the data from disk format to main memory format is more tedious. The adjacency information reflects data about a set of employees and might be represented on disk as a set of unique identifiers for employees. These unique identifiers should be converted to virtual memory pointers during the load process. Because virtual memory pointers are transient and depend on where the data is actually loaded in memory, the pointers cannot be reused in subsequent executions of the program. As such, disk pointers are fundamentally different from main memory pointers, and the load process must convert from one to the other. Similarly, when the data is written back to disk, the adjacency information may have been changed by the compaction routine, requiring a reverse conversion from main memory to disk representation.

Loading, converting, and then unloading and reconverting the data is a tedious effort that must be accomplished by the person who writes the compaction routine, (especially if a filesystem is used as a storage engine for the application). A better solution is to support persistent storage for the programming language in which the compaction routine is written. For purposes of exposition, suppose this is C++. As a result, the compaction routine would have a collection of data structures defined for its computation. One such declaration is provided in the following example:

```
integer I;
```

In a normal programming language, "I" is a transient variable, that is, it has no value unless initialized by the program. Its value is lost when the program terminates. Suppose persistent variables are allowed and declared, as follows:

```
persistent integer J;
```

In essence, the "J" integer is persistent. Hence, its value is automatically saved when the compaction program terminates. This value is also automatically available when the program is restarted. With persistent variables, the language support system is required to load and unload data, as well as to convert the data from disk format to main memory format and back. The person who writes the compaction routine must only write the algorithm and is freed from other details.

A persistent programming language offers the best DBMS support for this compaction application. With such a facility, the user can move from writing the code below:

```
main ()
{
read all employees;
read all floors;
compact();
write all employees;
}
```

to merely having to write the following code:

```
main ()
{
compact();
}
```

Fundamentally, a persistent programming language is closely integrated with a specific language. Clearly, the persistence system must understand the specific data declarations of the target language. Hence, if one writes a compaction routine in COBOL, then persistent COBOL is required, and persistent C++ is completely useless. As such, one persistence system is required for each language.

Notice that the application has the following DBMS requirements:

Query Language

None is required for this application.

Client Tools

The writer of a compaction routine is presumably using some sort of programming language tool kit, such as the one from Parc Place or Next. As such, he is expecting to obtain client tools from a programming language productivity company. Client tools from the persistent storage company are less critical.

Performance

The fundamental performance problem that this application must solve is the following. If the compaction routine runs on "vanilla" C++ and performs its own storage management, then the user obtains a certain performance. If the user runs the compaction routine on top of a persistent language, then the user may wish the compaction routine to run no slower than 10 percent. Hence, the main performance requirement for a persistent language is to "keep up" with a nonpersistent one.

Security

The above performance requirement is at the root of the architecture of persistent languages. Specifically, suppose the user executes the following command:

```
J = J + 1;
```

The above command increments J. If J is non-persistent, then this statement executes in one microsecond or less. On the other hand, if J is persistent, then this statement becomes an update. If the storage system runs in a different address space than the user program, then an address space switch must occur to process this command. As a result, the command will run two to three orders of magnitude slower than the non-persistent case. Such a performance hit is unacceptable to users, and causes the designers of persistent storage systems to execute commands in the same address space as the user program, as noted in Figure 2.

Avoiding an address space change generates much higher performance. However, it has one dramatic side effect: a malicious program can use operating system read and write calls to read and write any data that the storage system is capable of reading or writing. Since both run in the same address space, the operating system cannot distinguish the calls from a security perspective. As a result, any user program can read and write the entire database by going around the persistent storage system and dealing directly with the operating system.

For most companies, storing employee salaries in such a system is intolerable. No database administrator places sensitive data in a system where securi-

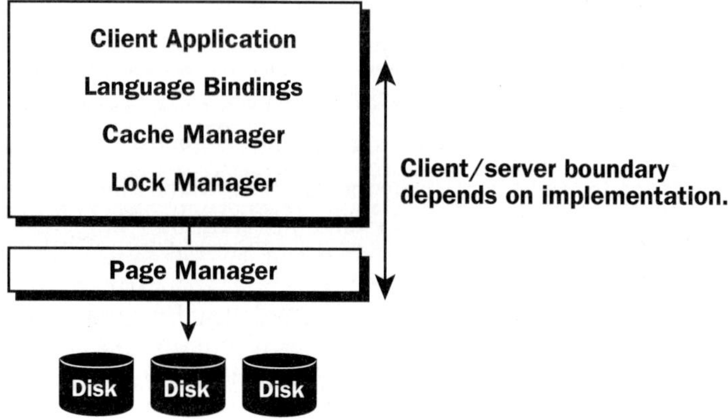

Figure 2: ODBMS architecture.

ty is severely compromised. Designers of persistent languages obtain very high performance by trading security. However, in the lower right-hand corner, this trade-off is often acceptable.

The reader might wonder why this discussion does not apply to relational DBMSs. There is a crucial difference between the two realms. In the persistent language realm, updates are "lightweight," that is, they take very small amounts of time. Note the following sample update:

```
J = J + 1;
```

This update takes, at most, one microsecond to complete. As such, the address space overhead is high. In a relational world, updates are heavier, that is, they require locating one or more records through a B+tree and then modifying the records. This requires a substantial path length, leading to updates that are two to three orders of magnitude heavier than in a persistent language realm. For example, the following SQL query is indicative:

```
select name
from emp
where age > 40;
```

This is the difference between expressing updates in a high-level language like SQL and a low-level language like C++. Because updates are relatively heavy in SQL, the cost of crossing the address space boundary is a small proportion of the total query cost. In the case of the light persistent storage updates, the address space cost forms a high proportion of the total transaction cost.

Systems that are focused on providing tight integration with a programming language, high performance for updates to persistent variables, and little (if any) focus on SQL are available for C++ and object-oriented DBMS vendors.

DBMS choices are quite easy. For an application in the lower right-hand corner, choose a vendor of a persistent language for the chosen programming language. That vendor is committed to the performance and features required in this corner of the matrix.

The observant reader might ask, "What will happen if I have a lower right-hand corner application and I run it on a relational DBMS?" The answer is quite simple. Note the following command:

```
J = J + 1;
```

The above command must be expressed in SQL to access a stored database. Since the type system of C++ is much more elaborate than that of SQL, the user must simulate the C++ type system in SQL. This simulation is time consuming and requires that the user manually map C++ variables into SQL reads and writes. Moreover, the user must perform a heavyweight client-server address space crossing on most commands. As a result, the application will be time consuming and slow. Stated differently, using a DBMS designed for one kind of application in a very different environment can result in a disaster. The net result is that relational systems are not ideal for solving lower right-hand corner problems.

The opposite question also bears asking, "What happens if I have an upper left-hand corner problem and I run it on an object-oriented DBMS?" Again, the result is less than satisfactory. Specifically, most object-oriented language vendors have very limited SQL, and several do not support updates from SQL at all. As such, the user must drop into C++ to express his transactions—resulting in a great deal more code. In addition, such products are typically not optimized to support 50 or 100 concurrent updaters, and tend to offer poor performance for large numbers of users. Put differently, using a DBMS designed for one kind of application in a very different environment can result in disaster. The net result is that object-oriented DBMSs are not ideally suited to work well on upper left-hand corner problems.

Upper Right-Hand Corner

We now turn to an application which is query-oriented and requires complex data. As such, it is representative of the upper right-hand corner. The State of California's Department of Water resources (DWR) is charged with managing most of the waterways and irrigation canals in California, as well as a collection of aqueducts, including the massive state water project. To document their facilities, DWR maintains a slide library of 35mm slides. Over time, this library has grown to 500,000 slides and is currently accessed daily by DWR employees and others.

The client typically requests a picture by content. For example, an employee might give a presentation in which a picture of "the big lift"—a massive pumping station that lifts Northern California water over the Tecahappi Mountains into Southern California. Another user request might be for a picture of San Francisco Bay at sunset, while a third requests a picture of a reservoir whose water level is very low.

DWR has found that it is difficult to find slides by content. Indexing all the slides according to a predefined collection of concepts is a prohibitively expensive job. Moreover, the concepts in which clients are interested changes over time. For example, low water in a reservoir was never of interest until the drought began seven years ago. Similarly, endangered species are currently a heated issue, but only in the last few years.

At the current time, there is a written caption about each slide. One such example is as follows:

Picture of Auburn Dam taken during scaffold construction.

A fairly primitive system can identify slides from specified keywords. However, this keyword system is not operating well because many concepts of interest are not mentioned in the caption and hence, the slides cannot be retrieved by keyword alone.

As a result, DWR is scanning the entire slide collection into a digital format and is constructing the following database:

```
create table slides (
   id        int,
   date      date,
   caption   document,
   picture   photo_CD_image);

create table landmarks (
   name      varchar(30),
   location  point);
```

Each slide has identifiers: the date that the slide was taken, a specific caption, and the digitized bits in Kodak Photo-CD format. In fact, the Photo-CD format is a collection of five images, ranging from a 128 x 192 "thumbnail" to the full 2K x 3K color image. At the current time, DWR has digitized about 20,000 images and is building a database with a projected size of 3 terabytes.

DWR is interested in classifying the images electronically. As noted above, classifying the images by hand is implausible. One of the attributes DWR wants to capture is the geographic location of each slide. The technique to accomplish this geo-registration involves a public domain spatial database from the U.S. Geological Survey. Specifically, DWR has the names of all landmarks which appear on any topographic map of California—along with the map location of the landmark. These landmarks are reflected as the table landmarks in the previous code example. Then, DWR proposes to examine the caption for each slide and ascertain if the caption contains the name of a landmark. If so, the location of the landmark is a good indicator of the slide's geographic position.

In addition, DWR is interested in creating programs which will inspect an image and ascertain attributes of the image. In fact, one can find "sunset" in this particular slide library by looking for the color orange at the top of the picture. Low water in a reservoir entails looking for a blue object surrounded by a brown ring. Many attributes of a picture in which DWR has an interest can be found using a fairly mundane pattern of matching techniques. Of course, some attributes are more difficult to isolate, such as ascertaining if the picture contains an endangered species. These attributes must wait for future advances in pattern recognition.

As a result, the previously mentioned schema contains a caption field that is a short document, a picture field that is a Photo-CD image, and a location field that is a type of geographic point. As such, this application is obviously on the right-hand side of our matrix.

Moreover, all the clients of this database submit ad-hoc inquiries. In one such inquiry, a user wishes to find a photo of a sunset taken within 20 miles of Sacramento. Users want a friendly interface to assist them in stating the following SQL query:

```
select id
from slides P, landmarks L S
where sunset (P.picture) and
contains (P.caption, L.name) and
L.location |20| S.location and
S.name = 'Sacramento';
```

This query can be explained as follows. First, it is necessary to find Sacramento in the Landmarks table. This table yields the geographic location of Sacramento (which is on several topographic maps). Then, other landmarks (L.location) are located which are within 20 miles of S.location. |20| is a user-defined operator defined for two operands, each of type point, which return true if the two points are within 20 miles of each other. This is the set of landmarks used to ascertain if any landmarks appear in the caption of a picture. "Contains" is a user-defined function which accepts two arguments, a document and a keyword, and ascertains if the keyword appears in the document. This function yields the set of pictures which are candidates for the result of the query. Lastly, sunset is a second user-defined function that examines the bits in an image to determine if the pictures have orange at the top. The net result of the query is the one desired by the client.

Obviously, this application entails "query mostly" on complex data. As such, it is an example of an upper right-hand corner application. The requirements for this kind of application will now be discussed.

Query Language

Notice in the example query about Sacramento sunsets, there are four clauses in the predicate of the query. The first contains a user-defined function, sunset, and is thereby not in SQL-92. The second clause likewise contains a user-defined function "Contains." The third clause contains a user-defined operator, |20|, which is not in SQL-92. Only the last clause is expressible in SQL-92. As such, this upper right-hand corner application requires a query language which allows at least user-defined functions and operators. The first standard version of SQL with these capabilities is SQL-3, now in draft form. Hence, the user requires an SQL-3 DBMS. Any SQL-2 DBMS is essentially useless on this application, since three of the four clauses cannot be expressed in SQL-2.

Tools

DWR would like to program the user's application by displaying a map of the state of California on-screen. Then, a pointing device can be used to circle the area of the state in which the user is interested. For example, on output, the user can see a map of Sacramento County with a "thumbnail" of each image positioned at its geographic location. With the ability to "pan" over the county, the user can examine thumbnails of interest. In addition, the user can "zoom" into given areas to obtain the higher resolution images stored in Photo-CD objects. Such a "pan and zoom" interface is typical of scientific visualization products, such as Khoros, Explorer, and AVS. As such, the user can benefit by the use of a visualization system which is carefully integrated with a DBMS. Notice that a standard 4GL is nearly useless on this application; there is not a business form in sight.

Performance

The user requires that queries, such as the Sacramento sunset, perform very rapidly. These are typically decision-support queries with significant predicates. To perform well in this environment, a collection of optimizations is required. For example, the sunset function typically consumes 100 million or more instructions. As such, if the query optimizer sees a clause of the following form:

```
where sunset (image) and date < "Jan 1, 1985"
```

the second clause should be performed first, thereby eliminating some of the images. The sunset clause is evaluated subsequently. A requirement in the upper right-hand corner of the applications matrix determines which functions are expensive to compute. Moreover, if many queries use the sunset function, then it is desirable to precompute its value for each image. Hence, the function would be executed once per image in the database, rather than once per each query that specifies sunsets.

Automatically supporting precomputation on image insertions and updates is a very useful optimization tactic. Lastly, in order to find the landmarks within 20 miles of Sacramento, it is necessary to efficiently execute a "point in circle" query. Such two-dimensional queries cannot be accelerated by B+tree indexes, which are one-dimensional access methods. As such, traditional access methods (B+trees and hashing) are not optimal for these clauses. Accelerating such spatial clauses requires a spatial access method, such as a grid file, R-tree, or K-D-B tree. A DBMS must either have such "object-specific access methods" or it must allow a user or system integrator to add an access method. Obviously, the best technical answer is the latter choice.

Notice that optimizing TPC-A is irrelevant to this application. There are essentially no transaction processing applications in the upper right-hand corner.

Security

Some upper right-hand corner applications have security requirements. As a result, the DBMS should run in a client/server architecture, as noted in Figure 1. Security is rarely tradeable for performance in this environment. Moreover, since this is a query world, the commands are "heavy," and the performance win in relinquishing security is much less dramatic than in the lower right-hand corner.

The DBMSs that support a dialect of SQL-3 (including non-traditional tools), and which optimize for complex decision-support SQL-3 queries, may be termed as object-relational DBMSs. These DBMSs are relational in nature since they support SQL; they are object-oriented in nature due to their support of complex data. In essence, these DBMSs are a marriage of the SQL from the relational realm and the modeling primitives from the object realm.

This article has already noted that an SQL-92 system will create an upper right-hand corner problem, since SQL-92 cannot express user queries. As a result, user queries must be executed in a user program, and this necessity places the burden on the user. In addition, if "sunset" is executed in user space, then a very large image must be transmitted over a client/server connection from the server space to client space. This transmission can potentially cause a severe performance problem. As such, a relational DBMS is too time consuming to solve upper right-hand corner problems.

Similarly, a persistent language does not provide a query language which can be used to express the user's query. Hence, the query must be expressed in a C++ program.

If a user has a lower right-hand corner problem, it is not recommended to use a relational DBMS solve it, as noted earlier. SQL is not the right kind of interface. Likewise, an SQL-3 system is not the correct choice, for the same reasons. As such, it is not recommended to use an object-relational DBMS on a lower right-hand corner problem.

Lastly, for an upper left-hand corner problem, usually an object-relational DBMS can be used to solve it. Similarly, SQL-3 is a superset of SQL-92, so it is possible to use an object-relational DBMS to solve an SQL-92 problem.

Summary

As explained previously, there are three different kinds of DBMSs—each with its own focus on a particular segment of the marketplace. These segments require very different query languages and tools, and are optimized with different kinds of engine enhancements. Moreover, the requirements for security differ among the segments. In effect, each kind of engine has carefully "scoped out" a segment of the marketplace and is optimized for that segment.

In addition, a DBMS oriented toward a specific segment generally introduces problems in a different segment. As such, the summary of this section is straightforward: classify your problem into one of the four quadrants, and then use a DBMS optimized for the quadrant. This advice is summarized in Table 2.

	Simple Data	Complex Data
Query	Relational DBMS	Object-Relational DBMS
No Query	Filesystem	Object-Oriented DBMS

Table 2: A classification of DBMS applications.

Many readers may ask, "How large is the upper right-hand corner?" Currently, the upper right-hand corner is largely the domain of start-up companies whose aggregate revenue is not large. However, the real question is: "How much potential resides in this quadrant?" This article provides two different answers to this question.

First, there is a significant number of applications that fit into this quadrant. These include medical imaging problems, digital library problems, asset management problems in the entertainment industry, and most scientific database applications. Based on these markets—which historically used filesystems because nothing better was available—the market for object-relational DBMS can be estimated to be of a size intermediate between the relational DBMS market and the object-oriented DBMS market. However, the second answer is perhaps more indicative.

In time, many of the applications in the upper left-hand corner may migrate toward the upper right-hand corner. For example, consider a typical insurance company which has a customer database and a claims database, presumably implemented as traditional business data processing applications in a relational DBMS. Additionally, the company plans to add a diagram for every accident site, the scanned image of the police report, the picture of the dented car, the latitude and longitude of the accident site, and the latitude and longitude of each customer's home. Then, the company wants to find the ten most dangerous intersections in each county and charge a "hazard premium" to each customer who lives within one mile of such an intersection. Besides finding high-risk customers, the insurance company also wants to find fraudulent body shops which charge excessive amounts for repairs. Eventually, the company also plans to add other kinds of decision-support functions.

As such, the typical insurance application will move from the upper left-hand corner area as it becomes an application with both upper left and upper right components. Simultaneously, the upper left-hand component will be subject to "technological depreciation." Specifically, the business data processing load of a typical upper left-hand corner application will increase slowly, perhaps at 10 percent per year. While the number of customers increases slowly, the number of incidents will grow slowly. As such, the load increases rather slowly. At the same time, the cost of the computers to execute this load declines. Currently, the cost of CPU cycles, disk storage, and main memory decreases at almost a factor of two per year. As a result, the cost of executing a given workload declines at almost a factor of two per year. This trend makes the business data processing workload technologically easier, at almost a factor of two per year. As such, not only is the application moving to the right-hand corner, but the upper left-hand corner applications are less expensive.

These trends will drive applications from upper left-hand to upper right-hand corners, thereby increasing over time the size of the object-relational DBMS market and, in turn, creating "the next wave."

About the Author

Dr. Michael R. Stonebraker is a co-founder of Illustra Information Technologies, Inc., and Chief Technology Officer of Informix. A noted expert in database management systems, operating systems, and expert systems, Dr. Stonebraker is Professor Emeritus of Computer Science at the University of California, Berkeley, where he joined the faculty in 1971. Illustra Information Technologies, Inc. represents the commercialization of Dr. Stonebraker's POSTGRES research project. In 1996, Informix acquired Illustra Information Technolgies, Inc.

Dr. Stonebraker founded INGRES Corporation (now the INGRES Products Division of ASK Computer Systems) in 1980 and served on the company's board of directors until 1993. Dr. Stonebraker recently authored the book entitled "Object-Relational DBMSs: The Next Great Wave."

9

AN INTRODUCTION TO ILLUSTRA'S ORDBMS CONCEPTS

by Matthew Eichler

The purpose of this article is to give the Informix developer an introduction to the Illustra server and the ORDBMS development environment. The Illustra extensions to the relational database offer the RDBMS developer a new frontier in application development. This article discusses several important considerations which are useful in planning an initial Illustra project.

What is Illustra?

Illustra Information Technologies was founded in 1992 to commercialize the POSTGRES "Object Relational Database Management System" project at the University of California at Berkeley (UCB). POSTGRES—initiated by the UCB Database Research Group under the leadership of Professor Michael Stonebraker in 1986—derived its name by being the next-generation DBMS after another UCB project, the Ingres RDBMS. Dr. Stonebraker later became the co-founder and Chief Technology Officer of Illustra.

The concept of extending RDBMS with rich types has been widely discussed since the mid-80's. However, it is only recently that businesses have recognized the need to manage all types of information assets with database systems. Along with the increase in multimedia applications and the incredible growth of the World Wide Web (Web), the scope of business information systems

(IS) has expanded beyond OLTP-structured data. Regardless of what type of data is used, the classic problems of manageability and scalability continue to plague IS shops.

Illustra's outstanding technology has come into the limelight as a radically new approach to databases. Illustra's Web site is at http://www.illustra.com, and the University of California at Berkeley POSTGRES project home page is at: http://s2k-ftp.CS.Berkeley.EDU:8000/postgres.

ORDBMS Concepts

Relational Database Management Systems (RDBMS) are widely popular due to the following reasons:

- SQL is an easy to use language—based on an open standard.

- The "flat" relational model allows changes to data structures—without cumbersome conversion processes that are required by older "network" and "hierarchical" database systems.

- RDBMS servers—such as INFORMIX-OnLine Dynamic Server—have evolved into highly scalable, cross-platform systems with robust administration tools. The developer can begin developing applications without worrying that the application will become too expensive to manage or grow beyond the means of the hardware or database server, (see Figure 1).

RDBMS technology has its disadvantages as well:

- Data must be highly structured and based on only a handful of built-in data types.

- There is no way for the developer to extend the functionality of the server. For example, there is no way to add "fuzzy-logic" text search server functions to a document-retrieval system that can be accessed through SQL.

- There is no way for the developer to define new datatypes with the usability of built-in types. For example, an application might require a three-dimensional (3D) spatial type that can be defined by points in space.

While RDBMS applications were well under way, Object-Oriented (OO) languages were also gaining popularity, for the following reasons:

RDBMS

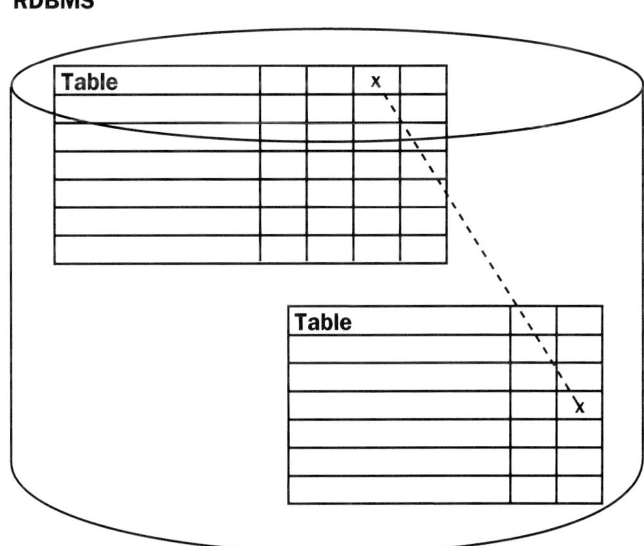

Figure 1: The Relational Database Management Systems (RDBMS) model.

- The developer can package data and functionality into reusable component libraries. These components can be easily "consumed" by other developers—without requiring an understanding of their inner workings. Thus, complex functionality is provided with simple interfaces.

- The developer can build "rich types" (such as the 3D-spatial type) for special purposes with all the functions and operators required to make the types usable as true data types.

Object-Orientated Languages

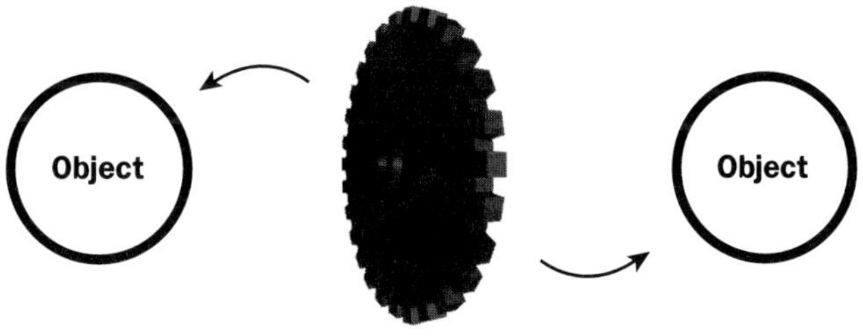

Interface Functions

Figure 2: Object-oriented languages.

The next step in extending the usefulness of objects is to apply database technology to manage the objects and to make them "persistent." Object Database Management Systems (ODBMS) have not gained wide acceptance, due to the following reasons:

- In terms of transaction management, recovery, availability, scalability and administration tools, ODBMS is not as robust as RDBMS technology.

- ODBMS has not benefited from an open, standard interface, such as SQL. Most vendors have proprietary APIs—which are harder to use and add to the cost of application development.

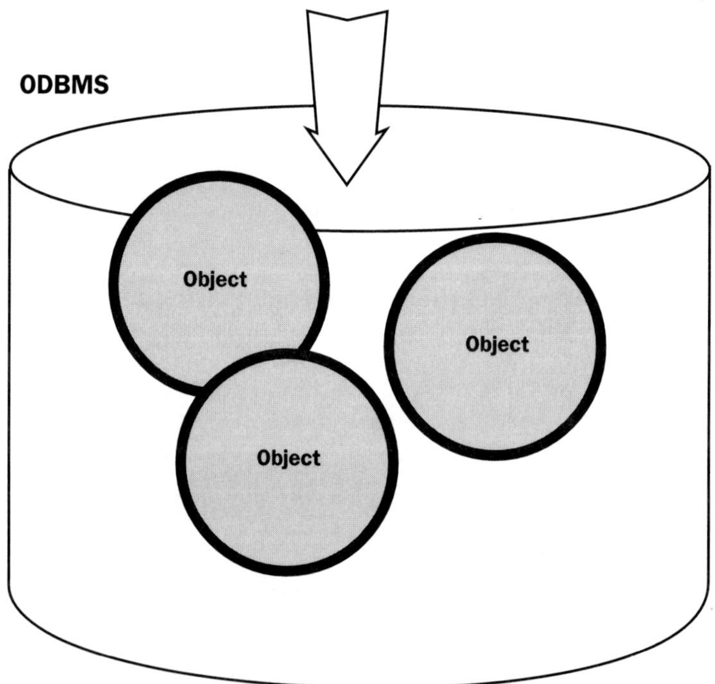

Figure 3: The Object Database Management Systems (ODBMS) model.

To add to the complexity of this technological landscape, there is a new generation of applications which the database developer must design for a wider variety of data types and complex functionality beyond traditional OLTP:

- Medical imaging;

- Mechanical CAD;

- Geographic Information Systems (GIS);

- Data warehousing/data mining;

- Text and document retrieval;

- Multimedia;

- Graphical User Interfaces (GUI); and

- Internet and World Wide Web.

The Illustra Object Relational Database Management System (ORDBMS) provides the best of the relational and object worlds:

- Illustra is SQL2 compliant—enabling the developer to work with a familiar interface (as opposed to the proprietary API of an ODBMS).

- Illustra provides extensions to SQL—allowing the development of complex, composite types (for example, arrays, sets, nested structures, and inheritance hierarchies).

- Illustra provides an API (*libmi*) which enables the developer to extend the server by building "server functions."

- Illustra provides the means for the developer to create complete rich types with the same usability as built-in types (for example, operators, rules, alerts, aggregates, casts, and index functions).

- Illustra provides DataBlades which extend the base engine with pre-built server functions and rich types (similar to an object library). For more information on DataBlades, refer to the next section of this article.

Consider the scenario of the Informix database developer who is working on a pilot Web site project. The project might include a mix of structured data from the RDBMS and files in the filesystem—including HTML pages and images. To minimize maintenance costs and plan for scaling up in size, the developer should minimize the number of files, including executables, which will be managed from the filesystem. Illustra solves these problems for the following reasons:

ORDBMS

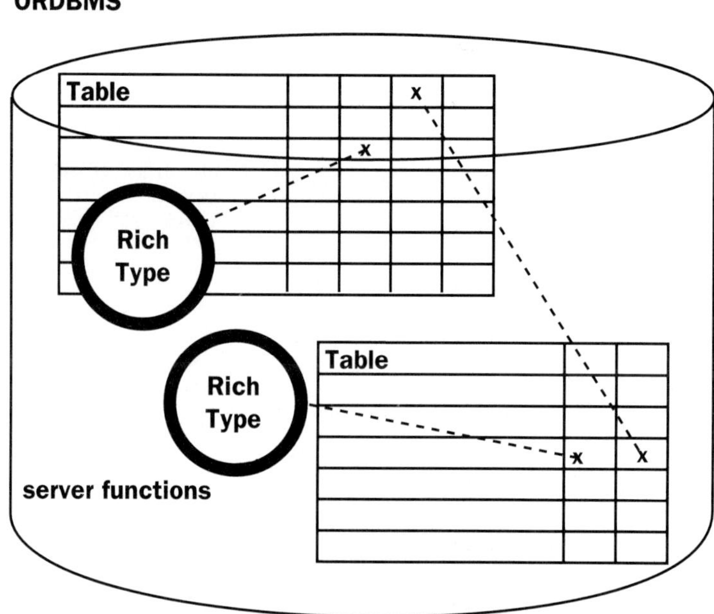

Figure 4: The Object Relational Database Management Systems (ORDBMS) model.

- Structured data can be handled with standard SQL tables;

- The Web DataBlade can be used to pass HTML pages to the Illustra server, where the special Illustra HTML tags can be interpreted. These tags allow the developer to imbed SQL commands within pages, and provide state and conditional logic;

- Text and Image DataBlades can be used to add text search and image management functionality to the application; and

- As the Web site grows, Illustra provides the foundation for the addition of new rich types—without losing manageability of the site. For instance, the developer can add video and sound objects. Additionally, the developer can enhance the user interface using Sun Microsystems' Java product. With Java, the developer can store compiled Java applets in the database.

What is a DataBlade?

A DataBlade is a type of object library that usually implements one or two rich types for a specific purpose. A DataBlade is installed into the database of choice. The developer can install more than one DataBlade in a database to implement all the required functionality. Note that casting functions are not always available to convert a type that was installed from one DataBlade to a type that was installed from another.

DataBlades are sometimes applications in their own right. For instance, the Web DataBlade provides an executable Webdriver which resides in the Web server's CGI executable directory, and passes requests to and from the browser and the Illustra server. This DataBlade also includes Application Page Builder pages which provide an environment for the developer to begin building an Illustra Web site immediately.

Other DataBlades include conversion and load utilities to convert filesystem data into a common format for use by the database or the Text DataBlade.

Following are some DataBlades which are currently available:

- Image DataBlade—Basic image management, manipulation, and retrieval;

- Text DataBlade—Basic text search;

- PLS Text DataBlade—Advanced text search;

- Drawing DataBlade—Storage and manipulation of 3D vector graphics;

- S-PLUS DataBlade—Advanced statistical and graphical data analysis;

- Timeseries DataBlade—Manipulation and analysis of time-sequenced data;

- 2D, 3D Spatial DataBlade—Manipulation and retrieval of spatial data; and

- Web DataBlade—Interface database to Web browsers, and the storage and manipulation of Web pages.

Illustra's Extensions to SQL

Illustra implements a number of object and rich type extensions to SQL. Since an ORDBMS is intended to function under the relational model, the extensions are object-based, but not purely object-oriented:

Data-Type Extensions

Text is a highly useful type in the development of Illustra databases which involve unstructured data (implemented differently than the TEXT BLOB type in Informix databases). Text is string data of variable length. The Informix user, in deciding between CHAR, VARCHAR, or TEXT data types for string data, contends with a series of trade-offs. CHAR is invariable in length and always uses the same number of bytes. VARCHAR supports a variable length, although it is limited to 256 bytes. TEXT can be of any length, but when it is a BLOB type, the type cannot be included as query criterion (except to test for NULLS), nor indexed. In using the Illustra text type, on the other hand, the developer is not required to make any of these trade-off decisions. Illustra provides a built-in implicit cast to Large Object when the string data can no longer fit in its own 8K page. Many of the examples provided by Illustra prefer the TEXT type over the fixed length CHAR type which is typically found in Informix applications.

```
create table         inventory
   ( part_id         text,
    description       text );
```

Other Illustra data-type extensions include native date/time types (an improvement over ANSI standard date/time and interval handling) and boolean.

```
create table web_pages
   (    title     text,
        page      text,
        active    boolean default 't',
        created   timestamp,
        expires   abstime );
```

Type Definition: create type

The developer can create abstract data-type structures which can be helpful later for the creation of tables. Types can be made of base types and other user-defined types. Tables can be made of a single type, or a mix of base types and user-defined types. Using types and data-structure extensions, the developer can create a complex data model of composite types, as opposed to the "flat" model of an RDBMS. Illustra also provides the developer with the ability to supply functions to cast from one type to another.

Typically, sample Illustra data models define types first, and then, tables are built from the types. In other words, for each table there is a corresponding type. Types can also take advantage of inheritance-tree structures.

```
create type zip_t
    ( code      char(5),
    plus_four char(4)  );

create type address_t
    ( street  text,
    city        text,
    state       char(2),
    zip         zip_t  );


create table address of type address_t;
```

References: OID and ref()

Illustra gives every object in the database (including individual rows in a table)
an object identifier (OID) which is unique to the server instance. A type or table
column can refer to an object ID using the ref() construct:

```
create type sched_t
    ( wbs_id        text,
    work_descr      text,
    start_date      abstime,
    end_date        abstime );
create type          project_plan_t
    ( title          text,
    description     text,
    current_work  ref(sched_t)  );
```

Multi-Dimensional Structures: arrays, setof()

Fixed-length arrays can be used in data structures:

```
create table time_card
    ( name           text,
    week_ending    date,
    hours            integer[7]  );


insert into time_card
    values
    ( 'Matt',
    '1994-03-05',
    '[8,8,10,8,8,8,0]'  );
```

Sets can be used if an unordered group of objects (of any type) of unlimited size is desired:

```
create type skill_t
    ( language     text,
      level         integer );


create table emp
    ( name          text,
      skills        setof(skill_t) );
```

Inheritance: under

The Ilustra developer can create OO-type inheritance trees for types and tables using the *under* clause in DDL statements. Unlike a pure OO environment, the inheritance only specifies data structures, not methods. In other words, a specialized type or table can inherit from a parent to add additional fields.

```
create type emp_t
(   name        text,base_salary numeric(12,2),
    manager     ref(emp_t) );


create type engineer_t
(   skills      setof(text),
    bonus       numeric(12,2) )
    under       emp_t;


create type sales_t
(   territory       text,
    commission      numeric(12,2) )
    under           emp_t;


create type techsales_t
    under engineer_t, sales_t;


create table employee of type emp_t;
create table engineer of type engineer_t;
create table sales of type sales_t;
create table techsales of type techsale_t;
```

In the previous example, the *engineer* table includes the columns of the employee table plus two additional ones. The *techsales* table includes all the columns of the *employee*, *sales* and *engineer* tables.

The developer can view the entire contents of a table in this inheritance tree by using the special construct:

```
select employee from employee;
```

This statement results in "jagged" rows, since the query includes the contents of several tables in the inheritance tree—each with a different number of columns.

Function Definition: create function

A high level of extensibility is achieved with Illustra from user-defined functions. Functions can be either SQL or dynamically linked code (written in C using *libmi*). Functions can be overloaded, since functions which take different numbers of parameters and/or different data types for parameters are considered unique.

An example of an SQL function:

```
create function update_by_pct (numeric, char(10))
   returns void
   as
   update inventory
        set price = price * ($1/100)
        where part_id = $2;
```

Below is an example of a C function using a dynamically-linked library built in C:

```
create function need_more (integer)
   returns boolean
   as
   external name 'MI_HOME/userfuncs/need.so' language C;
```

Rules and Alerters

Rules are a method to provide actions triggered by inserts, updates, deletes, or selects on tables, columns, views, and versions. The Illustra rule is more flexible than the Informix *trigger:*

- Rules can be triggered by selects, as well as inserts, updates, and deletes;

- There is no limit to the number of Rules on a table or column; and

- A Rule can cause an update on the same table or column which triggered the rule.

```
create rule employee_ctrl
    as
    on update to employees do
    insert into empl_audit
        values ( 'now'::abstime, user, current.name );
```

Alerters allow SQL events to trigger messages to the client. The client application must subscribe to a particular alerter in order to receive the message. Alerters can be used to monitor types of activities on the database.

```
create table sales_orders
    ( item_no      integer,
      unit_cost    money,
      quantity     integer);


create alerter big_order (mechanism = 'callback');


create rule verify_price
    as
    on insert to sales_orders
    where new.unit_cost * new.quantity > 1000 do
    begin
        insert into big_audit
        values ('now', user, new.item_no, new.quantity);
        alert big_order;
    end;
```

Casting: create cast

Illustra supports explicit casts and unambiguous implicit casts to one level. The Illustra developer can define casts by binding them to functions with the *create cast* DDL. In developing new base types, casting is an important tool and the developer must provide casts for all possible uses of the new type.

```
create type dollar under integer;
create type yen under integer;

create function yen_to_dollar(yen)
    returns dollar
    as return ( $1/100 );
create cast (yen as dollar with yen_to_dollar);
```

The developer can explicitly cast from one type to another using two colons (::):

```
create table japan_part
(   part        text,
    supplier    text,
    price       yen );


insert into japan_part (part, price) values ('part2', 100);


select part, price::dollar from japan_part;
```

Rich Types, Base Types

SQL extensions allow the Illustra developer to build new base types with rich functionality. A new base type can be designed with input, output, operators, aggregates, casting, and indexing functions so that it may be used anywhere in an SQL statement.

The following example begins to define a new base type, *complex,* by starting with input, output, addition, and multiplication functions—assuming the functions have been built in C using *libmi* into a shared library:

```
create function complex_in(text) returns complex
    as external name '/home/complex/complex.so' language C;


create function complex_out(complex) returns text
    as external name '/home/complex/complex.so' language C;


create type complex(
    internallength=8, input=complex_in, output=complex_out);


create function Plus(complex, complex) returns complex
    as external name '/home/complex/complex.so(add)' language C;
```

```
create function Times(complex, complex) return complex
   as external name '/home/complex/complex.so(times)' language C;

create function Times(complex, float) return complex
   as external name '/home/complex/complex.co(times_flt)' language C;
```

Illustra Query Tool

The *Illustra Query Tool* is a graphical tool that allows Windows 95 and Windows NT to issue Illustra SQL statements against a database. It is the graphical equivalent to Informix's *dbaccess*. This tool supports the special data constructs of Illustra—including complex nested structures, sets, and jagged rows (from inheritance hierarchies), as well as server function calls within statements.

libmi

The C library *libmi* provides a complete C language API for building Illustra client and server applications. When building a new base type with a complete interface in Illustra SQL, the developer will most likely require this library. *Libmi* can also be used to build client applications on the same platforms on which the database server is available, as well as 32-bit Windows and Macintosh. The library includes:

- Structures and functions to read and manipulate the environment passed from SQL;

- Structures and functions to use complex/variable length data types, sets, and jagged rows;

- Functions to connect to the database and execute SQL, including queries that fetch multiple rows;

- Functions to handle asynchronous events and alerts;

- Error handling and functions to raise SQL exceptions; and

- Functions to debug and trace query optimizer performance.

A client function must be statically linked to the client application. Therefore, the application must be installed to take advantage of a function. Server functions are compiled into dynamically-linked libraries and run in the same process space as the Illustra server. Illustra has provided the ability to build client functions mainly for development and debugging purposes. Afterwards, the functions can be "pushed" out to the server and deployed in server function libraries.

vblibmi

Vblibmi allows the developer to build Visual Basic client applications for the Illustra server. Most of the functionality of the C library *libmi* is exposed to the Visual Basic programmer.

C++ Interface

The Illustra client *C++ Interface* encapsulates the *libmi* functionality in C++ classes for the Microsoft Visual C++ and Microsoft Foundation Class Library developer.

Web DataBlade Application Page Builder

The *Web DataBlade Application Page Builder* is a set of HTML pages and forms that allow the Web developer to build an entire site based on the Illustra database—no other tools are required. Six special Illustra HTML tags are used to execute SQL statements, as well as to control state and logical flow within pages.

Project Considerations

Size

Although the SQL face is familiar, the Illustra ORDBMS still presents a radical paradigm shift for most developers—time and resource management can easily slip out of control. A key to success is to select a project of a manageable size—it probably should be smaller than the average project. Also, look for new applications with a relatively low profile which are not mission-critical to the enterprise.

Information Asset Management

A large part of an enterprise's information assets are still stored in the filesystems, due to RDBMS technology's limitations in handling the assets. An Illustra database can store all types of data in one place and structured, relational data ("metadata") serves to expose this rich repository of information to users—rendering it easy for users to search and retrieve exactly what they need.

Look for opportunities in the following areas:

- Document files, scanned documents, facsimiles, and text;

- Images, graphic artwork, photography, logos, icons, and video clips;

- Spreadsheets, and forms;

- Presentations, slides, and overheads;

- Audio clips, speeches, and music;

- Training materials, videos, and computer-based training files; and

- Sales materials, brochures, white papers, and fact sheets.

A New Base Type

A high level of re-usability is achieved in Illustra by building a new base type. New base types are useful when one particular type of data is used throughout an application and requires special input/output, conversion, retrieval or storage methods. The advantage is that the new datatype is completely accessible from SQL as though it were a built-in type. Thus, it is easy to use in many client applications. The disadvantage is the expense of ramping up in-house development and/or hiring consultants to use *libmi*. Do not underestimate the costs in undertaking a project which requires advanced C programming abilities. The alternative is to use the rich types already available in existing *DataBlades*.

Structured Versus Unstructured Data

Avoid using Illustra for an application with a high percentage of structured data that already fits in the standard RDBMS model. For instance, a straight conversion of an Informix schema would not make using Illustra worthwhile. On the other hand, adding unstructured data, such as large text objects, to existing structured data or remodelling an existing schema with complex types would be more appropriate for a pilot project. Note that no conversion utilities yet exist to convert between an Informix schema and an Illustra schema. Since ORDBMS is a paradigm shift, allow time and resources to carefully review and evolve the new data model. Remember that the Illustra TEXT type will often replace the Informix CHAR type. Also, look for opportunities to create types first in Illustra, before declaring tables.

Document Management

Businesses can often find opportunities to improve the document management of word processing files, scanned documents, facsimiles and/or ASCII text files. The key to success lies in the special text search capabilities which Illustra provides with both simple and advanced text *DataBlades*. These search capabilities include:

■ Keyword searches;

■ Phrase searches;

■ Natural language searches;

■ Proximity searches;

■ Fuzzy matching;

■ Conceptual searches; and

■ Weighted results.

Web sites can also benefit from intuitive text searches.

Conclusion

The Illustra ORDMS server is an excellent solution to the developer's ever expanding range of new data and information asset management challenges. Care should be taken to ensure the Illustra pilot project is successful.

About the Author

Matthew Eichler is a project manager in the Informix MIS Technologies group in Menlo Park, California. He can be contacted at matthew@informix.com.

The Data Warehouse

10

PARALLEL PROCESSING AND THE DATA WAREHOUSE

by William H. Inmon

One of the essences of the data warehouse environment is the accumulation and the management of large amounts of data. Indeed, it is said that if you manage large amounts of data well in the data warehouse environment, then all other aspects of the data warehouse design and usage come easily. And if you do not manage large amounts of data well in the data warehouse environment, then nothing else really matters because you will fail. It is true that the management of large amounts of data is the first and most critical success factor in the building and using of the data warehouse.

There are many design approaches and techniques for the management of large amounts of data in the warehouse environment, such as:

- Storing data on multiple storage media;

- Summarizing data when detail becomes obsolete;

- Storing data relationships in terms of artifacts;

- Encoding and referencing data where appropriate;

- Partitioning data for independent management of the different partitions;

- Choosing levels of granularity and summarization properly for the data warehouse, and so forth.

The Topic of Discussion

While all of these design and architecture techniques and approaches are valid and should be employed in any hardware environment, there is another approach to the management of large volumes of data for the data warehouse and that approach is to select technology that can manage data in parallel. Parallel technology is sometimes known as database machine technology.

This discussion will be on the management of large amounts of data warehouse data in a parallel environment. At this point, the reader should be very cautious about one aspect of this discussion. This discussion is for the data warehouse only. Occasionally, a developer will try to use database machine or parallel technology for operational processing. This discussion is not about that kind of environment. Also, a designer will try to use database machine technology for an environment that attempts to do both operational transaction processing and data warehouse processing at the same time on the same machine and on the same data. This discussion is not about that environment. This discussion is for the data warehouse environment only, where parallel technology has been selected as the (or one of the) primary storage and access method(s).

The Appeal of Parallel Technology

Parallel technology is technology in which different machines are tightly coupled together but work independently. The machines each manage their own collection of data independently. The spread of data in the data warehouse is orthogonal.

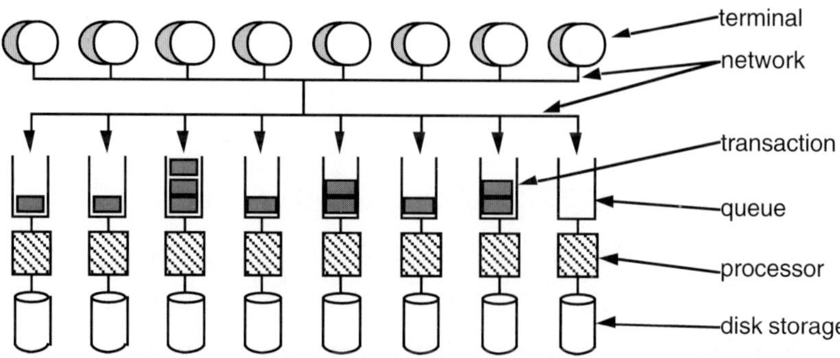

Figure 1: A typical parallel technology approach to the management of large amounts of data.

Figure 1 shows the basic configuration of processors working together and managing data independently.

In Figure 1, there are five basic components of interest—the transaction (or request), the queue in which the transaction is entered, the network connecting the processors, the processor, and the data controlled by the processor.

When a request enters the system, the processor to which the request is channeled determines the queue that the request will enter. In the case of a large transaction, the transaction may be broken into a series of requests for data and processing which, in turn, are routed to the appropriate processor. The request enters the queue, and the processor starts the execution of the request. Upon the completion of the work performed for the request, the results are sent to the requester.

While one processor services the requests that operate on data that belongs to it, another processor services the requests that have been channeled to it independently of the work performed by other processors. It is this independence of processing that has great appeal to the data warehouse architect because the independence of processing means that managing large amount of data is technologically possible. To manage large amounts of data merely requires the harnessing together of multiple processors. Said another way, in order to manage more data warehouse data, the data warehouse architect merely needs to add more processors to the tightly networked configuration, as shown by Figure 2.

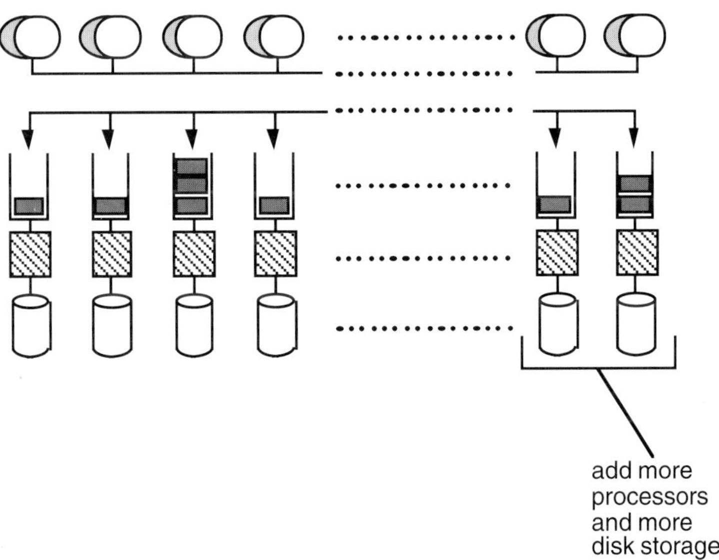

Figure 2: Adding capacity to a parallel environment is linear and easy to do—
you simply add more processors.

In non-parallel environments, adding large amounts of data to an already large environment can cause tremendous difficulties at the basic operating system level. Non-parallel environments have a threshold of data after which they operate inefficiently. Once this threshold of data is reached, there is nothing that can be done except to go to another technology. And transferring data and processing to another technology can be a disruptive, expensive, complex experience to be avoided if at all possible.

Parallel processing offers the possibility that the technology itself can be extended almost ad infinitum, avoiding the conversion of the data warehouse from one technology to another.

The independence of processing in the parallel environment leads to the observation that the speed of access of data is proportional to the number of processors that data is spread over. Suppose a parallel configuration has m independent processors with data spread evenly and optimally over the processors. Now suppose it takes a single large (non-parallel) processor n units of time to service a request. The elapsed time required for the parallel configuration to execute the service is n/m. Figure 3 shows this difference.

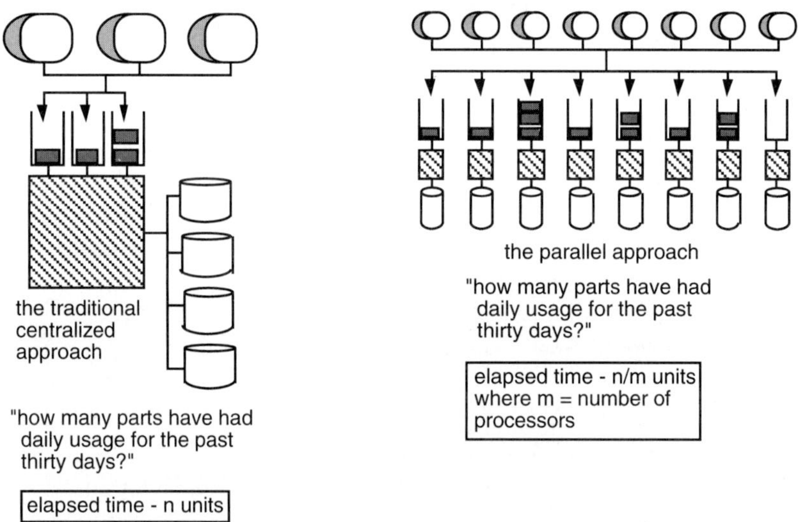

Figure 3: The parallel approach reduces the elapsed time of processing.

The savings in elapsed time by going to a parallel environment can be expressed:

n — (n/m) = elapsed time differential

It is worth noting that the work performed by the systems—either parallel or non-parallel—is the same in terms of I/O. The real difference is not in the total amount of work accomplished, but in the elapsed time required to perform that work.

Another observation about the parallel environment is that the marginal improvement in elapsed time decreases as the number of processors are added. In other words, when the number of processors in the parallel environment increases from one to two, there is an enormous improvement in elapsed time. When the number of processors increases from two to three there is a significant improvement in elapsed time. But as the number of processors increases, the improvement grows smaller. For example, increasing the number of processors from twenty to twenty-one may make no noticeable improvement in elapsed time at all.

The choice between a parallel approach to technology in the data warehouse and a standard centralized approach in the warehouse usually revolves around volumes of data. For small to modest sized data warehouses, a centralized approach makes economic and technological sense. But after a point (when the data warehouse starts to contain a very large volume of data), the amount of data is such that a parallel approach becomes economically and technologically advantageous. The choice always boils down to both technological and economic considerations.

Physical Organization

There are many ways in which the components of parallel technology can be arranged. The following is a discussion of the most common ways, but is hardly intended to describe all the possibilities. It is worth noting that each configuration and arrangement of the components of parallel technology have their associated trade-offs.

Figure 4 on the following page illustrates the (typical) dynamics of the inner workings of the components of the parallel environment.

The request can be a singular request for data that is routed to the appropriate processor or can be a general request that is broken down into a series of specific requests which are individually routed to individual processors.

The queue that the request goes into can be a single large queue that has access to all the processors or can be a series of queues, each of which is unique to different processors. When the queues are unique to different processors, the request must be assigned to a specific processor prior to execution.

The designation of data to a processor can be performed by means of a hashing algorithm or an index, (or ostensibly by both means). When a hashing algorithm is used, the data is divided across the different processors in a random manner based on the primary key of the record. When data is assigned to a processor by means of an index, data is usually (although not necessarily) assigned to a processor in groups.

Once the data arrives at the processor to which it is assigned, it is placed on disk storage and an index keeps track of its assignment. The data is stored in

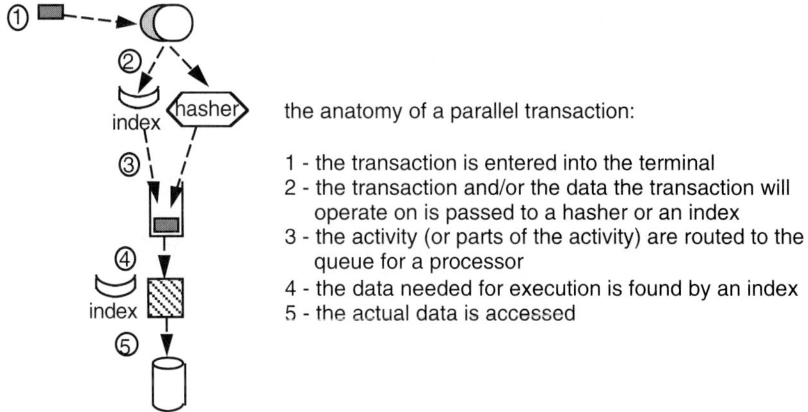

Figure 4: The anatomy of a parallel transaction.

physical blocks, which hold tables, which are made up of rows (or records), which contain columns (or fields).

As stated, there are many variations of the arrangement of the components of a parallel environment, each with its own strengths and weaknesses.

Hot Spots

The appeal of parallel technology is quite strong in the face of needing to manage large amounts of data and the ability to add processing resources in an incremental, non-disruptive fashion. At first glance, it appears that the parallel approach is the answer to the data architect's challenge—insofar as managing the volumes of data found in the data warehouse.

However, there are occasions where the parallel approach to the management of large amounts of data yields worse results in terms of performance than the traditional single processor approach.

The performance and the efficient utilization of the parallel approach to the management of large amounts of data depend on the data being spread evenly across the different processors, so that the corresponding workload is likewise spread evenly over the processors. When there is an even and equitable spread of data and processing, the parallel approach to the management of large amounts of data works quite well. However, if there is an imbalance in the spread of data across the parallel processors and there is a corresponding imbalance in the workload spread across the processors, then there develops what is known as a "hot spot," and the effectiveness of the parallel environment is compromised.

Figure 5 shows a hot spot.

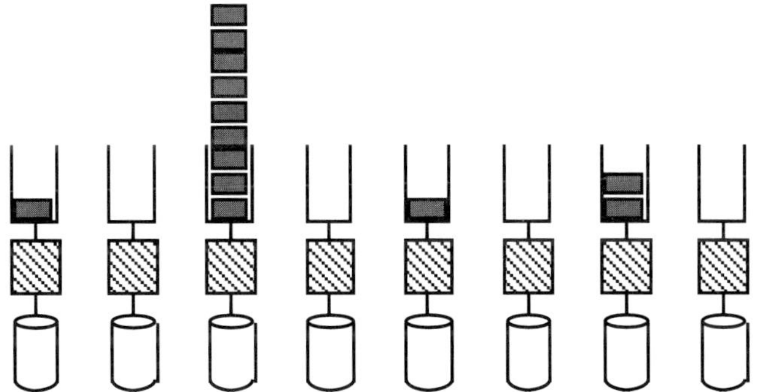

Figure 5: An unequal distribution of the workload results in a "hot spot."

The workload in Figure 5 is seen to be imbalanced and results in a hot spot. Some processors have no work at all and one processor has the majority of the work piled on it. In this case there might as well be a central management of data. Indeed, in this case a central approach to the management of data is much more effective and efficient than a parallel approach.

One of the problems associated with the data warehouse environment, and the world of decision-support systems [DSS] in general, is that the patterns of data access in a warehouse are unpredictable. Both the rate of access and the specific records to be accessed are very variable. This implies that for DSS processing hot spots are the norm.

Of course, hot spots can be remedied. To remedy a hot spot requires the redistribution of data to other or more processors. Figure 6 shows the remedying of hot spots.

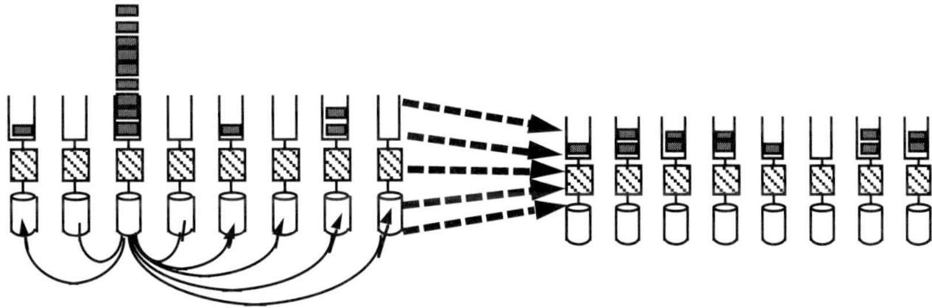

Figure 6: The distribution of data is altered so that the workload is distributed much more evenly over the parallel environment.

The problem with remedying hot spots in the data warehouse environment is that any remedy depends on a foreknowledge of the usage of data. Just because data has shown a pattern of usage in the past does not mean that it will exhibit the same pattern of usage in the future. Therefore, trying to identify and remedy hot spots in the parallel environment is a difficult task.

Operational/DSS Differences

The parallel environment can be used for the purposes of operational or data warehouse, DSS processing, but not both at the same time. There are several reasons why the two environments do not mix in the parallel environment. Figure 7.1, Figure 7.2, Figure 7.3 and Figure 7.4 illustrate some of those differences.

The first difference between the two environments is in the type of transaction that is being run. The operational environment runs many small transactions, each of which attach their processing to a single processor. The data warehouse environment has a very different transaction operating in it. On the other hand, the data warehouse environment contains a few very large transactions which operate on data spread all over the parallel environment.

The second major difference between the two environments lies in the internal structure of the data. The data warehouse environment contains data whose structure is optimized for massive sequential, non-update processing. The operational environment is structured for access of a limited amount of data where the data can be updated.

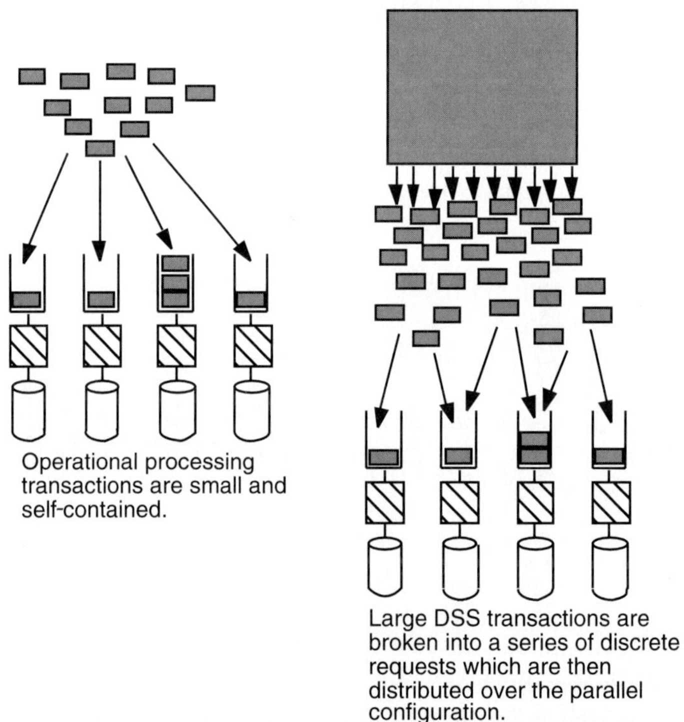

Figure 7.1: The transactions which are run in the operational and data warehouse environment are very different and are managed differently.

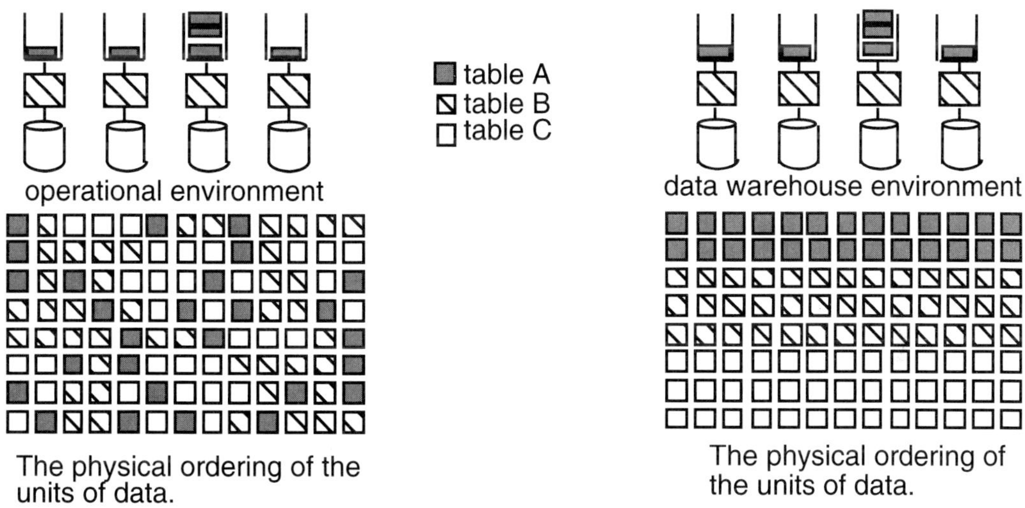

Figure 7.2: The physical structuring of the data is different for the two environments.

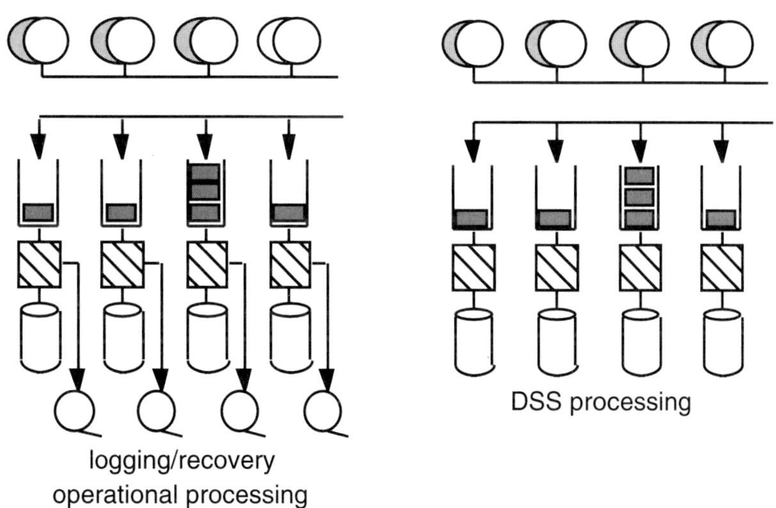

*Figure 7.3: An essential part of the operational environment is logging and recovery;
those facilities are not a part of the DSS environment.*

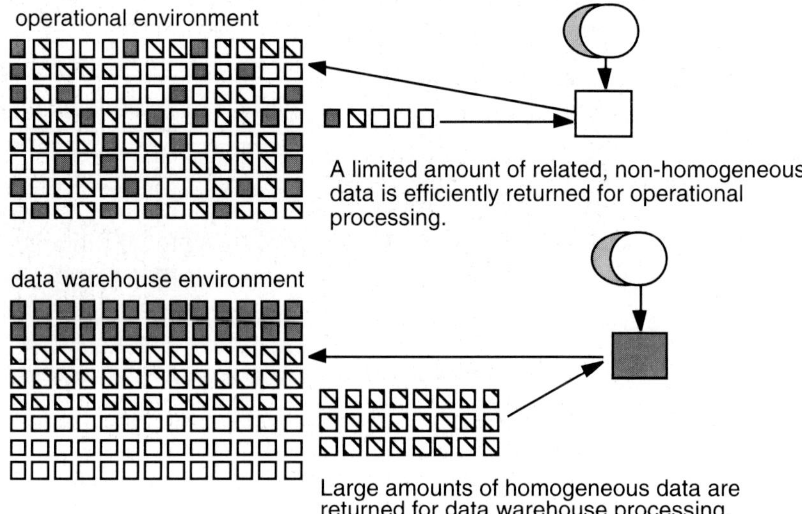

*Figure 7.4: The physical structure of the data has a profound effect
on the efficiency of the processing that occurs.*

In addition, the operational environment typically groups together data of different types, so that a transaction does not need to look into different locations in order to find the data. Data warehouse data, on the other hand, is stored homogeneously.

Another important difference between the operational environment and the data warehouse environment is in the logging of data. Since operational processing involves the update (or potential update) of data, there is a certain amount of overhead required. Logging is one type of overhead that comes with update processing. But data from a data warehouse does not require a log because no update is performed. Therefore, the basic system characteristics of the operating system are quite different.

These, then, are the basic reasons why the operational environment and the data warehouse environment do not mix, even in the face of a parallel management of data.

The Level of the Warehouse

The main benefit of the data warehouse which resides on parallel technology is that data can be accessed quickly and randomly. The details of data managed in this way are relatively easy to obtain. But a parallel management of data is expensive.

Most organizations try to position the current-detail level of the data warehouse in the parallel environment, and allow other levels of the data warehouse to reside on other technologies. Figure 8 shows this arrangement.

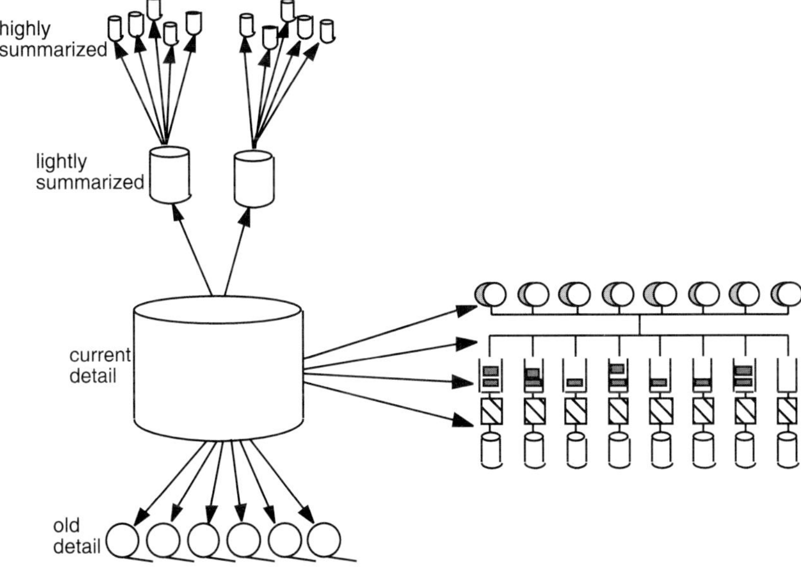

***Figure 8: Using parallel technology to manage only the current-detail portion of the
data warehouse.***

For a variety of reasons—economic and technological—the management of
current detailed data by parallel technology and other data by other technologies
is a very good solution.

Metadata in the Parallel Data Warehouse Environment

Metadata is one of the most important aspects of the data warehouse environment. The fact that the data warehouse resides on a parallel technology neither
diminishes nor enhances the role of metadata.

Typically the metadata stored with a data warehouse includes:

■ Data content;

■ Data structure;

■ The mapping of data from the operational environment;

■ The history of extracts; and

■ Versioning, etc.

Physical Design in the Parallel Data Warehouse Environment

The design of the data warehouse in the parallel environment proceeds exactly the same as the design of a data warehouse in the non-parallel environment in the early phases of design. The activities of defining the data model, defining the major subject areas, defining the system of record and so forth, are the same for both environments. The major difference in the design of a data warehouse in the parallel environment comes when the physical design is created. The spread of the data over the different processors is a major design issue.

The first issue is how many processors there will be. The next issue is how the data will be spread over the processors. Some of the relevant factors affecting this decision are:

■ The growth pattern of the data;

■ The initial volume of the data; and

■ The access pattern of the data.

Another important design issue is what the primary key of the data ought to be. The primary key affects the physical spread of the data over the different parallel processors in that the primary key is the discriminator that allows the data to be spread in the first place. A related important design issue is the placement of the secondary key of the data for units of data not directly related to the key. Secondary data may be placed randomly over the parallel processors or may be forced into the same physical location as the data relating directly to the primary key. The usage of the data dictates which is the better choice.

Partitioning of data is as important in the parallel environment as it is in the centralized data warehouse environment. Partitioning allows you to index data independently, to restructure data independently, to manage data independently, and so forth.

The assignment of data to parallel processor by means of the definition of keys is a very important design aspect in the data warehouse environment because the physical placement of data profoundly affects the pattern of access to data, which in turn has a profound effect on the effectiveness of the parallel management of data. Said another way, if the data is not spread properly over the parallel processors, the benefit of parallel processing is lost and the data may as well be managed by a single central processor.

A second important physical design aspect is the identification and support of derived (i.e., summary) data in the data warehouse environment. The storage of summary data makes sense when that data is used often and/or when an "official" calculation of data must be performed and there is concern that if calculation is accomplished more than once it will not be correct. Under these circumstances, summarization and the storing of data in the parallel environment makes sense.

An important physical design technique in the parallel data warehouse environment is that of the prejoining of data when it is known that the data will be joined as a regular matter of course. If it is known that data will be joined, it is much more efficient to join the data at the moment of load than it is to join the data dynamically.

Another physical design technique is to create artifacts of relationships in the data warehouse. Data relationships are important in the data warehouse. However, their implementation is quite different than that found in the operational environment.

Because data is much more quickly accessible in the parallel data warehouse environment, it is a temptation to store as much detailed data as possible, on the theory that you can never tell when you will be needing a scrap of data. There is, however, a cost of storing data in the warehouse, even in the face of a parallel technology. The following rules of thumb for the management of data hold true:

- If the data will not be used for DSS processing, it has no place in the data warehouse;

- If the data is very old, it should be considered for placement in "deep freeze," bulk storage; and

- If the level of detail is so granular that it is unlikely to be used, the data should be summarized.

Summary

The data warehouse can be managed by a parallel approach to technology. The parallel approach has multiple processors which operate on data independently and manage data independently. Because of the independent management of data, processors can be added linearly and independently.

The question as to whether to use a parallel approach or a centralized approach depends on the volume of data to be managed and the access to the data.

Even though the parallel approach offers a powerful alternative to the management of data, physical design issues are still very important in the design of the data warehouse.

About the Author

W. H. (Bill) Inmon, executive vice president of technology at Prism Solutions, is universally recognized as the father of the data warehouse concept. He has over 25 years of database technology management experience and data warehouse design expertise, and has published 30 books and more than 200 articles in major computer journals.

He is known globally for his seminars on developing data warehouses and has been a keynote speaker for every major computing association. He is responsible for the high-level design of the family of Prism products, as well as for the architecture of planned and future products. Before co-founding Prism, Mr. Inmon consulted with a variety of Fortune 1000 clients through his own firm, Forest Rim Technologies, offering data warehouse design and database management services. Prior to founding Forest Rim, he worked for American Management Services and Coopers & Lybrand.

About Prism Solutions

Prism Solutions provides data warehouse management software and services for a variety of IT and business projects, such as building decision-support systems, implementing client/server architectures, migrating and converting data between different computing platforms, and re-engineering legacy applications and business processes. Prism Solutions' corporate headquarters are located at 1000 Hamlin Court, Sunnyvale, California 94089; telephone: 408 752 1888.

## 11

Six Challenges Facing Data Warehousing Managers

by Alan Paller and Dr. Ramon Barquin

Foreword

The second half of 1995 is a period of important change for organizations involved in data warehousing. Until recently, most data warehousing projects were either experiments undertaken by early adopters or old projects, started years earlier in the name of decision support or marketing analysis, and re-labeled as data warehouses. By 1996, that profile of users will have changed radically.

A confluence of events have occurred that together move data warehousing out of the early adoption and experimental stage, and into the mass acceptance and broad deployment stage. The most important impact of that change is that, over the next three years, three times as many organizations will spend eight to ten times as much on data warehousing as in prior years.

Of the dozen or so events contributing to this transformation, the three most important include:

1. Broad coverage of data warehousing success stories in the technology press explaining benefits and architecture, explaining to non-technologists that data warehouses are valuable, and sometimes essential, for modern marketing programs.

2.   Mass adoption of the term "data warehousing" by hardware, database, and query tool vendors and the systems integration community in their advertising, white papers, and seminar programs—with particular emphasis on success stories that illuminate the benefits.

3.   The emergence of "complete-off-the-shelf" solutions made possible by industry alliances and system integrators that ensure the client that the parts of the data warehouse solution all fit together.

Those who sell hardware and software for data warehousing will enjoy a boom in the next three years, which can be compared only to the growth in mainframe downsizing and client/server computing that developed four to five years ago. And, to ensure the boom is real, those vendors are undertaking an unprecedented campaign to get the word out about their data warehousing solutions.

For database management professionals and data warehousing project managers, on the other hand, the blessings are mixed. Expectations have been raised. Timeframes have been cut. It is more difficult today to experiment. Managers in information systems (IS) and in the business units are willing to invest, but they want the job done right the first time. Hence this article, whose purpose is to point out the more common challenges that frequently delay the progress of data warehousing projects.

This article is based on research by the staff of The Data Warehousing Institute. The research involved interviews of data warehousing experts and meetings with active data warehousing project managers and IS executives. The goal of the research was to uncover the mistakes pioneers wished they had been able to avoid. The most common mistakes were published in July 1995 by The Institute in a booklet called "Ten Mistakes To Avoid for Data Warehousing."

Six Challenges for Data Warehousing Managers

1. Setting Expectations That Cannot Be Met and Frustrating Executives at the Moment of Truth

Data warehousing projects have at least two phases. Phase one is the selling phase in which executives are persuaded, through presentations, through vendor and consultant briefings, or through the text of articles, that a data warehouse will give users throughout the enterprise immediate access to all the information they need, when they need it, and in the right format. Along with that promise (explicit or implied) comes a bill for one-to-seven million dollars. Business executives who hear those promises and see those budgets cannot help but have high expectations. Phase two, then, is the colossal struggle to meet the expectations raised in phase one.

The truth is that users will not get all the information they need from a data warehouse. All data warehousing is, by necessity, domain specific, which means it focuses on a particular set of business information. If a question asked by an executive requires information from outside the domain, the answer is often, "We haven't loaded that information, but we can do so, at the cost of additional money and time." Executives feel enormous frustration when their expectations are dashed. They tend to focus that frustration on the person who made the promises.

2. Loading the Warehouse With Information Just "Because It Was Available"

Some inexperienced data warehousing managers send a list of tables and data elements to end users along with a request asking, "Which of these elements should be included in the warehouse?" Sometimes they ask for categories such as 'essential,' 'important,' and 'nice-to-have.' Typically, an answer to such a request includes long lists of marginally useful information that radically expand the data warehouse storage requirements and, more importantly, slow responsiveness. Extraneous data buries important information. Faced with the need to dig through long guides to find the right field name and having to deal with multiple versions of the same information, users quickly grow frustrated and may even give up entirely.

Extraneous data also leads to very large databases. One Chicago-area utility reported, for example, that their mainframe computing resources were being consumed to a greater and greater extent by analytical programs. Loads were growing, so the company decided to move the data to a new machine where it would be kept for analytical purposes. The users demanded the downloading of every data item and wanted the database updated every five minutes, but decided they could live with daily updates. Unfortunately, the relational database did not load well in parallel, causing downloads to consume more than 22 hours per day. Worse still, the performance during the remaining two hours was unbelievably slow.

The solution to this problem is not to ask better questions or to force users to limit their demands. Rather, the solution lies in a too-often missing step in data warehousing which involves synchronizing the data warehousing efforts with business process re-engineering efforts, thus deriving a business/data model to drive the warehouse project. This is such an important step that The Data Warehousing Institute has selected it as a major component of one of the "Five Disciplines Of Data Warehousing" that must be mastered by data warehousing staff.

3. Believing That Data Warehousing Database Design Is the Same as Transactional Database Design

Since the goals of transaction processing systems differ from the goals of data warehouses, the database designs must differ, as well. In transaction processing, the goal is speed to access and update a single record or a few records. Data warehousing is fundamentally different; the goal is to access aggregates—sums, averages, trends, and more. Another difference between the two types of systems is the user. In transaction processing, a programmer develops a query which will be used tens of thousands of times. In data warehousing, an end-user develops the query and may use it only once. Data warehousing databases are often denormalized to provide easier navigation for infrequent users. If, instead, the transaction processing database (with as many as 250 or more normalized tables) is used for data warehousing, infrequent users have no idea where to find the information they need or how to ask for it. Not surprisingly, users will have difficulties selecting the correct table name when 250 cryptic 8-character table names are arrayed in a table with only a few entries displayed at any given time.

An even more fundamental difference relates to content. Where transactional systems usually contain only the basic data, in data warehousing, users increasingly expect to find aggregates and time-series information already calculated for them and ready for immediate display. That's the impetus behind the multi-dimensional database market and the multi-dimensional extensions to relational database management systems.

4. Focusing on Traditional Internal Record-Oriented Data and Ignoring the Potential Value of External Data and of Text, Images, and Potentially, Sound and Video

In the early eighties, a White House study identified an interesting pattern in the way that senior managers obtain information. After interviewing CEOs and two other levels of management in over 50 large companies, the White House analysts concluded that "the higher a person is in the organization, the less value they place on internal data and the less time they spend using internal data." In fact, the analysts found that the highest level of executives rely on outside data (news, telephone calls from associates, etc.) for more than 95 percent of all the information they use.

Because of their focus on external sources of information, senior executives sometimes see data warehouses as irrelevant. It's not that they are uninterested in key operating indicators; they just don't have the time to bury themselves in the sort of detailed data that a warehouse provides. Without top management support, middle managers are less likely to continue supporting data warehouses. Therefore, if senior managers are part of your target user community, it's imperative to extend your project focus to include external information.

In addition, consider expanding the forms of information available through the data warehouse. Traditional record-oriented information transaction systems usually record the minimum possible amount of data to effect a business transaction. Frustrated users are starting to ask, "Where's the copy of the contract (image) that explains the information behind the data? And where's the ad (image) that ran in that magazine? Where's the tape (audio or video) of the key competitors at a recent conference talking about their business strategy. Where's the recent product launch (video)." An old saying goes, "When the only tool you have is a hammer, every problem is a nail." This is the age of television. Traditional alphanumeric data is two generations behind the current technology.

5. *Delivering Data with Overlapping and Confusing Definitions*

The Achilles heel of data warehousing is the requirement to gain consensus on data definitions. Conflicting definitions each have champions, which are not easily reconciled. Many of the most stubborn definitions have been constructed by managers to reflect data in a way that makes their department look effective. To the finance manager, sales means the net of revenue less returns. Sales to the distribution manager means products to be delivered. Sales to the sales organization is the amount committed by clients. One organization reported twenty-seven different definitions of sales.

Executives do not give up their definitions without a fight, and few data warehousing managers are in a position to bully executives into agreement. Solving this problem is one of the most important tasks of the data warehousing team, and to solve it, it's best to have powerful partners from the business side. If the problem is not solved, users will not have confidence in the available information. Worse, they may embarrass themselves by using the wrong data—in which case, they inevitably blame the data warehouse.

Some data warehousing managers suggest that definitions are not a data warehousing problem, but a user problem. They try to deliver all the data, representing all the different definitions, along with lengthy metadata lists that describe the origins and definitions of data elements. Then, they let the user decide which is appropriate. This is generally not a successful strategy. A well-known tale from the early days of decision support describes a meeting in which a president of Boston's Shawmut Bank, after sitting through a strident argument about whose data was accurate, told his senior managers, "If you people cannot agree on what data to use, I'll find people who can," and he stomped out of the room.

6. Focusing on Ad-Hoc Data Mining and Periodic Reporting, Instead of Alerts

This is a subtle error, but a very important one. Correcting this error can transform a data warehousing manager from a data librarian into a hero.

The natural progression of information in a data warehouse is as follows:

- Extract the data from legacy systems, sanitize it, and load it into the warehouse;

- Support ad-hoc reporting until most requirements are established; and

- Convert the ad-hoc reports into regularly scheduled reports.

In other words, first data is fed to the system; then, questions are asked, and reports are generated on the fly. Finally, managers request those reports daily, weekly, or monthly.

That's the natural progression, although it isn't the optimal progression. It leads to scores of reports that are produced automatically. It ignores the fact that managers are busy and that reports are liabilities rather than assets unless the recipients have time to read the reports. Reports are like inventory; if unused, they simply generate costs.

Alert systems are a better approach and can make a data warehouse mission-critical. Alert systems monitor the data flowing into the warehouse and inform all key people with a need-to-know message, as soon as a critical event takes place. Harris Semiconductor's industry-leading manufacturing alert server, for example, monitors patterns in semiconductor test data, and screams loudly (via e-mail) when wafer characteristics anywhere in the world (Malaysia, Singapore, or three U.S. sites) creep too far from the ideal.

Creating alert systems is a job that requires a data warehousing driver, a business person who is the bridge between the data warehousing manager and the business executive. The key to an effective alert system is infrequency. If alerts are sent too often, they become a burden rather than an asset. But to determine the contents and thresholds of critical information, it is necessary to understand the mind of the business person. As one experienced driver said, "To make an alert system an integral part of the day-to-day business, you have to be there when they (senior management) talk about the competition and about the future, and what's going to drive the business forward." Only drivers with great ties to other senior managers can do that job well.

However, after switching to an alarm system, you'll find the demand for periodic reports falls off, except for archival purposes. It's useful to rethink the manager's need. Does he or she really want reports from the data warehouse? Or, is an alert system better?

About the Authors

Alan Paller is president of the CIO Institute of Washington, D.C., and author of *The IS Book: Information Systems for Top Management,* published by Dow Jones Irwin, 1990.

Dr. Ramon Barquin is president of the Washington-based Data Warehousing Institute. He can be reached at tdwi@aol.com.

About the Data Warehousing Institute

The Data Warehousing Institute is a not-for-profit organization with the combined goals of (1) expanding the effective use of data warehousing technology and (2) enhancing the careers of data warehousing managers and their staff. It does this through the sharing of information about best practices and the lessons learned by data warehousing pioneers. It conducts courses, offers tips and techniques, provides references to outstanding speakers, consultants, and system integrators, and conducts an annual data warehousing user conference where experienced data warehousing managers and other professionals share the lessons they have learned about what works and what doesn't.

For more information, call Irene Fisher at 719 599 4303, or contact the Data Warehousing Institute by mail at: Box 295, The Data Warehousing Institute, 8902 Edgefield Drive, Colorado Springs, Colorado 80920.

=12 — IMPLEMENTING A PILOT DATA WAREHOUSE USING INFORMIX-OnLine DYNAMIC SERVER

by Dave Pepper

Introduction

There is a growing trend among companies to move from the traditional legacy informational environment to a more powerful and efficient model—the data warehouse. A data warehouse is a database which is separate from operational systems and is designed for decision support and analysis. This architecture, and the concepts surrounding it, were developed by William H. Inmon, who has written a series of books describing the architecture and how to implement it (please refer to the article in this section entitled "Parallel Processing and the Data Warehouse," by William H. Inmon). To briefly summarize, a data warehouse has the following basic characteristics:

- Its organization is subject-oriented as opposed to function-oriented;

- It integrates business information from multiple sources;

- It is a read-only repository of data snapshots taken over time; and

- It is an archive of summarized data used for decision-support and reporting applications.

Subject-oriented organization connotes that data is organized into subject areas, such as customer, vendor, or product. Integrating data for a particular subject area from operational systems in different functional areas gives a consistent view of that subject which can be used across an organization. This typically involves choosing between the various coding, naming, and measuring schemes used in different systems; data is required to go through a conversion process as part of the process of loading the warehouse.

Data in the warehouse is loaded once and not updated; relationships between entities were valid only when the data was loaded. The warehouse consists of a series of snapshots of operational data.

Data Warehouse Structure

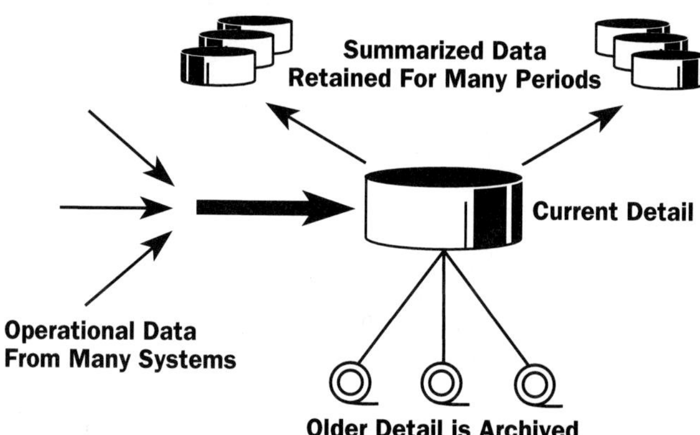

Figure 1: Data warehouse structure.

Data is taken from operational systems at the lowest level of detail available, and then is summarized in the warehouse to allow faster access to aggregate information and to reduce long-term storage requirements. The detail information can be archived when it is no longer current, and the summarized information can be retained and used to support historical analysis.

Pilot Methodology

A pilot is the first step in the process of developing a data warehouse and decision-support capability. This article uses as its example "Beacon", an internal decision-support pilot which was developed jointly by Informix MIS and several data warehouse partners. The work was organized into a series of steps, which were then reviewed and updated in successive iterations, as additional users and information were added to the warehouse. The steps are summarized as follows:

- Business analysis;

- Architecture and tool selection;

- Application development; and

- User evaluation and deployment.

The pilot's goal was to provide Informix's management with desktop access to worldwide revenue information. The pilot grew out of a business need to analyze revenue and shipment information from across the organization, without requiring that users navigate the intricacies of the various operational systems involved. Developed in approximately three months, Beacon served as a proof of concept for building quick, data warehouse based applications.

Business Analysis

At the onset, worldwide revenue constituted the focus of the project. However, it is always advisable to perform a business analysis study of a data warehouse. The study can bring greater visibility and support to the project. This step involved the interviewing of key decision makers across the organization. They were asked what information was needed to make good decisions and the monetary value assigned to the specific business decisions.

At its completion, the interview process yielded a good picture of the opportunities for decision support across the organization, as well as a decision matrix for prioritizing information areas for inclusion in future phases of the data warehouse. Also identified were a core group of business managers who worked with the Beacon team through the development of the pilot application, and examples of the current method of revenue analysis and reporting.

Defining the Pilot Scope

In order to meet the pilot timeframe, the project team worked with users to keep the scope of the pilot as small as possible for the first iteration. As the team iteratively defined the contents of the data warehouse, they continually made decisions about how much could be done, and what to defer into future phases.

Decision Support Analysis

Most of the analysis sought by users involved looking at summarized "cuts" of revenue information. For example, a sales manager wanted to see sales by sales region, comparisons between regions, or between current and prior time periods for a region, and also wanted to "drill down" to the branch level within a region to see how individual branches contributed to the total. Likewise, product managers wanted the same capability for a product line or product basis. These are used in combination as well, for instance, looking at product breakdowns by sales division, etc.

With the help of an experienced decision-support analyst, the team worked with users to design a "multi-dimensional" approach to the modeling and structuring of decision-support data. This approach is appropriate for environments where the kind of questions that will be asked are well-known. A set of information dimensions is chosen, and the data is organized around those dimensions. Each dimension is decomposed into a hierarchy of roll-up levels. In the Beacon pilot, the team chose four dimensions—customer, product, geography, and time—and focused on a small set of revenue and shipment metrics, including units sold, sales amount, and list price. The team found that users needed to differentiate between recognized revenue and actual shipment value, and so the data model includes both.

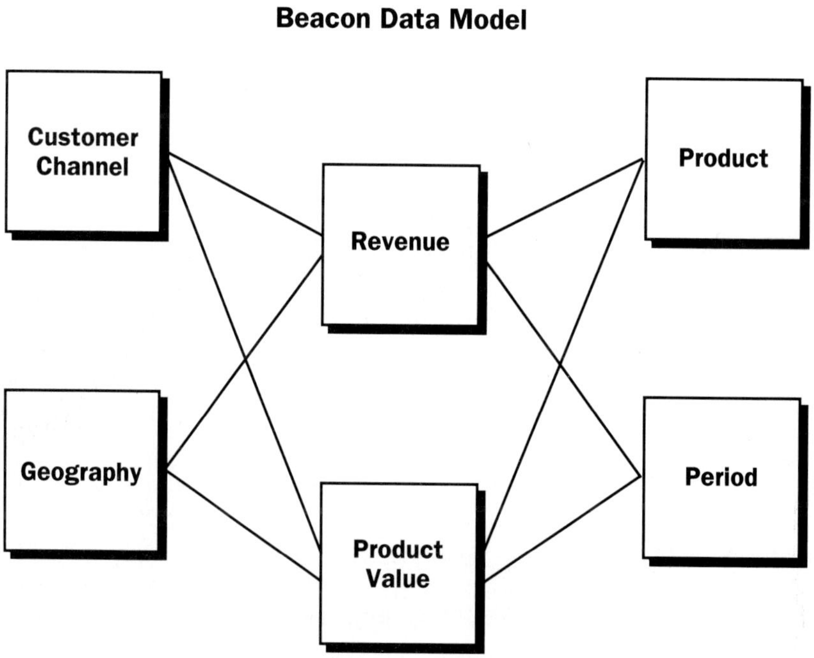

Beacon Data Model

Figure 2: Multi-dimensional data model.

Architecture and Tool Selection

In the architecture and tool selection step, the team looked at how to structure the components of the data warehouse environment, based on factors such as: volume of source data; distribution of source systems and users; and user requirements for response times, information sharing, and scalability. Based on our preliminary design, the team decided on a data structure specific to decision-support applications called a multi-dimensional or "star schema" structure. The architecture was designed to be highly scalable, and to optimize response time for the interactive navigation of the information.

There are a growing number of tools available on the market which support data warehousing, many of them from Informix partners. We looked at what tools would best fit our chosen architecture, and how the choice of tools would impact our design. We evaluated tools for extracting data from source systems, loading data into the warehouse, and accessing and navigating the information in the warehouse. The team expected to use a number of tools for different uses: multi-dimensional analysis, ad-hoc reporting, and so on.

Building the Pilot Application

Creating a Multi-Dimensional Data Structure

The data structure used in Beacon is a multi-dimensional or star-schema structure. At first glance, the schema may look odd. It's very denormalized, and intended to be used by a decision-support tool which expects this type of structure. Different decision-support tools expect variations on this general theme; the physical schema is both application and tool specific.

Creating Dimension Tables

The tables on the outside of the star, "product," "customer," "geography," and "period," are the "dimension" tables, or the reference tables which hold descriptions. Each is actually a denormalized hierarchy, with a "level" attribute specifying each row's level in the hierarchy.

For example, the time dimension (period) holds month, quarter, and year rows, which appear similar to Table 1.

Each of these "dimension" tables has a similar structure; for example, geography has sales territory, branch, region, and division attributes that represent each level of that hierarchy. A serial key is used to create a unique identifier for each row.

Month	Qtr	Year	Level	Description
Jan	1	1994	Month	January 1994
Feb	1	1994	Month	February 1994
Mar	1	1994	Month	March 1994
N/A	1	1994	Qtr	Q1 1994
Apr	2	1994	Month	April 1994
...				
Dec	4	1994	Month	December 1994
N/A	1	1994	Qtr	Q4 1994
N/A	N/A	1994	Year	1994
Jan	1	1995	Month	1995

Table 1: Time dimension example.

Dimension Tables

```
create table customer
  (
    cust_id serial not null constraint n210_76,
    descr char(45),
    level char(15),
    sale_type char(10),
    channel char(30),
    corp char(45),
    cust char(45),
    vert_mkt char(30),
    state_prov char(20),
    country char(15),
    org_cust_id char(20)
  );
revoke all on customer from "public";

create unique index ix103_1 on customer (cust_id);
create index ix_customer2 on customer (descr);
```

```
create table product
   (
      prod_id serial not null constraint n207_68,
      descr char(45),
      level char(20),
      offering char(20),
      line char(20),
      family char(20),
      version char(45),
      type char(45),
      platform char(45)
   );
revoke all on product from "public";

create index ix_product2 on product (descr);
create index ix_product3 on product (level);


create table geography
   (
      geo_id serial not null constraint n136_2,
      descr char(30),
      level char(10),

      division char(30),
      region char(30),
      branch char(30),
      territory char(10),
      geo_type char(15)
   );
revoke all on geography from "public";

create unique index ix101_1 on geography (geo_id);
create index ix_geography2 on geography (descr);


create table period
   (
      per_id serial not null constraint n137_3,
```

```
    descr char(15),
    level char(15),
    year char(4),
    quarter char(10),
    month char(10),
    sequence integer,
    per_num integer,
    cur_flag char(1)
  );
revoke all on period from "public";

create index ix_period2 on period (descr);
create unique index ix100_1 on period (per_id);
```

Creating Fact Tables

The tables in the middle of the star are the "fact" tables. These tables contain foreign key references to each dimension, as well as to the decision metrics or values which are pre-summarized at each level of the dimension hierarchy. The Beacon application contains sales and revenue related numbers, such as the units sold, list price, actual price and users. The different fact tables hold different types of revenue: shipment, contract, royalty, and cash.

The purpose of this structure is to allow interactive access in the answering of questions such as:

- How many copies of a product were sold in a particular sales region for a specific time period?

- What is the distribution of sales by territory?

- How do sales figures compare with last year's figures?

- How does one region compare to another?

- Who were the top ten customers using a specific product worldwide?

Since data is pre-summarized, certain information is readily available: for example, totals by year, region, product line, etc. The star structure minimizes the joins which are required.

Fact Tables

```
create table cash_rr
   (
     per_id integer,
     prod_id integer not null constraint n209_73,
     geo_id integer not null constraint n209_74,
     cust_id integer not null constraint n209_75,
     units integer,
     dollars money(16,2),
     list_price money(16,2),
     users integer,
     site_license integer
   );
revoke all on cash_rr from "public";


create index ix_cash_rr1 on cash_rr (prod_id,cust_id,geo_id,    per_id);
create index ix_cash_rr2 on cash_rr (cust_id,prod_id,per_id,    geo_id);



create table contract_rr
   (
     per_id integer,
     prod_id integer not null constraint n233_81,
     geo_id integer not null constraint n233_82,
     cust_id integer not null constraint n233_83,
     units integer,
     dollars money(16,2),
     list_price money(16,2),
     users integer,
     site_license integer
   );
revoke all on contract_rr from "public";


create index ix_contract_rr1 on contract_rr (prod_id,cust_id, geo_id,    per_id);
create index ix_contract_rr2 on contract_rr (cust_id,prod_id, per_id,    geo_id);
```

```
create table royalty_rr
   (
     per_id integer,
     prod_id integer not null constraint n234_84,
     geo_id integer not null constraint n234_85,
     cust_id integer not null constraint n234_86,
     units integer,
     dollars money(16,2),
     list_price money(16,2),
     users integer,
     site_license integer
   );
revoke all on royalty_rr from "public";

create index ix_royalty_rr1 on royalty_rr (prod_id,cust_id, geo_id,    per_id);
create index ix_royalty_rr2 on royalty_rr (cust_id,prod_id, per_id,    geo_id);




create table ship_rr
   (
     per_id integer,
     prod_id integer not null constraint n240_99,
     geo_id integer not null constraint n240_100,
     cust_id integer not null constraint n240_101,
     units integer,
     dollars money(16,2),
     list_price money(16,2),
     users integer,
     site_license integer
   );
revoke all on ship_rr from "public";

create index ix_ship_rr1 on ship_rr (prod_id,cust_id,geo_id,    per_id);
create index ix_ship_rr2 on ship_rr (cust_id,prod_id,per_id,    geo_id);




create table rec_rev
   (
```

```
   per_id integer,
   prod_id integer not null constraint n239_96,
   geo_id integer not null constraint n239_97,
   cust_id integer not null constraint n239_98,
   units integer,
   dollars money(16,2),
   list_price money(16,2),
   users integer,
   site_license integer
 );
revoke all on rec_rev from "public";


create index ix_rec_rev1 on rec_rev (prod_id,cust_id,geo_id,    per_id);
create index ix_rec_rev2 on rec_rev (cust_id,prod_id,per_id,    geo_id);




create table prod_value
 (
   per_id integer,
   prod_id integer not null constraint n238_93,
   geo_id integer not null constraint n238_94,
   cust_id integer not null constraint n238_95,
   units integer,
   dollars money(16,2),
   list_price money(16,2),
   users integer,
   site_license integer
 );
revoke all on prod_value from "public";

create index ix_prod_value1 on prod_value (prod_id,cust_id, geo_id,    per_id);
create index ix_prod_value2 on prod_value (cust_id,prod_id, per_id,    geo_id);
```

Extracting Data from Operational Systems

The data for the dimension and fact tables comes from operational databases. As the required data was determined for the pilot, the team began an analysis of existing systems to determine where data was available, and what transformations were needed to integrate the data.

Quite often, more than one system holds a particular set of data, such as customer records. One of the key steps for data warehousing is to determine the "system of record," or the authoritative source, for each type of information. In other cases, data is fragmented between systems, and must be joined together. This was the case for the Beacon project, with different invoicing and accounting systems used in different parts of the world.

Information was extracted from the invoicing and accounting systems on a monthly basis. All line item records for the given month were extracted, giving the fact metrics and the operational keys to the dimension information: customer IDs, part numbers, and sales territory codes. Dimension information was updated, based on the monthly line item extracts. Any new dimension elements in the monthly extract were added to the dimension tables.

Because the team worked in a homogeneous database environment, it was possible to use Informix tools to extract and load the data. In some cases, synonyms were created for operational tables in the warehouse database and the data was queried directly. In other cases, INFORMIX-4GL programs were written to extract the data and place it into unload format files.

Integrating and Mapping Data Into the Warehouse

Because of the timeframe of the project and the emphasis on the decision-support application, the initial data warehouse consisted of little more than a line item table, a set of tables for dimension information extracted from the operational systems, and the multi-dimensional tables.

The monthly load process included the following steps:

- Load operational data into the warehouse tables;

- Map system-specific values to common formats and codes;

- Load new dimension entries into the dimension tables;

- Map operational keys to dimension table keys; and

- Load the fact tables from the warehouse table.

In a mature warehouse environment, the rules for extracting, transforming and loading the data, as well as the structure of the warehouse and decision-support tables should be maintained as metadata in a repository. This is an area where automated tool support is very useful.

Creating Aggregates

Once the source data has been integrated and mapped to the dimension tables, a summarization process is used to create the fact rows for the different roll-up levels in the dimension hierarchy. In the Beacon implementation, the team aggregated from the detail information for all levels. A more efficient way to do this is to create the lowest-level aggregation first, and then use the aggregate values to derive the next level of aggregation, and so on, up to the last level.

Results of the Pilot

A three-month pilot proved to be a practical way to implement data warehousing technology and concepts, while delivering value to the organization.

On retrospect, the following factors greatly contributed to the pilot's success:

1. Tightly scoping the pilot around valuable and readily available data.
2. Forming a small team, including both an experienced decision-support analyst and people with a knowledge of existing systems.
3. Working closely with a core group of business managers to iteratively define and prototype the application.

Inevitably, certain roadblocks were encountered: for example, information about existing systems and data was not always well-documented to prove useful to the project, and additional research was sometimes required to determine how to interpret operational data.

Conclusion

The data warehouse pilot demonstrated a way to improve the delivery of management information. The pilot provided a basis for developing a warehouse in an incremental fashion, whereby users and information could be added, based on business priorities.

The Beacon pilot also helped to identify opportunities for improving data management in existing systems, as the team worked through the process of integrating data and reports from various systems. Although business requirements change, the Beacon pilot provides a technical foundation which offers scaleability as new users and information are added to the warehouse.

About the Author

Dave Pepper is a project manager at Informix MIS, Menlo Park, California.

=13= PRACTICAL DATA WAREHOUSE CONSIDERATIONS

by Jack Parker

What Are the Challenges We Cannot Meet With Existing Operational Systems?

Today's operational systems, which are frequently yesterday's operational systems, are meant to assist in the production of income-generating product, whether a material good or a service.

There is a set of continually developing questions asked by users of these systems. These questions are given to Information Systems (IS) groups. IS generally makes some modification to the operational systems to provide answers. Each of the answers to the questions in turn keys another question, until the operational system no longer bears any resemblance to its initial form, and may collapse under its own weight.

These operational systems have the following characteristics:

Well-Delineated Query Requirements

Reporting the weekly sales for a preceding period of time is a straight-forward activity. However, reporting how much product was sold to a specific niche of an industry over the same period of time might require data which is not necessarily housed in the sales-support system. Operational systems were designed to answer a few standard questions, but were not designed to answer "what if?"

questions or to present data which can be decomposed or broken down at the users' leisure.

Focus

Many operational systems are tightly focused to deal with a specific need. This need may not marry precisely with neighbouring systems' needs. While resultant data may be shipped to these systems, attempting to report data from both systems simultaneously can be difficult, if not impossible. Imagine then, the problem of combining data from a dozen such systems.

Definition and Ownership of Data Elements

Part_number to one system may be Component_number or Product_number to another. Part_revision may be built into the part number on one system and not another. There may also be some question as to the proper method for storing the Part_number, with or without the revision. There is also the question as to who is responsible for the maintenance of that attribute.

Time Element

Data from one system may not be of the same time period as data from another system. Suppose that a product costing program ran against sales. Such a request may appear simple at first; however, the part content of the product may vary over the time period for which such a report runs. Such time discrepancies are not always visible.

Priorities

Operational systems are generally concerned with transaction processing. Ad hoc and poorly formed user queries can wreak havoc on a heavily loaded system.

Data Integrity

Systems which are designed to fill one need are frequently pressed into service to fill another. Ingenious users force systems to work for them, even when it involves breaking the rules designed to ensure data integrity. Loading part revision information into the part number is a common example of forcing a system to handle revisions for which it was not designed. This makes perfect sense to the user, but destroys data integrity from an IS perspective.

Inflexible

Operational systems are generally not designed with change in mind, whereas the very nature of decision support is that of evolving questions. Attempting to support this change has created a backlog in many an MIS organization.

IS is plagued by user requirements which change with the nature of the results provided:

- Can you give me a total of failures across product lines?"

- Can you single-out shop floor failures from returns failures?"

- Could you break-out failures by component type?"

- Can you give me the data in a file which I can import into my spreadsheet program?"

The last question in the above set of requests is a sign that IS may have failed. In such a case, the user may be dissatisfied with the report turnaround time and prefers to manipulate the data with a familiar tool.

Operational systems are poor engines for decision-support requirements. IS requires a mechanism which allows for a more efficient and effective response to user requests.

What is an Information Warehouse?

The information warehouse is a tool specifically designed to meet decision-support requirements. The warehouse is a collection of data from diverse systems which is integrated (definition and data), write-only (old data is retained), and designed to service user requests as opposed to transaction processing. Rather than force a user to join fourteen tables with 'x' criteria, it is preferable to simply build a new view for the user. Warehouse data is structured to allow IS to respond more effectively to user requests, while at the same time allowing the user to navigate its structure in a facile manner.

Essentially, an information warehouse is a repository for data. Operational systems provide the necessary data, which is then reorganized into views and placed in a location where users can access the data with any given tool.

The information warehouse does not contain information related to the day-to-day running of the operational system. Key elements which "drop out" in data collection are flags, fields which signal that a process has occurred or which indicate a relationship to other data. Since data within the warehouse is normalized, it is no longer necessary to keep data which indicates such relationships.

There are differing philosophies regarding the parts of a warehouse and their names. In general, a warehouse consists of an archive, subject areas, and user views; following is a discussion of these three elements.

Archive

The archive is a detailed store of operational systems data. However, there may be a business need for only a portion of this data. The premise of this function is to anticipate a future demand from a user for specific historical information. The archive is a place where such information is kept off-line, and is easily recalled. In some cases, it is useful to convert incoming information into an "open" format: this can include resolving decimal points, using a common date format, converting currencies into a common monetary value, and so forth.

This data is then compressed and stored off-line. This level of data is further categorized by the level of detail that goes into it.

Subject Areas

Data which has a current use is stored in a normalized form in several SQL databases, one per subject matter. For example, one of the databases may be called "part" and have complete information describing all parts used by the company. Another might be called "supplier" and so forth. While there is a relationship between part and supplier, in that the latter provides to the former, there are a number of advantages to be realized by keeping subject areas separate from one another.

Size

Frequently, there is no possible way to estimate how large a subject area might grow. By keeping subject areas separate, it is possible to move any single subject area (or some collection thereof) to its own platform, if necessary.

Provenance

At some point, a better or more cost-effective warehouse for a subject area may become available. Since the databases are organized by subject matter in this fashion, and given the distributive power of SQL (Informix, in our case), it doesn't matter whether the supplier subject area is housed at the local site or at some remote location.

Logic

It is simple to view the 14 tables that belong to a subject area and understand how they relate to one another. It is more difficult to view 2,038 such tables, and attempt to determine which 14 relate to the subject matter in question.

At this level, data can be "lightly" summarized. The types of queries which run against this level are not prone to require the exhaustive detail of data from an operational system. Such detail is kept at the archive level, should it become necessary to restructure these subject areas.

User Views

Information which is stored in a subject area is of great use to IS staff. Queries against these normalized stores can be easily developed to extract required data.

However, this same structure may prove difficult for a user to navigate. This organization of data may lead users to make dreadfully expensive queries against these data stores. Finally, users' tools may not allow access to information from particular subject areas. To prevent such difficulties, a third layer of information, or the "user view," is given to the users.

The goal is to organize the data in the manner needed by the user. In this way, the user is not forced to navigate through obscure SQL structures. As users require a new view of the information, they can either access the subject area directly and retrieve it, or ask their IS department to build the new view for them. Fulfilling such a request is accomplished rapidly since all of the data is stored in the subject area. Information at this level is highly summarized (e.g., monthly or yearly totals).

Data Flows

Obviously, the data does not automatically appear in the user view. The final part of the warehouse structure is comprised of the data flows which stem from the operational systems and flow through the warehouse to the users' workstations or PCs.

"Strip," or extraction, programs retrieve data from the operational systems and deliver the data to the warehouse. In our case, data is stripped out of the operational systems and delivered by ftp to a UNIX warehouse platform.

At this point, each data flow is checked and converted into an open format. There is a single program which reads the metadata to determine what is contained in each file. This data is then converted, according to rules in the metadata. Any errors are rejected and noted. The resulting data is in an open format. In this manner, the data does not require the storage of older software. In 20 years, the data continues to stand on its own, long after the retirement of the originating systems.

That data is then routed: first into an SQL work area, and secondly to the archive itself. Unfortunately, many of the systems from which data is retrieved do not have a "date last updated" field. In such cases, it is difficult to determine if the data is new or old. In other words, a "snapshot" is accepted each time. A workaround is to archive the difference between the current snapshot and the most recent snapshot. This difference is stored in script form and can be applied directly against a preceding snapshot to make it current.

After several occurrences, a full archive of the snapshot is made. Thus, to rebuild a given day's worth of data requires only returning to the last full snapshot and applying all "difference" scripts to obtain the snapshot for that particular day. It may not be desirable to store such detail at the archive level, in which case the snapshots should be summarized accordingly. It is obviously not desirable to obtain a daily snapshot of a rather large file. Care should be taken to limit the use of this method. In practice, this method is a time-consuming use of the CPU and can produce scripts which are larger than the original data file.

The SQL work area serves as a "reservoir" into which data flows and is held until needed. SQL provides a natural environment in which to perform this next integration step. Periodically, according to a schedule, a number of integration programs can be run to build subject area data from this reservoir data. This same mechanism is used to populate user views from the subject areas.

All of the information required to process each data flow is collected and stored in the metadata. Building a new data flow can be affected by making an entry in the metadata, and describing what should be included. From this, new files can be accepted, data can be unearthed from the archives, and the integration code generated, thus populating the downstream portions of the warehouse.

Finally, data is delivered to the user view, where users have their own tools to view it. These user views can be housed in a multi-dimensional database with a specific front-end built for it, a third-party application, or another SQL database where generic tools can access the views.

As new tools become available, or as new demands are placed on the data structures, new views can be quickly built. In short, it is possible to meet new data demands on a time scale measured in hours, as opposed to the historical IS time scale of months.

Building a Data Warehouse, Additional Considerations

Politics

One of the challenges in building a warehouse is the political aspect to the effort. The collected data resides in multiple systems across multiple environments, owned by varying departments. Many owners of the data have no idea what a warehouse is and view any effort to use their data in another system as a threat—either to the system they support, or to the integrity of "their" data. In such cases, it is best to explain to them the concept of an information warehouse, that the data will not be diverted back, and emphasize that the information warehouse will relieve local owners of new reporting requirements.

Communication

The importance of communication cannot be stressed enough. While this is true for any large project, it is especially true for a warehouse project. A data warehouse project normally consists of many diverse professionals, each with a specific expertise and background. Understanding and commitment amongst these individuals must be continually reinforced.

Definition

Perhaps the second greatest challenge is to synthesize a single definition of the warehouse from the various mismatched concepts of the development group. As the first step of a warehouse project, it is important for the entire project team to agree on some base definition of what the warehouse will be. This agreement should be documented, and a mechanism for updating that agreement should be put in place.

There is a utopian warehouse that is probably impossible to build, or which would take several years to launch. The opposite extreme is yet another database which culls data from everywhere, allows anyone to add any data, and which is held together with bailing wire. It is important to steer a course between these two extremes.

Produce a Prototype

Any data warehouse you build will undergo change. Support for the effort may fade over time. Therefore, it is important to develop a working prototype in a short timeframe. This prototype will more clearly define the challenges ahead, and serves as a proof of concept for the warehouse itself. With this goal in mind, it is best to define a subset of your final product and deploy the prototype in a three-to-six month timeframe.

Summary

This article's intent is to provide a basic definition of a data warehouse and illustrates some of the basic building blocks required. For a more detailed discussion of data warehouse concepts, refer to William H. Inmon's book, *Building a Data Warehouse.*

About the Author

Jack Parker is an Information Technology engineer at Hewlett Packard, DMD/IS, Boise, Idaho.

DATA REPLICATION: USES AND REQUIRED FEATURES

by Marvin Miller

Introduction

With the increased use and popularity of data warehousing, client/server, and continuous-operation applications, businesses are looking for ways to manage not only large amounts of data, but data that is located in dozens of places. Data may be geographically dispersed and it may also be stored in different systems, even different RDBMSs. This article describes scenarios where data replication can be applied effectively, and discusses the design features that are required to make data replication accurate, dependable, and productive for document management and other data processing needs.

Data Replication Scenarios

In today's world of increasingly dispersed data, distributed database capabilities have become a necessity rather than a luxury. The continued growth of smaller local systems means more data locations and a greater need for individual users to access data from multiple and different systems. Over time, applications grow and are enhanced, but are rarely replaced. Corporate growth, acquisitions, and reorganization require that businesses adapt without losing existing functionality and processes.

Data replication answers these diverse needs by creating a data bridge between hardware systems, RDBMSs, and applications. Examples of data replication scenarios include:

- Data warehouses;

- Capacity relief;

- Migration and downsizing;

- Fault tolerance;

- Local data access;

- Data collection;

- Data merge;

- Mobile computing; and

- Continuous operations.

The Data Warehouse

The data warehouse is both a new and old concept in database systems. The purpose of a data warehouse is to make enterprise information available for planning and decision-support functions. This has been attempted in the past with varying results. Today's relational database management systems provide adequate performance, storage capacity, availability and, now, the tools to make this a reasonable expectation.

The industry has learned that operational data is not always suitable for planning and decision support for a number of reasons. Decision support queries usually interfere with the operational use of the data. This interference reduces the efficiency of the enterprise while trying to improve it. The solution to this interference is often to restrict ad-hoc data access to non-peak hours, or even outside of business hours, making access inconvenient for users.

To overcome this problem, some users take "snapshots" of their data at the end of the business cycle when the data is stable. Snapshots allow for the isolation of planning and decision-support functions from operational processing, thus improving response times for both functions. During the life of a snapshot, all requests yield consistent results. Snapshots, however, often require the transmission of large volumes of data at a single point in time, resulting in high network and system activity.

Snapshots suffer from another problem. Operational data is structured for the high performance of the functions that it serves and is usually not well-structured for planning and decision-support uses. For the effective use of the data warehouse, the data must be restructured with different keys and relationships. With a snapshot approach, this is difficult at best.

Data replication overcomes these problems by transmitting only the changes made to the database or table. Using data replication can dramatically reduce the total amount of information that must be transmitted. Consequently, data may be replicated on a more current basis. Since data replication can transmit changes based on time, updates can be scheduled to coincide with the end of the business cycle (day, week, month) and can be performed during low-activity periods.

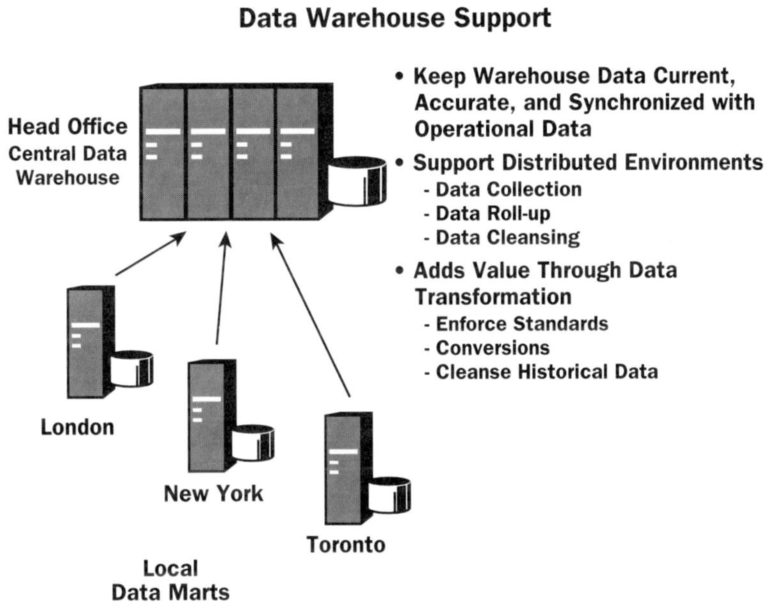

Data Warehouse Support

Figure 1: Replication needs for data warehouses.

In addition, as data moves from operational systems to the data warehouse, it is often necessary to transform raw data into useful information for business professionals. Data replication supports this requirement. Automated data enhancement routines can perform datatype transformations, arithmetic rounding, text justification, conversions to installation standards, and table lookups for encoding or decoding. Once defined, data replication can automatically apply enhancements to all replicated data updates.

Today's advanced applications use different data formats. Beyond FLOAT, CHAR, etc., there are new forms, such as EDI and BLOBs. Data replication assists in this area, too. Provided that the data structures are well understood, even BLOBs from different RDBMS sources can be replicated by replication tools.

Finally, data replication can take data that is maintained on mainframe platforms and move it to data warehouse platforms where the tools exist to aid the planning and decision-support functions. These tools are growing in number and capability on small-to-midrange platforms.

Migration and Downsizing

Application migrations are a way of life in Information Services (IS). New technologies improve operating efficiencies, and application migrations are necessary to take advantage of the efficiencies. As business changes its style and organization to improve responsiveness and competitiveness, IS must migrate systems to keep pace with the changes. And, IS must be fully available at every step in the migration—leading the way of change in the business instead of becoming a roadblock.

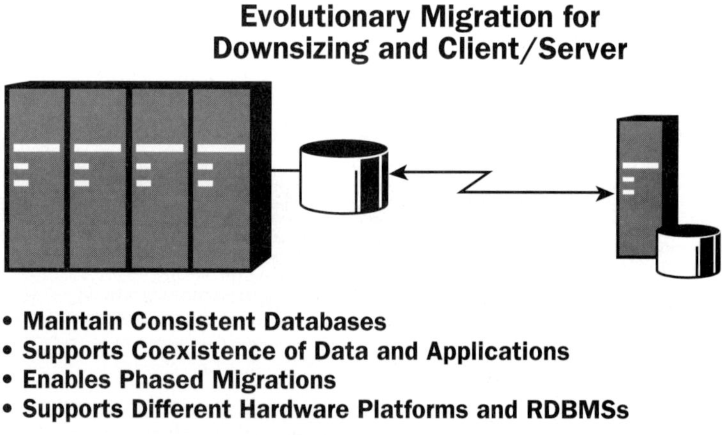

**Evolutionary Migration for
Downsizing and Client/Server**

• **Maintain Consistent Databases**
• **Supports Coexistence of Data and Applications**
• **Enables Phased Migrations**
• **Supports Different Hardware Platforms and RDBMSs**

Figure 2: Benefits of replication for migrations and downsizing.

Data replication can smooth migrations and permit the retention of the older system while the new system comes into existence. A new system can be put in place next to the existing system, as the new system is phased in gradually. The former database is reproduced in its new form on the new system. Updates to the existing database can be propagated by data replication to the new database without program changes in the old system. As individual functions are piloted and phased-in on the new system, the effects of data updates are propagated back to the old system and equivalent functions are discontinued on the old system.

Capacity Relief

As volumes continue to grow, installations often reach a point where growth is no longer possible within a single system. Yet, the application design still requires a single-system image. Data replication can relieve this condition by creating a second "mirror" system with replication maintaining the synchronization of data between the two systems. The careful allocation of users and applications to each system minimizes the likelihood of dual updates. The conflict detection and resolution routines necessary in data replication are designed to handle the occurrence of dual updates.

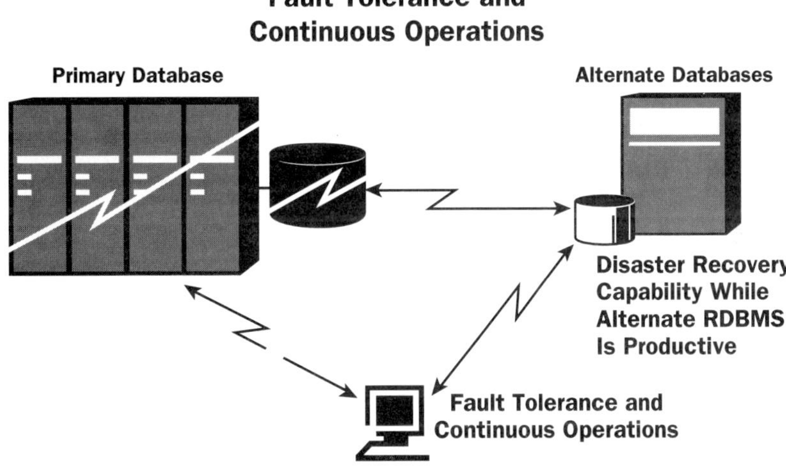

Figure 3: Replication supports fault-tolerant installation.

Fault Tolerance

System complexity tends to lead to a higher probability of system downtime. Centralized processing increases the risk of crippling an entire network of users. Complex systems and networks often use redundancy to avoid the risks created by a "single point of failure." Central databases suffer from this condition. If the network or central database node fail, all remote nodes become inoperable. Many elaborate designs exist to work around this problem.

With data replication, the solution is simple to implement. As each local site has its own copy of the required data, outages of the network or any one node rarely affect operations. When the unavailable resource is restored, the replicator will automatically resynchronize all copies. When multiple nodes update the same data and a network outage occurs, the ability to continue operations during the outage more than compensates for the effort of reconciling any conflicting updates.

Local Data Access

Remote site performance is dependent on a large number of variables. Line speeds are the first and most obvious. Assuming that the network is shared among a large number of users, there is also line contention. The data source system then becomes the next potential bottleneck. If the system is heavily utilized, all remote users compete for the system's resources.

Application Integration

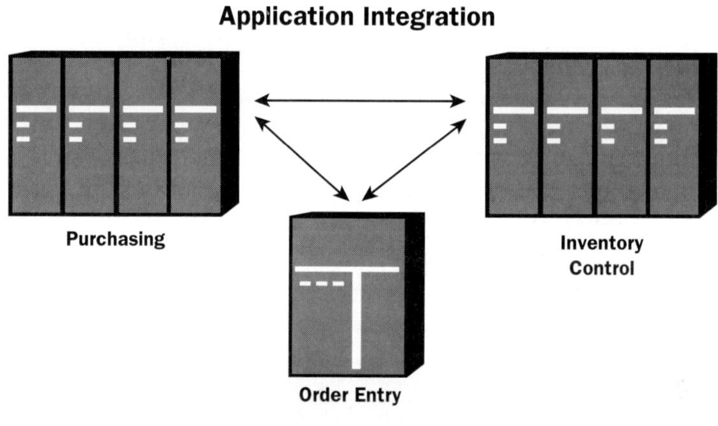

Figure 4: Replication supports application integration.

One alternative to problems of local data access is for each local system to maintain its own copy of the data for performance and control reasons. This is performed in many systems, but the result is the risk of inconsistent data across the enterprise. The cost is additional program development to create and maintain the local data. Data replication removes these problems by maintaining consistent copies of the data at any defined site—without additional application development effort.

Using data replication to maintain consistent copies of the data allows access that is both local and high-speed. There are no delays in responding to customer telephone inquiries. Should a customer call to change information, such as the ship-to location, an immediate local update can be accomplished, with the change replicated asynchronously to the appropriate operational database.

Data Collection

In any medium-to-large enterprise with a number of locations, data must be collected at one or more points. For instance, while warehouses maintain data on the volumes of goods shipped, manufacturing planning needs to know those same volumes from all warehouses, in order to schedule production facilities. Rather than developing an application to collect information from multiple sites, data replication can automatically replicate changes from the distributed points to one central site.

If data replication is asynchronous, it does not interfere with local operations. The actual transmission of data can be performed automatically during unattended low-usage hours, such as between midnight and 8:00 AM.

Data Merge

Similar to the case of data collection is data merging. In this case, a site wishes to collect all information on a series of related events. For example, an order moving through the enterprise may pass through order entry, manufacturing, shipping, returns, and accounts receivable. All are different functions and each has data organized around it in a way that promotes the efficient operation of that function. To the account manager who deals with the customer, however, the order is a single entity and these functions are transients in its life. The data must be collected from many different sources and must also be organized to meet customer support requirements.

Data replication makes data merging possible by defining the multiple points from which the data is generated. The data can be replicated and stored in a structure that is oriented to customers' activities. This is achieved by filtering the data at each source location and merging the data from the multiple sources at the target site.

Mobile Computing

With the popularity of the laptop computer, a new form of remote site has come into existence: the mobile computing site. These small systems exist throughout the enterprise in management, marketing, sales, education, technical support, and many other functions. One issue that laptops introduce is the difficulty of keeping them current with all the changes that may affect the user. Users do not want the extra work of finding and applying changes.

Data replication can address this problem. As changes to the database are made at the "home" site, users may log on daily to automatically receive replications of any updates applied to the "home." And, since only the changes are transmitted, the time to perform the update over phone lines is reduced. The problem of a laptop user who is on vacation for two weeks is overcome, as all the changes are queued and waiting when the user logs on to the central system.

Continuous Operations

As businesses move increasingly toward continuous operations, the problems of system and database maintenance become more difficult. Business operations call for 7-day, 24-hour operations, while the systems management group asks for more time to upgrade the systems for improved service and capability. Users demand the addition of new function but resist shutting down applications for a changeover. Data replication can assist in such situations.

To permit maintenance, a duplicate of the system may be created on the same or another system. Throughout the day, data replication keeps this backup database current. By switching the network to the backup system at a low-usage time, users are connected to a fully-operational and consistent version of their application. The replication process can then be stopped, effectively disconnecting the two systems.

Maintenance can now be performed on the primary system. Once maintenance is complete, replication may be re-enabled to propagate all data changes from the backup to the primary systems, even if the maintenance changes the primary database organization. At the completion of the resynchronization, the network may be switched back to the primary system. Any updates made on the backup database during switchover will be replicated to the primary database. The primary system will now be available with all maintenance complete. The maximum outage seen by users is the time to make two switches of the network. Data replication may again be stopped to permit the backup to be brought to the maintenance level of the primary system, after which it resynchronizes with the primary database and is ready for the next maintenance cycle.

Required Replication Features

Hierarchical

There are four principle strategies for database replication. These strategies are summarized, as follows.

Hierarchical, or "master/slave" replication, provides uni-directional transmission from the source. This is the typical strategy for read-only data warehouse implementations. For those systems where replication is desired to support local inquiry and reporting requirements, this implementation provides a simpler, faster technique than the bi-directional technique.

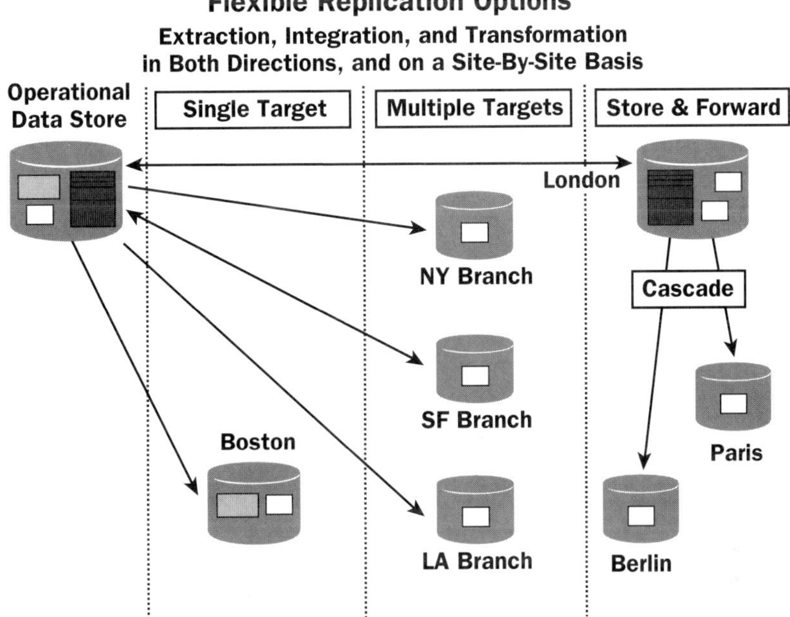

Figure 5: Typical replication uses.

When a hierarchical structure of replicated databases is implemented, data replication uses only a subset of its total functionality. There is no need for update conflict detection and therefore, the amount of data retained for checking is reduced. As a result, less logic is required to perform the update. This improves the performance of replication.

Broadcast

Data replication supports broadcasting replicas using only a single copy of the data to be replicated. In cases where a number of target sites receive the same information, such as price table changes replicated to a number of stores, data replication can take advantage of the commonality using a broadcast capability. This capability is implemented through a single storage of the data changes, along with transmission indicators for each destination. The result is reduced system time and greater storage efficiency.

Cascade

A cascade capability supports the target as a source for further replication. Thus, a system for an enterprise's corporate headquarters might replicate divisional data to a divisional system which could, in turn, replicate a subset to a regional system. This simplifies otherwise complex broadcast requirements and permits optional data enhancement and filtering at each level. In the inverse case, regional systems might replicate to divisional systems, which further replicate to the enterprise's headquarters. These staging steps permit each level to filter out data that is not appropriate at the next level.

Bi-Directional

Bi-directional capability makes no distinction in the priority of the systems. Either or both systems may update any data. Data replication assumes responsibility for detecting conflicts and either resolves them automatically, or presents them for resolution as the user specifies.

Bi-Directional With Collision Resolution

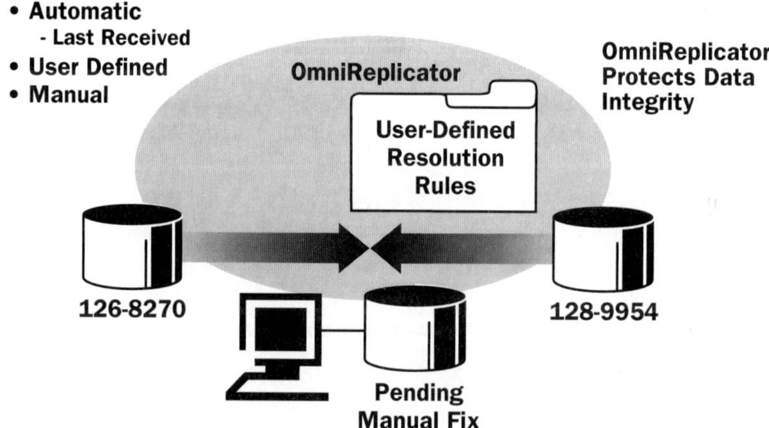

Figure 6: Bi-directional replication requires collision resolution.

Symmetric Implementation (Bi-Directional)

While replication is often thought of as a hierarchical approach with a source and some number of dependent (read-only) targets, that strategy limits the applications it can support. The dependent nodes in such a system are restricted to read-only, to prevent inconsistency with the source. Products, such as OmniReplicator from Praxis International, use symmetric data replication to avoid the restrictions of the hierarchical approach and employ a full symmetric architecture. All participating systems are potentially both source and target systems for the same data. This bi-directional architecture permits the establishment of a centrally updated system with additional query replicas, but also permits a fully-distributed transactional network where many local systems provide update capability. At the same time, these systems retain full access to the changes from all other systems.

A bank, for instance, could have local update capability for high performance, while all accounts are updated continuously for other branch activity. As with many types of transactions, it is unlikely for a bank account to be updated from two offices at the same instant, and if it occurs, data replication will discover the conflict and resolve it.

Multi-Table Data Consistency

Data replication must ensure integrity and consistency across multiple tables by using a transaction-oriented mode of replication. All updates for all tables of a user transaction are included in a single replication unit. This unit is a collection of remote requests which are incorporated within a single unit of work (the scope of commit) and it ensures integrity and consistency. An example is OmniReplicator, which maintains the sequence of updates and assures that updates to all tables by a single transaction are complete prior to the release of the data for use by the user. Of course, the sequence of transaction execution is also maintained. Just as the application ensures internal data consistency through its commit logic, data replication must ensure identical consistency throughout the replication. Users of a replicated database will not find inconsistency between tables due to delays in parts of the replication unit.

Filtering Data For Replication

Data replication must be capable of replicating all of the data in a table or set of tables. Thus, additional sites can maintain exact copies of the tables at the source and be assured that the data residing at the target is consistent with the data at the source. The target table can be on a different hardware platform and/or use a different vendor's database system.

In many cases, it is neither efficient nor desirable to replicate all changes. The most obvious concern is the volume of data shipped over the network, even at non-peak times. In addition, such concerns as privacy, security, and applicability must also be taken into account. Data replication must then provide the ability to independently define the data which will be sent to each target. A wide range of facilities for filtering the data (prior to sending) exist. For example:

- The billing department may receive only the portion of an order appropriate to the billing function. It may not be necessary for the department to be aware of product variables, such as color;

- The eastern marketing region may receive only the orders booked by eastern region personnel. They may not need access to the orders booked by other regions;

- For individual users, data may be selected by both row and column to provide the information required in its minimal form. Privacy is protected at the same time that storage at the user site and network traffic are minimized; and

- Data can be merged from multiple sources to a single target, to permit higher levels of the business to see a broader view.

Special Data Types

One example of unique data types is a Binary Large Object (BLOB). BLOBs contain a variety of information, from photographic images to corporate logos and other icons. Data replication of BLOBs can be tricky at best and, in some cases, not possible.

BLOBs have an internal organization, much like other data types. Rules for BLOBs must be followed. These rules can be defined, understood, and used in data replication. Provided that the data replication tool has a component for data filtration and transformation, BLOBs are also capable of being replicated. Even BLOBs created on different RDBMSs can be replicated, if the underlying data structure is defined and followed.

The analogy in PCs can be used as an example. Both .TIFF or .BMP files can be copied and understood by the receiving program. However, if the file format is unique, or not understood by the receiving program, the file consists of only a series of bits, and is rendered effectively useless.

Transmission Scheduling

Data replication architecture should support three basic means to control data transmission: continuous asynchronous, time of day, or manual initiation. To support this, the capture of changes is separated from the transmission, allowing these processes to occur independently. Changes are recorded in a persistent data store to await transmission.

Continuous asynchronous transmission provides a high degree of currency. As soon as a transaction's changes have been recorded, the data changes are queued for transmission and sent as the line becomes available. This technique can result in a nearly synchronous level of currency. It is appropriate for cases where the data is used for operational support.

In many cases, data is not required until a specific time, or is not needed before a certain period has expired. In cases such as these, data replication must support scheduled transmissions. For example, if billing is performed in a single run at 8:00 AM, it is not necessary to send updates at 1:00 PM, or if a shipping department does not require immediate notification of an order, since the order will not be assembled in the warehouse until the following day. Instead, replication transmissions can occur at non-peak times, thereby improving network utilization and response times during peak periods.

Finally, transmission may be manually initiated. In environments where activity is highly variable, operations can determine when the replication will take place. In other cases, users may not need continuous updates to local systems and prefer to request an update.

Fault Tolerance

Data replication cannot require that a network be continuously available. Since data replication should be asynchronous and operate in a store and forward mode, it can readily tolerate network and target node outages. Changes to be replicated are stored at the source for transmission. The replicator will attempt to transmit the changes based on the selected transmission scheduling algorithm. If the network or node is unavailable, the changes are retained at the source. The transmission takes place when the resource is available.

Ease of Use

Ease of use is an important feature of every system tool available today. The features should not require programming or elaborate scripts to set up, run, or maintain.

Ideally, a Window-based graphical user interface (GUI), such as the one incorporated in OmniReplicator, should be all that is needed to define replication requirements. Through the GUI, it is possible to use a mouse to simply select the replication source database from a drop-down list of available databases. Then, by using a mouse, a user should be able to select a graphical mapping of sources, targets, and the routings between them.

Everything required to initiate replication (selecting source columns and mapping them to target columns, applying pre-defined data enhancement routines to specific columns, defining replication scheduling, and setting protected or retransmit modes where applicable) can all be performed through the GUI. It is possible to define most elements by just pointing-and-clicking with a mouse. For items which require data input—such as selection criteria values and database connection strings—easy-to-follow dialog boxes should also be available to accept the necessary values.

Conclusion

Data replication can facilitate the development and redesign of distributed computing, data warehousing, continuous operations, and a host of other long-awaited applications. If implemented properly, data integrity can be maintained along with ease of use.

About the Author

Marvin Miller is a senior consultant for Digital Equipment Corporation, where he works closely with Informix on large-scale data warehousing opportunities. He has 25 years of experience in the computer industry, including large-scale system design, benchmarking, and migrations.

About Digital Equipment Corporation

Digital Equipment Corporation is the leading worldwide supplier of networked computer systems, software, and services. Digital pioneered and leads the industry in interactive, distributed, and multi-vendor computing. An international company, Digital conducts more than half its business outside the United States, developing and manufacturing products and providing customer service in the Americas, Europe, Asia, and the Pacific Rim.

The High Performance Database

=15

MULTITHREADING IN INFORMIX-ONLINE DYNAMIC SERVER

by Elliot Danziger

Introduction

The release of INFORMIX-OnLine Dynamic Server incorporates multithreading technology within the database server. This technology represents not only architectural changes to the traditional Informix two-process model, but also introduces new approaches to OLTP processing made possible by a multithreaded environment.

Note

Hereafter, to distinguish between the two distinct products, the article will refer to INFORMIX-OnLine Dynamic Server as "OnLine Dynamic Server" and to INFORMIX-OnLine as simply "OnLine."

This article will explore the design and key concepts of the new Dynamic Scalable Architecture (DSA). It is not the intent nor is it within the scope of this article to give an exhaustive description of the OnLine Dynamic Server tunables, utilities, and their options; that will be left for the documentation provided with the product. Rather, it is hoped that this discussion helps to substitute definitive concepts for any abstract notions of the multithreaded DSA engine.

To better understand the relative importance of the new multithreaded engine design, let us first review the current two-process model and examine some of the limitations inherent in this model which multithreading seeks to avoid.

The Traditional Two-Process Model

At its simplest, the current OnLine processing model consists of two processes: the front end or client process which formulates database requests, and the back end or server process which processes the database requests. During client/server communications, this model utilizes multiple processes to accomplish tasks: the front end (for example, an INFORMIX-ESQL/C program) resides on the client machine, a local back-end process communicates over a network to the server machine, a back-end process on the server machine actually performs the database requests, and another daemon (sqlexecd) runs on the server machine to fork server back-end processes. In summary, with OnLine, the client cannot talk directly to the server without requiring extra processes, context switches, and communication layers.

Whether dealing with client/server or local communications, the limitations of the two (or more) process model are clear, especially when taking overhead costs into consideration. Specifically, a larger number of processes place a heavier load on the UNIX kernel in that a greater amount of memory is allocated to kernel tables, and more instructions require execution by the scheduler for process aging. These are only a few of the administrative operating system tasks required.

Interestingly enough, among the most costly features of the two-process model are the restrictions inherent within the model itself. OnLine architecture requires that each engine process remain self-contained. Each engine process relies solely on itself to respond to user requests, perform disk I/O, and execute the logic of database accesses. For example, inserting a row into a table could potentially require operations consisting of the following steps:

a.   Processing the request;

b.   Writing to the physical log file;

c.   Writing to the logical log file; and

d.   Flushing dirty buffer cache pages to disk.

In the current architecture, all of these operations would perforce be accomplished synchronously, since they are all performed unaided by a single, standalone engine process. Furthermore, when running in a symmetric multiprocessing (SMP) hardware environment, these operations only utilize a single CPU at any given time to process, since the granularity for binding to a CPU occurs at the process level.

The new multithreaded architecture does not suffer from the aforementioned limitations; at the same time, it creates a platform that can support more advanced RDBMS techniques, which will be explained later.

The New Multithreaded Architecture

In many respects, multithreading within a process is analogous to UNIX multiprocessing within the operating system. Threads need to be created or forked, scheduled, switched in and out of processing, destroyed, along with other kernel-like tasks typically performed on processes in a multiprocessing operating system. Therefore, in order to understand the multithreaded process, it is imperative to first become familiar with how a single-threaded process (that is, a traditional UNIX process) operates. Armed with this knowledge, DBAs and users of INFORMIX-OnLine Dynamic Server systems will be in a position to more fully utilize the new DSA architecture.

Multithreading is a method to execute many iterations of a process for different users without having to fork many instances of that process at the operating system level. Instead, many threads are forked at the process level. This is a good time to do away with some preconceived notions. Multithreading is not simply a program that runs as a single-server process taking requests and responding to many client processes. Multithreading is a system-level concept whereby the multithreaded program executes machine-level instructions to manipulate a process. A process is thus enabled to execute for many users and not just for one. This manipulation is performed entirely within the user's process, without invoking any operating system routines. As far as UNIX is concerned, it still perceives it is running a single process like any other.

To further the analogy, think for a moment about the way that UNIX accomplishes multiprocessing. When running 1,000 processes, only one process is executed by UNIX at any given time. Each process runs for a specified time quantum before it is preempted by the kernel and the next scheduled process is run. When preempting a running process, enough information about the process must be saved so that the process can be restarted at a later time. This information is called the context of a process, hence the term *context switching.*

The context of a process consists of the user-level context, the register context, and the system-level context.

The user-level context consists of the following:

- TEXT segment   An addressable area within the process containing the machine instructions for a program.

■ DATA segment

An addressable area within the process for the storage of a program's global and static variables.

■ STACK segment

An addressable area within the process for the storage of the local variables used by a program's functions.

The register context consists of the following:

■ Program Counter

Specifies the address of the next instruction to execute.

■ Stack Pointer

Contains the current address of the entry in the stack segment.

■ General Purpose Registers

Contains the data generated by the process during its execution.

The system-level context is not critical to understanding concepts of multithreading and thus will only be described briefly here. The system-level context consists of the process table entry, the U area, region and page table entries, kernel mode stack frames, and the dynamic system-level context layers which handle exceptions and interrupts.

Now, let us consider the basics of a context switch. The kernel saves the context of the currently running process and loads the context of the next scheduled process. Loading the context involves the following steps:

1. Restoring the program counter, the stack pointer, and all general purpose registers (i.e., the register context) to the values saved by the kernel when the process was last preempted;

2. Remapping the text, data, and stack segments (i.e., the user context) in physical memory by way of the region and page table entries of the system-level context; and

3. Restoring the rest of the system-level context (for the kernel's own administrative needs).

The new process is now ready to run.

The CPU looks at the program counter, obtains the address of the next instruction in the text segment to be executed, loads the instruction, and then executes it, perceiving that the contents of the process' memory (the user segments) and all pointers to those offsets (the stack pointer, register offsets, etc.) have been restored. There is no magic involved in the way that the kernel saves and restores the context of processes. When saving contexts, it simply executes machine instructions which copy the contents of registers, program counter, etc., to preallocated data structures in memory which serve as the holding area for the contexts of different processes. When restoring contexts, this process is simply reversed.

What are Threads?

We will now transpose these concepts to threads. Let's say a program itself executes these machine instructions to copy the register context of its own process to data structures within its address space and then loads another saved register context to continue execution. The same result as described previously for kernel switching is thus achieved and, in fact, it is much simpler.

The same process continues to execute; thus, the user- and system-level segments remain mapped in memory. All that changes is the register context. The result is that the program counter points to a new instruction within the text segment, the stack pointer points to a different area of memory, and the general purpose registers are restored to the values which were previously saved for this context. It is, in effect, fooling UNIX to run a different flow of control sequence within the same running process. These sequential flows of control within a running process are called threads.

Many later versions of UNIX provide functionality for lightweight threads. Thus, it is possible to design a process to be multithreaded simply by utilizing a set of library routines available on the operating system to allow the programmer to execute the multithreading logic described in the previous section.

To implement multithreading in INFORMIX-OnLine Dynamic Server, a new multithreading (MT) layer containing these routines has been introduced underneath the existing relational logic (SQL) layers, as well as the access methods (RSAM) layer. This new MT layer is based on the Posix thread standard which makes it easy to map the MT calls to operating system calls (when the underlying operating system provides the functionality for lightweight threads conforming to the Posix standard).

Threads Used for Parallelism

One of the primary goals realized by the new Dynamic Scalable Architecture's multithreaded design is its ability to serve as a foundation for parallelism. Parallelism offers the potential for the significant speedup of operations by breaking large tasks into smaller subtasks and executing them in parallel. Parallel execution, however, requires that the executors of these tasks run concurrently. When traditional operating system processes are used as the executors of these concurrent subtasks, a significant load is placed on the system. For example, fifty jobs run in a serial processing environment would previously be executed by fifty operating system processes. If each of those fifty jobs were to be broken into ten subtasks (each being executed by a separate operating system process), a load of five-hundred processes must be sustained by the system.

This can have a negative impact on system performance, as the operating system must age many more processes, perform more context switches, allocate more memory for per-process private data areas which, in turn, results in more paging and swapping. These, as well as other limitations, are the result of operating system processes which are heavyweight in nature, that is, there is a fair amount of overhead associated with the masses. As users and tasks increase in this type of environment, the resulting load can overwhelm the operating system's ability to perform efficiently.

Threads, on the other hand, represent a much lower cost resource for parallelism with many hundreds of threads able to execute within a few operating system processes, (i.e., virtual processors), thus minimizing the load on the operating system. The threads themselves are lightweight (with little overhead). Thus, thread context switches are simple and fast, typically requiring twenty instructions or less to execute. Furthermore, for the efficient use of memory resources, all memory used by threads are allocated from a global pool. INFORMIX-OnLine Dynamic Server takes advantage of the low-cost nature of threads by offering a parallel index build feature. The next section will discuss the implementation of parallel index builds in the hope that the reader will appreciate the fact that software must be designed for parallelism. The execution of old, monolithic software methods on new parallel hardware machines does not guarantee that parallelism will be effected, nor does it ensure efficient paralleism (i.e., parallelism designed to make optimal use of a given parallel hardware architecture). DSA, on the other hand, is designed to efficiently execute on parallel hardware architectures, as will be clearly demonstrated by the following discussion.

Parallel Index Builds

When attempting to parallelize a task, one must first determine the individual components that comprise the task; these components, in turn, can be broken into subtasks and executed in parallel. The number of components identified is referred to as the vertical degree of parallelism, that is, the number of distinct forms of work which need to be executed to complete the overall task. There is another degree of parallelism that must be considered as well, namely, the horizontal degree of parallelism. The horizontal degree of parallelism refers to the number of iterations that each vertical subtask component uses to complete its piece of the overall task. Specifically, the task of building a B+tree is comprised of three components (i.e., its vertical degree of parallelism):

1.   Scanning the table for which this index is created;

2.   Sorting the data retrieved; and

3.   Placing each key into the B+tree.

Each of these components can have multiple iterations, (its horizontal degree of parallelism). For example, there may be three scanners scanning the table, three sorters sorting the retrieved data, and three appenders placing keys into the tree. In this example of horizontal parallelism, it would, of course, be unnecessary for each scanner to scan the entire table, each sorter to sort all the retrieved data, etc. That would result in simply performing the same task three times when the goal is to execute the same workload in less time. Rather, the work must be intelligently subdivided, so that each scanner scans a separate third of the table, each sorter sorts a separate third of the retrieved data, and each appender appends a separate third of the keys to the B+tree.

Efficient software design for parallel processing must also take interference into consideration, that is, when multiple tasks are executing concurrently to complete a job, each task should not slow another task. For example, if two scan tasks were to scan the same disk in parallel, the disk heads would resultantly thrash while trying to read two areas of the disk concurrently. Similarly, if all the parallel B+tree appenders were allowed to insert keys anywhere in the tree, the appenders could interfere with each other, (e.g., when trying to insert keys into the same node), forcing one appender to wait until another appender completed its current key insertion. This is actually one of the reasons the data scanned from disk is first sorted before being passed on to the B+tree appenders (the other reason is performance). Sorting the data allows each B+tree appender to work on a range of keys that does not overlap in value with those of another appender. In actuality, to ensure maximum non-interference, the B+tree appenders are not designed to work on the same tree. They each insert keys of their designated range of values into their own B+tree, creating a forest of trees. When all the trees are completed they merge to form a single tree which is actually the finished index. This concern for non-interference thus forces an additional vertical task to the index build process, that of merging the individual trees into a single B+tree. The incorporation of this additional step into the index build process is worthwhile, as the merge process is a simple algorithm that is much less costly than any of the interference that would otherwise be experienced as a result of colliding B+tree appenders.

The Design

Based on the aforementioned considerations, the parallel index build process has been designed with four basic components: scan, sort, append, and merge. The scan, sort, and append components can each have multiple iterations (horizontal parallelism) while the merge, since it is a very simple fast task, requires only one iteration. These four tasks form a vertical pipeline which, when parallelized horizontally, forms a producer-consumer environment, as shown in the following illustration:

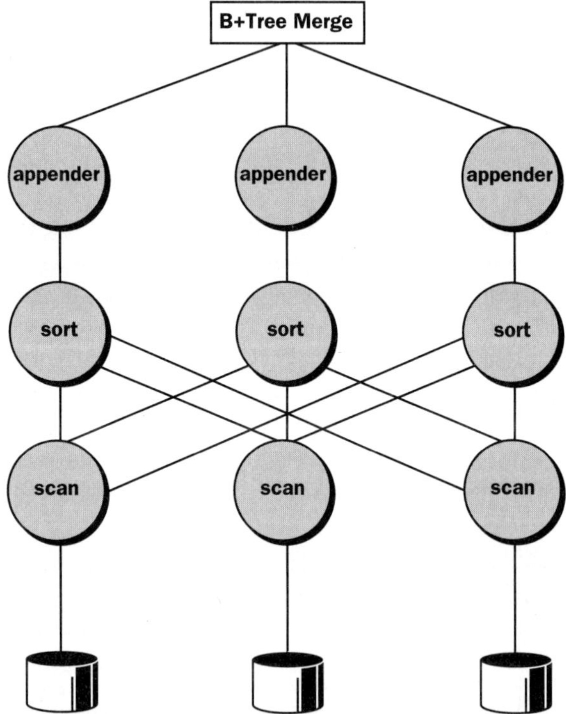

Figure 1: Task tree for parallel index builds.

For the purposes of our example, three scanners, three sorters, and three appenders are used, but the actual degree of horizontal parallelism can be different for each task. The number of scanners is determined by the number of chunks in the table to be indexed. The number of sorters is a function of the number of appenders and the number of processors specified in the PSORT_NPROCS environment variable. The number of appenders is a function of the estimated size of the B+tree and the number of available CPUs in the system.

The number of CPUs is important in these calculations, as this number ultimately determines how much real parallelism will take place. The actual ranges used by each sorter and appender are determined by taking data distribution samplings of the table. The goal in setting these ranges is to keep the load for each bin as evenly balanced as possible.

The lowermost tasks, the scans, produce the data which will be consumed by the sorts. There is one scan dedicated to each chunk that comprises the table to be indexed. Typically, one chunk is associated with one disk drive, so allocating one thread per chunk allows the multiple chunks that comprise the table to be read in parallel. As mentioned earlier, more than one thread scanning a single disk is not desirable, as it can result in disk head thrashing.

The sorts consume the data produced by the scans. As each row is scanned by a scan task, it must be redirected to the proper sort task, since the sorts are each working on sorting non-overlapping ranges of the overall data set. Sorting the data accomplishes two things:

1.   It allows for non-overlapping ranges to be handed off to each appender; and

2.   It also makes for more efficient B+tree insertion.

The appenders, in turn, consume the data produced by the sorts. Each appender, working on its own non-overlapping range of key values, inserts the keys contained within its range into a separate B+tree.

When all the appenders have completed, the merge task builds the final tree. The key to the simplicity of the merge task is the fact that the appenders create a forest of N trees in N non-overlapping ranges. The merge of the trees is accomplished only at the seams of the individual trees, as will now be explained. Figure 2 contains a forest of two trees with non-overlapping ranges. Tree 1 was built with key values ranging from 1 to 199, and tree 2 with key values ranging from 201 to 399.

The '>>>' notation refers to the infinity slot, a pointer to the node containing all values greater than the key values in this node. From this illustration, it can be seen that from a logical perspective the two trees can be viewed as one. If we were to put a root node above these two trees containing the keys, as follows:

199 | >>>

where 199 pointed to the "old" root node for tree 1, and >>> pointed to the "old" root node for tree 2, the result would be a single balanced B+tree, refer to Figure 2.

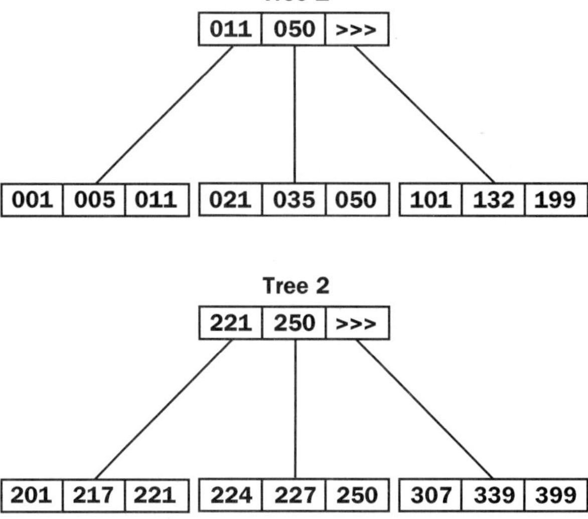

Figure 2: Two B+trees of two levels each having non-overlapping ranges.

This is actually how the merge is accomplished; however, some additional tasks must be performed, as well. Since the nodes within each level are linked to one another, the nodes on the right-most side of tree 1 must be linked with the nodes on the left-most side of tree 2. It is possible to picture these nodes as the seams of the trees and the merge as the act of "sewing" the trees together at the seams. When more than two trees are merged, (i.e., there are more than two appender tasks), the first two trees in the forest are merged, then the newly merged tree is merged with the third tree, which is then merged with the fourth tree, and so on, until all the N trees are merged. When trees are merged, it is possible that multiple appenders have created trees of varying levels. In that case, the merge task forces the trees with the smaller number of levels to have the same levels as their merge partners, before performing the merge described above. Once the individual trees are merged, the new root node is created and all of the former infinity slots within the former individual trees are updated to reflect the new single tree.

It may seem that there are many tasks which must be completed for parallel index builds, however, the keyword in this entire discussion is parallel. Actual tests, run by Informix and customers as well, demonstrate that index builds, which require hours or even days to complete on other systems, now execute in minutes or even seconds when parallel index builds are used.

During the course of this article, we have described the implementation of parallel index builds and how they have been designed for parallelism. The combination of parallelization at the core subtask level and the utilization of low cost threads as the vehicles for subtask execution allows INFORMIX-OnLine

Dynamic Server to set new standards for performance and scalability in the open system environment.

What are Virtual Processors (VPs)?

Multithreading significantly changes the architectural dynamics of INFORMIX-OnLine Dynamic Server. There are only a handful of virtual processors (VPs) which handle all server activities; Figure 3 depicts the configuration of VPs and system resources.

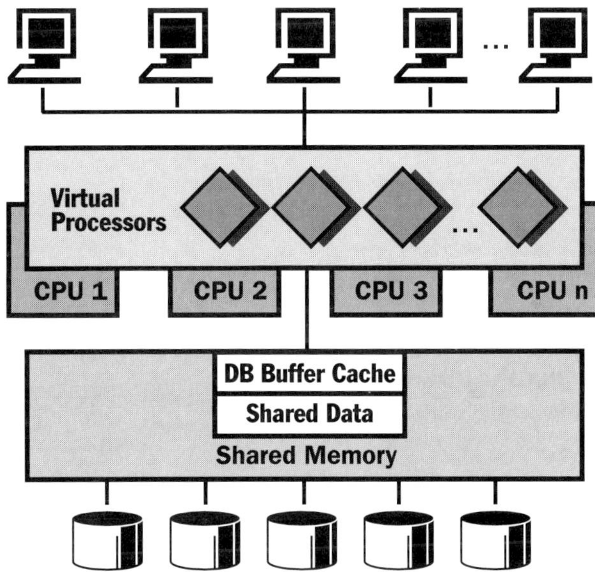

Figure 3: INFORMIX-OnLine Dynamic Server consists of a configurable pool of database server processes, called virtual processors, that respond to client requests.

VPs are individual UNIX processes (they each show up as 'oninit' in a 'ps' listing), each has the potential to handle many threads. VPs are divided into classes; as illustrated in the Figure 4, each class represents a different area of engine processing.

CPU VPs perform most of the work, including all SQL and RSAM processing. Therefore, on machines with many CPUs, the NUMCPUVPS processor is typically more than 1 (although the number of NUMCPUVPS should never be greater than the number of CPUs on the system). The I/O VPs handle disk I/O asynchronously at varying priorities. DSA also utilizes kernel I/O (KIO) to effect asynchronous I/O operations, when KIO is provided by the operating system vendor.

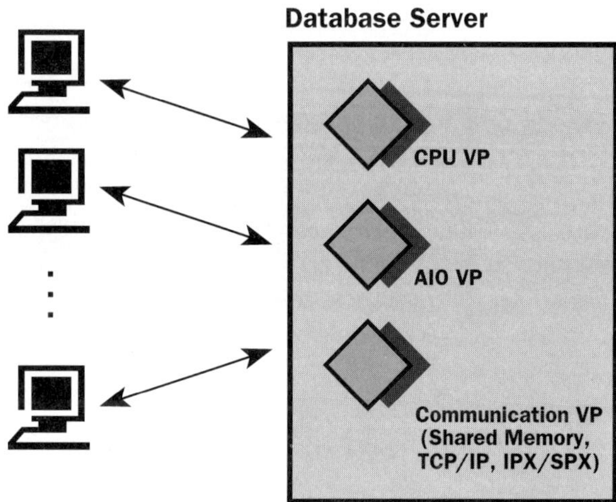

Figure 4: Virtual processors are grouped into classes which are optimized for a particular function. This illustration depicts three main classes.

The TLI, Socket, and Shared Memory (SHM) VPs are used for the client/server message passing system (remember pipes are no longer used). Any one of these message passing mechanisms—or a combination of all three can be used as long as the mechanisms are supported by the operating system. The user can configure the number and types of network VPs. There are other classes of VPs that are not configurable, such as logical log I/O VPs and physical log I/O VPs.

Built-In Connectivity

In case more than one type of communication mechanism is used, each client process specifies its mode of connection with an environment variable. SHM connections are faster than TLI and Socket connections, but are only good for local connections and are not as secure. TLI and Socket connections are, of course, used for remote connections. Since message passing is now an integral part of INFORMIX-OnLine Dynamic Server, there is no longer a need for the INFORMIX-STAR product.

Performance Gains in INFORMIX-OnLine Dynamic Server

One of the key advantages to INFORMIX-OnLine Dynamic Server is that it can have multiple VPs of the same class. This design can greatly improve performance in SMP environments by making sure that a VP running on one processor

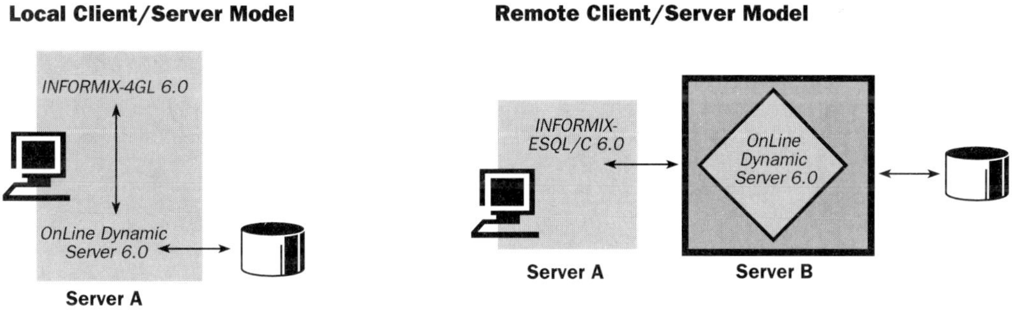

Local Client/Server Model   **Remote Client/Server Model**

Figure 5: INFORMIX-OnLine Dynamic Server includes built-in connectivity libraries; thus, it is client/server-ready directly out of the box.

does not become a bottleneck for user requests while other processors remain idle. For example, as pictured in Figure 5, an INFORMIX-OnLine Dynamic Server instance may be running three CPU VPs with processor affinity used to bind each VP to a specific physical processor. If the load on one of the CPU VPs becomes very large and if the remaining CPU VPs have completed their processing, the database requests of the busy CPU VP will be redirected to the two idle CPU VPs, thus load balancing the system's CPU processing.

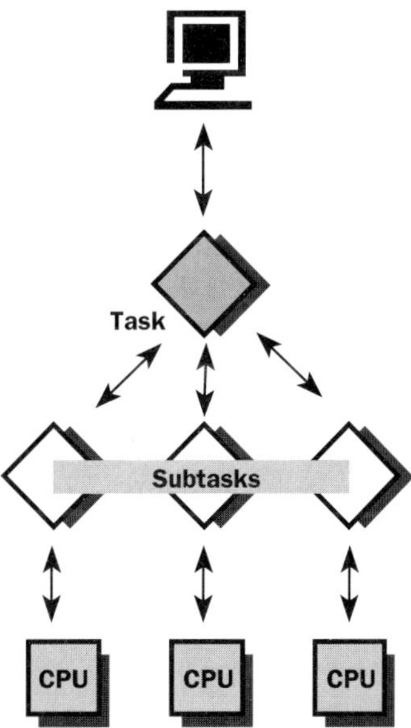

Figure 6: INFORMIX-OnLine Dynamic Server's core DSA technology takes full advantage of system resources; all allocated processors are in constant use, leaving no CPUs idle if there are databases requests to be processed.

In other words, this design allows threads to "migrate" from one VP to another VP of the same class. The previous discussion on multithreading explained how multiple threads could be maintained and executed by a single process. Thread migration is accomplished by keeping the critical parts of thread contexts (register context and stack) in shared memory, thus allowing any VP to address this information.

Conclusion

During the course of this article, the implementation of parallel index builds and their design for parallelism has been discussed. To conclude this discussion, let's move for a moment from the theoretical realm to the practical, and describe some strategies which will help to ensure that parallel index builds will operate at optimal levels of efficiency.

The "old" relationships between tables, chunks, and dbspaces should be rethought. Having many small chunks on one device, all belonging to the same dbspace, can cause sub-optimal performance for parallel index builds on tables within that dbspace. Since the parallel index build allocates one scan thread for each chunk which makes up the table being indexed, this scenario can cause the thrashing of the disk head, as multiple scan threads vie to position the disk over "their" portion of the disk. Logical Volume Managers (LVMs), used in many operating systems to stripe data across multiple disk drives (among other things), can have the opposite affect, namely, having too few scan threads allocated. When an LVM stripes data across drives, the actual OnLine chunk only points to the one "logical" device. Since there is only one OnLine chunk for that table, there would only be one scan thread allocated by the parallel index build, resulting in less parallelism.

One approach to consider is to "stripe" the table through INFORMIX-OnLine Dynamic Server. For example, if a table is estimated to have an initial size of 500 MB and there are seven disk drives available to stripe this table, a dbspace could be created containing seven chunks, with each chunk physically placed on the first 100 MB of each of the seven disk drives. When the data is loaded (with parallel index builds, it is always best to load before indexing), it would fill the first five chunks on five of the seven drives, leaving 200 MB available for indexes and data growth. This scheme has the added benefit of keeping the index pages on a device different from the initial data pages. When using strategies, such as this, it is useful to dedicate a dbspace to a single table. This helps to keep things logically and physically grouped, while at the same time provides table-level granularity for the DSA Archive and Restore utilities. Archive and restore in DSA allows archive and restore to take place at a dbspace level. If there is only one table per dbspace, then, in effect, a table-level granularity is achieved.

There are a number of configuration file tunables and environment variables which should be set for parallel index builds. PSORT_NPROCS is an environment variable which should be set to the number of CPUs that will participate in the parallel sort phase of the build process. The actual number of sort threads will be PSORT_NPROCS * (# of appenders). DBSPACETEMP can be specified in the environment and/or the configuration file; note, when both are set, the environment variable takes precedence. This should be set to the dbspace(s) which will be used for sort space. If more than 1 dbspace is specified, the dbspaces will all be used in Round-Robin fashion by the various sort threads. This being the case, it would be beneficial if these dbspaces could be made up of chunks which exist on their own dedicated disk drives or at least on disk drives which do not experience heavy I/O activity. This will ensure that the parallel sorters do not bottleneck on I/O to a small number of disks being used for temporary space.

The read-ahead configuration file parameters can also be useful in optimizing the index build process. Since each scan thread sequentially scans the chunk of the table that it has been assigned to, the server will use read-ahead to keep the buffer cache supplied with the pages that will be needed for the index build. This can potentially speed up the index build process in situations where the disk scan activity is accomplished in bursts that cause the other tasks involved in the build to wait for the I/O to complete.

There are two read-ahead configurables, RA_PAGES and RA_THRESHOLD. RA_PAGES refers to how many pages the server should read-ahead, while RA_THRESHOLD refers to the number of pages left from the last read-ahead that must still be processed before the next read-ahead is requested. The actual numbers used for RA_PAGES depends on the resources available in the system, the size of the table being read, how fast the I/O system processes the data, etc., and requires some trial and error to determine the best setting.

Start with a small number (for example, 10 or 20) and keep doubling the number as long as additional benefit is realized (one customer kept obtaining better performance until his RA_PAGES reached 200 which, while probably not the norm, indicates that every environment can be different). A good starting rule of thumb for RA_THRESHOLD is RA_PAGES / 2 but again, this varies depending on the environment. The new options available with the onstat utility supply detailed information for measuring everything from the number of threads used for parallelism to the exact I/O requests in use. This utility aids in selecting the exact numbers for tuning a particular environment.

Parallel index builds provide an example of how DSA has rearchitected database software to take advantage of parallelism. As DSA moves forward, other database tasks will be similarly rearchitected, such as Parallel Data Query (PDQ), which executes individual queries using vertical and horizontal parallelism. The combination of parallelization at the core subtask level and the use of low cost threads as the vehicles for subtask execution allows the INFORMIX-OnLine Dynamic Server to set new standards for performance and scalability in open systems databases.

About the Author

Elliot Danziger is a regional manager of the Advanced Technology Group (ATG) at Informix, Somerset, New Jersey.

=16

Implementing High Availability Informix Solutions with Unix

by Peter S. Simcox

Open Systems High Availability

High Availability (HA) continues to grow as a major consideration for database applications, particularly in mission-critical environments. HA features, commonly provided with proprietary systems, are now in demand as users downsize to open systems. High-availability functionality was the improvement most requested in a 1992 IDC study of UNIX sites [Morrell '92]. UNIX vendors are now including high availability features as an integral part of their hardware and operating system products.

Three broad approaches are used today to minimize system downtime, and increase application and data accessibility:

- Increased system resiliency;

- Continuous availability, or fault tolerance (FT); and

- High Availability.

Increased system resiliency is simply a combination of maximizing the reliability of the system and software. Fault tolerance provides the highest amount of coverage for system failure, but at a much higher cost. High availability systems combine cost-effective, fault tolerant features with fast recovery mechanisms.

Varying levels of high availability are attainable today, through a mixture of hardware technology, operating system extensions, and RDBMS features. Users can now choose the different features to meet their high availability needs, while minimizing any impact on overall system performance. In fact, HA features can often improve performance when configured correctly.

Note:

For more information on high availability, please refer to the article, *Planning and Tuning of Fragmentation Stategies in INFORMIX-OnLine Dynamic Server, Version 7.1,* by Subhash Bhatia. Also, please note that this article refers specifically to INFORMIX-OnLine Dynamic Server, version 6.0.

High-Availability Hardware Technology

Efforts to increase availability with hardware technology typically center around the I/O subsystem, CPU, and memory. Input/Output (I/O) is the first subsystem commonly addressed for added high availability. The principal reasons are:

- It holds the "valuable" data, as perceived by the customer; and

- It is the least costly subsystem in which to add redundancy.

Disk subsystem HA features, widely available in proprietary systems, such as disk mirroring, dual porting, and redundant I/O channels, have now become commonplace in UNIX systems. UNIX vendors are now developing advanced HA disk subsystems using RAID technology.

Redundant Array of Inexpensive Disks (RAID)

The term "RAID" originally stood for Redundant Array of Inexpensive Disks [Patterson '88]. The RAID Advisory Board now officially defines RAID as Redundant Array of Independent Disks. These systems are certainly not inexpensive, as first thought. Disk arrays are founded on the premise that I/O performance can be significantly improved by using a large number of small form-factor disks instead of a small number of large form-factor disks, i.e., increasing the number of drives for a given capacity requirement. The main problem with this approach, however, is system availability. A system with many disks is less reliable than one with fewer disks. RAID is the primary method used to overcome this problem in providing HA storage subsystems. RAID was first described in a paper by David Patterson, Garth Gibson, and Randy H. Katz of the University of California at Berkeley [Patterson '88]. There are six basic levels of RAID, 0 through 5. A higher number does not mean that the level of availability is any higher nor that performance is any greater. This article describes the following levels of array configurations.

RAID	Level Description
RAID Level 0	Disk array with striping but no parity. [Not referenced in the initial paper.]
RAID Level 1	Mirrored disk array with duplicated data.
RAID Level 2	Disk array with bit-level striping and hamming code protection.
RAID Level 3	Disk array with byte interleaved data and parity on one disk.
RAID Level 4	Disk array with block interleaved data and parity on one disk.
RAID Level 5	Disk array with block interleaved data and rotating parity.

Figure 1: The six basic RAID levels.

Three of these levels, RAID 1, 3, and 5, plus RAID 0 (not referenced in the original paper), are commonly found in HA disk subsystems today and will be discussed in the following sections.

RAID Level 0: RAID level 0 disk arrays provide generic striping of data across numerous physical disks. In this mode, data is divided into "logical blocks," referred to as a "stripe," which are written to different physical disks. RAID 0 configurations offer increased I/O performance, but no redundancy. Loss of a single disk in a RAID 0 group renders all the disks inaccessible.

RAID 0 configurations, therefore, are useful for non-critical data. Uses include UNIX temporary directories, such as "/tmp," "/usr/tmp," or "/var/tmp," and Informix temporary and sort files. Informix temporary files are held in the directory (or directories) specified by the DBTEMP environment variable. Informix parallel sort (PSORT) intermediary files are held in the directory (or directories) specified by the PSORT_DBTEMP environment variable.

Another use for RAID 0 is Informix temporary tables. By default, temporary tables are created in the root dbspace. Users can, however, choose a specific dbspace when creating an explicit temporary table.

INFORMIX-OnLine Dynamic Server stores both temporary files and implicit temporary tables in the rootdbs. This can be overridden using the DBSPACETEMP configuration parameter and environment variable. This option allows muliple dbspaces to be assigned for temprary usage. These dbspaces should be configured on RAID 0.

Use RAID 0 configurations in combination with the mirroring capabilities included with UNIX operating systems. RAID 0 combines high performance hardware disk striping with high availability software mirroring, and provides better overall performance than RAID 5 (see RAID 5) for write-intensive critical data.

RAID Level 1: RAID level 1 disk arrays use "hardware" mirroring for data redundancy. The two, or more, disks in a RAID 1 configuration include a data drive and one, or more, mirror (or shadow) drive(s). RAID 1 configurations can outperform standalone disks when reading data, since a request can be handled by any one of the drives in the mirror, and several requests can be serviced concurrently.

RAID 1 is the best choice for write-intensive data such as Informix physical logs and logical logs. Write-intensive tables should also be configured in dbspace(s) created on RAID level 1 arrays. For mission-critical applications in 24x7 environments, temporary files and tables should also be configured on RAID 1 for continuous operation and maximum performance.

The major disadvantage with RAID 1 is the cost incurred in duplicating the disk storage. Since one, or more, mirror disk(s) are required for every data disk, RAID 1 configurations have a 100 percent to 200 percent (or more) overhead associated with data redundancy. This is very expensive for all but the most critical data.

In addition, RAID 1 does not support the ability to break and re-synchronize a mirror, a feature commonly used for (non-Informix) on-line data backup. This, however, is not a problem with INFORMIX-OnLine, since on-line archiving is supported.

RAID Level 3: RAID level 3 is commonly called "Parallel Disk Array" technology since the disk drives operate in a parallel mode. During write operations, data is broken into "segments" which are stored across different physical disk drives in a single parallel operation. All drives operate in tandem.

During read operations, the process is reversed. Each drive seeks its data "segment" and transfers it to the controller in parallel. The time required to perform a single disk operation is reduced dramatically, particularly for large contiguous files. The parity information stored on a separate drive allows the array to reconstruct a drive's data in the event of failure. In a five-disk group, for example, one disk, i.e., 20 percent of the group's capacity, is dedicated to redundancy.

While a RAID 3 configuration improves the performance of a single I/O operation, it can only perform one operation at a time. All disks in the group are involved in every I/O. The disks are "lock-stepped" together, servicing each I/O request, one at a time. In OLTP environments, I/Os are queued, resulting in degraded performance.

Performance gains are achieved with RAID level 3 when large blocks of data must be moved quickly. It is, therefore, a good choice for storing INFORMIX-OnLine BLOBs. Graphics, video-on-demand, and imaging applications, in particular, have a high demand for such Binary Large OBject (BLOB) data storage.

INFORMIX-OnLine BLOB datatypes can be located in specific Blobspaces. Blobspaces are dedicated to storing BLOB datatypes. Because Blobspace Blobpages are allocated as contiguous space, it is more efficient to store BLOB datatypes in Blobpages sized according to the BLOB data. Configure these Blobspaces using RAID 3 arrays for high availability and best performance.

RAID Level 5: RAID level 5 uses hardware data striping to store data in "blocks" across several physical drives, similar to RAID 0. However, RAID 5 uses parity data, such as RAID 3, to provide for HA.

Each drive acts independently, performing separate I/O operations. This significantly increases the number of simultaneous operations compared to RAID level 3. In a RAID 5 configuration, the parity is not stored on a dedicated parity disk. Instead, the parity data is spread across all the drives in the array group, along with the data. This alleviates any bottleneck incurred through queued write requests to a dedicated parity drive.

RAID 5 configurations, however, incur a performance penalty when writing data. This results from having to update both the data and parity information in separate operations on separate drives. Write-intensive operations will experience performance degradation with RAID 5 arrays. Configure read-intensive tables only in dbspaces created on RAID 5 arrays to avoid performance degradation.

Recent advances in disk array technologies supplement the systems with large memory caches. The size of this cache is important in determining the write I/O rate and throughput. With such large caches, RAID 5 configurations can now support write-intensive data. However, there is an additional cost associated with such caches, which must be considered in a purchase decision.

RAID levels 1 through 5 only guard against a single disk failure. More recent advances in RAID technology attempt to address this issue. Standard definitions for these new RAID levels are not yet available. RAID levels 0 and 1 are often combined, providing mirroring and striping in what is often referred to as RAID 10.

Multi-RAID Configurations: New HA disk arrays provide for the configuration of multiple RAID groups, as well as standalone disks (non-RAID).

Concurrent access of multiple, different RAID levels within a single disk sub-system provide greater flexibility in configuring disk arrays to meet application needs.

For example, in a multi-user transaction-oriented INFORMIX-OnLine environment where both heavy read and write operations must be supported, configure disk arrays as follows:

- High read-oriented tables on RAID 5 groups;

- High write-oriented tables and logs on RAID 1 mirrored pairs;

- Blobspace data on RAID 3 groups; and

- Temporary directories and implicit/explicit OnLine tables and files on RAID 0 groups with optional software mirroring.

This configuration takes advantage of high-availability RAID technology, while also increasing total overall system performance.

High Available Disk Systems

RAID technology is at the heart of UNIX high-available disk systems. Through RAID and additional redundant hardware components, UNIX disk systems are providing a full complement of HA capabilities including:

- Multi-RAID level support;

- Online peripheral replacement;

- I/O path redundancy;

- Controller restart and failover;

- Multi-system configurations; and

- Storage failover/switchover.

Multi-RAID level support is implemented through dedicated I/O processors. These processors control access to the different RAID mode groups through additional I/O channels internal to the disk system. Multiple I/O processors are configured for increased HA and improved performance. On-line peripheral replacement provides for failed component replacement while the disk system remains up and running. This is commonly referred to as "Repair Under Power" (RUP). Multiple power and fan modules are configured to provide the necessary redundancy for continued operation while a failed module is replaced. There are several different ways in which failed disk components can be replaced or swapped. A "cold swap" requires system operation to be halted before the disk is replaced. With a disk "hot swap," the system does not need to be halted, but human intervention is required to replace the failed disk. If the disk replacement is pre-installed as a "hot standby," an "automatic swap" can occur without human intervention. Automatic swap configurations are popular with "darkened data centers".

RAID levels 1 through 5 include redundancy through mirrored or parity data. This enables the I/O processor to calculate the data held on a failed disk drive dynamically, allowing for continued access to data. The failed disk is replaced using "Hot Repair Disk Modules" or a "Failover Disk Drive." The data on the failed disk is rebuilt on the replacement using the data and parity information remaining on the other disks in the group. This, too, is performed by the I/O processor transparent to the computer system. The amount of disk subsystem I/O resources dedicated to recreating the data is often configurable.

I/O path redundancy allows for disk array connection to multiple disk controllers. The ability to restart controllers when one, or more, devices "hang" nullifies the need for computer system shutdown and reboot. Hence, only the applications accessing the devices on the restarted controller are affected, allowing continued availability of all other devices.

I/O path redundancy also allows for the failover of disks from one controller to another. In the event of a failure, the disks serviced by the failed controller are re-configured for access by an alternate controller. This HA functionality is also used to load balance disk access for best performance.

Use of protocols, such as SCSI, enables configuration of disk systems with other standard bus devices. This allows daisy-chaining multiple disk systems on the same channel in order to configure large "disk farms" common to proprietary HA commercial implementations.

By connecting the disk system to controllers from multiple computer systems, it is possible to share the disk system resources and switchover disks from one system to another. Storage switchover/failover support allows on-line switching of such dual-ported disk systems from one system to another. Fail-over is dependent upon both dual-ported I/O bus functionality and UNIX operating system extensions.

Manual and automatic failover solutions are available from leading HA system vendors. These loosely coupled configurations are the basis for the clustered systems being deployed today. CPU and memory availability, provided through failover, clustered systems, and/or redundant components, is paid for at a premium. In fact, such high levels of availability are more commonly catego-rized as "Fault Resilient," "Fault Tolerant," or "Continuous Availability" fea-tures. See [Patch '93] at the end of this article for an overview and discussion on HA terminology and definitions.

Advanced CPU and memory availability features de-configure failed CPU and/or memory modules using on-line diagnostics. This approach is based on new system designs which use field-replaceable CPU and memory modules. This modular design is suitable for UNIX multi-processor architectures and SMP kernels.

The level of data availability is important to determine. It will impact the cost of the HA system and its performance.

UNIX Operating System Extensions

System failover of high available disk systems is achieved through UNIX oper-ating system extension(s). Failover involves switching applications and accounts to another machine, while ensuring no data loss or corruption during the failover/switchover. Some or all of this process may be automated.

HA systems communicate with each other using a "heartbeat" [daemon] process. On system failure, the backup system goes into failover mode. Fail-over can be manual or automatic, with the user community logging off or waiting a brief period for failover completion.

Consider an HA disk system with two I/O processors dual-ported to a pro-duction system and a development system. Each computer system connects to both I/O processors via its own disk controller(s). Both systems are running INFORMIX-OnLine applications against databases held on disk(s) housed in the disk system. The development system is configured as a backup for the produc-tion system, using operating system extensions, in the event of a production sys-tem failure. The development system monitors the production system for such a failure using a "heartbeat."

On failure, the development system initiates failover of the physical disks comprising the production system applications and database(s). Once failed over, the development system checks any filesystems before running application spe-cific "initialization" script(s) developed to bring the production database on-line. The INFORMIX-OnLine production system enters fast recovery, automatically bringing the database(s) to a consistent state. Active transactions from the time of production system failure are rolled back, as in normal recovery. UNIX fail-over systems are provided with additional HA operating systems software exten-sions to quickly recover failed over applications and data. These and other com-mon HA extensions include:

■   Filesystem journaling;

■   Process fault isolation;

■   Transaction Processing (TP) monitors;

■   Auto-reboot on failure;

■   Filesystem re-sizing;

■   Online device controller configuration; and

■   Software disk mirroring.

Filesystem journaling supports "Fast Recovery Filesystems." A transaction-oriented logging technique is used to log updates to filesystem control structures (metadata). On failure, this critical metadata is reconstructed from information in the log, resulting in a faster reboot.

Consider using fast recovery filesystems for Informix data not supported by Informix recovery mechanisms. Informix product and application directories, including Informix users' home and working directories, are good candidates.

Process fault-isolation is employed with heavily-used system components, such as the filesystem. Fault-isolation ensures errors in a failed subsystem are isolated, and do not propagate throughout the system. For example, if a filesystem becomes corrupted, the UNIX "Logical Disk Manager" seals the disk partition, preventing further access. This limits the service disruption to the failed filesystem, extending integrity to valuable data and improving system availability. This is of particular value with Informix application software and with Informix data held in the UNIX filesystem.

"Logical Disk Managers" are given different names on different implementations of UNIX. Examples include the DG/UX "Virtual Disk Manager," the Open Software Foundation (OSF) "Logical Volume Manager" available from HP and IBM, and the UNIX International (UI) "Veritas Filesystem."

Use Transaction Monitors (TMs) with UNIX OS failover to build HA application environments. Specific application coding and administration is necessary to complement the transparent distribution and migration features a TM provides. Use a TM to manage seamless system failover and ensure no loss of data. Popular UNIX TMs include Tuxedo and Encina.

Automatic reboot from power or soft failures facilitates unattended restoration of service and dramatically improves mean time to recover. Rapid recovery is achieved through auto reboot, filesystem journaling, and intelligent fsck. Intelligent, selective fsck implementations do not check quiescent filesystems on reboot. A filesystem is quiescent when the metadata in memory is in-synch with that held on disk.

On-line configuration features allow disk, asynchronous, and local area network controllers to be re-loaded without system shutdown. Some implementations even allow for the removal of devices while the system is up and running. These are significant availability extensions to the operating system.

Finally software disk mirroring is an availability feature provided through a UNIX "Logical Disk Manager." A mirror is a logical disk built from several equally sized logical disk pieces (or partitions). Duplicate and triplicate mirroring is commonly supported. True mirroring implementations take advantage of concurrent I/O to achieve improved levels of performance.

For HA operation and data integrity, configure mirrors on different physical disk devices, located on different controllers, whenever possible. Take on-line UNIX backups from broken, synchronized mirrors. Use this feature with INFORMIX-SE (Standard Engine), which does not support on-line archiving. This is also useful for any other Informix UNIX files, such as Informix forms and reports.

UNIX OS mirroring uses less disk space than RAID level 1 hardware disk mirroring. Mirrors are configured using logical disks (partitions) in the OS versus physical disk with RAID 1. Therefore, UNIX mirroring is more cost-effective, but hardware mirroring yields better performance.

Informix Availability Features

INFORMIX-OnLine 5.0 Features

INFORMIX-OnLine 5.0 HA features, see (Informix 91), include:

- OnLine archiving;

- OnLine fast recovery; and

- OnLine disk mirroring.

An Informix archive is a copy of OnLine data at a specific point in time, stored on one or more tape volumes. Archives are created when OnLine is in quiescent or on-line mode. On-line archiving provides for continuous availability of data while the database(s) are copied to tape. Data is available for modification during an online archive.

Archiving creates a complete record on tape of all used disk pages at a single point in time. Both full and incremental archive capabilities are provided.

These archives, plus logical log backups, allow the state of an OnLine system to be recovered on data loss.

Fast recovery is an automatic, high-availability feature that OnLine executes when the operating mode changes from off-line to quiescent. Fast recovery returns OnLine to a state of physical and logical consistency with minimal downtime in the event of a system failure.

The physical log is used to return OnLine to the most recent point of known physical consistency, the most-recent checkpoint. The logical log file(s) are used to return OnLine to logical consistency, by rolling forward all committed transactions since the last checkpoint, and rolling back incomplete transactions.

During OnLine fast recovery, the physical log is checked to ensure it is empty. The log is empty when OnLine shuts down in a controlled manner. If OnLine was not shut down gracefully, the log will not be empty. This HA feature complements UNIX rapid recovery extensions by bringing OnLine up consistently and as quickly as possible.

INFORMIX-OnLine mirroring, performed by chunk, is configured for an entire Blobspace or dbspace. Chunks cannot be selected within a Blobspace or dbspace to mirror.

During OnLine processing, mirroring is performed by executing two writes for each modified page, one write to the primary chunk and another write to the mirror chunk. OnLine reads from the primary chunk only. If a failure occurs during a read, OnLine changes the primary chunk status to down and continues to read from the mirror chunk. If a failure occurs during a write, writes continue to the other chunk. Once the "down" chunk is recovered, reads are again performed on the primary chunk and writes return to both the primary and mirror chunks.

OnLine mirroring complements UNIX hardware and software mirroring. OnLine mirroring has a much finer granularity, configured by chunk, compared to software and hardware mirroring, configured by logical disk and physical disk, respectively. However, performance, in general, is the opposite. A mix of all three techniques is recommended depending upon the size of the system, the available disk space, and performance requirements.

INFORMIX-OnLine Dynamic Server 6.0 Features

New HA features available with INFORMIX-OnLine Dynamic Server, version 6.0, include:

- Performance mirroring enhancements;

- Parallel index build;

- Dbspace level archive and restore;

- Archive and tape management;

- Parallel recovery, and

- High available data replication.

Mirroring enhancements in INFORMIX-OnLine Dynamic Server split reads between a primary chunk and its mirror chunk, reducing disk seek time on average. Performance is further increased through asynchronous writes to both the primary and mirror chunks. Hence, writes are now performed in parallel rather than serially.

Parallel index build is another performance enhancement. It also improves availability by significantly reducing the time to re-build an index. A factor of ten in performance improvement is common, depending on the amount of data and the number of disks in use.

Online archiving under INFORMIX-OnLine, version 5.0, does not provide granularity for archive/restore. This is quite cumbersome when managing very large databases (VLDBs). A single disk failure requires a complete OnLine system restore.

The INFORMIX-OnLine Dynamic Server "OnArchive" utility allows the administrator to specify which dbspaces to archive/restore. This provides significantly faster restoration and therefore improved availability. Restoration of a dbspace is possible with other dbspaces on-line, increasing Informix system availability further. Such HA features position INFORMIX-OnLine Dynamic Server at the forefront of UNIX database managers.

Additional archive and tape management enhancements include archive and backup scheduling. Specific device lists and tape sets are associated with an archive. Multiple tape devices are supported, allowing for multiple concurrent dbspace archival/restoration. Additional availability features include "catastrophic restore," "multiple tape copies," and "restart restore." All these enhancements result in a feature-rich management system reducing time to archive/restore and increasing general system availability.

High Available Data Replication is used to maintain a "hot-site backup" of an OnLine system on a remote network node. This facility provides high levels of disaster recovery, vital in mission-critical OLTP environments.

Logical log information is extracted dynamically on the primary server and sent over a network to the secondary server. A server in secondary on-line mode receives logical log information over the network and applies it to a database copy using roll forward. Read-only access is allowed on the secondary server in this mode. On failure of the primary server, the secondary server can be changed to standard online mode, which allows write-access to the server. A failed server will restart in recovery mode, connect to its counterpart, and re-synchronize across the network using logical log information. Automatic switchover between the primary and secondary servers is possible.

Data replication assures the absolute minimum downtime when UNIX system failures occur. This provides an alternate approach to UNIX failover/switchover. INFORMIX-OnLine Dynamic Server data replication, however, relies on neither UNIX operating system extensions nor dual-ported disk array technology. Only a network connection is required.

Summary

Together, Informix and UNIX provide "Today's High Availability Solution." Users taking advantage of such leading price/performance systems now benefit from the HA functionality provided. The cost-effectiveness of these solutions is significant compared to the revenue lost due to unplanned system downtime.

For example, a typical system may be reliable 99 percent of the time, which may account for more than 83 hours of downtime a year. A 1992 study [Computerworld '92] of 450 information executives at Fortune 1,000 companies showed the hours lost to downtime per year to be 37.3 hours, resulting in total losses of $4 billion from downtime.

A high availability solution is achieved through a mixture of hardware technology, operating system extensions, and RDBMS features. The level of HA selected carries a related cost, especially for fault tolerant hardware features requiring special-purpose technology and redundancy.

References

[Morrell '92] John Morrell, "Assessing High-Availability Requirements for UNIX Systems," International Data Corporation, October 1992, IDC#:6997, Vol:1, Tab:3 Operating Systems / Architectural Issues.

[Patterson '88] David Patterson, Garth Gibson, Randy H. Katz, "A Case for Redundant Arrays of Inexpensive Disks (RAID)," 1988 ACM0-89791-268-3/88006/109.

[Patch '93] Kimberley Patch, "Highly Available Open Systems—Expanding Today's Definition," Patricia Seybold Group, Open Information Systems, Guide to UNIX and Other Open Systems, Vol. 8, No. 2 ISSN:1058-4161, February 1993.

[Informix '91] Informix Software, Inc., "INFORMIX-OnLine Database server Administrator's Guide," Version 5.0, December 1991, Part No. 000-7106.

[Computerworld '92] Melinda-Carol Ballou, "Survey Pegs Computer Downtime Costs at $4 Billion," Computerworld, August 10, 1992.

About the Author

Peter S. Simcox is a client services engineer at Informix, Somerset, New Jersey.

PLANNING AND TUNING OF FRAGMENTATION STRATEGIES IN INFORMIX-ONLINE DYNAMIC SERVER, VERSION 7.1

by Subhash Bhatia

Overview

The purpose of this article is to describe various planning and tuning aspects of INFORMIX-OnLine Dynamic Server, version 7.1, in order to obtain the best fragmentation strategy to meet target goals. This article also discusses several tools and techniques available to the user for monitoring and tuning the selected fragmentation scheme. Several case studies are included which provide insight into the alternate choices of fragmentation schemes available to the user and discuss some tradeoffs. The case studies have been selected from a spectrum of industry sectors representing applications in areas as broad as telecommunication, retail, banking, and the TPC-D benchmark. Our experience indicates that building a right fragmentation scheme is an iterative process. One can build a macro level (sub-optimal) fragmentation scheme by using the general guidelines described in this article, and later fine-tune the selected fragmentation scheme for best performance by executing the queries on the target system, and performing an analysis of the data collected using the diagnostic and monitoring tools, as described in this article.

Introduction

Data fragmentation allows users to control where data is stored at the table level. It is an INFORMIX-OnLine Dynamic Server feature which enables users to define groups of rows or index keys within a table, and place them according to some algorithm or scheme. This allows data to be spread across multiple disks and therefore reduces I/O contention. The distribution scheme and the set of dbspaces in which the fragments are located make up the fragmentation strategy. There are two broad types of fragmentation schemes: fragment by round-robin (RR) and fragment by expression. As the name suggests, the RR scheme places data rows into a table in a round-robin fashion. The first fragment, in which data is to be inserted, is also selected randomly. This scheme is generally used in situations where the data access patterns of queries are not known in advance. Fragmentation by expression involves defining a range based on single or multiple column(s) of a table. The user is allowed to define a range rule while creating the table. This scheme is used in situations where query characteristics (filters, access patterns, etc.) are known, so that scanning of some fragments can be eliminated during query execution.

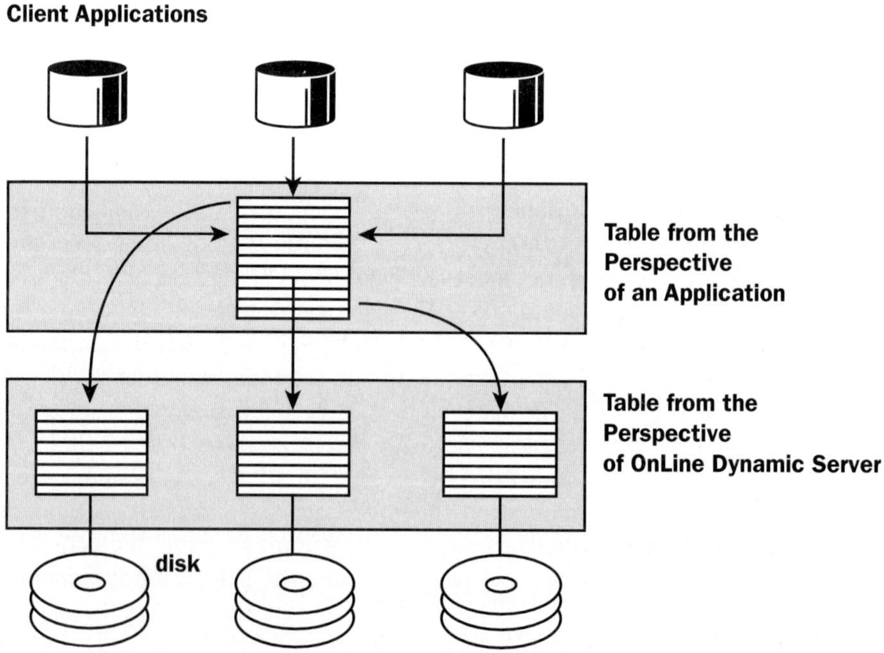

Figure 1: Data fragmentation; INFORMIX-OnLine Dynamic Server routes requests for data from client applications. Each fragment resides on a separate disk drive.

The use of fragmentation for both data and indexes provides several opportunities to improve overall application performance. Fragmentation improves query performance by allowing INFORMIX-OnLine Dynamic Server to scan fragments spread across multiple disks in parallel which results in intra-query parallelization, refer to Figure 1. Intra-query parallelization helps reduce the overall response time of an individual complex query. Fragmentation can be used in conjunction with the Parallel Data Query (PDQ) features of INFORMIX-OnLine Dynamic Server. This allows INFORMIX-OnLine Dynamic Server to assign multiple threads to retrieve data from all the fragments in parallel. Moreover, it is possible to scan only those fragments which contain the data requested. The result is a dramatic improvement in overall system performance. The DATASKIP feature allows the user to skip a fragment which is either down or does not contain the data requested. This allows higher data availability in situations where some of the data is not available. Inter-query parallelization is achieved by spreading the data onto multiple disks using a large number of fragments. This reduces the I/O contention on a single disk when a large number of users are trying to access data from the same table. Overall system throughput is improved in terms of the number of transactions completed per second. Fragmentation also allows a fine granularity of archive and restore since each fragment is stored in a single dbspace, which can be individually archived.

Fragmentation Schemes

This section describes, in brief, the fragmentation schemes available in INFORMIX-OnLine Dynamic Server, version 7.1. More detailed information can be found in the product documentation noted in the References section. Fragmentation schemes can be used for both data tables and creating indexes. The indexes can be attached or detached from their associated data. An index is considered attached when it follows the fragmentation strategy of the table data. On the other hand, if the fragmentation scheme of the indexes is different from that of the data, then it is called a detached index. In this situation, the indexes are placed in the dbspaces specified in the index fragmentation scheme.

There are two broad categories of data fragmentation types: the round-robin scheme or the expression based scheme, as illustrated in Figure 2.

Round-Robin Scheme

The round-robin (RR) scheme uses a rule defined internally by the INFORMIX-OnLine Dynamic Server server. In this scheme, as a new record is added, it is placed into the next fragment in a round-robin fashion. The first fragment, in which a record is inserted, is also determined randomly.

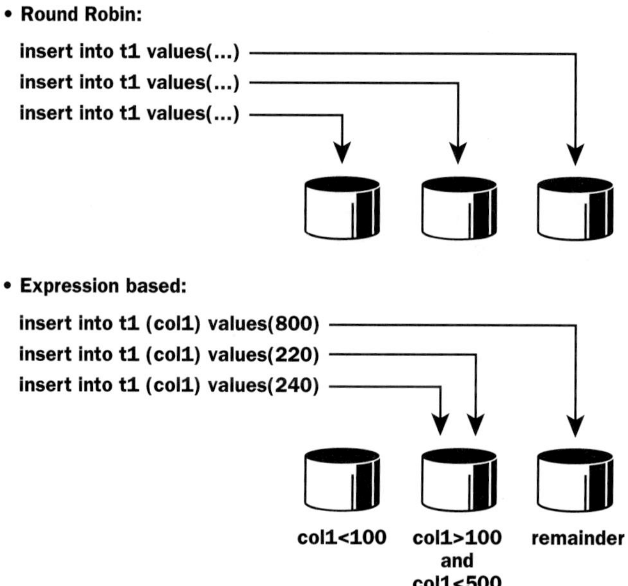

Figure 2: Types of fragmentation schemes.

For example, the following syntax is used to create a table named xyz:

```
CREATE TABLE xyz FRAGMENT BY ROUND ROBIN IN
dbspace1, dbspace2, ...dbspaceN
```

Index creation using the round-robin scheme is not supported, as it leads to performance degradation. The advantage of using this strategy is that the fragments are loaded more or less evenly and it does not require the moving of records when updates occur. One drawback of this scheme, however, is that all fragments must be scanned when evaluating a query. Therefore, this scheme cannot make use of the DATASKIP facility and does not allow INFORMIX-OnLine Dynamic Server to eliminate entire fragments during query execution, if correct results are desired. If DATASKIP is not set and if one fragment is unavailable, then the query is forced to fail, since it cannot determine if any records in the unavailable fragments have met the selection criteria. This scheme can be useful when fast data loading is important, data access patterns are not known in advance, queries are update intensive, or data distributions are unknown.

Expression Based Scheme

For an expression based fragmentation scheme, the user can provide a rule definition which belongs to one of the following two classes:

- Range rule

- Arbitrary rule

Range Rule

A range rule uses SQL relational and logical operators to define the boundaries of each fragment in a table. A range rule can contain relational operators, such as >,<,>=,<=, or may have logical operators, such as an AND. A range rule should preferably refer to only one column in a table, but may use two or more columns. The latter case is inefficient, as more computation is needed each time a row is inserted into the table. All rows that do not satisfy any expression condition fall into the REMAINDER dbspace. The goal of the range-based Expression scheme is to set up fragmentation in such a way that INFORMIX-OnLine Dynamic Server selects and scans only those fragments which contain the requested data.

An example of creating a table using an expression based on a range rule is as follows:

```
CREATE TABLE xyz (aa integer, ...)
FRAGMENT BY EXPRESSION
aa < = 1000                 IN   dbspace1
aa > 1000 AND aa < 2000  IN   dbspace2
REMAINDER                   IN   dbspace3
```

Arbitrary Rule

An arbitrary rule uses SQL relational and logical operators. Unlike range rules, this method allows the use of any relational and logical operator to define the rule. In addition, any number of table columns can be referenced using this method.

Example:

```
FRAGMENT BY EXAMPLE
zipcode = 94536 OR zipcode = 94538 IN dbspace1
zipcode = 94025 OR zipcode = 92310 IN dbspace2
REMAINDER IN dbspace3
```

In this scheme, it is essential to know the distribution of the number of rows for each zipcode in order to balance all the fragments so that INFORMIX-OnLine Dynamic Server can reduce the number of fragments scanned. The distribution scheme must be defined in such a way that none of the fragments overlap (or are tightly bound). Additionally, the fragments are defined without a REMAINDER.

General Guidelines

Fragmentation expressions should be kept as simple as possible, since the evaluation of complex expression is CPU intensive. Also, it is not necessary that every table in a database is fragmented, if a significant benefit from fragmentation is not perceived. The expressions should be such that they balance the I/O across the disks; although, this does not necessarily mean an even distribution of data. If a majority of the queries access only a small portion of data in a table, the expression should be set up such that most frequently accessed data is spread on more disks, even when this results in an uneven distribution of data. The expression should be arranged such that the most restrictive part is first in order. The goal of re-arranging the expression is to reduce the number of expression evaluations, per data access, in order to reduce CPU overhead. If the first inequality of an expression is false, then the entire expression will be false; thus, the rest of the expression is not evaluated. For example, in order to insert the value 25, the following expression requires the evaluation of six inequalities:

```
x >=      1          and   x <= 10  in  dbspace1,
x >       10         and   x <= 20  in  dbspace2,
x >       20         and   x <= 30  in  dbspace3
```

The following re-arranged expression requires the evaluation of four inequalities:

```
x <=      10 and   x >=      1    in  dbspace1,
x <=      20 and   x >       10   in  dbspace2,
x <=      30 and   x >       20   in  dbspace3
```

The expressions which use data conversion should be avoided. For example, a date datatype is internally converted into an integer. Fragmenting on columns which change frequently results in additional administrative overhead. For example, if a date column is used for fragmentation and rows with older dates are deleted, then the fragment containing older dates will eventually be empty. This results in a need to drop the old fragment and add a new fragment for most recent dates.

Fragmentation Strategy Planning

A fragmentation strategy consists of a distribution scheme and a set of dbspaces in which fragments are placed. Formulating a fragmentation strategy requires several decisions, depending on fragmentation goals and the availability of database information, such as hardware/software characteristics, query characteristics, and data distributions. Also, it is useful to know whether an existing non-fragmented database needs to be converted or an application needs to be created from scratch. In the former case, the query execution patterns are known and can be exploited. It is also important to take into consideration any future growth patterns, such as the addition of regions and/or accounts in a database.

Fragmentation goals, as described earlier, may include maximizing intra-query parallelization, inter-query parallelization, data availability, finer granularity of archive/restore, or improving data load performance.

Fragmenting for Intra-Query Parallelization refers to the ability of INFORMIX-OnLine Dynamic Server to process an individual complex query in parallel, taking advantages of the fragmentation and PDQ functionality. This is the primary goal for Decision Support System (DSS) type applications which are characterized by a small number of SELECT oriented queries with long execution times. The DSS queries perform sequential reads of a large number of the rows in a table. Fragmentation of rows of tables are recommended in this situation. When to select a RR or an Expression based scheme depends on other factors, such as query characteristics and data distributions. Generally, the use of the RR scheme is recommended when one cannot identify a column in the table using an Expression based fragmentation scheme to evenly spread the data across disks, or the data access pattern is unknown. The fragmentation of indexes is not recommended in such situations, as a scan may be required to cross a fragment boundary for that index, resulting in performance degradation. The fragmentation strategy should be such that the rows are evenly distributed over different fragments, resulting in the even completion of parallel sequential scans.

Fragmenting for Inter-Query Parallelization refers to the ability of INFORMIX-OnLine Dynamic Server to maximize performance when the applications are characterized by a large number of users running short queries which return a small amount of data. These are, generally, On-Line Transaction Processing (OLTP) applications which require real-time response time for a large number of users. The queries access a small portion of the data at a time and involve many updates and deletes on a random set of rows. These queries usually involve indexed scans. In this scenario, both the data tables and index tables should be fragmented by an expression which allows queries to eliminate fragments from the scan. The data fragments and index fragments may reside on the same disk and use the same fragmentation strategy in situations where I/O contention is not an issue. On the other hand, on large systems where additional disks are available and disk I/O may be the potential bottleneck, indexes may be built on separate disks. It is also possible to build indexes using a different expression than the data fragmentation scheme, e.g., when the index is built on a key value and every query uses the same key value for accessing the row. In this case, a different column must be used than the one used in the WHERE clause. The RR scheme may serve best for data fragmentation, where the queries are update-intensive and there are few deletes or additions of rows.

Again, the degree of success in optimizing the fragmentation strategy depends on the information available regarding the data distributions and the distribution of queries against the tables. The goal is to distribute the data in such a way that there is no I/O bottleneck, although the data may not be evenly distributed within each fragment.

Fragmenting for Increased Data Availability refers to the capability of a database to accept queries from applications, even when some of the data is not available due to fragment non-availability caused by a non-operational disk/device. This is achieved using the DATASKIP feature of INFORMIX-OnLine Dynamic Server. This feature works well with applications which do not require access to unavailable fragments all the time, and those that accept the unavailability of data. An example of the former case is a situation where data is fragmented, based on a region or time period (for example, months of a year) and the queries are for individual regions or months of a year. For simple queries, INFORMIX-OnLine Dynamic Server can determine if a row is contained in a fragment without accessing the fragment. If the requested data is contained in the available fragments, then the query succeeds, although some of the data was unavailable. In the latter case, applications are designed in such a way that partial data is acceptable. This is typical of DSS applications which perform queries in order to obtain statistical data using sampling techniques. These applications allow the fragments to be skipped by executing a SET DATASKIP statement before executing a query. The results may be skewed, depending on how many fragments have been skipped.

Fragmenting for Finer Granularity of Archive and Backup involves a discussion of levels of granularity. The smallest granularity used by an On-Archive unit is a dbspace. With non-fragmented tables, it is not possible to archive a small portion of a very large table. With the use of a fragmentation scheme, the finest granularity of storage can be a few data rows of a table or several key values from an index stored in a fragment. The key to obtaining the best performance is to keep the fragments small and to carefully group the rows. Small sized fragments reduce recovery time due to corrupt fragments or hardware failures. On the other hand, the fragments should not be so small that query performance is degraded. If a device containing a dbspace fails, all the rows contained in the fragment are inaccessible. This may help to determine which rows should be grouped together in a particular way. An expression based scheme should be used for the appropriate grouping of rows in a fragment.

Fragmenting for Improved Data Load Performance is especially useful for large applications which require the periodic loading of Gigabytes of data and therefore, fast-loading techniques. Fragmenting data into multiple disks lends itself to the parallel loading of data. This is accomplished by using multiple I/O streams to write into fragments (dbspaces) residing on different disks. The round-robin fragmentation scheme promises to be the fastest for data loading, since the evaluation of complex expressions tends to be CPU intensive. The data load performance for the expression based scheme can be improved by using simple expression schemes and placing each fragment on a separate disk.

Following are the general steps necessary in order to come up with a reasonable fragmentation strategy:

Hardware/Software Characteristics

- Identify the hardware platform used for the application, i.e., CPU speed, the number of CPUs, number of disks, size of each disk, speed of disks, number of disk controllers, and number of disks attached to each controller. This information is useful in identifying the number of fragments to be used for each table and to layout the fragments (one dbspaces per fragment) over the disks such that the I/O is minimized. There are some upper limits on the number of fragments to be used per table, apart from the disk storage resources used. These limits relate to the fragmentation goal. If the primary goal is to maximize intra-query parallelization, then the number of hardware CPUs available on the system and the bus bandwidth limits the maximum number of parallel scans which are possible on one table. On the other hand, if the goal is inter-query parallelization, one may have more fragments than the total number of CPUs. This would facilitate distributing the data on more disks, thus allowing concurrent users to access different disks in an OLTP situation. However, when fragments are smaller, the likelihood increases that range searches must scan multiple fragments and merge the results. This degrades the performance of such queries.

- For systems with a high CPU speed and slow disks, the number of fragments per table may exceed the number of physical CPUs.

- The type of operating system and compilers used on the selected hardware platform is also an important factor in the selection of a fragmentation scheme. Some operating systems have more efficient MOD and data conversion operations than others.

Study Query Characteristics

- Identify whether the application is an OLTP or decision-support application. Identify whether the queries are mostly SELECT statements or are update and/or delete intensive. If the queries are mostly SELECT statements, identify the complexity, i.e., group by, order by, etc.

- Examine the frequency concerning the execution of the queries executed. This determination will help in balancing the I/O and eliminating bottlenecks.

- Examine the selectivity of each SELECT query, i.e., the percent of rows returned. An index may be necessary for a query which has a very low selectivity.

- Examine if the query involves JOINS and identify the primary keys for each join. If particular tables are always joined together in a DSS query, the fragments for these tables should be spread across multiple disks in order to avoid I/O bottlenecks.

- Examine the FILTERS used in each query. It is best to draw a matrix of the queries versus the columns of each of the tables involved. Then, fill the matrix with a cross in the row where a table column is used as a filter in a particular query. With this matrix, one could identify which filters are most commonly used in all the queries. This information, combined with the frequency of execution of each query, can help to identify which columns maximize the benefits from expression based fragmentation.

- Examine how data is accessed, i.e., accessed via a sequential scan or an indexed scan. The SETEXPLAIN for each query, combined with table scheme information, may be used for this purpose.

Data Distributions and Characteristics

- Identify the ranges of values for the table columns used in the query filters.

- Identify the number of rows for each range of values of a column in a table. In many decision-support type applications, data is collected which is based on geographic regions or the months of a year. In such situations, it is easy to identify the number of rows per state or city, or the number of entries per month in the latter case. If most queries have a state or month as a filter, these columns may be good candidates for an expression based fragmentation strategy.

- Identify the rate at which the table data is modified, i.e., added, deleted, and/or updated.

Tools and Techniques

INFORMIX-OnLine Dynamic Server, version 7.1, provides several tools which can be used for diagnostics and the tuning of fragmentation schemes in order to improve performance.

Set Explain

The Set Explain facility within SQL/ESQL allows users to determine how fragmentation will be used within a specific query. It produces a file named sqexplain.out which displays, besides other things, the number of fragments which will be scanned during a sequential scan and the number of secondary threads used. This data indicates the efficiency of the fragmentation scheme implemented. In many situations, the optimizer may choose to scan all the fragments, although the data is contained in fewer fragments; this may be due to the lack of an explicit bound on fragment ranges. This situation can be corrected by adjusting the fragmentation scheme, such that each expression has a clearly defined lower and upper bound. When using cursors, it is not necessary to run the query to obtain the sqexplain output. Solely by preparing the query, opening a cursor and not issuing the execute command, one can obtain the sqexplain.out file for that query. However, this is true only if no host variables are used in the query.

Usage

Insert the following statement in the application before the query is executed:

```
SET   EXPLAIN ON
```

The following query plan is stored in the file called sqexplain.out:

```
QUERY
——-

SELECT amount FROM bank_account ORDER BY acct_num;

Estimated Cost: 3333
Estimated # of rows returned: 99999
Temporary Files Required For: order by

1) informix.account: SEQUENTIAL SCAN(Parallel, fragments: ALL)

#of secondary threads  = 6
```

As shown in the example, the number of secondary threads indicates the maximum number of threads which will be used to process this query. In the example, there may be, at most, six fragments to be scanned in parallel.

Dbschema

The Dbschema utility within INFORMIX-OnLine Dynamic Server provides a facility to capture the tables and index information from an existing database which needs to be migrated to INFORMIX-OnLine Dynamic Server, version 7.1. This utility accommodates fragmented tables and indexes. It displays fragmented syntax so that fragmented tables can be recreated from the output file called the schema file. This file can be edited to change database object characteristics, such as access privileges, lock mode, extent sizes, and dbspaces where a table may be stored.

Dbschema can be examined using the following command:

```
Dbschema -d database -hd table
```

Onstat

The Onstat utility is an administrative and performance monitoring tool which can help users look for fragment loading and usage. **Onstat** with the **-d** option may be used to look at the fragments being loaded. **Onstat -g ppf** may be used to monitor the fragment usage. This command shows the number of read/write calls for each fragment which is currently open. Although the read/write calls do not show how may disk read/writes occurred, yet a reasonable estimate is provided of the I/O activity on the disks which contain these fragments. **Onstat -g iof** displays the number of reads from each chunk and the number of writes to each chunk. If some chunks have a disproportionate amount of I/O activity, these chunks may be acting as a system bottleneck. This option is very useful in monitoring the distribution of I/O requests against the different fragments of a fragmented table. Based on the output returned by this utility, one may adjust the fragmentation scheme in such a way that the activity is uniform on all fragments, thus yielding better performance.

SMI

The Systems Monitoring Interface (SMI) allows users to write SQL queries to the system tables within INFORMIX-OnLine Dynamic Server. The following query may be used to examine the partition numbers from the sysfragments table within INFORMIX-OnLine Dynamic Server:

```
SELECT tablename FROM sysfragments, systables
WHERE sysfragments.tabid = systables.tabid
```

The systabnames table displays one row per fragment and lists the partition number, database name, owner, and table name. Similarly, the sysextents table displays one row per extent and lists the extents used by each fragment.

The SMI can be used after creating the fragmented tables to validate that the correct fragments and extents are built for each table.

Dbaccess—Use of ALTER FRAGMENT

An option within the Dbaccess utility provides a facility to alter the existing fragmentation scheme. The fragmentation scheme can be modified by adding, dropping, initializing, attaching, and detaching a local fragment. The fragmentation expression can also be modified using this facility. For example, if an application is fragmented using an expression based scheme comprised of geographic regions, one may need to add a new region by adding a local fragment. Similarly, a fragment for another region may be archived and dropped. If many entries of two regions have been deleted, they can be combined to become one new fragment. On the other hand, if a given fragment has become full, it can be split into two fragments. In this way, the fragmentation scheme can be tuned for performance improvements without bringing the database server down.

There are other INFORMIX-OnLine Dynamic Server tools available for monitoring the fragments within dbspaces. These utilities include OnPerf and DBCockpit. More detailed information is noted in the References section.

Case Studies

This section discusses four case studies. The customers in the first two cases participated in the INFORMIX-OnLine Dynamic Server, version 7.1, beta program. The other two cases were customer benchmarks. The applications covered are from the telecommunication, retail, banking industries, and TPC-D benchmark.

Case A: Telecommunication Service Application

The customer in this case is a telecommunication service provider with a large decision-support database used to store subscribers' historical data for performing trend analysis. The customer's interest was to move their current applications from another proprietary system to an HP T500 running INFORMIX-OnLine Dynamic Server, version 7.1. The initial tests were performed using a subscriber database consisting of three large tables which collectively consume 14 Gigabytes (GB) of space. One of the tables alone was almost 8 GB in size. The tests were run on an HP T500 with 6 processors, 1 GB of RAM, and 90 single-ended SCSI disks of 2 GB each. The testbed consisted of an HP T500 attached to a private LAN with additional HP workstations and PCs. The workstations and PCs were used to remote log into the HP T500. INFORMIX-OnLine Dynamic Server, version 7.1, was installed on the HP T500.

Workload Description

The test database contained 14 GB of unindexed data. Three main tables of the database were used: customer service (serv), account (acct), and demographics (dmg). The customer service table was the largest table, with approximately ~8 GB of data. There were 21 columns with a total row size of 129 Bytes. The account table was ~4 GB. The number of columns in this table were 53 with a total row size of 402 Bytes. The demographics table which was ~ 2 GB with 56 columns and a row size of 119 Bytes. Twelve DSS queries, representing major parts of the application, were used. The application appeared to be a true DSS in the sense that it was used as read-only data with no update activity. The key characteristic of the data appeared to be that it was collected based on the geography of the United States (U.S.), i.e., state by state. The count of the number of rows for each state in a table was also available. The data was collected for a total of 39 states. This fact rendered the states as the logical choice for partitioning the account table. However, to balance the number of rows in each fragment, several states needed to be grouped together.

First, the data was loaded into non-fragmented tables using INFORMIX-OnLine Dynamic Server, version 6.0. The queries were executed with SET EXPLAIN to determine the path chosen by the optimizer.

Table A depicts query characteristics. The profile was created by observing the query characteristics and execution of queries on INFORMIX-OnLine Dynamic Server, version 6.0. Based on this profile and the availability of data access patterns, the RR scheme was eliminated, since the use of the expression based scheme provided a good possibility of eliminating some fragments. Moreover, the results above showed that only index joins were performed.

The objective was to come up with a fragmentation scheme which would avoid indexed joins and force hash joins which have a distinct advantage over the former when the selectivity of the queries is high. The join keys were eliminated as a possible choice for an expression based scheme. No fragmentation scheme was used to build the indexes.

Fragmentation Scheme for the Customer Service Table

Table 'serv' is used in queries 1,2,3,4,5,8 and 9. The possible choices regarding the columns for an expression based scheme for this table included: unit_cd,

Table A: Query characteristics.

Query	Tables	Join Key	Characteristics	Filters	Optimizer
Q1	acct,serv,	blg_tel,	None	edt_ind, blg_tel, clac,	Seq. Scan,
	dmg	svc_data,clac		svc_dat, unit_cd	MergeJoin, Index
Q2	serv,dmg	pdct_svc	group & order	unit_cd, pdct_svc	Seq. Scan/Index
Q3	serv	-	group, & order aggr.	unit_cd	Seq. Scan
Q4	serv	-	group & order aggr.	pdct_svc, state	Seq. Scan/ Index Path
Q5	serv,dmg	seq_no	group	seq_no, revenue -	
Q6	acct,dmg	seq_no	group, aggr. UNION	toll_rvn, seq_no	Seq. Scan/Index
Q7	acct,dmg	seq_no	,,	linekeeper, seq_no, state	Seq. Scan/Index
Q8	serv,dmg	seq_no	group, aggr.	unit_cd, seq_no	Index/Index
Q9	serv,dmg	seq_no	group, aggr.	revenue, unit_cd, seq_no	Seq. Scan/Index
Q10	acct,dmg	seq_no	group	cnvrn_tm, seq_no	Seq. Scan/Index
Q11	acct,dmg	seq_no	group	ia_rcd_cnt, seq_no	Seq. Scan/Index
Q12	acct,dmg	seq_no	group	edt_ind, seq_no	Seq.Scan/Index

state, blg_tel, pdct_svc, seq_no and revenue. Of these filters in the WHERE clause, the unit_cd appears in five out of seven queries. Thus, it was selected as the column of choice for an expression based scheme. The amount of disk space was sufficient to build one fragment on each disk. Particular attention was given so that the disks, selected to place dbspaces containing the fragments used in this table, were not clustered on the same disk controller. Since the total data in this table was 8 GB, a minimum of four fragments were required. However, a total of six hardware CPUs were available and there was a good possibility of eliminating a few fragments in a query execution. Therefore, in order to maximize on parallel scans, it was decided to select eight fragments initially, and tune further if necessary. The next logical step was to group unit_cd, such that the data was distributed evenly within the eight fragments. This was achieved by running some test queries on the INFORMIX-OnLine Dynamic Server, version 6.0, system with selected values of unit_cd in the WHERE clause, and thus, obtain a row count. For example, note that the following tuning statement provides the total row count for all rows with unit_cd='CCCC001':

```
Select count(*) from serv WHERE unit_cd = 'CCCC001'
```

Based on the results computed above, the following fragmentation scheme was developed.

```
CREATE TABLE serv (...)                        Percent data
 FRAGMENT BY EXPRESSION
 unit_cd = 'CCCC001'        in   cdbspace1,      16.88%
 unit_cd = 'CAAA001'        in   cdbspace2,      13.36%
 . . . .                         . . .               . . .
 unit_cd >= 'CAAA000'       in   cdbspace7,      10.23%
 unit_cd >= ' '            in   cdbspace8       12.03%
```

The percentages shown under percent data, in the previous example were obtained after loading the data into the INFORMIX-OnLine Dynamic Server, version 7.1, database. The results show reasonably balanced fragments, except for the fragment in dbspace cdbspace1. The RR scheme was not considered for this table since apriori knowledge was available about the data distributions and query characteristics.

The fragmentation scheme was later modified, as shown below, due to the fact that the above scheme fragments do not have an explicit bound on ranges. Running these queries using INFORMIX-OnLine Dynamic Server showed that all fragments were being scanned.

```
FRAGMENT BY EXPRESSION
unit_cd = 'CCCC001'        in   cdbspace1,
unit_cd = 'CAAA001'        in   cdbspace2,

. . .    . . .

unit_cd >= '        '  AND unit_cd <= 'CATM     'in   cdbspace7,
unit_cd > 'CATM    '   AND unit_cd <= 'zzzzzzz'  in   cdbspace8
```

With the changes above, performance improvements of up to 50 percent were observed in the execution of queries 3, 8, and 9.

Fragmentation Scheme for the Account Table

The table called account is used in queries 1, 6, 7, 10, 11, and 12. The RR scheme, although useful in balancing the amount of data on several fragments, was not chosen in this case for the following reasons: the availability of data distributions, the possibility of an increase in the number of account regions, and the opportunity to eliminate the scanning of some fragments to improve performance. The columns selected for an expression based scheme were: edt_ind, oll_rvn, linekeeper, state, cvrn_tm, blg_tel, clac, svc_dat, seq_no, and ia_rcd_cnt. The seq_no, svc_dat, and clac were already used as join keys. Other than these columns, all others occur only once in a different query. Thus, other criteria was necessary to choose one of these columns for an expression. The selection criteria can include: importance of one of these queries over another, frequency in the usage of a particular query, a column which creates a reasonable balance of rows in a fragment, or the need to divide the accounts into geographical regions (allowing for the potential for growth in the account regions). The column for building an expression was "state," due to the latter two reasons. A total of six fragments were selected for this table. The states were grouped in such a way that, on average, 16 to 18 percent of the rows were loaded into a fragment. The fragmentation scheme designed for this table is shown below.

```
CREATE TABLE acct (....)
FRAGMENT BY EXPRESSION
state = 'CA'                       in  adbspace1,  20.20%
state <= 'GA'                      in  adbspace2,  16.35%
state <= 'KS'                      in  adbspace3,  16.07%
state <= 'NY' or state = 'SC'      in  adbspace4,  15.67%
state >= 'UT' or state = 'OH'      in  adbspace5,  15.88%
state <= 'TX'                      in  adbspace6   15.83%
```

This fragmentation scheme has some shortfalls, as is shown in Table B. The expressions are not tightly bound. As a result, all fragments are scanned initially, until INFORMIX-OnLine Dynamic Server, version 7.1, determines at run time that all fragments do not require scanning, since the fragmentation scheme does not set explicit ranges. Thus, the current version of INFORMIX-OnLine Dynamic Server is unable to determine the correct fragment for an "OR" expression at compile time. At runtime, only the potentially active fragments are searched, however, a thread is started for all fragments and each thread determines if its fragment should be active. Nevertheless, more threads are used than are truly necessary, resulting in performance degradation. In such situations, the construction of non-relevent threads can be eliminated by repartitioning the table in the following way:

```
FRAGMENT BY EXPRESSION
state = 'CA'                                        in  adbspace1,
state <= 'GA'                                       in  adbspace2,
state > 'GA'  AND state <= 'KS'                     in  adbspace3,
state > 'KS' AND state <= 'NY' OR state = 'SC'      in  adbspace4,
state > 'TX' or state = 'OH'                        in  adbspace5,
state > 'NY' AND state <= 'TX'                      in  adbspace6
```

Demographics Table

The table demographics contained 56 non-null columns of mixed datatypes. For this table, the 'clac' code was arbitrarily selected to create an expression based fragmentation strategy:

```
FRAGMENT BY EXPRESSION
  clac_cd  <   '132'        in   ddbspace1,      34.59%
  clac_cd  <   '48'         in   ddbspace2,      32.70%
  clac_cd  >=  '48'         in   ddbspace3       32.72%
```

Later, this scheme was modified to the RR scheme, to provide better performance. Also, load performance improved by selecting the RR scheme.

Index Creation

Detached and non-fragmented indexes were built using the seq_no column. The following are indexes:

```
CREATE UNIQUE INDEX xxx ON account (seq_no) fillfactor 100 in acfi1dbs;


CREATE INDEX yyy ON customer (seq_no) fillfactor 99 in csfi1dbs;


CREATE UNIQUE INDEX zzz ON demographics (seq_no) fillfactor 100 in dmfi1dbs;
```

Results show that the index was used only in query 9. The use of fragmentation eliminated the need for a large number of indexes, and thus freed some disk space and reduced the overhead of index administration.

Below are optimizer selection paths, as observed in the set explain, which resulted when the queries were executed in INFORMIX-OnLine Dynamic Server, version 7.1. Also shown are the number of fragments scanned and the total thread allocation during query execution. The results show that a fewer number of threads are needed when all fragments are not scanned, resulting in efficient resource utilization.

Also, most of the queries now use a hash join as opposed to an index join, as observed in the INFORMIX-OnLine Dynamic Server, version 6.0 case, as shown in Table A. Queries 3, 8, and 9 benefit from the expression based fragmentation scheme by providing fragment elimination.

Table B: Query Characteristics.

Query	Tables	SCANType	# of Fragments	JOIN Method	Total # of Threads
Q1	acct	sequential	ALL	—	
	serv	sequential	ALL	Dynamic Hash	
	dmg	sequential	ALL	Dynamic Hash	23
Q2	serv	sequential	ALL	—	
	dmg	sequential	ALL	Dynamic Hash	15
Q3	serv	sequential	2	—	8
Q4	serv	sequential	ALL	—	14
Q5	serv	sequential	ALL	—	-
	dmg	sequential	ALL	Dynamic Hash	17
Q6	acct,dmg	sequential	ALL	"	45
Q7	acct,dmg	sequential	ALL	"	36
Q8	dmg	,,	,,	"	
	serv	sequential	2	"	12
Q9	serv	sequential	1	—	
	dmg	index	ALL	Index	7
Q10	dmg,acct	sequential	ALL	Dynamix Hash	15
Q11	dmg,acct	sequential	ALL	Dynamic Hash	15
Q12	dmg,acct	sequential	ALL	—	15

Case B: Retail Application

The customer in this case study comes from the retail industry. This customer uses several small HP machines, each running INFORMIX-OnLine Dynamic Server, version 6.0, with part of a large database containing data related to a different type of merchandise. Each HP machine holds 40 MB rows of a large table within the database. The objective was to integrate all the components of this large database using an HP T500 running INFORMIX-OnLine Dynamic Server, version 7.1; this was only possible by using the fragmentation feature of INFORMIX-OnLine Dynamic Server, version 7.1. They also identified the requirement to store and access 10 Terabytes of information, and wanted to verify that Informix provided a viable solution to their DBMS strategy. The test system configuration was an HP T500 with six processors and 30 single-ended SCSI disk drives (2 GB each) attached to ten disk controllers (three disk drives per controller).

Workload Description

The application used for tests involved about 20 GB of data. OLTP type queries were performed. The customer runs this application using INFORMIX-OnLine, version 5.0. The customer emphasized that the database named SKU was used to manage the inventory for all of the retail stores. Three main tables are used in the database: business_unit, stock_keeping_unit (SKU), and merchandize_family. The sample queries were tested on the stock_keeping_unit table which had a row size of 43 Bytes, ten columns, and a maximum of 450 million rows.

The queries have the following characteristics:

Table C: Query Characteristics.

Query:	Tables	Characteristics	Filters	Scan Type	# of Frag. Scanned
Q1	sku	None	business_id, quantity	Index	1
Q2	sku	None	business_id	Index	1
Q3	sku	None	business_id	Index	1
Q4	sku	None	family_id	Sequential Scan	ALL
Q5	sku	None	family_id	Sequential Scan	ALL
Q6	sku	Group By, Avg	—	Sequential Scan	ALL
Q7	sku	Group By	business_id	Sequential Scan	1

Twelve fragments were selected, based on the fact that there were six hardware CPUs, and a parallel scan of two disks per CPU did not pose an I/O bottleneck. Also, the minimum number of fragments required was 10 in order to accommodate 20 GB of data. Each fragment was placed in a dbspace located on a separate drive. Based on the above characteristics, it was possible to eliminate a scan of some fragments due to the filters business_id and family_id. The business_id was selected as the column on which to base the expression based fragmentation, since it was used in most of the above queries. Moreover, simple queries 1 and 2 were used most often. Running the queries using INFORMIX-OnLine Dynamic Server, version 7.1, showed that queries 1, 2, 3, and 7 scanned only one fragment. The remaining queries scanned all the fragments, as they do not use bus_id as a filter; thus, these queries were found to have low selectivity. The index was also built using the same fragmentation strategy, except that two expressions used for the table were collapsed into one fragment for the index, and the dbspaces selected were other than those used for the table data.

The following example displays the table and index fragmentation scheme designed for the SKU database.

```
CREATE TABLE sku (....)


FRAGMENT BY EXPRESSION
  ((business_id <= 294369 ) AND (business_id >= 0 ) ) in dfrag1,
  ((business_id <= 294553 ) AND (business_id >= 294370 ) ) in dfrag2,
  ((business_id <= 294741 ) AND (business_id >= 294554 ) ) in dfrag3,
   . . .
  ((business_id <= 370320 ) AND (business_id >= 295991 ) ) in dfrag11,
  ((business_id <= 2099999999 ) AND (business_id >= 370321 ) ) in dfrag12


CREATE INDEX sku_index


FRAGMENT BY EXPRESSION
  ((business_id <= 294369 ) AND (business_id >= 0 ) )         in ifrag1,
   . . .
  ((business_id <= 295106 ) AND (business_id >= 294924 ) ) in ifrag5,
  ((business_id <= 295283 ) AND (business_id >= 295107 ) ) in ifrag6
```

The query characteristics table indicates the advantages gained by using this scheme. Eleven out of the twelve fragments were eliminated in four out of seven queries, thus reducing the amount of time required to scan the data. This also resulted in a lower number of secondary threads allocated per query, further freeing system resources for use by other queries running concurrently.

Case C: Banking Application

This customer is a financial institution which provides banking and credit card services. The customer's plan is to develop a data warehouse which will be used to perform financial analysis on their credit card operations. Initially, their application was benchmarked using INFORMIX-OnLine Dynamic Server, version 7.1. The test database size was 20 GB (data plus index). Data access patterns were unknown, since end users were expected to perform ad-hoc queries against this database. The customer wanted to evaluate performance based on a wide spectrum of queries, and compare the results with those of competitive products.

Hardware/Software Environment

The testbed set-up consisted of an HP T500 with eight CPUs and 1 GB of memory, and 16 single-ended 2 GB SCSI disks. The operating system used was HP-UX 9.04.

Workload Description

There were four tables in the database containing data for a one-month period. The same data file was used to build 13 months' worth of data for each table.

Table Name	#rows size	Table size (MB) (one month)	Total (13 months)
VOP_A	2.7M	360	4.6GB
VOP_B	5400	0.35	4.55MB
VOP_C	291K	13	169MB
VOP_T	6.4M	141	1.9GB

The sample query characteristics were as follows:

```
Select sum(amount) from vop_t where month=1 and tran_id in (21,24);
Select (sum(acct_cd)* 100) from vop_c
where group_num > 0 and dt_cd in ('M')  and month=4;
Select sum(amount)/(sum(avg_balance)) from vop_t t , vop_c c
where month = 2 and trab_cd in (4,8) and split_cd 'A" and t.seq_num = c.seq_num
```

Fragmentation Strategy

The competition partitioned the data at the schema level (they had no other options). A separate table was created for each month, striped across 13 disks.

As an end user can perform any ad-hoc query, the actual queries to be executed were not available. The options available to the users included trend analysis (spanning tables across multiple months), aggregate, group by, and order by on a one-month table. In this benchmark, the month field was not part of the schema. If the partition was performed based on 'month,' it was then necessary to create a month field for use during data loading. Two possible fragmentation strategies were identified as:

OPTION 1: Add a month field and partition on a month field.

- Provide one logical table for all 13 months; hence, some queries can be simplified (to run fast) instead of using joins and unions.

- Simplify the schema and physical design.

- The queries across multiple months will benefit compared to the competition's strategy.

OPTION 2: Use a separate table for each month and partition each month on some other filter (column), such as an account category.

- This allows for the exploitation of fragmentation features, such as parallel scan and fragment elimination within a table (one month of data).

- Indexes must be kept in a separate dbspace in order to avoid I/O bottleneck.

Based on the above options, it was decided to build a table fragmented on 13 dbspaces (13 disks), based on a month field, i.e., month 1 in dbspace1, and so on. The index on two fields (smallint, int), fragmented into 13 partitions, was also built with the fragmentation strategy, in the same manner as the data table, but using different dbspaces. The dbspaces for the table and indexes shared the same set of 13 disks, although the fragment data for month 1 was not placed on the same disk as the index data for that month.

```
disks:          1   2   3   4   5   6   7   8  . . .13
data(month):    1   2   3       5   6   7   8  . . .13
index(month):  13  12  11  10   9   8   6   7  . . .1
```

The fragments for the 'VOP_A' table were stored in dbspaces 1 through 13. The fragments for the other two tables were stored in dbspaces 2_1 through 2_13. Thus, the same month's data for two major tables resides on two different disks, with the expectation that doing so facilitates joins on these two tables.

The customer also tried to partition one month's worth of data. One month's data for VOP_T was fragmented over 13 disks, using expression based partitioning on the filter column. The partitions were created, based on the data distribution and filter criteria. The select statement, which took 100 seconds with a non-fragmented month, finished in less than three (3) seconds. A query on one month's data, using RR strategy over nine disks, finished in 37 seconds. Scanning the table VOP_T across all 13 months of data took about 250 seconds.

In this case, an expression based scheme provides better performance than an RR scheme due to the possibility of scanning only those fragments which contain the requested data. The benchmark was quite successful and the performance was better than that of the competition in many areas (particularly during stress testing).

Case D: Telecommunication Service Provider

The customer performed the standard TPC benchmark and then converted their marketing application from INFORMIX-OnLine Dynamic Server, version 6.0, to INFORMIX-OnLine Dynamic Server, version 7.1. The benchmark was the TPC-D suite. The marketing application is a DSS used for targeting potential customers. The workload consists primarily in the testing of existing queries and the loading of large amounts of data. The number of DSS users is between 10 and 30.

Hardware/Software Environment

The hardware used for the benchmark was a Sequent Symmetry 5000/SE60 system with eighteen Pentium processors, 1.5 GB of main memory, four SCSI disk controllers, 154 X 2.1 GB disks (130 dbspaces), and 12 8mm 0.5 GB tape units.

TPC-D Draft 6.4 Benchmark Suite is a decision-support benchmark developed by the Transaction Processing Performance Council (TPC). The main components of the TPC-D database are defined as consisting of seven separate individual tables: parts, suppliers, partsupp, customers, lineitem, orders, and time. The tables are described as follows:

```
1.   Table part row size = 151 number of columns = 9 index size = 45
     create table part (p_partkey integer, p_name char(50),
        p_mfgr char(25), p_brand char(10),
        p_type char(25), p_size integer, p_container char(10), p_retail
price money(16,2), p_comment char(14) )


2.   Table supplier row size = 145 number of columns = 8 index size = 130
     create table supplier (s_suppkey integer, s_name char(25), s_address char(25)
        s_nation char(25),s_region char(25), s_phone char(15), s_acctbal
money(16,2), s_comment char(17) )


3.   Table partsupp row size = 145 number of columns = 5 index size = 30
     create table partsupp (ps_partkey integer, ps_suppkey integer,
ps_availqty integer,    ps_supplycost money(16,2), ps_ comment char(124))
```

```
4.   Table customer row size = 165 number of columns = 9 index size = 76
     create table customer ( c_custkey integer, c_name char(25),
c_address char(25),      c_nation char(25),c_region char(25),
c_phone char(15), c_acctbal money(16,2),
     c_mktsegment char(10), c_comment char(27) )

5.   Table order row size = 109 number of columns = 9 index size = 64
     create table order (o_orderkey integer, o_custkey integer, o_order
status char(1), o_totalprice money(16,2), o_orderdate date, o_orderpriority char(15),
     o_clerk char(15), o_shippriority integer, o_comment char(49) )

6.   TABLE lineitem row size = 161 number of columns = 16 index
     size = 69
     create table lineitem ( l_orderkey integer, l_partkey integer, l_
     suppkey integer,
        l_linenumber integer,l_quantity integer, l_extendedprice
money(16,2), l_discount integer, l_tax integer, l_return
flagchar(1),l_linestatus char(1),l_shipdate date, l_com
mitdate date, l_receiptdate date, l_shipinstruct char(25), l_ship
mode char(10), l_comment char(27))
```

The seventh table, Time, was not fragmented. The database Scale Factors (SF) used were 100 (10 GB) and 1000 (100 GB). In this benchmark, the tables called Lineitem and Orders collectively contain almost 90 percent of the data; thus, the fragmentation effort focused on these two tables.

The queries have the following characteristics:

Table D: Query characteristics.

Query:	Tables	Join Keys	Characteristics	Other Filters
Q1	lineitem	-	group,order, sum,avg.	l_shipdate
Q2	parts,suppliers, partsupp	partkey, suppkey	subquery	p_size,p_type,s_nation,ps_supplycost
Q3.	customers, orders,lineitem	custkey, orderkey	group,order, #loops10	c_mktsegment,o_orderdate,l_shipdate
Q4	orders	-	group,order, subquery	o_orderkey, subquery:lineitem,orders;filters: l_orderkey,o_orderdate,l_commitdate

Table D: Query characteristics (continued).

Query:	Tables	Join Keys	Characteristics	Other Filters
Q5	customers,orders lineitem, suppliers	custkey, orderkey, suppkey	group,order, sum	c_nation,s_region,o_orderdate
Q6	lineitem	-	sum	l_shipdate,l_discount,l_quantity
Q7	suppliers,orders, lineitem, customers	suppkey, orderkey, custkey	group,order, view	s_nation,l_shipdate
Q8a	suppliers,orders, lineitem, customers	partkey, orderkey, custkey	sum,view	o_orderdate,p_type
Q8b	all_nations (res.8b)	-	group,view	nation
Q8c	all_nations	-	group,view	region
Q8d	sum_nation (res.8b&8c)	year	-	-
Q9a	parts,suppliers, lineitem, partsupp, orders	suppkey, partkey, orderkey	View	p_name
Q9b	-	-	Group,order	-
Q10	customers,orders lineitem	custkey, orderkey	group,order, sum,loop20	o_orderdate,returnflag
Q11	partsupp, suppliers	suppkey	sum	s_nation
Q11b	partsupp, suppliers	suppkey	order whileloop	s_nation
Q12	orders,lineitem	orderkey	group,count UNION,order	o_orderpriority,l_shipmode, l_commitdate,l_shipdate,l_receiptdate
Q13a	lineitem, orders	orderkey	view,extract	o_clerk,returnflag
Q13b	performance (res.13a)	-	sum,group, order	-

Table D: Query characteristics (continued).

Query:	Tables	Join Keys	Characteristics	Other Filters
Q14a	lineitem, parts	partkey	view,group	l_shipdate
Q14b	allsales(res.14a)	-	view,sum	-
Q14c	allsales(res.14a)	-	view,sum	-
Q14d	sum_promo_sales-	-	-	
Q15a	lineitem	-	view,group, sum	l_shipdate
Q15b	suppliers, revenue(res.15a)	suppkey	-	subquery:revenue(res.15a)
Q16	partsupp,parts	partkey	group,order, count	p_brand,p_type,p_size
Q17	lineitem,parts	partkey	sum	p_brand, p_container,l_quantity subquery:lineitemL1 Filter:partkey

The above matrix displays the tables used in each of the seventeen TPC-D queries. Also shown are the join keys, complexity of queries, and the filters. As indicated, some of these queries loop multiple times, thus increasing the frequency of use. Many of the queries have subqueries as filters. Queries 8, 9, 11, 13, 14, and 15 have a set of small queries, where the result of first is stored in a temporary table for use by subsequent queries.

Fragmentation Schemes

Table Part

The parts table is used in queries 2, 9, 14, 16, and 17. The possible choice of filters for expression based fragmentation includes: p_brand, p_container, p_type, p_size, and p_name. Of these filters, p_type (part type) is used in at least two queries and appears to be the logical choice. Column p_type is a random string of ASCII letters; there are eight types in all. The choice of a fragmentation scheme is fragmentation by expression, using an arbitrary rule over four dbspaces located on separate disks.

```
fragment by expression
    p_type = 'ALUMINIUM' or p_type = 'BRASS'   in dbsp1,
    p_type = 'COPPER' or p_type = 'BRONZE'     in dbsp2,
    p_type = 'NICKEL' or p_type = 'STEEL'      in dbsp3,
    p_type = 'TIN' or p_type = 'PROMOTIONAL'   in dbsp4
```

Table Suppliers

The suppliers table is used in queries 2, 5, 7, 8, 9, 11, and 15. The possible choice of filters for expression based fragmentation includes: s_nation and s_region. Of these filters, nation is used in four queries and appears to be the logical choice. The column called nation is a random string from Nations and there are 25 nations in all. The choice of a fragmentation scheme is fragmentation by expression using an arbitrary rule over four dbspaces located on separate disks. Queries 2, 5, 7, and 11 benefit from this fragmentation scheme.

```
fragment by expression
s_nation = 'ALGERIA' or s_nation = 'ARGENTINA' or s_nation = 'BRAZIL' or
s_nation = 'CANADA' or s_nation = 'EGYPT' or s_nation = 'ETHIOPIA'in sdbsp1,
s_nation = 'FRANCE' or s_nation = 'GERMANY' or s_nation = 'INDIA' or
s_nation = 'INDONESIA' or s_nation = 'IRAN' or s_nation = 'IRAQ'  in sdbsp2,
s_nation = 'JAPAN' or s_nation = 'JORDAN' or s_nation = 'KENYA' or
s_nation = 'MOROCCO' or s_nation='MOZAMBIQUE' or s_nation= 'PERU'  in sdbsp3,
s_nation = 'CHINA' or s_nation = 'ROMANIA' or s_nation= 'SAUDI ARABIA' or
s_nation = 'VIETNAM' or s_nation = 'RUSSIA' or
s_nation = 'UNITED KINGDOM' or s_nation = 'UNITED STATES' in sdbsp4
```

Table Partsupp

The suppliers table is used in queries 2, 9, 11, and 16. The only possible choice of a filter for this table is ps_supplycost. Column supplycost takes a random value between $1.00 and $1,000.00. The choice of a fragmentation scheme is fragmentation by expression, using a range rule over eight dbspaces located on separate disks. Only query 2 benefits from this fragmentation scheme.

```
fragment by expression
    ps_supplycost >   0.00 and ps_supplycost <= 125.00    in pdbsp1,
    ps_supplycost > 125.00 and ps_supplycost <= 250.00    in pdbsp2,
    ps_supplycost > 250.00 and ps_supplycost <= 375.00    in pdbsp3,
.. .. ..
    ps_supplycost > 875.00 and ps_supplycost <= 1000.00 in pdbsp8
```

Table Customer

The customer table is used in queries 3, 5, 7, 8, and 10. The possible choice of filters for expression based fragmentation includes: c_mktsegment, c_nation, and c_region. Of these filters, c_nation is used in at least two queries and appears to be the logical choice. Column nation takes a random string from Nations from a list of 25 nations. The choice of a fragmentation scheme is fragmentation by expression, using an arbitrary rule over eight dbspaces located on separate disks. Queries 5 and 7 benefit from this fragmentation scheme.

```
fragment by expression
 c_nation='ALGERIA' or c_nation='ARGENTINA' or c_nation= 'BRAZIL'  in cdbsp1,
 c_nation = 'CANADA' or c_nation = 'EGYPT' or c_nation = 'ETHIOPIA'  in cdbsp2,
 c_nation = 'FRANCE' or c_nation = 'GERMANY' or c_nation = 'INDIA'in cdbsp3,
 c_nation = 'INDONESIA' or c_nation = 'IRAN' or c_nation = 'IRAQ' in cdbsp4,
 c_nation = 'JAPAN' or c_nation = 'JORDAN' or c_nation = 'KENYA'  in cdbsp5,
 c_nation = 'MOROCCO' or c_nation = 'MOZAMBIQUE' or c_nation = 'PERU'  in cdbsp6,
 c_nation= 'CHINA' or c_nation= 'ROMANIA' or c_nation= 'SAUDI ARABIA'  in cdbsp7,
 c_nation= 'VIETNAM' or c_nation= 'RUSSIA' or
 c_nation= 'UNITED KINGDOM' or c_nation = 'UNITED STATES'  in cdbsp8
```

Table Order

The order table is used in queries 3, 4, and 12. The possible choice of filters for expression based fragmentation includes: o_orderdate, o_shipdate, and o_order-priority. Of these filters, orderdate is used in at least two queries and appears to be the logical choice. Column o_orderdate is uniformly distributed between STARTDATE [1992-01-01], and ENDDATE [1998-12-31] - 151 days, for a total of seven years. The choice of a fragmentation scheme is fragmentation by expression, using a range rule over 12 dbspaces located on separate disks. Queries 3 and 4 can benefit from this fragmentation scheme.

```
o_orderdate <= 33816 and o_orderdate >= 33603 in odbsp1,
o_orderdate <= 34028 and o_orderdate >= 33817 in odbsp2,
o_orderdate <= 34242 and o_orderdate >= 34029 in odbsp3,
o_orderdate <= 34454 and o_orderdate >= 34243 in odbsp4,.. .. ..
o_orderdate <= 35734 and o_orderdate >= 35521 in odbsp10
o_orderdate <= 35946 and o_orderdate >= 35735 in odbsp11,
o_orderdate <= 36160 and o_orderdate >= 35947 in odbsp12
```

Table Lineitem

The lineitem table is used in queries 3, 5-10, 12-15, and 17. The possible choice of filters for expression based fragmentation includes: l_shipdate, l_shipmode, l_receiptdata, l_quantity, and l_commitdate. Of these filters, l_shipdate is used in at least 7 queries and appears to be the logical choice. Column l_shipdate is orderdate, plus a random value between 1 and 121. The choice of a fragmentation scheme is fragmentation by expression, using a range rule over 42 dbspaces located on separate disks. Queries 3 and 4 benefit from this fragmentation scheme.

```
l_shipdate <= 33663 and l_shipdate >= 33603 in ldbsp1,
l_shipdate <= 33724 and l_shipdate >= 33664 in ldbsp2,
l_shipdate <= 33785 and l_shipdate >= 33725 in ldbsp3,
   .. .. ..
l_shipdate <= 35976 and l_shipdate >= 35916 in ldbsp39,
l_shipdate <= 36038 and l_shipdate >= 35977 in ldbsp40,
l_shipdate <= 36099 and l_shipdate >= 36039 in ldbsp41,
l_shipdate <= 36160 and l_shipdate >= 36100 in ldbsp42
```

Index Fragmentation

Below are the fragmentation schemes used for the indexes.

1. Table Lineitem

```
Index order_key

fragment by expression
l_orderkey > 0 and l_orderkey <= 10000000 in ildbsp1,
l_orderkey > 10000000 and l_orderkey <= 20000000 in ildbsp2,
l_orderkey > 20000000 and l_orderkey <= 30000000 in ildbsp3,
..

..
l_orderkey > 130000000 and l_orderkey <= 140000000 in ildbsp14,
l_orderkey > 140000000 and l_orderkey <= 150000000 in ildbsp15;


Index l_partkey on lineitem (l_partkey)
fragment by expression
l_partkey > 0 and l_partkey <= 1333 in il2_dbsp1,
l_partkey > 1333 and l_partkey <= 2666 in il2_dbsp2
l_partkey > 2666 and l_partkey <= 3999 in il2_dbsp3,
...

...
l_partkey > 17329 and l_partkey <= 18662 in il2_dbsp14,
l_partkey > 18662 and l_partkey <= 20000 in il2_dbsp15;
```

2. Table Order

```
Index o_ckey on Order

fragment by expression
o_orderdate <= 34114 and o_orderdate >= 33603 in iodbsp1,
o_orderdate <= 34625 and o_orderdate >= 34115 in iodbsp2,
o_orderdate <= 35136 and o_orderdate >= 34626 in iodbsp3,
o_orderdate <= 35647 and o_orderdate >= 35137 in iodbsp4,
o_orderdate <= 36160 and o_orderdate >= 35648 in iodbsp5;
```

3. Table Parts

```
Index p_pkey on part (p_partkey)

fragment by expression
p_type = 'ALUMINIUM' or p_type = 'BRASS' or
p_type = 'COPPER' or p_type = 'BRONZE' in dbsp75,
p_type = 'NICKEL' or p_type = 'STEEL' or
p_type = 'TIN' or p_type = 'PROMOTIONAL' in dbsp78; }
```

4. Table Suppliers

```
Index s_k_n_r on supplier (s_suppkey,s_nation,s_region)

fragment by expression
s_suppkey <= 250000 and s_suppkey > 0 in dbsp180,
s_suppkey <= 500000 and s_suppkey > 250000 in dbspE36,
s_suppkey <= 750000 and s_suppkey > 500000 in dbsp186,
s_suppkey <= 1000000 and s_suppkey > 750000 in dbspE42;
```

As a result of the above fragmentation scheme, the 17 complex queries had the following run characteristics, as shown by the query plans.

Table E: Query characteristics.

Query	Table	Scan Type	# Fragments Scanned	Join Type	# Threads
Q1.	lineitem,	SEQ.	41/42	-	59
Q2.	partsupp	SEQ.	ALL	Dy. Hash	27
	supplier	SEQ.	1/4	-	
Q3.	order	SEQ	6/12	-	32
	customer	SEQ.	ALL	Dy. Hash	
	lineitem	Index	ALL	Index	
Q4.	order	SEQ.	ALL	Dyn. Hash	62
	lineitem	SEQ.	2/42		

Table E: Query characteristics (continued).

Query	Table	Scan Type	# Fragments Scanned	Join Type	# Threads
Q5.	customer	SEQ	ALL	Merge	72
	order	SEQ.	3/12	Merge	
	lineitem	SEQ.	ALL	-	
	suplier	SEQ.	ALL	Dy. Hash	
Q6.	lineitem	SEQ.	7/42	-	25
Q7.	customer	SEQ.	2/8	Dy. Hash	33
	order	SEQ.	ALL	-	
	supplier	SEQ.	1/4	Dy. Hash	
	lineitem,	Index.	ALL	Index	
Q8a.	order	SEQ.	4/12	-	30
	customer	SEQ.	All	Dyn. Hash	
Q8b.	lineitem,	SEQ.	ALL	Dyn. Hash	66
	result.8a,	SEQ.	-	Dyn. Hash	
	supplier,	SEQ.	ALL	Dyn. Hash	
	part	SEQ.	1/4	-	
Q9a	partsupp	SEQ.	ALL	Dyn. Hash	34
	supplier	SEQ.	ALL	Dyn. Hash	
	part	SEQ	ALL	-	
Q9b	lineitem	SEQ.	ALL	Dy. Hash	62
Q9c	order	SEQ.	ALL	-	31
Q10	customer	SEQ	ALL	-	28
	order	SEQ.	2/12	Dy. Hash	
	lineitem	Index	ALL	Index	
Q12.	order	SEQ.	ALL	Dyn. Hash	144
	lineitem	SEQ.	ALL	-	
Q13.	lineitem,	SEQ.	ALL	Index.	30
	order	SEQ.	ALL	-	
Q14a.	lineitem,	SEQ.	1/42	Merge Join	21
	part	Index.	ALL	-	
Q14b	all_sales (res.14a)	SEQ.	-	-	19
Q14c	all_sales (res.14a)	SEQ.	-	-	19
Q14d.	res.14b,	SEQ.	-	-	19
	res.14c	SEQ.	-	-	
Q15a	lineitem	SEQ.	3/42	-	21
Q15b.	supplier	index	ALL	Index	40
	revenue (res.15a)	SEQ.	-	-	-

Table E: Query characteristics (continued).

Query	Table	Scan Type	# Fragments Scanned	Join Type	# Threads
Q16.	partsupp,	SEQ.	ALL	Dy. Hash	30
	part	SEQ.	ALL	-	
Q17a.	lineitem,	SEQ.	ALL	Dyn. Hash	64
	part	SEQ.	ALL	-	
Q17b.	res.17a	SEQ.	-	Index	19
	part	Index	ALL		

The results above show that the fragmentation scheme designed for the TPC-D Benchmark helped to improve the performance of queries Q1-Q8, Q10, Q14, and Q15 by the elimination of some of the fragments. Since most of the data is in the tables Lineitem and Orders, it is easy to observe that, by design, these tables were affected the most.

Summary

This article has described various planning and tuning aspects of INFORMIX-OnLine Dynamic Server, version 7.1, which were used to obtain the best fragmentation strategy to meet target goals. Also discussed were several tools and techniques available to the user to monitor and tune the selected fragmentation scheme. Several case studies were provided to offer insight into the alternate choices of fragmentation schemes and to discuss some tradeoffs. The case studies were selected from a spectrum of industry sectors representing applications in areas as broad as the telecommunication, retail, banking industries, and TPC-D benchmark. Our experience indicates that building the right fragmentation scheme is an iterative process. One can build a macro level (sub-optimal) fragmentation scheme by using the general guidelines described in this article. Later, the selected fragmentation scheme can be fine-tuned for best performance by executing queries on the target system, and analyzing the data collected using the diagnostic and monitoring tools provided by INFORMIX-OnLine Dynamic Server, version 7.1.

Acknowledgments

The author acknowledges the assistance of Pete Simcox, Dinesh Kumar, Blake Hughes, Jason Sango (Technology Investments), Robert Hartman, Tom DeMott,

Jeff Fried, Jerry Bortvedt, and other colleagues, in providing feedback and the review of material.

References

1. *INFORMIX-OnLine Dynamic Server, Version 7.1, Administrator's Guide*, Volumes I and II.

2. *Informix Guide to SQL: Syntax.*

3. *INFORMIX-OnLine Dynamic Server Performance Guide.*

4. *INFORMIX-OnLine Dynamic Server Performance Tuning Guide,* Part No. 502-5-268-1-99999-1.

5. *INFORMIX-OnLine Dynamic Server: Archive and Backup Guide,* version 7.1, December 1994.

6. *DB/Cockpit User's Manual.*

7. *TPC Benchmark D, Working Draft 6.4,* Transaction Processing Performance Council, 1993.

About the Author

Subhash Bhatia is a software development manager for INFORMIX-OnLine Extended Parallel Server OEM Labs at Informix, Menlo Park, California.

Schema Optimization

by Kevin Fennimore

Introduction

The database schema is comprised of table definitions, index definitions, permissions, etc. Optimizing the schema involves creating tables that make efficient use of system resources (i.e., disk space, reduced maintenance and I/O requirements, etc.) and allow the database to access data in an efficient manner. An inefficient schema can result in tables that require more disk space, are hard to maintain, and require more I/O to access data. All of these factors can lead to poor performance. The intent of this article is to suggest ways in which schemas can be optimized for improved performance.

Column Definitions

A discussion regarding optimization should first address the type of columns defined in the table. Often, character strings are used in place of integers; this is sometimes a result of standards which require all fields that are not used in mathematical calculations to be characters. This practice leads to inefficiency for two reasons.

The first inefficiency relates to space. An eight-character field containing only numeric values uses eight bytes for each record. If this field is numeric, such as an integer, it is large enough to store the data and only occupies four bytes of storage per record. Thus, if the column is used as a key in an index, the key size will be smaller and the record's size will be smaller. The benefits of smaller row sizes will be discussed later in this article.

Customer table	Inaccurate column definition	# of bytes	Accurate column definition	# of bytes
customer_num	char (8)	8	integer	4
lname	char (30)	30	char (20)	20
fname	char (30)	30	char (15)	15
credit_limit	decimal (11,2)	7	decimal (7,2)	5
last_update	datetime year to fraction(s)	11	datetime year to minute	7
Total		86	vs.	51

Figure 1: For a table with 1,000,000 rows, the second column definitions would save 35-million bytes or approximately 35 megabytes of storage.

The second inefficiency concerns comparisons. The database engine requires more time to compare two eight-character fields than two integer fields. The engine must compare each character in the string to determine equality. In contrast, only one comparison is necessary for integer fields.

Another issue related to column definitions concerns the size of the fields. It is very common for fields to be oversized, especially when the database is first designed and it is difficult to determine the actual scope of all future data. For example, if a price column is defined in the database as `money(11,2)`, it is capable of containing a value up to $999,999,999.99. However, if such a large denomination is unlikely, it is preferable to define the column as `money(5,2)`, allowing for values up to $999.99 and also saving two to three bytes per record.

The same concept applies to other datatypes such as datetime. Most applications define these fields as datetime year to `fraction(5)`. Yet most UNIX machines do not support fractions of a second past the hundredths or thousandths. Although some of these space savings may seem trivial, nevertheless, a few bytes here and there on a table containing one-million rows adds up.

Primary and Foreign Keys

Another common schema design mistake is to use large primary keys as the foreign keys in other tables. For example, if the primary key of an orders table consists of a 20-character order number, it is efficient to use that primary key as the foreign key in the order items table.

However, a better alternative is to define a serial field in the orders table and carry the serial value for an order into the order items table. This conserves space in the order items table and speeds up the join between the two tables, since the tables are joined by an integer field. There is one drawback to this alternative: the order items table cannot be accessed directly by the order number; the orders table must be accessed first.

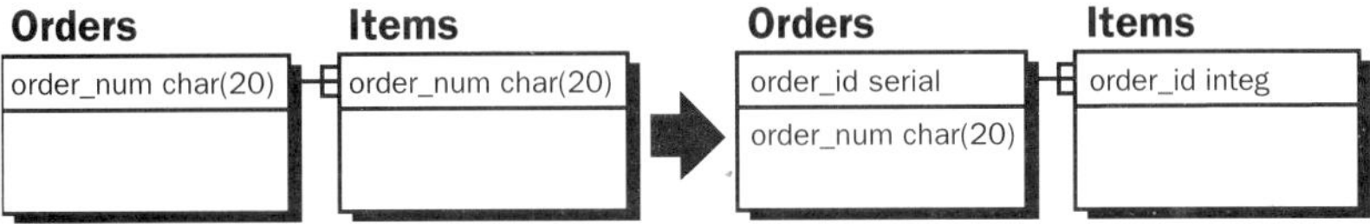

Figure 2: An example of using an integer instead of a larger character string as a foreign key.

Denormalization

Performance gains can also be realized by "denormalizing" the database. Typically, a normalized database does not contain derived data; yet derived data sometimes yields performance gains. For example, let's assume that a commonly queried value is the total price of an order and that it is important for this query to return as quickly as possible.

One way to perform this query is to obtain a total for all of the items associated with an order. For a system with a few items for each order, this may not be a problem. However, if several hundred items exist for each order, more I/O is required to obtain the sum. Alternatively, an order total field can be kept in the order table; this method obtains the order total for a given order by only reading a single record from the database. (See Figure 3.)

Another example of denormalizing for performance is repeating data in a detail table. Let's say a table contains information about cartons in inventory and a detail table lists the contents of each carton. The carton table contains the status of the carton, while the carton_detail contains the names of the actual items in the carton. When looking for all of the available cartons in inventory which contain a specific item, it is necessary to join the carton and carton_detail tables as follows:

```
select *
from carton, carton_detail
where carton.id = carton_detail.id
and carton.status = "A"
and carton_detail.item = some_item
```

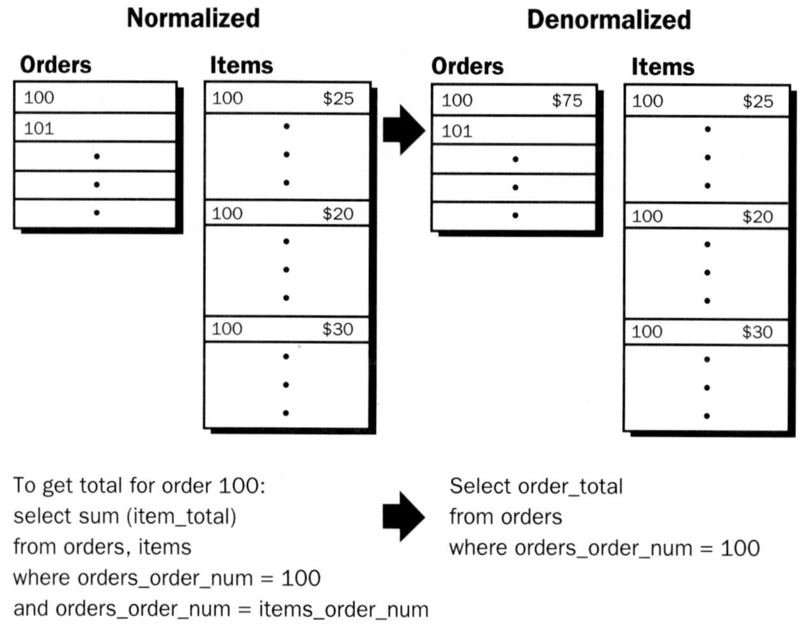

Figure 3: An example of using derived data to speed up a query.

If this is a common query, it is best to move the status to the carton_detail table—eliminating the need to join the carton table. In this case, an index can be built on item and status in the carton_detail table, allowing the query to run very quickly.

Typically, "denormalization" is frowned upon, due to the additional overhead and programming required to maintain derived and repetitive data. There is also the risk of compromising data integrity, if the derived or repeated data is not updated properly. For example, if the status in the carton table is updated, yet the status in the carton_detail records is not, a data integrity problem can result. All of these problems can be addressed by using triggers and stored procedures to maintain the denormalized data. Although there are trade-offs when the schema is denormalized, the key is to achieve better query performance.

Wide Tables

It is common to store all information about an entity (i.e., order) in one table which can produce a very large row. A table with a large row size is called a wide table. Wide tables are inefficient for several reasons, one of which is the amount of caching that is performed.

For example, when a row is read from the disk, the entire page containing that row is read into shared memory. Then, the row is read from shared memory. If additional rows are required which are on pages already in shared memory, the pages are read from memory and are not physically read from the disk (this is called *caching*). In other words, if more rows can be put on a page, there are more rows eligible to be read from memory.

Typical Data Page For:

Wide Table (row size = 300)   **Thin Table (row size = 20)**

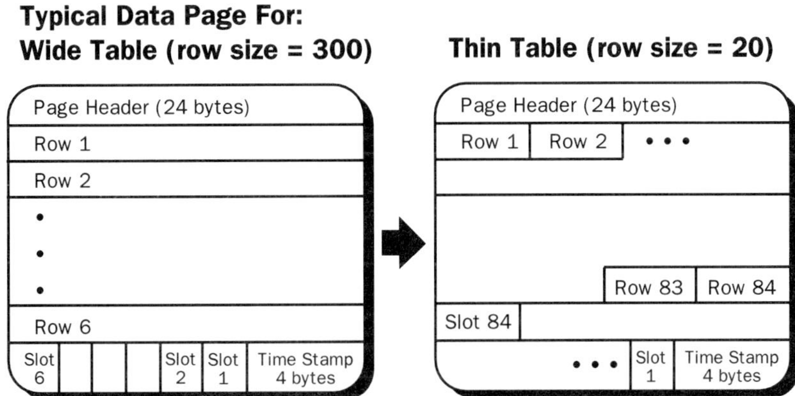

Figure 4: Contents of a data page for wide and thin tables. Note the smaller row size allows more rows on a page, thus increasing caching.

Another performance problem related to wide tables is logging. When a row is updated, inserted, or deleted in a database with logging, the entire record is written to the transaction log. Updates are the biggest problem, since an update causes the before image and the after image of the record to be written to disk.

Let's look at an example of an order table which contains all possible information about an order (i.e., status, billing, and shipping information). Assume that the record is 300 bytes long (20 for status information, 80 for billing, and 200 for shipping).

When an order is placed, all of this information is entered into one table. As the order is processed, the status information is accessed frequently and sometimes changed; however, the billing and shipping information is accessed infrequently and does not change. When the status_flag (one character) is updated, which is the most common update, the before and after image of the entire record—for a total of 600 bytes—is written to the transaction log. This results in a large overhead for an update on a one-character field. Also, when the status information of a record is accessed, the entire row is read. With INFORMIX-OnLine Dynamic Server, the entire page containing the row is read; as a result, 280 bytes are read and not used.

To correct these inefficiencies, break the table into three tables with a one-to-one correspondence. In all, there would be an order_status table (20 bytes), an order_billing table (80 bytes + order_num), and an order_shipping table (200 bytes + order_num). In this case, when the order_status is updated, only 40 bytes are written to the log. Also, in an INFORMIX-OnLine Dynamic Server system with a 2 K page size, the order_status table would contain 84 records per page, as opposed to only 6 records per page when the record size was 300 bytes. As a result, more rows are cached and performance is increased.

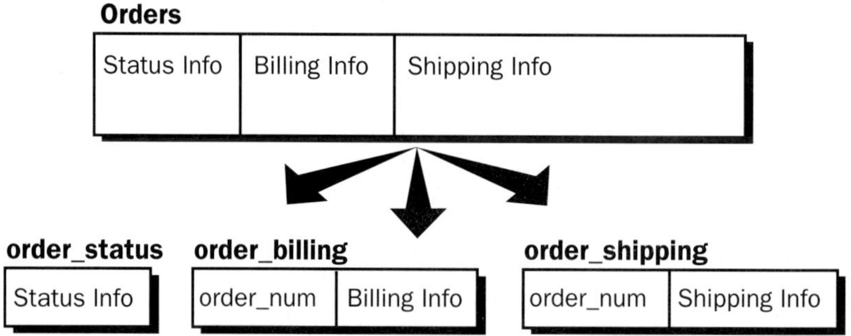

Figure 5: Break up a wide table by the type of information which is stored in the table.

Long Tables

A long table is a table with many rows. Typically, systems contain data for several years, but only access recent data for day-to-day activities. This may be the case with a patient information system. Data for patient visits might be retained for years, but most of the daily activity and reporting is performed on the most recent three months. All data prior to the last three months can be considered historical and has a negative impact on the daily operations of the database, since it is still part of the indexes and must be scanned when searching for "current" data.

To improve performance, a historical table can be created to contain all data older than three months. This enables applications to use the current table or to select from the historical table, if necessary. Selecting from the two tables is accomplished by using a union.

A table that contains rows with distinct purposes can also create long tables. An example is a log table that contains log information which is uploaded to a central machine; table log records are used for local tracking alone. This type of table can be divided into separate tables: one for local tracking and one for uploaded information. This methodology improves performance for selects which are run for local tracking information or for newly uploaded information.

Another way to separate long tables is to use table fragmenting, which is available with INFORMIX-OnLine Dynamic Server, version 7.10 or later. With table fragmenting, tables can be separated into separate fragments based on a

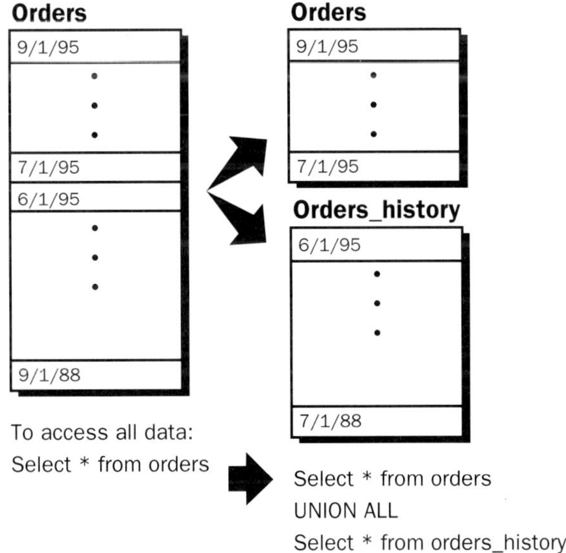

Figure 6: Break up long tables into current and historical tables.

value or round-robin scheme. In the historical data example above, the table can be fragmented by a date—the most recent three months in one fragment, and the historical information in another. This gives the application the appearance of one table. However, if a query runs with a date criteria within the last three months, the optimizer only looks at the fragment with the most recent three months and skips the other fragment.

Conclusion

This article discussed some of the most common problems with schema design. As with query optimization, the goal of schema optimization is to reduce I/O and processing time. By using the right datatypes, using appropriate foreign keys, denormalizing the database, and splitting wide and long tables, the amount of I/O and processing time for queries is greatly reduced and thereby increases performance.

About the Author

Kevin Fennimore is a consultant with UCI Consulting, Germantown, Maryland.

=19=

CUSTOMIZING SUPERTABLE FUNCTIONALITY

by Art Taylor

Introduction

The INFORMIX-NewEra SuperTable provides the programmer with both database manipulation, and screen input and output capabilities. Through the use of object-oriented and event-driven programming features, the programmer has significant flexibility in customizing the functionality of the SuperTable. However, the way in which the SuperTable retrieves rows from the database may be one area where customization is desirable.

SuperTable Row Retrieval Modifications

When rows are retrieved by INFORMIX-NewEra using the SuperTable **retrieve** method, NewEra will attempt to retrieve all of the rows that qualify for the query up to the maxrows SuperTable parameter value. The number of rows retrieved is controlled by the SuperTable maxrows parameter. By default, the maxrows parameter is set to zero, which allows all rows to be retrieved. If there are a large number of rows that qualify for the query, the INFORMIX-NewEra application may use all available disk space to retrieve the rows, a situation which could wreak havoc on a PC running Microsoft Windows™.

"

One alternative is to set the maxrows parameter to a value which will limit the number of rows retrieved. This eliminates the problem of using all available disk resources to support the application, but could also be constraining for the user. It is preferable to allow the user to retrieve up to the maxrows number of rows and then optionally choose to retrieve additional records, yet retain a limit for the total number of records retrieved.

This article presents an approach to creating a custom handler for the SuperTable `rowretrieved` event. In this approach, the application displays a prompt and allows the user to retrieve records, in increments of 25, without an upper limit. In practice, this increment could be modified and an upper limit set on the number of records retrieved.

Desired Functionality

The desired functionality allows the user to enter query criteria in the usual manner. The user can press the Retrieve button to begin retrieving rows. When the rows retrieved match the `maxrows` parameter, a prompt indicates that the maxrows parameter has been reached. The user has the option of retrieving more rows. The user could then press the "yes" button to retrieve more rows, or press a "no" button to quit retrieving rows, refer to Figure 1.

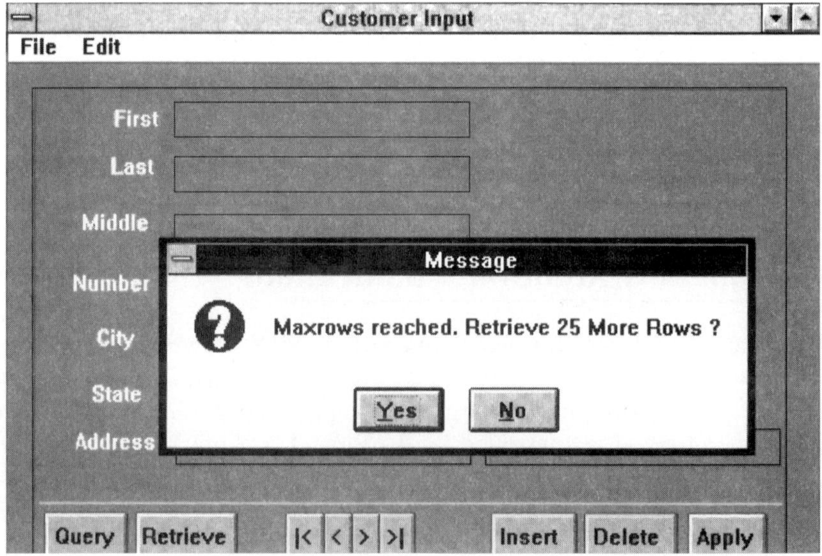

Figure 1: SuperTable row retrieval prompt.

If the user presses the "yes" button, then the maxrows parameter (a public variable within the SuperTable object) for the SuperTable is modified. In the example shown in this article, the user is prompted to retrieve 25 more rows; thus, the maxrows parameter is increased by 25. The event handler returns and the SuperTable continues to retrieve more rows until it is finished or until the new maxrows parameter is reached.

The Maxrowsexceeded Event

The **maxrowsexceeded** event handler is called when the number of rows retrieved matches the value of the maxrows parameter. This event does not return a value. It is intended to allow the programmer to display a message to the user indicating that more rows exist to fulfill the query than have been retrieved.

It is preferable to use this event handler to prompt the user to retrieve additional rows. However, when this event is raised, the SuperTable facilities have **finished** retrieving rows from the database. There is no simple way to allow the SuperTable to retrieve more rows at this point. For this reason, the **rowretrieved** event handler is used instead.

The Rowretrieved Event

The SuperTable **rowretrieved** event is raised after each row is retrieved from the database. It is called from within the retrieval loop which brings rows back to the client from the database server. Since this event is called after each row is retrieved, it is possible to determine how many rows have been retrieved and, when necessary, allows the adjustment of the **maxrows** parameter to suit the user's needs. The code used to provide this functionality from within the **rowretrieved** event handler is shown below.

```
HANDLER ixSuperTable::wind1_cust_st_rowRetrieved(theRow ixRow) RETURNING BOOLEAN
variable retval smallint
variable str char(10)


- must look at maxrows - 1, else maxrowsexceeded event is tripped


if wind1.cust_st.getnumStoredRows() = (wind1.cust_st.maxrows - 1 ) then - prompt
the user to continue
   call messagebox( title:   new ixString( "Message" ),
        message: new ixString("Maxrows reached. Retrieve 25 More Rows ?" ),
```

```
                    iconstyle:    ixQueryicon,
                    buttonstyle: ixYesNo )
                                         returning retval
if retval = ixYesButton then   -increment maxrows
    let wind1.cust_st.maxrows = wind1.cust_st.maxrows + 25
end if

end if
return TRUE
END HANDLER-ixSuperTable::wind1_cust_st_rowRetrieved
```

In the code above, the value of the total number of rows currently retrieved is tested. This value is retrieved using the **getnumstoredrows** method. This value must be tested for a value one less than the maxrows parameter. A test for the exact value of the maxrows parameter can not be used because when this value is reached, the SuperTable stops retrieving rows and executes the **maxrowsexceeded** event. This precludes the possibility of retrieving more rows for the current set.

If the user does not request the retrieval of the additional rows retrieved, then this code does not interfere with the normal SuperTable functionality. If the user replies by pressing the "no" button in answer to the prompt to retrieve more rows, the SuperTable will continue to retrieve exactly the maxrows number of rows. In this case, the event handler merely allows the SuperTable to continue retrieving rows until the number of rows retrieved matches the maxrows parameter.

If the number of stored rows, as returned by **getNumStoredRows()**, is one less than the value of the maxrows parameter, a message box is displayed to prompt the user to continue. There are two buttons on the message box: a "Yes" button and a "No" button. This style of buttons is provided by using the **ixYesNoButton** style with the INFORMIX-NewEra messagebox function. The return value that is important is the return value which indicates the user has pressed the "Yes" button. This value is indicated by the return value of **ixYesButton**, an integer of constant value contained in the **ix4gl.4gh** include file.

If the user has pressed the "Yes" button, then the value of maxrows contained in the SuperTable object is changed. This value is incremented by 25. If the user has pressed the "No" button, control simply passes to the return statement at the end of the handler. In this case, the SuperTable will continue retrieving rows until the maxrows number of rows is retrieved or until no additional rows can be retrieved.

The final line of code in the handler returns a BOOLEAN value, as required by the handler signature. In all cases, this handler returns a value of TRUE, allowing the SuperTable to continue processing the row just retrieved. Returning a value of FALSE would have rejected the row that was just retrieved, which is not the goal of this modification.

Adding Additional Functionality

These minor changes to the rowRetrieved handler significantly alter the behavior of the SuperTable. The user can now retrieve additional rows for query rather than resort to the creation of a query to retrieve a smaller number of rows which fit within the maxrows value.

However, it may still be desirable to set a total limit on the number of rows retrieved. This maximum value can be entered into the code shown above to limit the total number of rows retrieved. An example of this approach appears on the following page.

```
HANDLER ixSuperTable::wind1_cust_st_rowRetrieved(theRow ixRow)
   RETURNING BOOLEAN
variable retval smallint
variable str char(10)

if wind1.cust_st.getnumstoredrows() = 200   then
    call messagebox( title: new ixString( "Message" ),
        message: new ixString( "Maximum Number of Rows Total Retrieved.")
            returning retval
        let wind1.cust_st.maxrows = 200
    return TRUE
end if


- must look at maxrows - 1, else maxrowsexceeded event is tripped
if wind1.cust_st.getnumstoredrows() = (wind1.cust_st.maxrows - 1 ) then
  call messagebox( title:   new ixString( "Message" ),
        message: new ixString("Maxrows reached. Retrieve 25 More Rows ?" ),
        iconstyle:   ixQueryicon,
        buttonstyle: ixYesNo )
        returning retval
if retval = ixYesButton then   —increment maxrows
        let wind1.cust_st.maxrows = wind1.cust_st.maxrows + 25
end if
```

```
end if
return TRUE
END HANDLER-ixSuperTable::wind1_cust_st_rowRetrieved
```

In the example above, a specific value is tested against the number of rows currently retrieved. If this value has been reached, then a message box is displayed to the user, refer to Figure 2. Once the user confirms that the message has been read, the handler returns immediately. This prevents the remaining code from being executed and limits the SuperTable retrieval to the fixed number of rows. The remainder of this sample code is identical to the code shown previously.

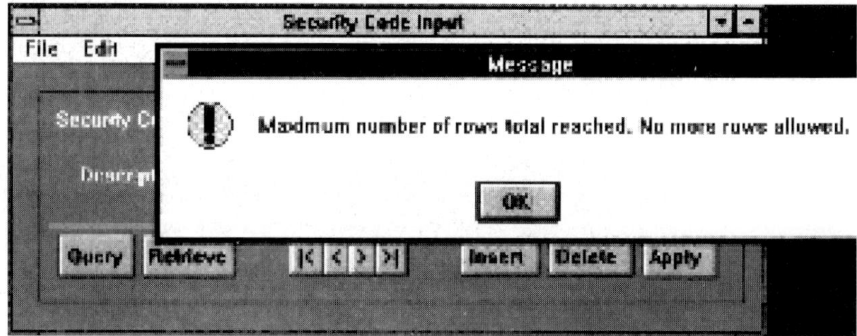

Figure 2: Total rows limit message.

Adding Informational Messages

It is useful to provide informational messages for the user at various points during the retrieval and browsing of data. For instance, when the user has reached the end of the current set and is attempting to move past the end of the set, a message can be displayed which indicates that there are "no more rows" available, refer to Figure 4. Another useful message can be displayed when the user has entered a query and no rows were found, refer to Figure 3.

By default, the INFORMIX-NewEra SuperTable does not provide this functionality. It is also important to note that there are no handlers which allow code to be entered to provide these features. To implement these functions, the default code for the various SuperTable buttons must be changed.

In this example, the SuperTable "next row" default button code has been modified. The **rowposition** variable is set using the return value from the SuperTable **getCurrRowNum** method. This value is incremented by one, since the user is attempting to move to the next row; the value of the **rowposition** variable is thus the *target* row. This value is tested against the value of the total

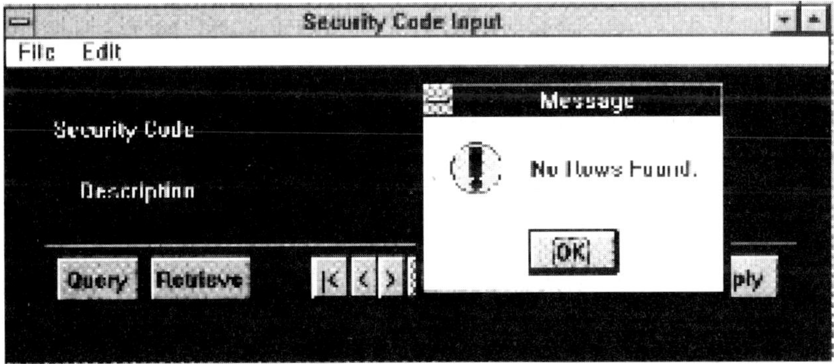

Figure 3: No rows found error message.

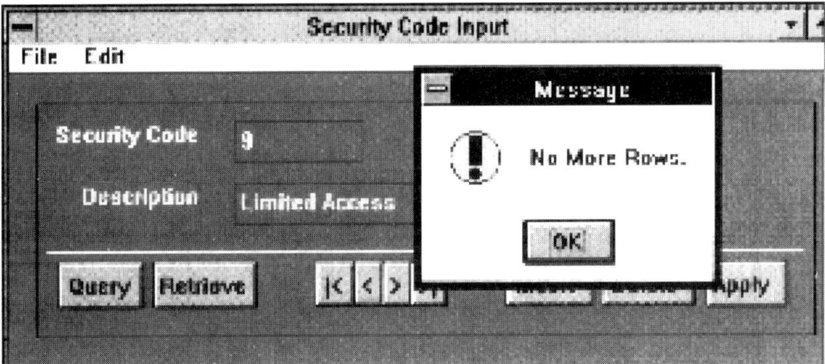

Figure 4: No more rows message.

number of rows in the SuperTable set as returned by the **getnumstoredrows** method. When this function is called with a NULL parameter (the default), it uses the current set.

If the **rowPosition** is determined to be beyond the number of rows available, then a messagebox is displayed to indicate that there are no additional rows available. This is the code inserted to implement the user message. The **rowPosition** is then set to the SuperTable value for the last row in the set (**SuperTable::lastrow**). The SuperTable **setcurrentcell** method is subsequently called to set the current cell to the value of the **rowposition** variable.

```
HANDLER ixButton::wind1_Button32_activate() RETURNING VOID
VARIABLE ok BOOLEAN
variable retval smallint
VARIABLE superTable ixSuperTable
```

```
VARIABLE rowPosition INTEGER

LET superTable = (getVisualContainer() CAST ixSuperTable)
LET rowPosition = superTable.getCurrRowNum() + 1

IF rowPosition > superTable.getNumStoredRows(NULL) THEN
     call messagebox( title: new ixString( "Message"),
                         message: new ixString( "No More Rows." ),
                         iconstyle: ixExclaimIcon )
             returning retval

     # get the number of rows for the current displayMode
     LET rowPosition = ixSuperTable::lastRow

END IF

LET ok = superTable.setCurrentCell(rowPosition,
                                   ixSuperTable::currentColumn)

END HANDLER-ixButton::wind1_Button32_activate
```

Using a Template Window

If a number of INFORMIX-NewEra windows are being developed, it is useful to encapsulate much of the desired functionality and thus avoid re-programming these features for each window. This can be accomplished by creating a set of template windows which provide the desired features. Following is a sample template window. The features provided in this window are listed in Table 1.

Obviously, re-programming these features for each window could be time-consuming and tedious. However, by creating a template screen with these features, the task of window development can be simplified.

To simplify the process of using the template screen, the code entered for the various features should be as generic as possible; it should not contain specific names of screen objects. For example, the event handler code for the rowretrieved event (shown previously) used the specific name of the SuperTable with the reference, as noted below.

```
if wind1.cust_st.getnumstoredrows() =
(wind1.cust_st.maxrows - 1 ) then ....
```

Feature	**Programming Required**
"no rows found" message	Code entered in the handler code for the activate event of the Retrieve button.
"no more rows" message	Code entered in the handler code for the activate event of the Next and Previous buttons.
Prompt for the retrieval of more rows if the **maxrows** number of rows has been reached	Code entered in the event handler for the rowretrieved event of the SuperTable.
File menu option with exit choice	Use the menu editor to create the menu and to enter the code for the exit option.
Edit menu option with clipboard options	Use the menu editor to create the menu and to enter code for the edit options.
VCR-type buttons for SuperTable set traversal	Insert buttons and modify the button "title" parameter.
Color and font of window	Enter window properties.

Table 1: Template window features.

A more general reference is needed if this code is to be inserted into other applications. This general reference can be provided with the **self** identifier. The **self** identifier references the containing object for the method or handler. For example, in the case of the **rowretrieved** event, the self identifier references the SuperTable being used (this connection to the SuperTable is accomplished by the Window Painter in the code generated for the SuperTable handler). Thus, the following code could be used for the **rowretrieved** event handler.

```
variable retval smallint
variable str char(10)
variable st ixSuperTable
if self.getnumstoredrows() = (self.maxrows - 1 ) then
    call messagebox( title: new ixString( "Message" ),
        message: new ixString("Maxrows reached. Retrieve 25 More Rows ?" ),
            iconstyle: ixQueryicon,
            buttonstyle: ixYesNo )
        returning retval
```

```
   if retval = ixYesButton then
      let self.maxrows = self.maxrows + 25
   end if


end if


return TRUE
```

This code segment is identical to the code provided above (in the Rowretrieved Event paragraph) with the exception of the **self** identifier used as a reference to the containing object. The use of the **self** identifier allows this code to be used without modification in other applications where the name of the SuperTable object is unknown.

Using the Template Windows

A template window contains all of the features listed in the previous table. The programmer can open this window, select the SuperTable object, and paste table or SuperView columns into the SuperTable frame.

Once the database columns have been pasted into the SuperTable frame, several database properties must be set. These properties are specific to each SuperTable instance and are not part of the template window. The *primary key* must be identified and a locking mode must be selected. This allows the update buttons *(insert, apply)* to be operational. If these buttons are not needed, they can be deleted from the window. Also, it is necessary to identify the type of the window and to modify the *startup* property.

Once these changes have been made, the window should be saved using the "save-as" option; indicate a new name for the window.

Free-Form and Grid-Form SuperTable Templates

The grid-form and free-form SuperTables retrieve data using the same method; however, the presentation of the data is different. With the grid SuperTable, traversal of the current set can be accomplished using the scroll buttons on the grid box; the next and previous buttons are not needed to move through the data set. It is important to note that, if used, the next and previous buttons will move the user through the data on the screen; refer to Figure 5.

When a SuperTable is inserted into a window, its "layout" parameter is set to the type of SuperTable being used. This parameter is locked by the Window Painter and cannot be changed. For that reason, when using template windows,

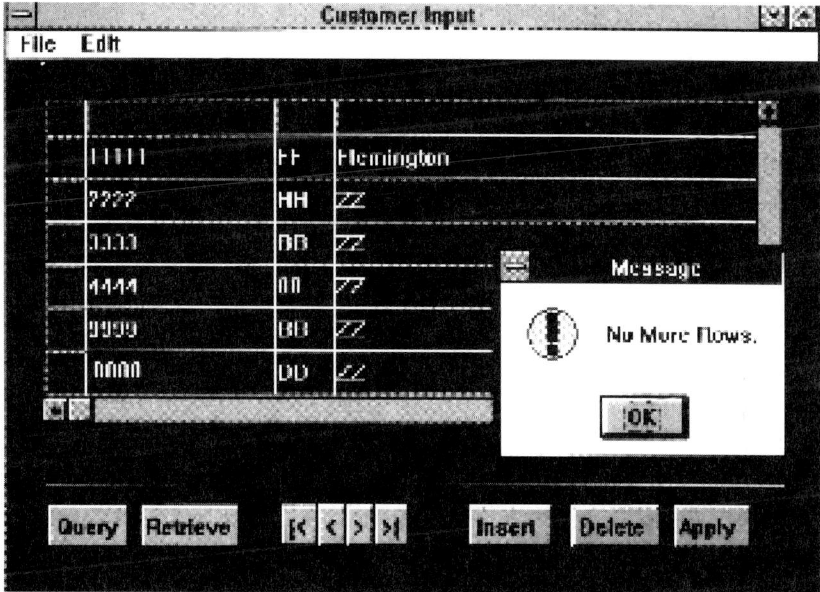

Figure 5: Grid-form SuperTable from template.

a separate template window must be provided for both grid-form and free-form SuperTables.

Conclusion

As this article has shown, using window templates to develop application windows can promote consistency throughout an application. For example, a series of templates can be developed for different types of windows. These features can be distributed to a team of programmers. Additionally, the templates add another layer of efficiency to the process of using the Window Painter. Thus, programming is reduced and maintainability enhanced through the added functionality and consistency.

The classes supplied with INFORMIX-NewEra can be easily extended. This article has demonstrated the ease of altering the rowRetrieved event of the SuperTable class to limit the number of records retrieved by the user. Such a change can be easily accomplished and, as shown previously, can be saved in a window template for use by other programmers.

The rich features of the INFORMIX-NewEra language allow the power of object-oriented programming to be utilized. Although not demonstrated in this article, the alterations to the SuperTable class can be placed in a custom class which is derived from the SuperTable class. To use this custom class only requires the substitution of the custom class name for the **`ixSuperTable`** class within the Window Painter. It is also necessary to include the class library files in the program file list within the Application Builder. This approach has the added benefit of allowing a change in the custom class to be realized in the application code, which already uses the custom class, by simply recompiling the code using the new custom class library.

This article, by Art Taylor, is an excerpt from "INFORMIX-NewEra: A Guide for Application Developers" by Art Taylor and Tony Lacy-Thompson, be published by Informix Press/Prentice Hall PTR.

About the Author

Art Taylor is a project leader at Informix, New Jersey.

## 20

Using SMI Tables in INFORMIX-OnLine Dynamic Server to Broadcast Messages to Users

by David Ranney

Introduction

INFORMIX-OnLine Dynamic Server provides monitoring information, previously restricted to the UNIX command line, in the form of SQL tables. These tables, known as System Monitoring Interface (SMI) tables, provide an unparalled ease of access to INFORMIX-OnLine Dynamic Server system information. One possible application of this easily available information is a stored procedure which broadcasts a message to every user currently attached to the current OnLine instance.

Overview

This article covers the following topics:

- The SMI Tables;

- The syssessions SMI table;

- Specific issues related to the example of a stored procedure;

- An example of a stored procedure which broadcasts a message to all users; and

- Running the example of a stored procedure.

The SMI Tables

When INFORMIX-OnLine Dynamic Server is first initialized, a message appears in the message log saying that a database called "sysmaster" was created. This database contains all of the SMI tables. Each OnLine instance has its own sysmaster database. The tables within the sysmaster database are a combination of regular disk-based SQL tables and views into shared memory known as pseudo-tables. The SMI tables are treated the same as SQL tables within the query language, thus the full power of SQL is available to retrieve information on the current OnLine instance. It is important to realize that INFORMIX-OnLine Dynamic Server relies on the data within these tables; therefore, altering the tables or updating the data can produce unpredictable results. You should consider the SMI tables to contain read-only information.

The SMI tables allow for the monitoring of such things as disk usage, table status, chunk status, system profiling, archiving status (for On-Archive) and many other types of information. For more information about the SMI tables, see Chapter 36 of the INFORMIX-OnLine Dynamic Server Administrator's Guide, version 6.0.

The syssessions Table

Since the example provided in this article will broadcast a message to all current users, the SMI table "syssessions" is particularly important. This table contains information about each user who is connected to the current OnLine instance. When a user attaches to the engine, a new entry appears in this table. When the user detaches, his entry disappears. Among the columns available in this table, the following are the most important elements for the stored procedure in this article:

    sid—Session Id: Useful when joining to other SMI tables
    username—User Id: The user's UNIX login

hostname—Hostname of Client: The user's client machine
tty—User's Stderr File: The full path on the client

There are many other columns available in the syssessions table, including information about the current status of the user's session. However, this information is not necessary for the procedure in this article. These columns are documented in the INFORMIX-OnLine Dynamic Server Administrator's Guide.

Specific Issues Related to the Example Stored Procedure

First, it is necessary to explain some specific issues regarding the stored procedure's algorithm and specific syntax.

Initially, the procedure performs a simple echo into the tty device to write to the screen of a remote user. Since there is no standard remote "write" command across all UNIX platforms, this method suffices for the sake of expediency.

Note that the hostname and tty columns in syssessions are only 16 characters long. On some systems, this length is insufficient to fully specify a terminal device or machine name.

Also, note that the """" syntax appears in this procedure; this is the method to include a double quote within a string in the Stored Procedure Language (SPL).

An Example of a Stored Procedure

```
public address.sql
_____________________ CUT  HERE___________________
_  ***************************************************************************
_  *
_  * Procedure:
_  * public_address
_  *
_  * Author:
_  * David Ranney
_  *
_  * Input:
_  * msg_file: A string containing a sufficient path to an ASCII file with
_  * the appropriate message.
_  *
```

```
- * Description:
- * This procedure will broadcast a message to all appropriate users on a
- * given OnLine instance. This procedure makes use of the SMI tables which
- * are only available in INFORMIX-OnLine Dynamic Server.
- *
- * If a user is connected more than once to the OnLine instance, each
- * connection receives the message to ensure that the user saw it.
- *
- * This procedure supplies the basic functionality for demonstration purposes
- * only. It can be modified to meet more general needs.
- *
- ************************************************************************************
CREATE PROCEDURE public_address (msg_str CHAR(80))

 DEFINE user_name CHAR(10);
 DEFINE mach_name CHAR(16);
 DEFINE tty_name CHAR(20);
 DEFINE cmd_line CHAR(160);

 FOREACH c_user_list_1 FOR
    SELECT UNIQUE
        username,
        hostname,
        tty
    INTO
        user_name,
        mach_name,
        tty_name
    FROM
        sysmaster:syssessions
    WHERE
        username IS NOT NULL AND
        username != " " AND
        hostname IS NOT NULL AND
        hostname != " " AND
        tty IS NOT NULL AND
        tty != " "

 LET cmd_line = "rsh "||mach_name||" ""echo '"||msg_str||"' > "||tty_name||
```

```
" " " ";
 SYSTEM cmd_line;


 END FOREACH


END PROCEDURE - public address;
___________________ CUT HERE___________________
```

Running the Stored Procedure

Since the above example is a basic stored procedure which runs against the sys-master database, executing it is straightforward. To prepare and run the stored procedure, perform the following steps:

1. Bring up dbaccess and attach to a regular database (not sysmaster).
2. Run the above statement from the Query Language.
3. Inform users in the current OnLine instance that a message will appear on their screens.
4. From the Query Language, run the following command: EXECUTE PROCEDURE public_address("Hi Vern");
5. Confirm that "Hi Vern" was sent to all users, whether local or remote.

Conclusion

This article demonstrated one simple application of a single SMI table. With all the information now present in the SMI tables and the ability to bring the full power of SQL and the various front-end utilities to bear, the possibilities for using SMI information are far greater than indicated by this example. Any number of extremely helpful utilities can be based on the SMI tables, depending on your specific needs.

About the Author

David Ranney is an associate project manager at Informix, Menlo Park, California.

## 21

A Database Comparison Utility

by Guy A. Molinari

Introduction

Anyone engaged in maintaining databases which consist of many tables and columns will appreciate a utility that compares two similar SQL Data Description Language (DDL) scripts. SCHEMADIFF is a program that generates an SQL script which incrementally modifies the database structure of a source database to achieve parity with a target database schema. This generated script consists of alter table, create index, and drop index sequences which alter the structure of individual database tables.

SCHEMADIFF compares the database schemata one table at a time, generating add, modify, and drop sequences as appropriate. Tables that exist in the target schema—which are not in the source schema—are created. Tables existing in the source schema—which are absent from the target schema—are dropped. A command line switch can disable this function. Indices are handled in a similar fashion but with one difference, modified indices are dropped and re-created. SCHEMADIFF handles the conversion of duplicate/unique indices; however, some care must be taken, as there is no way for the utility to determine if the data is unique. The order of the tables within the schemata may differ without any adverse effect. The program also contains logic to avoid dropping indices on tables that are themselves dropped, thus avoiding unnecessary operations.

Command line usage is as follows:

```
schemadiff {-d} [sourcefile] [targetfile]
```

The '-d' option prevents the dropping of tables and indices in the source schema file which are not contained in the target file. SCHEMADIFF returns a status of 0 if the source and target files do not differ. A status of 1 is returned if any differences are found. The script containing differences is generated to standard output, where it may be redirected as desired. Rudimentary syntax checking is performed on both the source and target files. Error messages and status are indicated with corresponding line numbers, where applicable.

Example 1

An example illustrates the output of this utility.
The file 'test1.sql' contains the following SQL script:

```
{ test1.sql }

create table test1
  (
    datacol1 decimal(10,2),
    datacol2 integer,
    datacol3 char(20),
    datacol4 date,
    datacol5 char(5)
  );
create unique index idx1 on test1 (datacol2, datacol5);


create table test2
  (
    apples char(10),
    oranges char(10),
    pears char(10),
    grapes char(10)
  );


create table dropit
```

```
   (
     goodbye1 char(1),
     goodbye2 char(1)
   );
create index idx2 on dropit (goodbye1);
```

Example 2

The file 'test2.sql' contains the following SQL script:

```
{ test2.sql }

create table test2
   (
     apples char(10),
     oranges char(10),
     pears char(10)
   );
create index idx3 on test2 (apples);

create table test1
   (
     datacol1 integer,
     datacol2 integer,
     datacol3 char(20),
     datacol3b char(20),
     datacol3c char(20),
     datacol5 char(5),
     datacol5b char(6)
   );
create index idx1 on test1 (datacol2, datacol5, datacol3);


create table newtable
   (
     new1 integer,
     new2 integer,
   );
```

Example 3

When the line below is entered:

```
schemadiff test1.sql test2.sql
```

the following is displayed on your screen:

```
{ SCHEMADIFF Version 1.0 - Guy A. Molinari }
{ Copyright(c) 1995, All Rights Reserved }

alter table test2
  drop (grapes);

create index idx3 on test2 (apples);

alter table test1
  modify (datacol1 integer),
  add (datacol3b char(20) before datacol4),
  add (datacol3c char(20) before datacol4),
  add (datacol5b char(6)),
  drop (datacol4);

drop index idx1;
create index idx1 on test1 (datacol2,datacol5,datacol3);

create table newtable
  (
    new1 integer,
    new2 integer
  );

drop table dropit;
```

SCHEMADIFF Code

SCHEMADIFF was written in 'C', and is highly portable to other platforms and environments.

```c
//
// SCHEMADIFF.C V1.1 - Compare schemas and generate SQL DDL script
//
// Copyright (c) 1995, Guy A. Molinari, All Rights Reserved


//
// Guy A. Molinari
// Unitek Computer Systems
// 19109 36th Avenue West
// Suite 102
// Lynnwood, WA 98036
// (206) 672-1304
//


#include <stdio.h>
#include <string.h>
#include <ctype.h>

#define FALSE 0
#define TRUE 1

typedef struct s_collist
{
    char tabname[20];
    char colname[20];
    char attrib[50];
    int       b_drop;
} st_collist;

typedef struct s_idxlist
{
    char idxname[20];
    char idxtable[20];
    char idxspec[255];
    int       b_unique;
    int       b_drop;
```

```c
} st_idxlist;

static char *get_token();
static char *get_name();
static void parse_file();
static void addlist();
static void addidxlist();
static void gendiff();
static void genidxdiff();
static void coldrops();
static void tabdrops();
static void idxdrops();
static void different();

static st_collist *orglist;
static st_idxlist *idxlist;
static char *outbuf, *outptr;
static int orglistend = 0;
static int idxlistend = 0;
static int b_different = FALSE;

/*****************************************************************************
MAIN
*****************************************************************************/
main(argc, argv)
int        argc;
char **argv;
{
    int filepos1, filepos2;

    if ((argc != 3 && argc != 4) || (argc = = 4 && strcmp(argv[1], "-d")))
    {
    printf("SCHEMADIFF V1.1 - Copyright (c) 1995 - Guy A. Molinari\n\n");
        printf("Usage: schemadiff {-d} [srcfile] [destfile]\n");
        printf("       : {-d} Don't drop tables/indexes (optional).\n");
        printf("       : [srcfile] Source schema script.\n");
        printf("       : [destfile] Destination schema script.\n");
        printf("       : Differences are generated to standard output.\n\n");
        exit(-1);
```

```
}

if (argc == 3)
{
    filepos1 = 1;
    filepos2 = 2;
}
else
{
    filepos1 = 2;
    filepos2 = 3;
}


orglist = (st_collist*) calloc(5000, sizeof(st_collist));
idxlist = (st_idxlist*) calloc(500, sizeof(st_idxlist));
outbuf = (char*) malloc(8192);
if (orglist == NULL || idxlist == NULL || outbuf == NULL)
{
    fprintf(stderr, "Memory allocation error.\n");
    exit(-2);
}
outptr = outbuf;

parse_file(argv[filepos1], addlist, addidxlist);
parse_file(argv[filepos2], gendiff, genidxdiff);
gendiff(NULL, NULL, NULL);
if (argc == 3)
{
    tabdrops();
    idxdrops();
}

free(orglist);
free(idxlist);
free(outbuf);

if (b_different)
    exit(1);
```

```
        else
            exit(0);


}


/****************************************************************************
PARSE_FILE
****************************************************************************/
void parse_file(fname, actionfunc, indexfunc)
char *fname;
void (*actionfunc)();
void (*indexfunc)();
{
        char            currtable[20];
        char            currcolumn[20];
        char            currattrib[50];
        char            currindex[20];
        char            currindextable[20];
        char            curridxspec[255];
        char            buf[255], *bufptr, *ptr2;
        int             b_intable;
        int             b_unique;
        int             linecnt;
        FILE*           fileptr;

        if((fileptr = fopen(fname, "r")) == NULL)
        {
            fprintf(stderr, "Error opening file: %s\n", fname);
            exit(-3);
        }

        /* parse table */
        b_intable = FALSE;
        linecnt = 0;
        while(fgets(buf, 254, fileptr) != NULL)
        {
            linecnt++;

            if(!b_intable)
```

```c
{
    /* look for 'create table' */
    if((bufptr = get_token(buf, "create table")) != NULL)
    {
        bufptr += strlen("create table");
        memset(currtable, '\0', 1);
        if((bufptr = get_name(bufptr)) == NULL)
        {
          fprintf(stderr, "[%s.%d] Error: missing table name.\n",
                  fname, linecnt);
            exit(-4);
        }
        else
            strcpy(currtable, bufptr);
        if(fgets(buf, 254, fileptr) != NULL)
        {
            linecnt++;
            if((bufptr = get_token(buf, "(")) != NULL)
                b_intable = TRUE;
            else
            {
              fprintf(stderr, "[%s.%d] Error: Missing '('.\n",
                      fname, linecnt);
                exit(-5);
            }
        }
        else
        {
            fprintf(stderr,
          "[%s] End of file reached looking for '('.\n", fname);
            exit(-6);
        }
    } /* end if get_token("create table") */
}
else /* if (!b_intable) */
{
    /* check for end of table definition */
    if((bufptr = get_token(buf, ");")) != NULL)
    {
```

```c
            b_intable = FALSE;
            strcpy(buf, "\n");
        }
        else
        {

            /* get column name */
            bufptr = buf;
            memset(currcolumn, '\0', 1);
            if((bufptr = get_name(bufptr)) == NULL)
            {
              fprintf(stderr, "[%s.%d] Error: missing column name.\n",
                    fname, linecnt);
                exit(-7);
            }
            else
                strcpy(currcolumn, bufptr);
            bufptr += strlen(currcolumn) + 1;


            /* get attribute */
            while(isspace(*bufptr))
                bufptr++;
            strcpy(currattrib, bufptr);
            bufptr = currattrib;
            while(isprint(*bufptr))
                bufptr++;
            *bufptr = '\0';
            if(!strlen(currattrib))
            {
                fprintf(stderr,
                    "[%s.%d] Error: missing column attribute.\n",
                    fname, linecnt);
                exit(-8);
            }
            bufptr = currattrib + strlen(currattrib) - 1;
            if (*bufptr == ',')
                *bufptr = '\0';
```

```
                (*actionfunc)(currtable, currcolumn, currattrib);

    } /* if((bufptr = get_token(buf, ");")) != NULL) */


} /* end if (!b_intable) */


if(!b_intable)
{
    if((bufptr = get_token(buf, "create index")) != NULL ||
        (bufptr = get_token(buf, "create unique index")) != NULL)
    {
        if (!strncmp(bufptr, "create unique index",
            strlen("create unique index")))
        {
            bufptr += strlen("create unique index");
            b_unique = TRUE;
        }
        else
        {
            bufptr += strlen("create index");
            b_unique = FALSE;
        }

        if ((bufptr = get_name(bufptr)) == NULL)
        {
        fprintf(stderr, "[%s.%d] Error: missing index name.\n",
                fname, linecnt);
            exit(-9);
        }
        else
        {
            strcpy(currindex, bufptr);
            bufptr += strlen(currindex) + 1;
        }

        if ((bufptr = get_token(bufptr, "on")) == NULL)
        {
          fprintf(stderr, "[%s.%d] Error: missing 'on' keyword.\n",
                    fname, linecnt);
```

```c
            exit(-10);

        }
        else
            bufptr += strlen("on") + 1;



        /* Get index table name */
        if((bufptr = get_name(bufptr)) == NULL)
        {
            fprintf(stderr, "[%s.%d] Error: missing table name.\n",
                fname, linecnt);
            exit(-11);
        }
        else
        {
            strcpy(currindextable, bufptr);
            bufptr += strlen(currindextable) + 1;
        }

        /* Get index specifier */
        ptr2 = curridxspec;
        while (*bufptr)
        {
            while (isspace(*bufptr))
                bufptr++;
            while (!isspace(*bufptr) && *bufptr)
                *ptr2++ = *bufptr++;
        }
        *ptr2 = '\0';

        /* is this line terminated */
        if (*(ptr2 - 2) != ')' && *(ptr2 - 1) != ';')
        {
        if (fgets(buf, 254, fileptr) == NULL)
        {
        fprintf(stderr,
        "[%s] End of file reached in create index.\n",
                        fname);
```

```c
                    exit(-12);
                }
                bufptr = buf;

                while (*bufptr)
                {
                    while (isspace(*bufptr))
                        bufptr++;
                    while (!isspace(*bufptr) && *bufptr)
                        *ptr2++ = *bufptr++;
                }
                *ptr2 = '\0';
            }

            (*indexfunc)(currindex, currindextable, curridxspec,
                b_unique);


    } /* end if ((bufptr = get_token(buf, "create index")) != NULL) */

    } /* end if (check for create index) */

    } /* end while(fgets "fileptr" */

    if(b_intable)
    {
        fprintf(stderr, "[%s] End of file reached looking for
');'.\n",
            fname);
        exit(-13);
    }

}


/***********************************************************************
GET_TOKEN
*********************************************************************/
char* get_token(buf, token)
```

```c
char *buf;
char *token;
{
     char first = *token;
     char *chrpos;
     int  i, len;

     chrpos = buf;

     while((chrpos = strchr(chrpos, (int) first)) != NULL)
     {
         if(!strncmp(chrpos, token, strlen(token)))
             return chrpos;
         chrpos++;
     }
     return NULL;

}


/***********************************************************************
GET_NAME
***********************************************************************/
char* get_name(buf)
char* buf;
{
     char *retbuf, *ptr2;

     while(isspace(*buf))
         buf++;

     if(*buf == '"')
     {
         while(*buf != '.')
             buf++;
         buf++;
     }

     retbuf = buf;
```

```c
    if(isalpha(*buf))
    {
        while(isalnum(*buf) || *buf == '_')
            buf++;

        if (!isspace(*buf))
            for (ptr2 = buf + strlen(buf) + 1; ptr2 > buf; ptr2--)
                *ptr2 = *(ptr2 - 1);

        *buf = '\0';
        return retbuf;
    }
    else
        return NULL;

}


/******************************************************************
ADDLIST
******************************************************************/
void addlist(table, column, attrib)
char *table, *column, *attrib;
{
    strcpy(orglist[orglistend].tabname, table);
    strcpy(orglist[orglistend].colname, column);
    strcpy(orglist[orglistend].attrib, attrib);
    orglist[orglistend].b_drop = TRUE;
    orglistend++;

}


/******************************************************************
ADDIDXLIST
******************************************************************/
void addidxlist(idxname, idxtable, idxspec, b_unique)
char *idxname, *idxtable, *idxspec;
int b_unique;
{
    strcpy(idxlist[idxlistend].idxname, idxname);
```

```c
        strcpy(idxlist[idxlistend].idxtable, idxtable);
        strcpy(idxlist[idxlistend].idxspec, idxspec);
        idxlist[idxlistend].b_unique = b_unique;
        idxlist[idxlistend].b_drop = TRUE;
        idxlistend++;


}


/************************************************************************
GENDIFF
************************************************************************/
void gendiff(table, column, attrib)
char *table, *column, *attrib;
{
        static int          colpos = 0;
        static char         currtable[20];
        static int          b_create = FALSE;
        static int          b_alter = FALSE;
        static int          b_terminate = FALSE;
        int                 fndpos;


        if (strcmp(currtable, table))
        {
            /* lookahead for drop columns */
            if(colpos >= 0 && !strcmp(orglist[colpos].tabname, currtable)
                && !b_alter && orglistend > 0)
             {
             outptr += sprintf(outptr, "alter table %s\n", currtable);
             b_terminate = TRUE;
             }


            b_alter = FALSE;


            coldrops(currtable);


            strcpy(currtable, table);


            if(b_terminate)
            {
```

```c
            different();

            if(b_create)
                printf("\n   );\n\n");
            else
            {
                outptr -= 2;
                outptr += sprintf(outptr, ";\n\n");
                printf("%s", outbuf);
                outptr = outbuf;
            }
            b_terminate = FALSE;
        }


        if ((colpos = findtable(table)) == -1 && table != NULL)
        {
            different();
            b_create = TRUE;
            printf("create table %s\n", table);
            printf("   (\n");
            printf("      %s %s", column, attrib);
            b_terminate = TRUE;
        }
        else
            b_create = FALSE;

    }
    else
    {
        if (b_create)
        {
            printf(",\n      %s %s", column, attrib);
            b_terminate = TRUE;
        }
    }
}

/* alter table mode */
if (colpos != -1 && column != NULL)
```

```
{

    if (strcmp(orglist[colpos].colname, column) ||
        strcmp(orglist[colpos].attrib, attrib))
    {
        if(!b_alter)
        {
            b_alter = TRUE;
            outptr += sprintf(outptr, "alter table %s\n", table);
            b_terminate = TRUE;
        }



        if (strcmp(orglist[colpos].colname, column))
        {
            if ((fndpos = findentry(table, column)) == -1)
            {
                if (strcmp(orglist[colpos].tabname, table))
            outptr += sprintf(outptr, "  add (%s %s),\n", column,
                        attrib);
                else
        outptr += sprintf(outptr, "  add (%s %s before %s),\n",
                        column, attrib, orglist[colpos].colname);
            }
            else
            {
                /* skip over drop columns */
                colpos = fndpos + 1;
                orglist[fndpos].b_drop = FALSE;
            }
        }
        else
        {
        outptr += sprintf(outptr, "  modify (%s %s),\n", column, attrib);

            orglist[colpos].b_drop = FALSE;
            colpos++;
        }
```

```
            }
        else
        {
            orglist[colpos].b_drop = FALSE;
            colpos++;
        }

    } /* end if (strncmp(currtable, table, strlen(table))) */


}


/**************************************************************
GENIDXDIFF
**************************************************************/
void genidxdiff(index, idxtable, idxspec, b_unique)
char *index, *idxtable, *idxspec;
int b_unique;
{
    int fndpos;

    /* make sure all line termination has been done for table processing */
    gendiff(NULL, NULL, NULL);

    if ((fndpos = findindex(index)) != -1)
    {
        idxlist[fndpos].b_drop = FALSE;
        if (strcmp(idxlist[fndpos].idxspec, idxspec) ||
            idxlist[fndpos].b_unique != b_unique)
        {
            different();
            printf("drop index %s;\n", index);
            if(b_unique)
             printf("create unique index %s on %s %s\n\n", index, idxtable,
                    idxspec);
            else
                printf("create index %s on %s %s\n\n", index, idxtable,
                    idxspec);
        }
```

```c
        }
        else
        {
            different();
            if(b_unique)
                printf("create unique index %s on %s %s\n\n", index, idxtable,
                    idxspec);
            else
                printf("create index %s on %s %s\n\n", index, idxtable,
                    idxspec);
        }
}


/****************************************************************************
COLDROPS
****************************************************************************/
void coldrops(table)
char *table;
{
    int     listcnt;

    if ((listcnt = findtable(table)) != -1)
    {
        while (listcnt < orglistend && !strcmp(orglist[listcnt].tabname,
            table))
        {
            if (orglist[listcnt].b_drop)
            {
                outptr += sprintf(outptr, "  drop (%s),\n",
                    orglist[listcnt].colname);
            }
            listcnt++;
        }
    }
}


/****************************************************************************
TABDROPS
****************************************************************************/
```

```c
void tabdrops()
{
    int        listcnt, b_dropall, fndpos;
    char currtable[20];

    memset(currtable, '\0', 1);

 /* Add a dummy entry in case last table in list needs to be dropped */
    addlist("XXX", "XXX", "XXX");
    for (listcnt = 0; listcnt < orglistend; listcnt++)
    {
        if (strcmp(orglist[listcnt].tabname, currtable))
        {
            if (strlen(currtable))
            {
                if (b_dropall)
                {
                    different();
                    printf("drop table %s;\n\n", currtable);
                    /* Cancel index drops for this table */
                    fndpos = -1;
                    while ((fndpos = find_table_index(currtable,
                        fndpos + 1)) != -1)
                        idxlist[fndpos].b_drop = FALSE;
                }
            }
            b_dropall = TRUE;
            strcpy(currtable, orglist[listcnt].tabname);
        }

        if (!orglist[listcnt].b_drop && b_dropall)
            b_dropall = FALSE;
    }
}


/*****************************************************************************
IDXDROPS
*****************************************************************************/
void idxdrops()
```

```c
{
    int        listcnt;


    for (listcnt = 0; listcnt < idxlistend; listcnt++)
    {
        if (idxlist[listcnt].b_drop)
        {
            different();
            printf("drop index %s;\n\n", idxlist[listcnt].idxname);
        }
    }
}


/*****************************************************************************
FINDENTRY
*****************************************************************************/
int findentry(table, column)
char *table, *column;
{
    int  i;

    for (i = 0; i < orglistend; i++)
        if (!strcmp(orglist[i].tabname, table) &&
            !strcmp(orglist[i].colname, column))
            return i;

    return -1;

}


/*****************************************************************************
FINDTABLE
*****************************************************************************/
int findtable(table)
char *table;
{
    int  i;
```

```c
    for (i = 0; i < orglistend; i++)
        if (!strcmp(orglist[i].tabname, table))
            return i;

    return -1;

}


/*****************************************************************
FINDINDEX
*****************************************************************/
int  findindex(index)
char *index;
{
    int  i;

    for (i = 0; i < idxlistend; i++)
        if (!strcmp(idxlist[i].idxname, index))
            return i;

    return -1;

}


/*****************************************************************
FIND_TABLE_INDEX(table, startpos)
*****************************************************************/
int find_table_index(table, startpos)
char *table;
int startpos;
{
    int  i;

    for (i = startpos; i < idxlistend; i++)
        if (!strcmp(idxlist[i].idxtable, table))
            return i;

    return -1;
```

```
}

/*****************************************************************
DIFFERENT
*****************************************************************/
void different()
{

    if(!b_different)
    {
        b_different = TRUE;
        printf("{ SCHEMADIFF Version 1.0 - Guy A. Molinari }\n");
        printf("{ Copyright(c) 1995, All Rights Reserved }\n\n");
    }


}
```

Conclusion

Once the generated script has been applied to the target database, run the INFORMIX dbschema utility and direct this output to a file. SCHEMADIFF will check this file against the target schema script to identify any remaining differences.

SCHEMADIFF is used primarily to manage large deployments involving hundreds of systems which run the same application. It provides an easy method to distribute updates to application programs when database changes are made. Even if the reader does not deploy applications in this fashion, this utility can be used in a number of other ways. Some developers like to maintain a separate copy of an application for testing and deployment, while another version is used for work-in-process. SCHEMADIFF can ease the process of updating the test application.

There is an excellent article in *Informix Tech Notes,* Volume 3, Number 4, 1993, that describes an elegant method of using the UNIX "make" utility to trigger the recompilation of INFORMIX-4GL sources when table changes occur. This technique involves storing separate "create table" DDL scripts for each table checked into Source Code Control System (SCCS). This method has the unfortunate down side of creating more files that need to be maintained. If a copy of the database schema from a prior stable version of a project was instead compared with the current output of dbchema, the resulting output could be searched with the UNIX "grep" utility to determine if a particular table was modified. This technique is especially helpful if the project involves a large number of tables and/or programs.

About the Author

Guy A. Molinari is a senior software engineer at InfoSoft, Inc., Seattle, Washington.

About InfoSoft, Inc.

InfoSoft, Inc. is a software development and consulting organization whose core expertise is focused on INFORMIX-OnLine Dynamic Server and INFORMIX-New Era. InfoSoft concentrates on turn-key development, and the migration and porting of unique business-critical applications. Based in the Silicon Valley—with additional offices in Kansas City and Seattle—InfoSoft's customers include Hewlett-Packard, Sun Microsystems, Silicon Graphics, KPMG–Peat Marwick, and others. For more information, please contact Martyn Crew, Vice President of Sales and Marketing at 408 366 9710, or visit InfoSoft's web site at the following location: http://www.infosoft.com.

## 22

SCRIPT WHICH FREES SHARED MEMORY SEGMENTS IN INFORMIX-ONLINE DYNAMIC SERVER

by Gary D. Cherneski

Introduction

The script provided in this article identifies the *oninit pids* which are associated with a particular OnLine instance. The script then populates an executable "kill file" to remove those pids, thus freeing the shared memory segments.

When an INFORMIX-OnLine Dynamic Server engine aborts, the shared memory segments will not clear due to active oninit pids which are associated with those segments. Since `onstat` commands are not available, the best method to find and remove the oninit pids is to trace the pids through the shared memory segments which are still active or appear with a "D" status that will not clear.

Script Which Frees Shared Memory Segments

The find_oninit_pids script polls for all shared memory segments owned by Informix using the "ipcs" command. The script then prompts the user to select an instance by SERVERNUM, and traverses the associated pid structure to locate all oninit processes. When the processes are found, a file is created which contains the "kill -9" command, followed by the pids. The script outputs to the user the location of the "kill file." The created file has 700 permissions and must be executed to remove the pids.

Lastly, this script reports to the user all dbaccess, onmonitor, and oncheck processes on the system. Since these are separate processes, which could prevent the instance from clearing, and because it is not possible to associate those processes with a specific instance, it is necessary to manually determine their connection.

Script Syntax

The syntax for the script described in this article is as follows:

```
find_oninit_pids
```

Requirements

This script is a korn shell script and must be run as user Informix. The script requires the use of the following: ksh, awk, and nawk.

When copying the script, ensure that no white space appears after the |\ characters.

The find_oninit_pids Script

Following is the find_oninit_pids script.

```
####################################################################################
#!/bin/ksh


# Written by Gary D. Cherneski   18 May 1995


# Problem Description:
# When an OnLine DSA engine aborts, the shared memory segments will not
# clear due to active pids that are associated with those segments.
# Because the onstat commands are not available, the best way to find
# and remove the oninit pids is by tracing them through the shared
# memory segments that are still active or with a "D" status that will
# not clear. This can be a sizable and time consuming task.
```

```
# Script Description:
# This script will poll for all shared memory segments owned by Informix
# and prompt the user to select an instance. The script will then traverse
# the associated pid structure to find all of the oninit processes. Once it
# finds the processes, a file will be created that has the kill -9 command
# followed by the pids. The file created will have 700 permissions and must
# be executed to remove the pids. Lastly this script will report to the user
# all dbaccess, onmonitor, and oncheck processes on the system.  Since these
# are separate processes that could prevent the instance from clearing and
# because there is no way of associating those processes with a specific
# instance, it will be necessary to manually determine their connection.

# Notes:
# This tool should be run as user informix.
# This tool has been tested on a Sun Microsystems system running Solaris 5.4
# and Informix 7.10.

# Requirements: ksh, awk, and nawk

# Hints for copying script:
# make sure there is no white space after the |\

# Design:
#      *get parsed data
#           *determine row size
#           *convert hex number of ipcs KEY
#      *which instance
#           *output to user instance numbers to choose from and get reply
#      *get associated pids
#          *trace through three levels of pid structures defining only oninit
#             processes and their pids.
#           *create file that contains a "kill -9" followed by the pid.
#            *output to user location and name of file
#      *display other processes
#           *display to user dbaccess, onmonitor, and oncheck processes

# Conclusion:
# Only the first three levels of pids are checked.  This should be more
```

```
# than sufficient for most OnLine instances.  This script will also
# come in handy when running multiple instances on one box and an
# individual instance goes down. The script can be altered to have
# automatic execution of the kill -9. It was designed to go to a file to
# give the user one last chance before killing the oninit pids.
################################################################

# Function will prompt the user to press enter to continue

function pause_return
{
    REPLY=""
    print -n "Please press ENTER to continue —> "
    read $REPLY
} # end function pause_return


################################################################

# This function will get the hex shared memory address and the pid of the creator of
# that shared memory address process

function get_parsed_data
{
    ipcs -ma|\
    grep informix|\
    awk '{if ( NF = = 14 )   # if NATTCH and SEGSZ run together (large
SEGSZ)
                {print $3"x"$10}
            else {if ( NF = = 15 )
                    {print $3"x"$11}}}'|\
    awk '{FS="x"} {printf ("%.4s %d\n",$2, $3)}'|\
    awk '{
            total=0
            converted_subtractor=21078   # 0x5256 in decimal
            determinate=length($1)    # length of hex part of sh mem address
            original_address=$1
            creators_pid=$2

            # map hex numbers to decimal prior to conversion
```

```
        for ( i=1; i<=determinate; i=i+1 )
        {
            num=substr(original_address,i,1)
            if ( num == "a" ) { hex_no=10 }
            if ( num == "b" ) { hex_no=11 }
            if ( num == "c" ) { hex_no=12 }
            if ( num == "d" ) { hex_no=13 }
            if ( num == "e" ) { hex_no=14 }
            if ( num == "f" ) { hex_no=15 }
            if ( num ~/[0-9]/ ) { hex_no=num }

            # Perform hex to decimal conversion
            if ( i == 1 ) {
                total=(total + ( hex_no * 16 )) }
            else {
                    if ( i !=  determinate )
                        total=(( total + hex_no )*16)
                    else total=(total + hex_no) }
        } instance_no = total - converted_subtractor
          print instance_no"|0x"original_address"4808|"creators_pid
        | awk'!/^-/{print $0}' >> $
} # end function get_parsed_data


#################################################################################
# This function will get all of the associated pids to a specific shared memory
# segment

function get_associated_pids
{
    killfile=/tmp/$$killfile
    >$killfile
    nawk '{FS="|"}{
        if ($1 = = '$ans')
            { system ("ps -ef|egrep "$3" ")}
        }' $outfile|\
    nawk ' /oninit/ {print $2"\n"$3} # get only oninit processes'|\
    sort -u -r|\
    nawk '{ pid[NR] = $0 }    # read into array
        END {if (pid[NR] = = 1) {NR=NR-1}  # delete pid of 1 from kill list
```

```
                     {for (i = NR; i > 0; i—)      # dump level 2 pids to array
                        {system ("ps -ef|egrep "pid[i]"|egrep -v grep")}}}'|\
nawk ' /oninit/ {print $2"\n"$3} # get only oninit processes'|\
sort -u -r|\
nawk '{ pid[NR] = $0 }     # read into array
      END  {if (pid[NR] = = 1) {NR=NR-1}     # delete pid of 1 from kill list
              {for ( i = NR; i > 0; i—)       # dump level 3 pids to array
                 {system ("ps -ef|egrep "pid[i]"|egrep -v grep")}}}'|\
nawk ' /oninit/ {print $2"\n"$3} # get only oninit processes'|\
sort -u -r|\
nawk '{ pid[NR] = $0 }
        END  {if (pid[NR] = = 1) {NR=NR-1} # delete pid of 1 from kill list
          {for ( i = NR; i > 0; i—) print "kill -9 "pid[i] }}' > $killfile


chmod 700 $killfile
clear
print "\n\nThe file containing all of the pids to kill for instance $ans is"
print "$killfile. Execute this file and the pids will be killed.\n\n"
pause_return
} # end function get_associated_pids


############################################################################


# Function to prompt the user to select an instance

function which_instance
{
    REPLY=""
    clear
    print "\nWhich instance do you want to clean up...\n"
    awk '{FS="|"}{printf ("%10s\n",$1)}' $outfile
    print -n "\nYour selection please —> "
    read $REPLY
    ans=$REPLY
    print "\nThis process may take a while depending on the number of pids"
    print "associated with the shared memory segment...\n"
    return $ans
```

```
} # end function which_instance

#####################################################################

# Function will display any oncheck, dbaccess, and onmonitor processes since
# they cannot be tied back to a specific instance.

function display_other_processes
{
    clear
    print "\nChecking for other processes (onmonitor,oncheck,dbaccess)...\n\n"
    ps -ef|awk ' /onmonitor/ /dbaccess/ /oncheck/ {print $0}'|grep -v awk
    print "\n\nIf your shared memory segment will not clear, check these process-
es.\n\n"
} # end function display_other_processes

#####################################################################

# main

# declarations
outfile=/tmp/$$awkfile
export OPEN_MAX=10      # maximum number of concurrent pipes allowed open

get_parsed_data $outfile
which_instance $outfile
get_associated_pids $ans $outfile
display_other_processes

# cleanup
rm $outfile
```

<u>Conclusion</u>

Only the first three levels of pids are checked. This suffices for most OnLine instances. This script is also useful when running multiple instances on one machine and an individual instance goes down. The script was designed to output to a file, which allows the user to deliberate before killing the oninit pids.

About the Author

Gary D. Cherneski is a database administrator at the Arrowhead Consulting Company in Englewood, Colorado. He is currently contracted to MCI in Colorado Springs, Colorado, to work on MCI's data warehouse. Gary is also a member of the Informix User Group of Colorado board of directors.

=23

SOLID-STATE DISK: A SOLUTION TO I/O BOTTLENECKS

by Peter S. Simcox

Introduction

The intent of this article is to describe the advantages of solid-state disk (SSD) technology, and how it may be used to solve INFORMIX-OnLine I/O bottlenecks.

Historically, the SSD has been viewed as a small, optional layer in the hierachical storage management (HSM) pyramid, see Figure 1. The META Group [R1],* recommends that SSD be considered as a high-performance tool in UNIX server RDBMS environments by users who seek ultra-fast OLTP and DSS performance. SSD can fill the growing performance gap between CPUs and I/O subsystems. Fast RISC processors and large-scale SMP configurations are outpacing the speed improvements in magnetic storage subsystems by a factor of 4-to-1. This discrepancy, coupled with the immaturity of integrated HSM subsystems and the relatively small caches available for magnetic disks, provides for several strategic uses of SSD technology with INFORMIX-OnLine Dynamic Server. These uses will be discussed in this article.

Notations such as [R1] through [R7], and [V1] through [V3], refer to the "References" and "Vendor References" sections, respectively, at the end of this article.

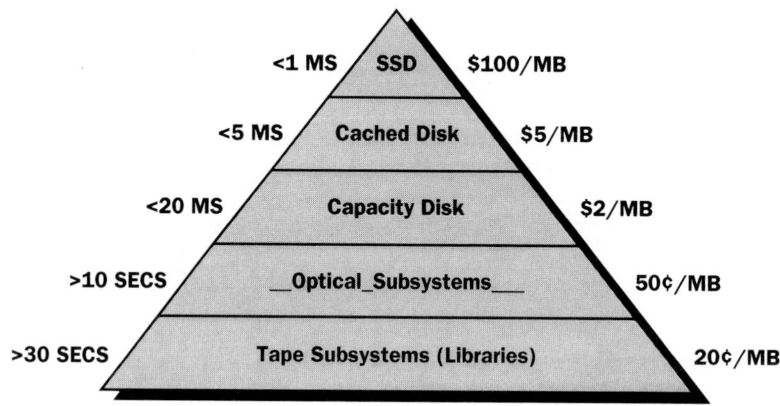

Figure 1: The Hierarchical Storage Pyramid. Source: META Group, Inc. [R1].*

Overview

This article covers the following topics:

- What is Solid-State Disk (SSD)?

- SSD vs Magnetic Media

- Why use SSD?

- Using SSD for Logging

- Using SSD for Temporary Storage

- Using SSD for "Hot" Tables and Indexes

- Using SSD for UNIX System Device(s)

- SSD Flexibility

- SSD Reliability

- A Case Study: Aromat Corporation

- Configuring DES SSDs on HP/UX

- Database Exceleration Systems (DES) Solid-State Disks

- Imperial Technology—MEGARAM Solid-State Disk Storage Systems

- Avastor (Digital) Solid-State Disks

- SSD Pricing

- Conclusions

What is Solid-State Disk (SSD)?

Solid-State Disk (SSD) is memory based disk storage that, for all practical purposes, looks to the computer exactly like a magnetic storage device, i.e., a disk. Dynamic Random Access Memory (DRAM) chips and ultra-fast semiconductors are used to store data while the system is powered on. DRAM increases data access and eliminates I/O bottlenecks.

An SSD has sectors on it and performs essentially all the functions of a traditional disk drive. An SSD is therefore, in effect, a memory device that communicates with a host computer via a disk interface. SSDs typically plug into a computer's I/O controller SCSI interface. No special operating system drivers are required when using the ANSI-standard SCSI interface.

SSD emulators are either "volatile" or "non-volatile." Non-volatile SSDs retain data when the system is powered off. While DRAM alone is volatile, SSDs designed with an integrated backup system provide for non-volatile storage devices. When power is lost, the backup system guarantees that no data is lost. Availability is also provided through multiple SCSI interfaces for device sharing and failover.

SSD versus Magnetic Media

Most of the UNIX systems on which Informix servers run today use the SCSI interface for disk I/O. SCSI performance has improved with new implementations of the standard: SCSI-1, SCSI-2, FAST & WIDE SCSI-2. While other connectivity protocols are supported by SSD vendors, including DSSI, SDI, and SMD, this article will focus on SCSI.

Disk performance can also be improved by using a larger number of smaller spindles, and by improving the aggregate I/O per spindle through data striping. Striping is a method of data distribution, through which data can be evenly distributed across a number of physical devices, which collectively constitute a logical device.

Striping is implemented in a number of ways. Redundant Arrays of Inexpensive Disks (RAID) technology supports several RAID levels which perform hardware disk striping. For more information on RAID levels, refer to the article entitled "Implementing High Availability Informix Solutions with UNIX," in *Informix Tech Notes*, Volume 5, Issue 1, 1995. UNIX operating system (OS) implementations support software striping through logical and virtual disk management subsystems.

INFORMIX-OnLine provides limited data striping by locating dbspace chunks on different physical devices. This mechanism allows a dbspace to span multiple disks, but is far less granular compared to the hardware and OS software techniques. INFORMIX-OnLine Dynamic Server, beginning in version 7.0, supports table partitioning, also referred to as *table fragmentation* [R6]*. This horizontal partitioning provides for table row level striping, a significantly finer level of granularity compared to all other techniques.

Magnetic disks are limited to about 50 small block I/Os per second. Boak [R3]* quotes a 20-disk farm with an aggregate I/O rate of about 800 I/Os per second using striping. Cached disks rely on high read-to-write and cache-hit ratios for performance. Although cache improves disk subsystem write performance, especially for write-intensive RAID5, SSD systems deliver 100 percent hit ratios and are especially well-suited for write-intensive applications.

According to Boak [R3]*, SSD performs both reads and writes at memory speeds, over the whole disk, regardless of data locale. Using a powerful controller, SSDs can match the controller at more than 2,500 I/Os per second for small block I/O, including operating system overhead. They are also faster at sequential I/O, transferring data at 20 MB per second, limited only by channel bandwidth and operating system overhead. This performance is achieved independent of the amount of CPU or controller cache available, and independent of the locality of the data. The best numbers are the same as the worst numbers. Access times are virtually constant for reads and writes.

Why Use SSD?

CPU performance gains have far exceeded those of magnetic disk. A CPU can execute over 100,000 instructions in the time required for a single magnetic disk I/O. The growing discrepancy between CPU and magnetic disk performance results in I/O bottlenecks which severely impact system performance. Data partitioning, available with INFORMIX-OnLine Dynamic Server, version 7.0 and later, is the great enabler for parallel execution, providing the mechanism through which data can be scanned in parallel. This is of particular value when the percentage of data being accessed is high.

However, all data is not created equal under all processing environments, and must be managed accordingly. Storage options must be configured to match the performance, capacity, and cost requirements of the application environment. Simply adding more spindles to the traditional disk farm may not solve the storage performance dilemma, even with data partitioning.

Using the appropriate mix of storage devices will assure the right data is in the right place, at the right time, for the right price. This becomes even more important with the integration of Hierarchical Storage Management (HSM) systems with INFORMIX-OnLine Dynamic Server. In some application environments, it is common to find a small percentage of the data receiving a large percentage of the I/O requests, see Figure 2. In OnLine OLTP environments, this could be log space, temporary space, or a number of very active "hot" tables and/or indexes. This is potentially a good technology fit for SSDs and INFORMIX-OnLine Dynamic Server.

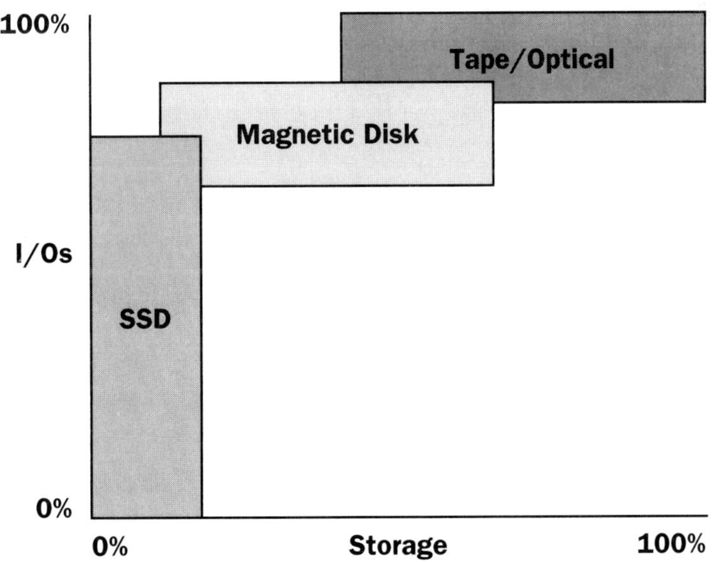

Figure 2: Why buy SSD?—I/Os versus storage. Source: DES [V1], 1993.*

Using SSD for Logging

INFORMIX-OnLine Dynamic Server (OnLine Dynamic Server) employs a physical log to store before-image copies of pages modified in the shared memory buffer cache, and logical logs to store transaction records (i.e., transaction logs). Both types of logs can be very I/O intensive in dynamic OLTP environments. Under most circumstances, this is primarily write activity, as the logs are only read intensively during fast recovery and restore.

Both logs are buffered, i.e., writes to a log are buffered in a shared memory cache before being written out to the log. The extent of the log buffering is dependent upon the buffer(s) size, shared memory page buffer cache flushing, and checkpointing. Logical log buffers are also flushed when a transaction is committed within a database that uses unbuffered logging. Because all write activity is by definition written to the end of a log buffer, there is no benefit to striping the disks—no matter how many devices are available. OnLine Dynamic Server always writes to only one device per log type at any one time, namely, the disk holding the current log.

Granted, if the stripe granularity is very fine, say several kilobytes, and the log size(s) are very large (greater than several kilobytes), then a log write could result in concurrent physical writes to multiple devices, depending on the striping technology employed. RAID solutions provide for such fine granularity of striping at the hardware level [R5]*. Further, RAID level 3 allows for parallelized physical writes for a single I/O. A single n-block log flush [= single write] results in n/m-block parallelized writes to m devices, using a m+1 device RAID3 group. Figure 3, "RAID3 Logical to Physical Write Mapping," shows a log flush write of 8 KB to a single RAID3 logical device. This results in 2 KB [n/m] parallelized writes to five [m+1] physical devices, four [m] 2 KB data writes and one 2 KB parity write.

However, although using these striping and parallelized technologies, it is still reasonable in large systems that disk I/O access rates will reach capacity. Under a heavy system load, such logging contention can result in performance degradation as high as a factor of 20, according to Boak [R3]*. The addition of SSD for appropriate logging devices can completely eliminate this as a source of system degradation—assuming each SSD has a dedicated channel.

Using SSD for Temporary Storage

OnLine Dynamic Server uses temporary storage for tables and files. Prior to version 6.0 of OnLine Dynamic Server, files were used extensively for temporary storage. Environment variables, including $DBTEMP and $PSORT_DBTEMP, were available to specify the operating system directories used to hold these tem-

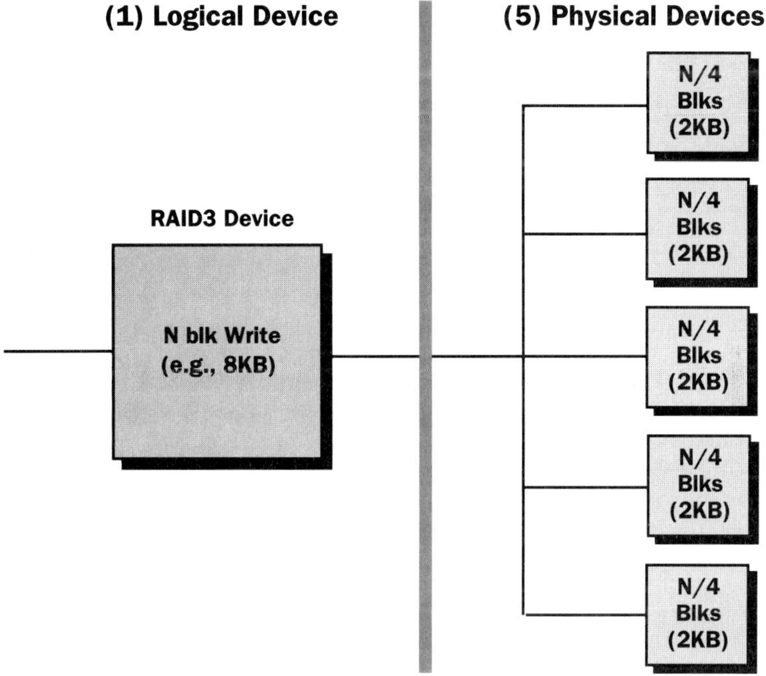

Figure 3: RAID3, logical to physical write mapping.

porary files. Temporary tables were stored implicitly in the root dbspace, and explicitly in specified dbspace(s).

With OnLine Dynamic Server, temporary files are now also held in dbspaces. The root dbspace is again used as the default. However, with OnLine Dynamic Server, multiple dbspaces can be specified for use implicitly as temporary storage. The configuration parameter, DBSPACETEMP, allows a number of dbspaces to be defined for such use system wide. The environment variable $DBSPACETEMP allows the system-wide setting to be overridden on a per-user session basis. Dbspaces can also be created explicitly for temporary storage use. Any temporary tables or files stored in a temporary dbspace are dropped whenever OnLine Dynamic Server is initialized. Logging is suppressed for temporary dbspaces.

This enables temporary data to be distributed across multiple devices, reducing I/O contention. Temporary dbspaces are chosen by OnLine Dynamic Server using a round-robin strategy. This granularity of dbspace usage, however, may still not alleviate all I/O contention under heavy temporary space usage. The use of SSD-based temporary dbspace(s) will enable such contention to be addressed. Through the use of the configuration parameter and the environment variable, specific users and/or applications can be given sole access to such SSD-based temporary dbspace(s).

Using SSD for "Hot" Tables and Indexes

In OnLine Dynamic Server application environments, it is common to find "hot" tables and/or indexes. The DBA will use a configuration strategy to attempt to keep these objects cached in shared memory. OnLine regular buffers, versus log buffers, are used to store the object dbspace pages which are read from disk.

As a general guideline, regular buffer space should range from 20 to 25 percent of physical memory [R6]*. The buffer cached read and write percentages can be improved up to a point, by tuning the number of regular buffers. However, care must be taken so as not to oversubscribe to shared memory resources, resulting in excessive operating system paging. In general, such an operation profile can only be addressed through the configuration of more physical memory.

Under circumstances where the buffer cache effectiveness is skewed by heavy access to a particular table and/or index, it is possible to alleviate the performance degradation by configuring these "hot" objects on SSD. While the cached percentages would not be improved, the throughput to these objects is greatly increased. Decision-support (DS) queries and batch-oriented report operations often fall into this category.

Beginning with OnLine Dynamic Server, version 7.0, it is possible to configure the "fragments" of a table in different dbspaces through horizontal partitioning [R7]*. SQL expressions can be used to isolate specific table and/or index subsets (partitions) within particular dbspaces. Using data partitioning, it is possible to isolate specific "hot" object subsets (partitions) on dbspaces configured on SSD. This flexibility allows the total of required SSD to be minimized, thus reducing overall cost.

Using SSD for UNIX System Device(s)

Boak [R3]* suggests that SSDs may be effective at the OS level as a system swap device when a large proportion of system activity is devoted to swapping. If a swap device is I/O bound, a swapped process will see a delay of several seconds, as process contexts are swapped. Even if the system is not swapping, heavy paging activity can lead to significant performance degradation. Both swapping and paging use CPU cycles and disk channel bandwidth.

OnLine Dynamic Server installations usually use raw devices to hold data, while buffering database pages in shared memory. More importantly, the UNIX buffer cache is not used to hold such pages. Therefore, heavy swap-device operations probably result from a very large number of processes and/or very large filesystem I/O. Both cases put a heavy demand on physical memory. The amount of memory is governed by the system architecture. Large symmetrical multiprocessor (SMP) systems can now be configured with up to 5 GB of memory. However, if a large percentage of memory is configured for OnLine shared memory use, the amount of memory available for the OS, application processes, and file I/O may be insufficient. An SSD configured as a swap device may be the answer.

In application environments where large UNIX file I/O is required, an SSD should be considered for holding OS filesystems. The performance of these applications is often governed by the throughput of the OS filesystem. While OS striping can be used to spread large files across multiple physical disks, performance is still paced by the throughput of a single device and the OS kernel filesystem layer(s), when the file is accessed sequentially. Such large files will "flood" the OS buffer cache, and may also induce paging, as discussed earlier. Enhanced UNIX versions have kernel parameters which can be used to "throttle" this behavior. However, to improve the actual I/O performance, an SSD should be considered as a filesystem device to improve performance and prevent the filesystem from pacing the application throughput.

SSD Flexibility and OnLine

SSDs can be considered as "plug-and-play." They use industry standard interfaces, primarily SCSI (SCSI-1, SCSI-2, F&W-SCSI), which allow for easy hardware installation. The SCSI software device drivers, provided with the UNIX OS, are used to access the device. The SSD simply appears as a disk to the host system.

SSDs are field upgradable for capacity changes. Memory arrays are commonly available in 64 MB and higher increments. Capacities greater to 4 GB can be configured. An SSD chassis will hold several such *memory arrays* for fast and easy upgrades. This flexibility also helps to control the cost of entry for SSD technology. Auto sizing automatically reports the new size directly to the host CPU.

A completely self-contained ANSI 19-inch rackmount chassis, the most common type of cabinet in the industry, assures ease of installation into open systems. This saves on floor space, and provides cosmetic compatibility with existing CPU and storage cabinetry.

This flexibility allows SSD technology to be easily introduced into existing environments to address OnLine I/O bottlenecks. The necessary OnLine DBA modifications—to use SSD to address logging and temporary storage disk contention—are straightforward. The additional changes necessary to locate "hot" objects requires altering the table and/or index, or reloading the table (unload/load) and rebuilding the indexes. The extent of these changes is dependent upon the size of the object and the partitioning strategy employed. Since OnLine Dynamic Server uses parallelism for all these maintenance operations, their performance has been greatly improved.

SSD Reliability and OnLine

An SSD "variable backup timer" is commonly provided for a switch-selectable backup delay. This sets the time that the SSD will operate on batteries before backup to disk. Two-and-a-half hours' battery backup is common. This also allows the SSD to remain on-line and available during short power outages, preventing nuisance backups. Custom SSD UPS power supplies feature on-line battery backup and zero-time failover.

The internal backup device provides for high-speed hard disk backup of the DRAM, using a separate SCSI port. It contains the SSD low-level format and is an exact mirror of the SSD. The device is used for automatic backup during long power failures; data is automatically restored when power returns. The backup device can also directly replace the SSD DRAM in an emergency, for maximum data availability.

This level of reliability obviously provides both integrity and availability for all OnLine Dynamic Server data objects stored in dbspaces which are configured on SSD. SSD is therefore an excellent fit for the root dbspace, for log dbspaces, and for mission-critical tables and indexes that require a high level of availability.

A Case Study: Aromat Corporation

Aromat Corporation, a division of Matsushita Electric of Japan, designs and manufactures electronic relays and distributes them throughout its North American distribution centers. In 1992, an entirely new Distribution Resource Planning (DRP) system was implemented to improve real-time processing.

The system, which manages all distribution, inventory management, and accounting/financials for North America, was designed using the Man-Trak Distribution and Manufacturing System as a base with additional decision-support features, for optimal inventory and order management. Man-Trak is developed in INFORMIX-4GL using an Informix engine. The system utilized was a Hewlett-Packard (HP) 9000/847 with more than 90 user logins.

When the system went live on January 1, 1993, I/O bottlenecks quickly developed and caused the overall system response to plummet below acceptable performance levels, according to DES [R4]*. Aromat's time-critical environment dictated that disk I/O improve by at least 400 percent. To achieve this level of performance, HP recommended upgrading to a more powerful CPU—a HP 890 Data Center system.

Informix Enterprise Consulting Services analyzed the application environment and isolated several causes for I/O contention, including: poor table distribution, poor extent sizing, large row sizes, and poor isolation-level usage. Informix also recommended a number of general optimizing techniques which were not being used in the application(s). Additional application-specific changes were recommended to remove redundant processes and temporary tables which were explicitly locked by each instance of the application.

The decision-support reports were the main culprits. Much of the I/O bottleneck was traced to the exceedingly large row sizes on many of the highly utilized tables. In extreme cases, only two rows were allocated per page. Informix recommended schema modifications to split these tables along functional lines, to localize frequently used columns in smaller table(s). These changes would also require application changes.

Due to the time and cost involved in redesigning the schema and application(s), Aromat and the developers of the Man-Trak DRP system chose to use an SSD from Database Exceleration Systems (DES) to address I/O performance. After installing the SSD emulator on the system and moving some of the "hot" files onto the disk, a 750 percent performance increase was realized. The addition of the SSD reduced Aromat's 5-hour (300 minute) packing-slip process to 40 minutes.

Aromat's decision to use the SSD saved them the cost of CPU upgrading, or redesigning the database schema and application(s).

Configuring DES SSDs on HP/UX

A 128 MB DES 800S from Database Exceleration Systems was installed at Aromat Corporation on a 9000/847 running HP-UX release A.08.02. Aromat was running INFORMIX-OnLine, version 4.10.UG1. DES provided the necessary "/etc/disktab" entry for a 128 MB unit: DES800SDES_800S, see disktab(4). Disktab is a simple database that describes disk geometries and disk section characteristics. The DES entry included the following values:

:ty=winchester	[Type of disk (e.g., removable, winchester)]
:ns#128	[Number of sectors per track]
:nt#8	[Number of tracks per cylinder]
:nc#510	[Total number of cylinders on the disk]
:s2#261120	[Size of section <2> in sectors]
:b2#8192	[Block size for section <2> in bytes]

      :f2#1024   [Fragment size for section <2> in bytes]
      :se#512   [Sector size in bytes]
      :rm#3600   [Revolution per minute]

The HP-UX mediainit(1) command was used to verify the SSD media integrity. The SSD was configured into HP-UX as device node "/dev/[r]dsk/c8d0s2. Section 2 corresponds to a single partition for all the device, see "/etc/disktab." Two hard links were used to create device nodes "rootusa1" and "manusa5" in "/dev/rdsk." The two chunks were sized at 20000 KB and 107500 KB respectively for a total of 127500 KB. After relocating the "hot" tables to corresponding dbspaces, a large percentage of the I/O was monitored to these two chunks, see tbstat -D.

From this example installation process, it is possible to demonstrate how simple SSDs are to install. Since all leading UNIX platforms employ SCSI technology, with the device driver(s) included in the OS, SSDs are nearly plug-and-play.

Database Exceleration Systems (DES) Solid-State Disks

Database Exceleration Systems (DES), formerly Disk Emulation Systems, is an Informix partner based in Santa Clara, California—see [V1] for contact information. DES Solid-State Disks are supported on SCSI, SCSI-2, and F&W SCSI-2 interfaces. All SCSI (F&W) hosts are supported including: Data General, DEC, Hewlett-Packard, IBM, Silicon Graphics, and Sun Microsystems.

Key Specifications and Features:

Performance: (SCSI-2 F&W)

- 18 microsecond average access time
- Seek Time: 0
- Latency: 0
- 17,900 I/Os per second
- 20 megabyte/second data rate (synchronous)

Configurability:

- Uses OEM software drivers
- Field upgradable for capacity changes
- Memory arrays available in 134 and 268 megabyte increments
    —536 megabyte increments are also available

- A cabinet can hold from 1 to 16 arrays (134 MB to 4.2 GB capacity)
- Auto sizing automatically reports new size to host CPU
- Self-contained rackmount chassis
    - —Full ANSI spcc. 5.25" 19" chassis

Reliability:

- Switch-selectable backup delay
    - —SSD remains on-line during short power outages
- Custom SSD UPS power supply
    - —Zero-time failover to battery backup
- High-speed hard disk backup
- Automatic backup during long power failures
- Automatic restore when power returns
- Manual initiation of backup and restore is keylock enabled
- 2.5 hours battery backup
    - —Dual internal batteries support DC power supply
- RS232 diagnostic port

Imperial Technology—
MEGARAM Solid-State Disk Storage Systems

Imperial Technology is an Informix InSync partner based in El Segundo, California—see [V2]* for contact information. MEGARAM Solid-State Disk Storage Systems are supported on SCSI and SCSI-2 Fast & Wide interfaces.

Key Specifications and Features:

Performance: (SCSI-2 F&W)

- Transfer rate up to 20 megabytes per second
- Access time less than 35 microseconds

Configurability:

- Available in 8-inch, 5-1/4 inch, and 3-1/2 inch form factors
- Storage capacity ranges from 64 MB to 3 GB
- Configurable with four SCSI interface controllers
    - —Multi-porting for simultaneous data access
- No special drivers or software changes to incorporate

Reliability:

- Internal battery backup for temporary power loss
- Internal disk backup module for extended power interruptions
- Automatic data restore on power restoration
- Operator initiated backups and restores
- 1,500,000 hours MTBF for a 200 MB storage module
- RS232 port-service adapter

Imperial Technology also markets their technology as a "MEGACACHE" for disk arrays. The unit is dual-ported between the host system and the array, caching all I/O transfers to and from the disks in the array. The cache can be configured from 64 MB to 800 MB.

SSD Pricing

According to the META Group, SSD is currently priced at $100/MB, see Figure 1: "The Hierarchical Storage Pyramid." This compares with $5/MB for "Cached Disk," and $2/MB for "Capacity Disk." SSD is therefore 20 to 50 times more expensive than regular disk, depending on the disk technology being compared.

Memory prices are on average $150/MB for larger memory volumes. SSDs are therefore very competitively priced compared to memory, and provide many RAD Reliability, Availability, and Durability (RAD) benefits.

Conclusion

The price/performance advantages for SSD versus memory and other disk technologies must be calculated on a per installation basis. The cost of alternate hardware technologies (CPU/memory/disk), and software enhancements (database and/or application re-design) must be evaluated in each case to determine the true price/performance benefits of each option.

References

[R1] "Cache-ing out on Solid State Memory," META Group, Inc. *Open Computing & Server Strategies,* August 29, 1994.

[R2] "Solid-State Disks," Jerry Lazer, *VARBUSINESS,* August 1993.

[R3] "Data Supercharger: Improving Database Performance using Solid-State Disk," James Boak (technical director), *Migration Software*, April 6, 1994.

[R4] *Solid-State Disk Emulators increase Man-Trak's Performance By Up to 750 Percent,* Database Exceleration Systems (DES).

[R5] "Implementing High Availability INFORMIX Solutions with UNIX," Peter S. Simcox (senior consultant), Informix Software, Inc., *Informix Tech Notes,* Volume 5, Issue 1, 1995.

[R6] *INFORMIX-OnLine Dynamic Server, Administrator's Guide,* Version 6.0, December 1993.

[R7] *INFORMIX-OnLine Dynamic Server Enhancement, Guide to Version 7.0 Functionality,* Version 7.0, February 1994.

Vendor References

[V1] Database Exceleration Systems (DES), Inc.
3080 Oak Mead Village Drive
Santa Clara, CA 95051
408 727 5497

Contact: Mike Precobb, VP of Sales

[V2] Imperial Technology Inc.
2305 Utah Avenue
El Segundo, CA 90245
800 451 0666 (in North America)

Contact: John Jory, VP of Marketing and Sales

[V3] Digital Equipment Corporation

OEM Marketing: 508 841-3111
StorageWorks Resource Center: (800) 786 7967

About the Author

Peter S. Simcox is a principal engineer in the Advanced Technology Group at Informix, Somerset, New Jersey.

=24

DISK ALLOCATION FOR LARGE INFORMIX DATABASES ON HP-UX SYSTEMS

by Robert Fisher

Introduction

This article is an attempt to present information obtained while consulting with a large telecommunications company. Part of this consulting involved planning and configuring the disk space for almost a dozen large Informix database systems on Hewlett-Packard (HP) 9000 HP-UX systems. The article covers topics related to Informix storage management, the HP-UX Logical Volume Manager, and disk drives and arrays.

The trend toward increasingly larger databases is expected to continue. Data warehouses are now built to encompass vast amounts of data from within the enterprise and to make that data available for on-line analysis. In the next few years, over 90 percent of Fortune 2000 companies will develop data warehouses. In most cases, the data warehouses are used to analyze customer profiles and service data that is downloaded from legacy mainframes. Typically, initial database sizes range from 100 to 300 GB, however, the databases are usually expected to grow considerably larger. Therefore, proper disk configuration is extremely important in these types of environments—both from a capacity and performance perspective.

Besides an increase in the size of databases, the requirement for higher database availability experiences rapid growth. High-availability features—such as RAID disk arrays and mirrored disks—are also very important for systems with large configurations. System and application failover products—such as MC/ServiceGuard, QuickSwitch, and SwitchOver/UX—all rely on clearly designed logical volume configurations.

The first portion of this article provides a brief introduction to the HP-UX Logical Volume Manager (LVM) and some background on associating Informix data structures to LVM logical volumes. The HP-UX LVM has been clearly positioned as the software which will be used to allocate disk space. It provides a flexible and manageable way to control disk allocation, as will be illustrated in the remainder of this article. Some knowledge of the issues surrounding the allocation of disk space will be assumed. While most examples are based on the HP-UX 9.04 release, notations related to version 10.x of HP-UX are also included.

A Logical Volume Manager Primer

The HP-UX LVM provides many advantages over fixed partitions. HP-UX LVM enables partitions—also known as *logical volumes*—to span disk drives, thereby balancing I/O loads and allowing the maximum size of a partition to expand beyond a single disk drive. HP-UX LVM also allows up to three copies of identical data to be stored and updated simultaneously through the HP MirrorDisk/UX product. Additionally, HP-UX LVM provides the ability to dynamically expand, contract, and move logical volumes between disks. HP-UX LVM also allows for a group of disks belonging to a particular application to be exported off of one system and imported to another.

The LVM provides a way to combine one or more disks into a pool of available space, called a *volume group*. Subsequently, that pool can be subdivided into customized logical volumes to hold databases, filesystems, swap space, or any other disk data. The pooled space belonging to the volume group can be allocated without regard to the physical boundaries of each volume group's disks. Through LVM, logical volumes can be placed on specific drives; this is usually accomplished for performance reasons.

Generally, there are four principal objects to be dealt with when working with the LVM. The first objects are the disks, or *physical volumes*. Disks are converted to LVM *physical volumes* through the **pvcreate** command. This command writes LVM data structures to the beginning of the disk. Secondly, *volume groups* pool the physical volumes into a large virtual space from which the third object, *logical volumes*, are allocated. Volume groups are created and assigned a number of disks with the **vgcreate** command. Logical volumes are, in turn, created with the **lvcreate** command. Several parameters are set when a volume group is created. These parameters dictate the volume group's ability to grow within a given application. These parameters must be carefully considered before the volume group is created, since the parameters cannot be altered without rebuilding the entire volume group.

The fourth object is the *physical volume group*. This object subdivides the disks belonging to a volume group, based on hardware characteristics. Physical volume groups are configured with mirroring to assure that the space allocated to both parts of a mirrored logical volume reside across different I/O cards; this is known as *I/O channel separation*. A given volume group may contain all the disks hooked to "SCSI card A," while a second contains the disks connected to "SCSI card B." Physical volume groups are also created using the **vgcreate** or **vgextend** commands.

Volume groups and logical volumes can be extended, reduced, displayed, or certain of their characteristics can be changed. Correspondingly, the commands for volume groups are **vgextend, vgreduce, vgdisplay,** and **vgchange.** Likewise, for logical volumes, there are the **lvextend, lvreduce, lvdisplay,** and **lvchange** commands. In addition, there are commands for managing mirrors, such as **lvsync, lvsplit,** and **lvmerge.** Commands for moving volume groups to other systems, and for maintaining volume group configurations, include **vgscan, vgcfgbackup,** and **vgcfgrestore.**

The System Administration Manager (SAM) can also be used to issue LVM commands. However, with large complex configurations, it is more straightforward to create LVM scripts which become part of the system documentation. There are also some LVM features which cannot be performed using SAM—such as allocating logical volumes to a particular drive or striping a logical volume across multiple disks. Both features are essential for large database configurations.

There are basically two ways to allocate volume group space for logical volumes. The first way is to simply request space from the volume group—without regard for the physical volumes on which the volume group will reside. The space for such a logical volume is satisfied from the volume group disks in the order in which the disks were added to the volume group. This type of allocation is abstract in that the database administrator (DBA) need not be concerned about the underlying media. Physical volume groups support mirroring by providing I/O channel separation when this first type of allocation is used.

In many cases, however, it is desirable to use a second type of logical volume allocation which allows data to be placed on a particular drive—either for performance reasons or as a second method to obtain I/O channel separation when using mirroring. Logical volume placement is particularly important for a database such as INFORMIX-OnLine Dynamic Server, version 7.1, which requires I/O channel and drive separation to achieve improved response times for highly parallelized queries. The **lvextend** command, not the **lvcreate** command, provides the ability to specify a particular device within a given volume group. More details on the individual LVM commands are provided in a subsequent section of this article.

Informix and LVM

It is necessary to work with the DBA to determine all requirements before creating the logical volume layout for a given database environment. However, understanding certain key Informix terms and concepts is a necessary precursor to such a step. Note that this article does not specify the sizing of the different Informix logical structures; particulars related to sizing are left to the DBA, their spreadsheets, Informix manuals, and user requirements.

Physical Structures

The basic building blocks of Informix databases are *chunks*. Chunks are created using HP-UX logical volumes. When creating a chunk, simply specify the character logical volume device file to be contained in the logical volume.

An Informix database space or *dbspace*, is comprised of one or more chunks. A dbspace roughly performs the equivalent function of an LVM volume group. The dbspace is a logical pool of space out of which the different types of logical Informix structures—such as tables, indexes, logs, etc.—are created. When an Informix database server is first initialized, a *root dbspace* consisting of a single chunk is created. Since the maximum size of an Informix chunk is limited to 2 GB, logical volumes created for Informix databases should not exceed this limit. A character logical volume device file used by Informix should have its user and group set to Informix, and its permissions set to read/write for both the group and owner.

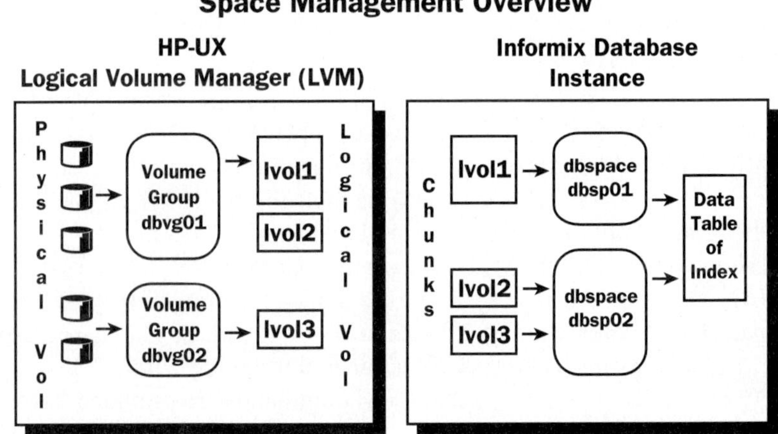

Figure 1: The Logical Volume Manager's relationship with Informix.

There are also several other Informix terms used to track the physical space of an Informix environment. Informix tables and other logical structures are allocated in terms of 2 K *pages*. Pages are allocated from dbspaces in groupings called *extents*. Tables are initially allocated a certain group of pages called the *initial extent size*, and are allowed to grow in units termed the *next extent size*. An Informix extent is always contained entirely in a given chunk and must be contiguously allocated within the chunk.

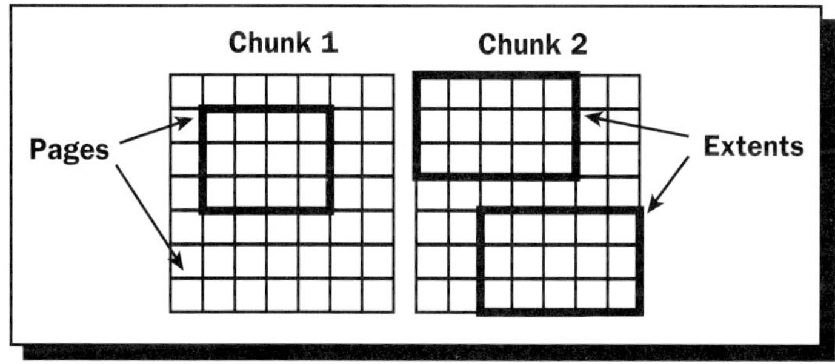

Figure 2: Informix disk space management.

The last concept associated with the allocation of Informix physical space is the *offset*. Offsets permit the subdivision of logical volumes into smaller chunks. From the perspective of the HP-UX operating system, a chunk is a stream of bytes. An offset can indicate the number of kilobytes of a logical volume which are needed to reach a given chunk. For example, suppose a 1 MB logical volume is created. The logical volume is then divided into two chunks of 500 KB each. An offset of zero can mark the beginning of the first chunk and an offset of 500 KB can mark the beginning of the second chunk. An offset can be specified whenever a dbspace is created, a chunk is added to a dbspace, or a chunk is dropped from a dbspace.

While Binary Large Objects (BLOBs), *blobpages*, and *blobspaces* are not discussed in this article, they require careful disk space allocation. For additional information, refer to the *INFORMIX-OnLine Dynamic Server Administrator's Guide*.

Logical Structures

Now that the physical aspects of allocating Informix space have been discussed, it is time to cover the logical Informix structures. The physical space is actually allocated to the logical Informix structures. The first structure is that of the

Informix instance, also referred to as the INFORMIX-OnLine Dynamic Server database server or engine. The Informix instance is the environment in which Informix databases are built. An Informix instance has one root dbspace which it uses to keep track of the environment's contents in a large number of internal tables. The Informix logs help to maintain the environment's ACID properties and are also associated with the Informix instance, not an individual database. It is possible to have more than one Informix instance on a given system.

The logical structures that must be sized by the Informix DBA include *tables* and *indexes, temporary space*, both logical and physical logs, and database catalogs, which contain information about each of the individual databases within an Informix instance. Ensure that space for all these entities is provided in the physical layout. The *INFORMIX-OnLine Dynamic Server Administrator's Guide* provides guidelines governing the placement of Informix structures. These guidelines take into consideration performance, high availability, and recoverability.

Informix Server Products

INFORMIX-OnLine Dynamic Server (version 6 and later) is well suited for data warehouse applications due to its parallel query and table partitioning capabilities. The maximum size of an INFORMIX-OnLine (version 5.x) database is approximately 130 GB in size, while the maximum size of an INFORMIX-OnLine Dynamic Server database can exceed 4 terabytes. Obviously, the logical volume layout will be very different between INFORMIX-OnLine Dynamic Server and INFORMIX-OnLine.

When allocating disk space for an INFORMIX-OnLine database, it is typical to take advantage of logical volume striping. Striping spreads across a number of disks the logical volumes that will be mapped to Informix chunks. Also, striping allows processes to query or update the same table with a degree of I/O parallelism that can greatly improve performance. This is all accomplished at the logical volume level and is transparent to the Informix DBA.

In INFORMIX-OnLine, there is a limitation in the number of chunks that can be specified. This limit is dictated largely by the length of the fully-qualified logical volume names with which the chunks are associated. For INFORMIX-OnLine Dynamic Server, the limit is 2,048 chunks. Also, there is a limited amount of space in which to store the logical volume names in INFORMIX-OnLine. To reach the maximum number of chunks for a given Informix instance, it is necessary to make the logical volume names exactly three characters or less (for example, "/aa"). This is typically accomplished using soft links placed in the / directory. The `ln -s` command is used to create the soft links.

INFORMIX-OnLine Dynamic Server requires the DBA to be more aware of the specific drives on which data is placed—for maximum parallel performance. Additionally, INFORMIX-OnLine Dynamic Server, version 7.1 supports a new table partitioning feature called *fragmentation* that will be discussed in the next section.

With versions 6 and 7.1 of INFORMIX-OnLine Dynamic Server, temporary space can be allocated either within Informix chunks or externally. However, with version 5 of INFORMIX-OnLine, temporary space is allocated only externally. By default, INFORMIX-OnLine uses the /tmp directory for temporary space, but can be pointed at other directories by adjusting certain Informix parameters.

Fragmentation

Fragmentation is an Informix feature used to define groups of rows or index keys within a table according to some algorithm or scheme. Each group or fragment (also referred to as *partitions*) can be stored in a separate dbspace associated with a specific physical disk. The fragments can be created and assigned to dbspaces using SQL statements. The *fragmentation scheme* defines how different rows are grouped. Row distribution is based either on key values within a row—termed *expression-based* fragmentation—or a simple *round-robin* allocation method. A table fragment uses a dbspace as its unit of storage. A fragmented table uses many dbspaces, as illustrated below:

```
CREATE TABLE SUPPLIER...FRAGMENT BY EXPRESSION
supplier_id > 1000 AND supplier_id <= 2000 IN dbspace1,
supplier_id > 2000 AND supplier_id <= 3000 IN dbspace2,
supplier_id > 3000 AND supplier_id <= 4000 IN dbspace3,
supplier_id > 4000 IN dbspace4
```

Code Example 1: Implementing Informix expression-based fragmentation when creating a table.

Fragmentation can considerably increase the responsiveness of decision-support type queries. Consider a table that is fragmented in equally-sized partitions based on some key value. The Parallel Data Query (PDQ) feature of version 7.1 of INFORMIX-OnLine Dynamic Server allocates multiple threads to retrieve data from fragments in parallel and eliminates unnecessary fragments. For example, if a query requests all records greater than supplier_id 2100, parallel I/O will be initiated only on the fragments. If each fragment resides on a different drive, I/O parallelism will be enhanced. This technique is especially effective when used with SMP-based hardware. When allocating logical volumes and chunks for dbspaces involved in a fragmentation scheme, it is important to maintain the I/O separation of each dbspace.

Disk Drives and Arrays

When discussing disk drives, issues related to performance and failure rate are usually discussed first (followed closely by cost). While the mean-time between failure has risen dramatically over the last few years, disk drives are still the most likely point of hardware failure—especially on systems with hundreds of drives. High-availability features—such as RAID arrays and mirrored disks—provide protection from most disk failures. The latest disk arrays, coupled with the new HP-UX LVM, version 10.0, also provide protection against failures of the interface cards, cables, controllers, and power supplies.

In the area of performance, as a rule of thumb, stand-alone disks generally offer better performance than disk arrays configured at RAID 3 or RAID 5 modes. While RAID 5 arrays can have higher throughput when random-read concurrency is high, and RAID 3 arrays have an advantage in performing large sequential writes, the best choice for both general performance and high availability are mirrored stand-alone disks. The cost effectiveness of each solution must also be analyzed.

When disk arrays are selected as the high-availability solution for a given disk configuration, there is the question of which RAID mode is most appropriate. The RAID choices available until recently on the HP 9000 server systems are modes 3 and 5. RAID 3 offers good performance for large sequential disk requests and is also preferable if the write-to-read ratio is high. RAID 5 offers high I/O concurrency and is best at handling high read-to-write ratios in random access environments. Mixing the two modes on the same system is often a good strategy. Use RAID 3 arrays for the filesystems that contain large amounts of sequentially accessed data, and RAID 5 for an OLTP database. RAID 3 is also a good choice for decision-support databases.

An issue that often surfaces with disk arrays is that of interface card and controller throughput. Since so much data is accessed through one connection, it is best not to configure more than three (3) to five (5) arrays per interface card. Although each array holds a large amount of data and stripes this data internally across the array's drives, it is still important to ensure a good spread of data across individual arrays and interface cards. An individual array can handle a large amount of I/O requests. The newest A3232A Model 10 and 20 arrays can handle over 300 I/Os per second and can hold between 21 and 42 GB, respectively.

Both arrays and stand-alone mechanisms have internal memory caches. Drive caching can significantly improve the performance of both reads and writes. Drive caching can be manipulated on some HP disk arrays using the `dcc` command. Immediate reporting of writes can be enabled on stand-alone SCSI drives using the `scsictl` command. By default, read caching is typically enabled. Write caching, or immediate reporting, must be specifically enabled due to data integrity issues. If a drive loses power with immediate write reporting enabled, it may lose I/O, even though the drive reports a successful completion to the system. Systems which utilize a UPS are in a better position to take advantage of this feature.

```
dcc -won /dev/rdsk/c14d0s2
scsictl -m ir=on /dev/rdsk/c0d0s2
```

Code Example 2: Enabling immediate reporting for writes;* dcc *for disk arrays, and* scsictl *for stand-alone disks.

After the drives have been installed on the system, any selected disk arrays must be converted to the proper RAID mode. The HP C2430D Cascade arrays are typically configured in RAID mode 5. The configured RAID mode can be checked by using SAM or the **dsp** command found in the **/usr/hpC2400/bin** directory. It is not recommended to use SAM for checking or reconfiguring arrays on large disk configuration systems. SAM can take over five minutes to enter the disk configuration menu and this menu must be re-entered each time that the status of a single array is checked. In addition, SAM can only configure one array at a time. Array reconfiguration can take over 30 minutes per array and can be performed in parallel outside of SAM. The **newarray** command can be used to reconfigure disk arrays in parallel. This command references pre-defined array configurations in the file **/usr/hpC2400/etc/arraytab**. Note **Raid_3_5d** in the following example.

```
newarray -NRaid_3_5d /dev/rdsk/c44d0s2 &
newarray -NRaid_3_5d /dev/rdsk/c64d0s2 &
newarray -NRaid_3_5d /dev/rdsk/c72d0s2 &
newarray -NRaid_3_5d /dev/rdsk/c79d0s2 &
```

Code Example 3: Simultaneously converting four arrays to RAID mode 3.

Creating the Logical Volumes

This section describes the LVM commands used to layout the actual logical volumes. Sections of actual scripts have been included to illustrate some important concepts.

Initializing Disks for LVM Usage

The first step in building the disk configuration is to turn the disks over to the LVM. This is accomplished by using the **pvcreate** command, as shown in the figure below. This command simply writes some information to the beginning of each disk in preparation for including the disks in a volume group. The **-f** option is used to force the command to overwrite any previously existing information on the specified disk. There is another option used with **pvcreate** to reserve space for system boot structures; this option will be discussed later.

```
pvcreate -f /dev/rdsk/c25d0s2
pvcreate -f /dev/rdsk/c26d0s2
pvcreate -f /dev/rdsk/c27d0s2
pvcreate -f /dev/rdsk/c28d0s2
pvcreate -f /dev/rdsk/c29d0s2
pvcreate -f /dev/rdsk/c30d0s2
pvcreate -f /dev/rdsk/c31d0s2
```

Code Example 4: Making a list of drives for LVM physical volumes.

Planning the Volume Group Configuration

Creating a volume group requires a certain amount of planning. Typically, disks that will be used with a specific application or database are grouped together in a single volume group. It may be useful to consider creating more than one volume group. For example, it is best to separate disks into two different volume groups if different types of disks are involved—such as a mix of stand-alone SCSI disks and disk arrays. One of the parameters required by the **newfs** command is a disk type. The disk type information is used to optimize the filesystem for a particular disk. Therefore, if a logical volume is built which spans two different disk types, some of the filesystem accesses may experience worse performance than others.

Data which will be striped within the volume groups is another reason to partition disks that belong to a single database into multiple volume groups. For a very large database striped at a fine level of granularity, logical volume striping can take days to complete. By separating the disks into multiple volume groups, it is possible to stripe multiple logical volumes one-by-one, since only one logical volume within a volume group can be effectively striped at a time. Note that breaking disks into multiple volume groups limits the extent to which data can be striped—that is, the data will be spread across fewer drives. Additionally, a logical volume can only be striped across the disks which belong to its own volume group.

Other reasons to use multiple volume groups involve MirrorDisk/UX and simply the performance of each LVM command. When using mirrored disks and selecting the Mirror Write Cache (MWC) option for mirror consistency, performance may be better with fewer disks in a volume group. All mirrored logical volumes in a volume group share the same MWC and it could potentially become a point of contention. More information on MWC will be presented in a subsequent section. Finally, each LVM command that modifies a volume group's configuration must update every physical volume in the volume group. With more than 30 or so disks, the time required for each LVM command to complete can be a time-consuming process.

There are a number of ways to break a database environment into multiple volume groups. The data for different databases within the database environment can be placed into separate volume groups, or the database environment's root dbspace and log files can be put into a separate volume group. The disks can also be separated on a basis of I/O channel configuration—to make spreading data across I/O channels more obvious to the DBA. Keep in mind that basing the volume group partitioning on the hardware configuration is not always advisable if the hardware configuration is likely to change.

Creating Volume Groups

First, decide on the volume group's name. The system volume group, by default, is named *vg00*. Other volume groups can continue in that pattern as *vg01*, *vg02*, or have names that reflect their usage, such as *dbvg01* or *dbadmin*. Before using the **vgcreate** command, a directory must be created under **/dev** with the same name as the volume group. This location specifies where the logical volume device files, both raw character and block files, will be stored. In addition, build within that directory a character device file that will be used internally by the LVM to access the volume group. This device file must be named *group*. This file's minor number must have the UNIQUE hexidecimal volume group number in the most significant two digits of this six-digit number. The maximum number of volume groups on a system is ten; however, this number can be increased by modifying a kernel parameter. Before reusing a volume group number, it may be necessary to restart the system.

```
mkdir /dev/dbvg02
mknod /dev/dbvg02/group c 64 0x040000

vgcreate -p 32 /dev/dbvg02 /dev/dsk/c25d0s2 /dev/dsk/c26d0s2 \
/dev/dsk/c27d0s2 /dev/dsk/c28d0s2 /dev/dsk/c29d0s2 \
/dev/dsk/c30d0s2 /dev/dsk/c31d0s2 /dev/dsk/c73d0s2 \
/dev/dsk/c74d0s2 /dev/dsk/c75d0s2 /dev/dsk/c76d0s2 \
/dev/dsk/c77d0s2 /dev/dsk/c78d0s2 /dev/dsk/c79d0s2
```

Code Example 5: Creating a new volume group which will allow a maximum of 32 physical volume members.

The **vgcreate** command creates the actual volume group and assigns to it the physical volumes. There are several parameters associated with the volume group that can only be set at volume group creation time. Thus, the values to be set for the volume group must be carefully considered. The **-p** option defines the maximum number of physical volumes per group. The default is 16 physical volumes. If volume groups are particularly large, the default setting must be modified. The **-l** option specifies the maximum number of logical volumes which can be allocated from the volume group. Its default is the maximum of 255 logical volumes; as such, it should never be necessary to alter this parameter. The **-e** and **-s** options are also important, and will be discussed in the next section. All of these parameters are responsible for sizing disk-resident data structures which cannot be changed after creating the volume group. The size of these data structures is relatively small compared to today's large disk drives. Thus, it is advisable to be generous in sizing the data structures. The **vgextend** command can be used to add more disks to a volume group.

Creating Logical Volumes

Logical volumes are created with volume groups using the **lvcreate** command. A name may be specified using the **-n** option, or allow the command to return the next default name. The default name follows this sequence: **lvol1, lvol2, lvol3**, etc. Allocating a sequence of default names and subsequently deleting some of the names results in the reuse of the deleted logical volume names. When a logical volume is allocated, two device files are created in the volume group directory. The block device file will have the name of the logical volume. The raw character device file will also have the logical volume name, but it will be preceded by the letter **r**. The number in the default logical volume name sequence corresponds to the logical volume number, which is also reflected in the least significant four (4) hexidecimal digits of the device file's minor number.

Logical volumes are sized internally in terms of extents. Extents are portions of disk space ranging in size from 1 to 256 MB—depending on how the volume group was created. The **-s** option on the **vgcreate** command sets the extent size for a given volume group. The default value for extent size is 4 MB. This value is rarely changed—except in the case where finer granularity is required for disk striping. The **-l** option on **lvcreate** permits the logical volume size to be specified in extents, and the **-L** option is used to specify the size in megabytes.

It is necessary to use the **lvextend** command in conjunction with **lvcreate** to allocate logical volumes on specific disks within a volume group. The **lvextend** command is typically used to increase the amount of space allocated to a logical volume. In addition, this command can be used to specify on which disk or disks the additional space is to be allocated. Use the `lvcreate` command to create a zero-size logical volume, followed by one or more `lvextend` calls to allocate the disk space. Notice that space is always specified in both commands as the total space for the logical volume. The incremental space added with an individual `lvextend` command is the difference between the new size parameter specified and the previous total size of the logical volume. In the example below, the logical volume **svcnpa** is first allocated 10 extents of space on disk 34, and then allocated 10 more extents on disk 59.

```
lvcreate -n cmpy /dev/raid3a
lvcreate -n svcnpa /dev/raid3a
lvcreate -n npa /dev/raid3a

lvextend -l 10 /dev/raid3a/cmpy /dev/dsk/c39d0s2
lvextend -l 10 /dev/raid3a/svcnpa /dev/dsk/c34d0s2
lvextend -l 20 /dev/raid3a/svcnpa /dev/dsk/c59d0s2
lvextend -l 10 /dev/raid3a/npa /dev/dsk/c71d0s2
```

Code Example 6: Creating logical volumes and allocating their disk space on specific drives.

Logical Volume Mirroring

Disk mirroring is an excellent way to provide protection from disk failures. It also provides the best all-around performance of all other disk protection methods. MirrorDisk/UX is a separately purchased and installable product.

MirrorDisk/UX permits the specification of multiple mirrors for the same logical volume. When creating a logical volume, it is possible to specify the number of mirror copies. Singly mirrored data is an original plus a copy. Doubly mirrored data is an original plus two copies. Doubly mirrored data provides higher availability, although it correspondingly consumes more disk space. By doubly mirroring data, it is possible to take one copy off-line for backup, while still maintaining high availability through the duplicate copy.

There are two choices for maintaining mirror consistency in the event of a failure: Mirror Write Cache (MWC), and mirror consistency recovery. Using the MWC, the system recovers consistent data as fast as possible, although routine performance is impacted. The MWC tracks each write of mirrored data to the physical volumes and maintains a record of any mirrored writes that have not yet successfully completed at the time of a system panic. Therefore, during recovery, only those physical extents with I/O in progress must be made consistent. The frequency of MWC writes is small for sequentially accessed logical volumes, such as database log files, but increases when access is more random. Therefore, when performance is more critical than recovery time, logical volumes containing database data, or filesystems with few or infrequently written large files, should not use the MWC.

Mirror consistency recovery—also known as non-MWC recovery—initiates a full-mirror copy for each mirrored logical volume. When the system is restarted after a failure, background tasks are launched for each volume group. These tasks begin producing complete mirror copies of all the logical volumes using this recovery method. The logical volumes are made consistent in a serial fashion. While the copies are created, the logical volumes are still accessible. However, high-availability characteristics are not in place until the mirror copies are complete.

Mirroring can also be accomplished without any LVM mirror consistency mechanism. This approach is useful when running an application program which has its own means to maintain or recover consistent data, or to rebuild its data largely from scratch. System swap space is an example of data that does not require any consistency recovery method. LVM provides commands for manually synchronizing logical volumes that contain stale extents. The **vgsync** or **lvsync** command can be issued to perform this task.

Quickly creating large mirrored logical volumes is an involved process. First, create the logical volume without allocating any disk space. Then, allocate a single extent on the first disk of the mirrored disk pair. Next, create the mirror. Part of the mirror creation process requires copying all extents from the original logical volume to the new mirror. In this case, only one extent must be copied. Finally, extend the logical volume to its full desired size. Since the mirror has been created already, extending the size of the logical volume does not result in any additional data copying. This is the fastest procedure to create a new mirrored logical volume. Adding a mirror to an existing large logical volume can take up to a half-hour to synchronize both sides of the mirror.

```
lvcreate -M n -c y /dev/dbvg02
lvcreate -M n -c y /dev/dbvg02


lvextend -l 1 /dev/dbvg02/lvol1 /dev/dsk/c25d0s2
lvextend -m 1 /dev/dbvg02/lvol1 /dev/dsk/c73d0s2
lvextend -l 500 /dev/dbvg02/lvol1 /dev/dsk/c25d0s2
/dev/dsk/c73d0s2


lvextend -l 1 /dev/dbvg02/lvol2 /dev/dsk/c26d0s2
lvextend -m 1 /dev/dbvg02/lvol2 /dev/dsk/c74d0s2
lvextend -l 500 /dev/dbvg02/lvol2 /dev/dsk/c26d0s2
/dev/dsk/c74d0s2
```

Code Example 7: Creating and mirroring 2 GB logical volumes with non-MWC mirror consistency.

The MWC is enabled with the **-M y** option on the **lvcreate** and **lvchange** commands. If MWC is not enabled, then the **-c y** option specifies that non-MWC recovery is to take place after a failure. The **-m 1** or **-m 2** options on the **lvcreate** or **lvextend** commands specifiy singly or doubly mirrored logical volumes, respectively. Managing mirrors during a disk failure is discussed in a subsequent section.

Logical Volume Striping

Logical volume striping is an excellent way to distribute disk access across a number of drives—while hiding the inherent complexity from applications. LVM allows logical volumes to span individual drives. LVM striping takes this concept to the extreme by distributing small portions of a logical volume across a number of drives in a round-robin fashion. This gives applications that use the data a better response time duc to better I/O concurrency. There is no impact to the end user in accessing a logical volume that is striped versus a volume that is not striped.

Each individual portion of the logical volume that is allocated during striping is called a *stripe*. The size of a stripe is typically a single LVM extent. However, the stripe can consist of any number of LVM extents. The selected stripe size should be influenced by the access pattern of the data intended for the striped logical volume. If access is to be random and well-distributed, a fine striping granularity is not necessary. If access to the data is random and highly clustered, keep the stripe size as small as possible—even to the point of reducing the volume group default extent size to a minimum of 1 MB. Striping can also improve sequential access by allowing the fetch-ahead algorithms to achieve some degree of I/O parallelism.

```
numstripedisks=5
stripedisk[1]=/dev/dsk/c39d0s2
stripedisk[2]=/dev/dsk/c34d0s2
stripedisk[3]=/dev/dsk/c59d0s2
stripedisk[4]=/dev/dsk/c54d0s2
stripedisk[5]=/dev/dsk/c71d0s2

i=1
stripesize=50
maxlvsize=500
lvsize=$stripesize
while [[ lvsize -le maxlvsize ]]
do
    lvextend -1 $lvsize /dev/vg02/custdem00 ${stripedisk[i]}
    let lvsize=lvsize+stripesize
```

```
        if [[ i -lt numstripedisks ]]
        then let i=i+1
        else i=1
        fi
done
```

Code Example 8: Striping a 2 GB logical volume across five (5) disks using a 50 extent (200 MB) stripe size.

A major drawback to LVM striping is the amount of time required to stripe a large logical volume with a small stripe size. Each **lvextend** command must write information to every physical volume in the volume group. Hundreds of **lvextend** commands are required to stripe a large logical volume. At a stripe size of 4 MB and with seven disk arrays in the volume group, it can take over 12 hours to complete one disk-striping task.

The amount of time required for striping can be greatly reduced by breaking the disks to be striped into multiple volume groups. Logical volumes within a volume group cannot be striped in parallel. However, logical volumes in different volume groups can be striped in this manner. It is also important to note that creating additional volume groups limits the number of disks over which a given logical volume can be striped.

Note

Create all volume groups before initiating any of the striping scripts, since volume group commands cannot execute while other LVM activities take place. However, this is not true for logical volume commands.

The LVM on HP-UX, version 10.0, has striping built into the **lvcreate** command. Therefore, no additional scripting is required. However, the above method is still a compatible option.

LVM striping is different from disk array striping. Disk arrays employ block or byte striping to distribute data across internal drives. LVM striping can be used in conjunction with disk arrays to distribute the logical volume data across a number of individual disk arrays. This improves the I/O concurrency at a higher level than the disk array striping.

Creating Physical Volume Groups

Physical volume groups are used in conjunction with mirrored logical volumes to provide I/O channel separation when disks are not explicitly specified. For a given volume group, place all the disks attached to one I/O card (or set of I/O cards) in one physical volume group, and all the disks attached to another I/O

tem, patch levels, and whether or not the system has been restarted since the failure. Synchronization of a logical volume can be checked with the **lvdisplay -v** command. If stale extents are found, synchronization is required. Keep in mind that this procedure only restores the logical volumes to the disk—additionally, the user must restore data on the affected logical volumes.

There are a number of commands that can be used to obtain information which is useful in isolating LVM problems, see Table 1.

Command	*What it displays*
pvdisplay -v <drive>	All logical volumes that have extents on this drive.
vgdisplay -v <volgrp>	All physical volumes, logical volumes, and physical volume groups, and their characteristics.
lvdisplay -v <lvol>	Logical volume characteristics, as well as all the physical volumes that this logical volume spans.
lvlnboot -v	All the volume groups that contain boot disks, as well as the locations of root, primary swap, and dump volumes within those groups.
vgscan -pv	Scans all disks on the system and displays the volume group associated with each disk.
vgcfgrestore -n <volgrp> -1	Physical volumes belonging to particular volume groups at the time a **vgcfgbackup** command was issued
ioscan -fkC disk	All disks connected to the system.

Table 1: Commands for isolating LVM problems.

LVM is tied into the system boot process. If there are problems with the system drives during startup, LVM may prevent the system from booting up. To correct LVM problems that affect system startup, there are two special command options to specify on the boot string. The first is **-lm** (i.e., ISL> hpux -lm (;0)/hp-ux). This option boots the system into LVM maintenance mode. Maintenance mode is a special way to boot a system that bypasses the normal

LVM structures. It is similar to single-user mode, since it bypasses many of the processes that are normally started—as well as many of the system checks that are typically performed. It is intended to allow a system to be booted long enough to repair damage to the system's LVM data structures, and then allows the system to be booted normally.

If LVM does not allow a system to boot since some of the system volume group disks are not available, use the `-lq` option on the boot command to override volume group quorum. A quorum of disks at boot time is defined as one more than half the total number of drives in the volume group. Thus, if a system volume group consists of two drives mirroring the system logical volumes—and one of the drives fails—use the quorum override option to start the system until the mirror drive is repaired.

To properly recover from problems and manage a complex disk layout—as required for a very large database—it is extremely important to have documentation that shows the system layout respecting the logical volumes. The next section of this article provides diagrams which can be used to troubleshoot problems. This section also provides some helpful suggestions on documenting the LVM configuration. For more information, refer to the *Solving HP-UX Problems* manual, which was provided with your Hewlett-Packard documentation. Reviewing the LVM-related chapters of the above manual—as well as the *System Administration Tasks* and the *How HP-UX Works: Concepts for the System Administrator* manuals—is also recommended.

Case Studies

This section describes two different systems which illustrate many of the concepts discussed in this article. The intent of both systems is to support the sales organization of a large telecommunication company by providing specific information on customer profiles and rendered services. The designers of both systems faced the challenges and complexities of creating databases that exceed 100 GB in size.

Case Study 1

This first case study concerns a system that maintained customer profiles and summarized service information. The customer databases were populated from billing information obtained from a mainframe. Thereafter, the system regularly received regular updates containing service information and accommodates manual updates of customer records. This system, and a second system, were designed to hold over 400 GB of user information.

The system selected for this application is an HP 9000 T500 8 with 2 GB of memory. The system provided 428 GB of disk space. The system also included 30 Fast/Wide SCSI Cascade disk arrays with five 2 GB mechanisms each, and sixty-four 2 GB stand-alone mechanisms. The 30 disk arrays were configured in a high-availability RAID mode and all stand-alone drives were mirrored, bringing the system's total disk space to 304 GB.

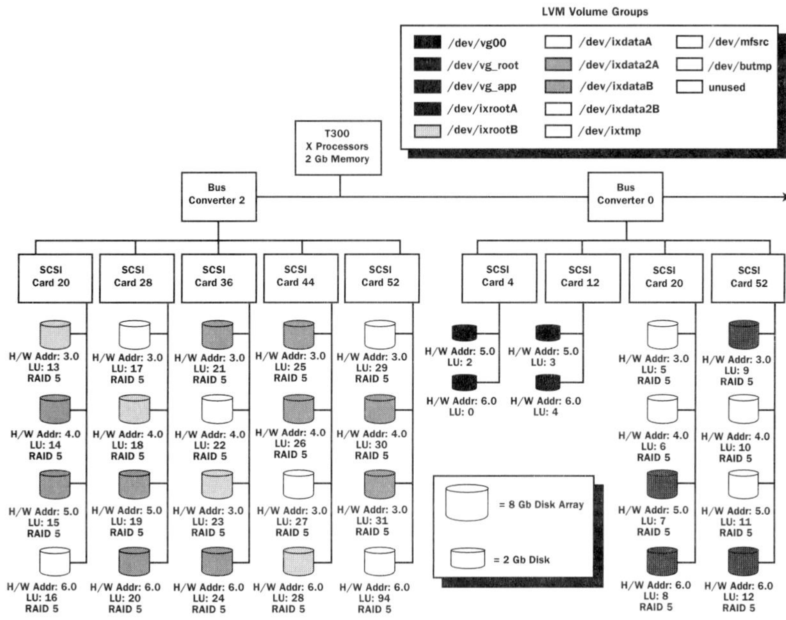

Sample 1: Disk configuration with volume groups, part 1.

HP-UX, version 9.04 was the chosen operating system and INFORMIX-OnLine was the selected database. Due to the limitations of INFORMIX-OnLine, each database instance held between 120 and 130 GB of data. Thus, four separate database instances were required to hold all the data for each customer region. Each region had its own database—with several databases per Informix instance.

Besides the disks drives, the other supporting hardware was configured for optimal performance and connectivity. The disks were spread across three bus converters—each capable of sustaining an I/O rate of 21 MB/second. There were a total of 16 SCSI F/W cards—each capable of handling 7-10 MB/second. Refer to the previous diagram for further configuration details.

The majority of disk arrays in this configuration were intended to hold the Informix databases. These disk arrays were configured in RAID 5 mode to facilitate highly concurrent random-read access. Two of the 30 disk arrays were

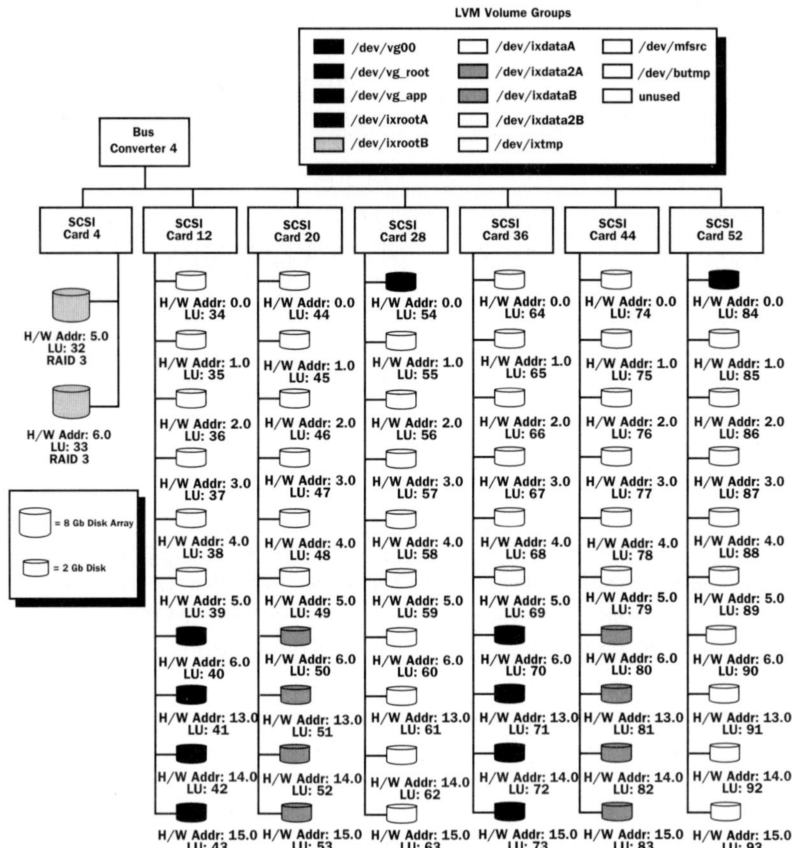

Sample 1: Disk configuration with volume groups, part 2.

assigned to the database backup directories and were subsequently configured in
RAID 3 mode to facilitate the typically large sequential transfers which are
characteristic of this kind of work. Immediate-write reporting was disabled on all
drives, while drive-read caching was enabled.

Each database instance was divided into three volume groups. One volume
group consisted of six stand-alone 2 GB drives, used for the database root and
catalogs, physical logs, and logical logs. Each of these entities were placed on
separate disks and the logical volumes containing them were mirrored to separate
drives. Informix recommends using mirrored stand-alone drives versus using disk
arrays for root and logs. The second of the two volume groups were created to
hold the database tables and indexes. Each volume group consisted of seven
arrays over which 28 logical volumes of 2 GB each were striped, since the maximum size of an Informix chunk is 2 GB. The disks selected for each volume

group were evenly spread across the individual I/O cards. In addition, the SCSI bus address priorities were also considered prior to allocating each drive. Striping the four large volume groups that comprised the two database instances was performed in parallel and took approximately 14 hours to complete.

In addition to the six database volume groups, three additional volume groups were closely tied to the database. The first, **/dev/mfsrc**, stored down-loaded files from the mainframe. This volume group consisted of a   large number of stand-alone drives and used physical volume groups to assure I/O channel separation for mirroring. Implemented on two RAID 3 disk arrays, the second was the **/dev/butmp** volume group. This volume group held unloaded database table information prior to copying to an optical jukebox. The volume group held four 4 GB logical volumes for containing HP-UX filesystems. The third volume group, **/dev/ixtmp**, contained the HP-UX filesystems to be used as temporary work space. Physical volume groups were not used with this volume group. Each logical volume was manually placed to optimize disk separation between the different database instances. Using physical volume groups does not guarantee that two logical volumes will not reside on the same disk. The MWC was disabled for this volume group, due to the expectation that much of the I/O would be random. The MWC was used with all other mirrored logical volumes.

In addition to the volume groups described above, the system used three other volume groups to maintain HP-UX application binaries and user work space. The system was configured with two bootable system volume groups, **/dev/vg00** and **/dev/vg_root**. Each of these volume groups contained a single mirrored boot disk. Two boot volume groups protected the user from human error (for example, scripts that delete the operating system) and protected from mechanism failure by mirroring. The third volume group, **/dev/vg_app**, contained some application-related directories.

One potential area of concern was the total number of I/O devices on the final bus converter (address 4). I/O loads across this converter were monitored. All stand-alone drives connected to this bus converter were not in simultaneous use during normal production. Many drives on this converter were only used when the database was loaded or backed up. This is an important consideration to keep in mind when loading I/O channels.

Case Study 2

This second case study involved a system designed to perform analysis on detailed telecommunications service information. Data was downloaded from a mainframe at specific intervals and loaded into an Informix database. Enough disk space was required to hold three-days worth of service data. Large decision-support type queries were executed against the data. The majority of queries originated from a standard set of queries that showed variations in service within regions. However, some queries were ad hoc in nature. The standard queries were supported by indexes and took advantage of Informix's Parallel Data Query (PDQ) and table fragmentation features. The entire database (logs, tables, indexes, catalogs, and temporary space) was sized at about 100 GB.

The key design criteria for this system focused on high performance; thus, mirrored disks were selected over disk arrays. The system was also to be highly available, using both SPU switchover mechanism and LVM disk mirroring. Note that a system utilizing both these technologies is difficult to set up and writing the LVM scripts requires special care. Besides detailed system diagrams and documentation, a uniform logical unit (LU) numbering scheme was a requirement for both systems. In some cases, it is necessary to reset logical unit numbering after HP-UX installation by using the **rmsf** and **insf** commands.

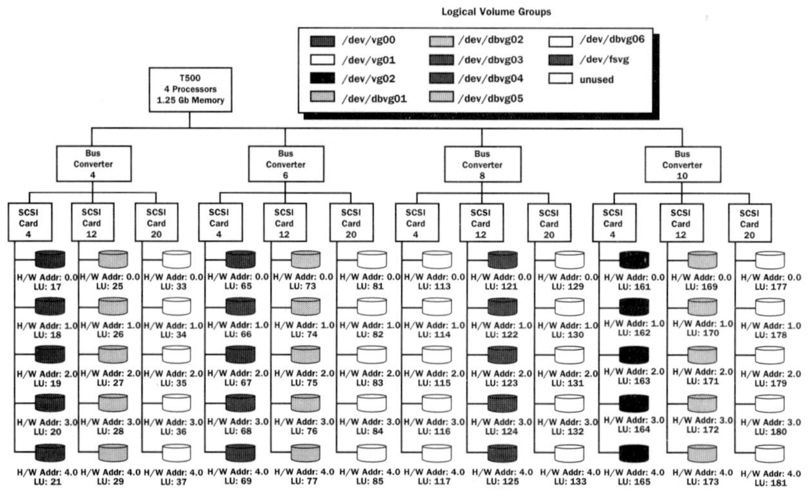

Sample 2: Disk configuration with volume groups, part 1.

This application made use of an HP 9000 T500 4-way system with 1.25 GB of memory. The system had a total of 240 GB of disk space consisting of 120 Fast/Wide SCSI stand-alone 2 GB disks. All disk space was mirrored, bringing the effective disk space to 120 GB. Only eight drives were not included in the SPU switchover setup. The two systems used as the switchover pair had identical I/O configurations; thus, the actual total number of drives attached to a single system was 232. Immediate-write reporting was disabled for all drives. The disks were spread across a seven bus converters for future growth and to support the large number disks required for the switchover configuration. See the previous diagrams for more information. Note that the I/O cards and channels required for the switchover system are not shown in this diagram.

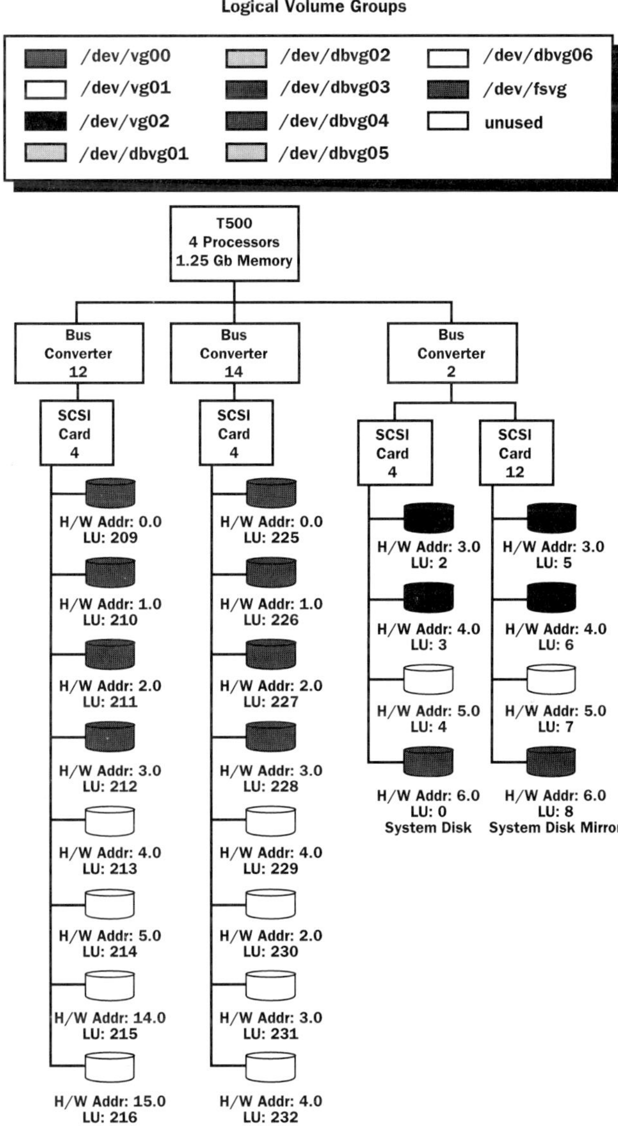

Sample 2: Disk configuration with volume groups, part 2.

INFORMIX-OnLine Dynamic Server, version 7.1—with its parallel data query and extensive table partitioning functionality—was selected as the database engine. Since OnLine Dynamic Server, version 7.1, allows the DBA to fragment tables at the database level, it was decided that logical volume striping would not be needed. This puts the responsibility for distributing the I/O for a given large table in the hands of the DBA.

There are different performance advantages to implementing data mirroring at either the operating system or database level. Because LVM uses the shortest disk queues for each disk, it has the benefit of optimizing read performance by selecting the mirror disk with the least I/O activity. LVM mirroring also lessens the complexity of the DBA's administration requirements. This greatly improves I/O throughput when a table has multiple accessors. Likewise, with INFORMIX-OnLine Dynamic Server, a feature called split-reads is used to reduce the disk-seek time. Read requests are serviced by either the primary or mirror chunk, depending upon the location of the desired data page. Write operations were performed to both mirror drives in parallel for both the Informix and LVM implementations.

The database instance on this system was broken up into six volume groups. Each volume group contained a set of disks with a F/W SCSI card in common. Each logical volume was mirrored to another set of disks with a single F/W SCSI card in common. Therefore, the DBA can fragment large tables across different I/O cards by selecting logical volumes from different volume groups. Each logical volume was sized at 2 GB and manually placed on specific drives. Separating each logical volume onto its own drive allowed parallel queries to achieve maximum I/O parallelism (assuming that the common queries correspond with the chosen fragmentation scheme).

A seventh volume group, */dev/fsvg*, was set up to contain downloaded files from the mainframe. I/O channel separation was maintained with physical volume groups. The system volume groups were also mirrored.

The LVM Mirror Write Cache was not used with any of the database logical volumes. The MWC was disabled to improve throughput during operations. However, in the event of a failure, the system will be significantly impacted while the six volume groups resynchronize all their logical volume mirrors. However, the volume groups will be accessible during this resynchronization.

Conclusion

Improvements in software and hardware technology are allowing databases to reach ever increasing sizes. Business requirements are driving these sizes to new heights. When creating large databases, it is important to avoid the pitfalls, and build the databases on reliable and extensible foundations to meet overall performance goals. Hopefully, the information covered in this article will help the reader to build future implementations of large Informix databases.

About the Author

Robert Fisher is a technical consultant in the General Systems division of Hewlett-Packard, Cupertino, California.

About Hewlett-Packard

Hewlett-Packard (HP) is the second-largest computer supplier in the United States, with computer-related revenue of $19.6 billion in its 1994 fiscal year. HP is a leading global manufacturer of computing, communications, and measurement products and services recognized for excellence in quality and support. For more information about HP, access the HP home page at the following Web location: http://www.hp.com.

## 25

Raising the Standard for Enterprise Document Management in Informix Environments

by Matt Shanahan and Dick Hoffman

Introduction: Enterprise Foundations

"Documents will increasingly be used to describe business processes, and to embody and animate business rules. As a result, entire industries will change their business practices based on the availability of new integrated document and output management technologies." This quote is from the *Integrated Document and Output Management Scenario: The Document Assumes its New Role in the Enterprise,* Gartner Group, July 13-14, 1995.

Although much of Informix Software's history of leadership in database management focused on the area of transaction processing and the management of structured data within large enterprises, Informix's vision of data management clearly goes far beyond transactions and structured datatypes. As evidenced by their stated directions with object extensions to their parallel server technology, the growing success of their object-oriented product, INFORMIX-NewEra, and the recent acquisition by Informix of Illustra, Informix's future clearly encompasses the management of all types of customer data, including text, drawings, images, sound, and video. The purpose of this article is to describe the model and requirements for enterprise document management systems, and to present a solution based on the use of Informix database technology and Documentum's products.

The Gartner Group estimates that up to 80 percent of the valuable information in organizations—the "intellectual capital" of major corporations and governments—is in formats and/or locations that are inaccessible to the vast majority of people within those organizations. Thus, the vast stores of corporate assets are untapped by the majority of people who could benefit from the information.

As indicated by the introductory quote to this article, the document is taking on an increasingly strategic role in today's businesses. In growing numbers, companies are turning to document technology as the foundation for capturing business rules, shaping and automating key business practices and policies, and managing intellectual capital effectively across the enterprise.

Collaborating to Meet Enterprise Needs

To meet the needs of enterprises, Documentum and Informix announced an alliance to port Documentum's Enterprise Document Management System (EDMS) to INFORMIX-OnLine Dynamic Server, version 7.1 in mid-September, 1995. The alliance serves to enhance both companies' position of extending solutions across the enterprise and to align the support for customers' requirements in managing unstructured data, including text, documents, images, audio, and video. Documentum's collaboration provides Informix with core abilities to handle additional datatypes, allowing it to become a major presence in the synergistic management of structured and unstructured information.

Documentum and Informix share a close synergy in their approaches to assisting customers in the management of critical corporate information. The synergies in technology direction, partnership philosophy, and vision of the document management market make the two companies a perfect match for providing "information management" solutions to global customers. The proven strengths of their technologies ensure document management solutions that provide high performance, scalability, and interoperability across the enterprise.

Enterprise Foundations for Business Advantage

According to the Harvard Business Review (September–October 1995), information technology accounts for more than 50 percent of the capital-goods dollars spent in the United States (U.S.) today. CEOs around the world now view document management technology as a valuable ingredient in business solutions that integrate business processes and deliver competitive advantages.

Enterprise foundations provide several key business advantages:

- Companies can deploy solutions that not only meet the needs of individual departments, but can immediately scale to the entire enterprise;

- Companies can execute their best business practices without imposing artificial technical barriers that limit productivity and time to market; and

- Companies can leverage their valuable intellectual capital to build document management solutions to capture and sustain competitive advantages.

Enterprise Requirements

Fortune 1000 CIOs and MIS managers were polled on their most essential information technology requirements—the technologies that would meet their enterprise needs into the coming decades. The responses centered around three important criteria:

- *Flexibility*. The technology must accommodate the widest possible selection of application configurations, deliver maximum systems interoperability, and support a broad range of information formats—both now and in the future.

- *Scalability*. The technology must scale easily at every level to meet the changing needs of the enterprise. It must be able to handle very large numbers of users, sites, business processes, documents, and document types. This system must also leverage the full power of the market leading database, INFORMIX-OnLine Dynamic Server.

- *Extensibility*. The technology must be highly tailorable—enabling a company to easily modify applications to reflect the changing business and to embed rules which are truly reflective of individual business practices. The technology must also be accessible and extensible through development tools, such as INFORMIX-NewEra.

Enterprise Flexibility

Corporate customers have identified a number of flexibility requirements for document management technology. First, they want maximum flexibility in the way users access and use information. Information should only have to be created once to be reused an infinite number of times, and in an infinite variety of combinations with other information. Second, users want to search and retrieve documents on demand, at any time and from any location. Users also need the ability to capture not only the documents themselves, but information about the documents and any associated business processes. For this reason, workflow is a critical component in any enterprise document management system, since it encapsulates and manages business processes.

Additionally, companies need document technology that is flexible enough to run in the organization's existing computing and document environment. The technology should enable the deployment of document repositories in whatever configuration which conforms to user and business needs, rather than requiring users and networks to conform to the constraints of the repository. Finally, flexibility in document technology means the ability to save and store documents at any level of granularity—from a multi-megabyte sized image to a single paragraph from an operating manual.

Another important criterion for enterprise information delivery is the flexibility to accommodate multiple viewing and editing requirements. Additionally, it is necessary to provide the ability to support and maintain multiple content renditions for a single document. For instance, a document's content can be stored in native format for versioning and editing, in HTML for publishing, and in Adobe Acrobat for review and annotations—all within the same reusable document object. Since all renditions represent the same object, the system assures that the content remains synchronized if any of the renditions changes. Finally, a document management system should also support an enterprise's dynamic storage requirements by delivering mechanisms for moving information easily between on-line, near-line, and off-line storage devices.

Enterprise Scalability

There are several key scalability requirements for enterprise document management. First, the technology must deliver guaranteed continued high performance in a distributed environment—without imposing artificial limitations that hamper the system's growth. The system must be able to optimize network, database, and server resource usage in order to deliver maximum capacity and throughput. The system must be optimized to deliver high performance for document storage and access regardless of the size of the document or document fragment. Finally, the system should be able to minimize or eliminate any network bottlenecks that result from file transfers and data movement. All of this is made possible by the Documentum server and INFORMIX-OnLine Dynamic Server.

Enterprise Extensibility

Additionally, customers require extensible document management technology to deliver solutions that help them sustain competitive advantage and differentiate themselves from their competition. Their extensibility requirements begin with a rich set of off-the-shelf document management services that add immediate value without requiring customization. At the same time, these services must be tailorable at any level so that business-specific rules or system administration policies can be easily embedded at any point in the architecture. In addition, companies require the ability to build custom applications using the development tools of their choice, in order to leverage existing development skills and ensure maximum productivity.

Architectural Considerations

To deliver flexibility, scalability and extensibility, a document mangement system must have the appropriate technology foundation. The following architectural considerations should be examined prior to building the foundation for a document management system.

- *Three-Tier Architecture.* A three-tier client/server architecture is a prerequisite for today's information environments. In a three-tier architecture, a broad range of clients access network services that deliver common business rules and document services.

- *A Parallel Three-Tier Architecture.* This architecture ensures that storage, network, and server capacity can be added to increase performance and throughput as more clients are added to the network. This enables a company to easily scale the system at any tier, as needed, to accommodate growth and change. It also provides the flexibility for optimizing client/server hardware.

Three-Tier Architecture

Client/server computing has become a standard fixture in corporate information systems (IS) environments and has now entered its next generation: three-tier architecture. For document management solutions, a three-tier client/server architecture has several important advantages over earlier-generation two-tier configurations.

First, three-tier architecture ensures that common document services are made available to all necessary client applications—without requiring the services to be redeveloped on each client. A three-tier architecture also enables application partitioning, in which presentation, core application, and database services are developed as separate object modules and deployed on separate computers in the network. In this manner, three-tier architecture helps to improve application performance, minimizes network bottlenecks, and leverages network computing power.

Beyond Three-Tier: A Parallel Architecture

As powerful as it is, three-tier architecture alone is not enough to satisfy the essential requirements of enterprise document management. The three-tier architecture must also be parallel—delivering the scalability to relieve bottlenecks at any level and continually adapting to ever-changing computing requirements.

Scalable document, workflow, search, and security services must also be provided in a common manner, based on consistent business rules, to all clients through servers in the network. This gives customers maximum flexibility in choosing network clients, such as Documentum Workspace, a World Wide Web browser, or application-specific clients. At the same time, network servers can be tuned for the optimal use of system-level components, such as the filesystem, database, full-text indexing engine, and other resources. Finally, the parallel architecture is easy to scale—simply by adding additional computing capacity at tier 2 or 3, to increase network capacity for access, refer to Figure 1.

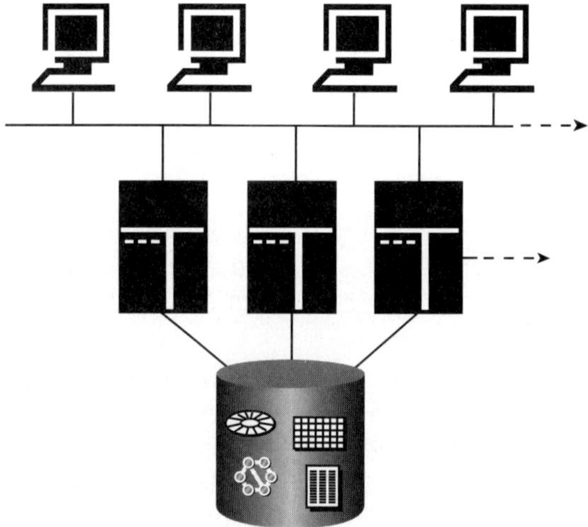

Figure 1: Documentum's parallel architecture.

Document Modeling

The document repository's modeling of documents—specifically, the way it profiles, indexes, stores, and accesses documents—has an important bearing on a system's ability to deliver on the key corporate requirements of flexibility, extensibility, and scalability.

Most of today's document management systems model documents as rows in a relational database. This relational model is the current standard for corporate database applications and is a cornerstone in the client/server architecture. INFORMIX-OnLine Dynamic Server has set the new standard. Relational technology offers the maturity and reliability of a tried-and-true standard—with robust systems features such as transaction control, security, flexible data access, scalability, and relationship management.

Some document management systems model documents as reusable, modular objects in an object database with many attributes for searches. Through such concepts as abstract data typing, inheritance, object identity, and polymorphism, the object model provides a mechanism for representing and manipulating real-world business entities. Some database companies, such as Informix, are attempting to implement document management systems based on an object-relational model, which integrates both object and relational technology to provide a foundation for profiling and indexing documents. Informix's next generation server is INFORMIX-Universal Server, a product which encompasses both object and relational technology.

While relational databases and object databases both solve different aspects of the document management problem, neither addresses the entire set of document requirements nor the actual informational content—the true source of a document's value.

Object-Orientation

Object-oriented programming, which encapsulates data together with the operations (also called *methods*) to be carried out on the data, offers many key business benefits, including increased developer productivity and reduced long-term maintenance costs. Object-orientation delivers these benefits through such features as extensibility, code reusability, the ability to create specialized software components, and the ability to model applications closely on real-world processes. True object-oriented systems employ four key concepts:

- *Abstract data typing*, which enables developers to create types of objects by defining a common structure and behavior that applies to every object within the type.

- *Inheritance*, which enables new types of documents to be created from existing types.

- *Object identity*, which enables developers to give a specific global identity to every object, so that it can be referenced individually throughout the system.

- *Polymorphism*, which enables developers to define a reusable operation that can be applied with different results to different types of objects.

Documents can be modeled as objects because they have attributes that need to be captured (such as author, title, and date) as well as methods to be carried out (such as routing and printing). But a document has two additional informational components that need to be captured, controlled, and managed: the actual content of the document, and the document's relationship to other documents and workflows.

Content Architecture and Relationship Management

Reusable document components provide the mechanism for storing documents and their content. They also encapsulate any information about the documents and how they're managed, including attached workflow objects, integrity rules, and other business rules (refer to the following figure). For example, Documentum's reusable document component, the Docobject™, contains four parts: the document's content, attributes or metadata (name, title, author, etc.), operations, and relationships to other Docobjects, refer to Figure 2.

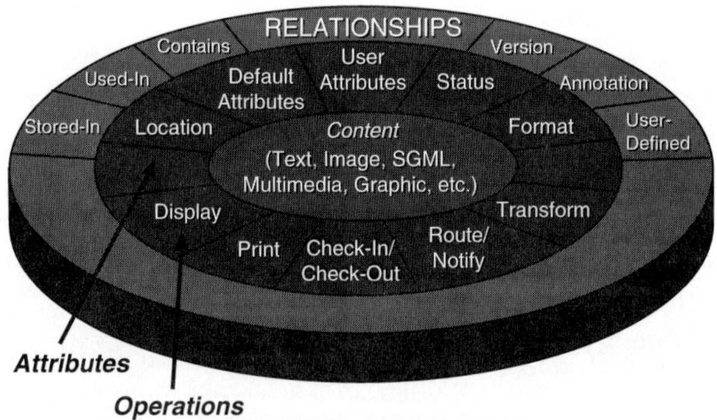

Figure 2: The Documentum Docobject.

The document is stored on the network either in a database or a filesystem, and is indexed by Documentum's full-text retrieval engine. The attributes are stored and indexed in INFORMIX-OnLine Dynamic Server.

Ideally, a reusable document component is, at its core, content-aware—meaning it understands how to efficiently store, index, and manage its own content. These objects can represent various format or information types, including complex formats, such as multi-file CAD drawings or multi-page fax images.

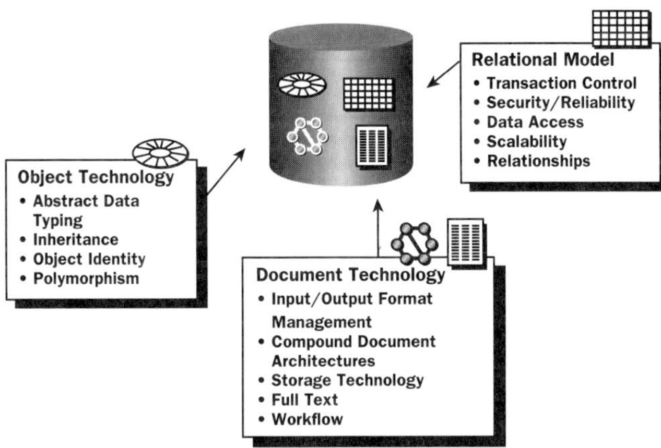

Figure 3: A document relational architecture incorporates object, relational, and document technologies for managing complex document formats.

It is also necessary to set up a subsystem to manage the movement, indexing, and storage of a document's content. The relationship management capabilities should also provide another important function: preserving the relational integrity between related objects, such as a document and its annotations. Relational integrity ensures that if a document is deleted, all of its associated objects and annotations are deleted as well. Likewise, the user only needs to delete the object once to ensure that it will be deleted everywhere it's used.

Scalability Through Parallel Three-Tier Architecture

The database industry has recently validated the increased performance delivered by three-tier architecture through published TPC benchmarks. Document transactions, however, are different from database transactions—a user will need to check out a document for perhaps several days to make edits, as opposed to a database transaction which is completed in a matter of seconds. In order to deliver scalability, a three-tier architecture for enterprise document management must be able to deliver the same levels of responsiveness as database transactions, but at the same time conserve server resources while a user works on a document. Likewise, scalability means that throughput and response times can be easily maintained as demand increases and the application grows. Documentum's parallel three-tier architecture delivers this scalability by making it easy to add capacity at any level as required to head off bottlenecks.

Optimally, a document management system should scale at every hardware level. The system should also provide a routable client/server protocol which enables the customer to increase network capacity by adding additional routers on the network backplane. For example, the Documentum EDMS system supports symmetric multiprocessing (SMP) at the processor level and massively parallel processing (MPP) at the server level, therefore taking advantage of the new INFORMIX-OnLine Dynamic Server features and the capabilities of upcoming Informix products.

At the network level, a document management system can utilize a tunable client/server protocol to optimize the message size between the client and server, as well as software fault-tolerance. Software fault tolerance ensures that if a server in the network fails, a backup server will recover the connection and complete the client's requested operations in a way that is completely transparent to the user.

Scalability Through the Document-Relational Model

Scalability is not just a hardware or software issue. The majority of document management repositories fail to deliver required scalability because they cannot capture and search on the broad array of object types found in the enterprise. Most systems cannot accommodate the number of document types required in an enterprise deployment and their search capabilities are not optimized for millions of documents. When used with INFORMIX-OnLine Dynamic Server, Documentum's Docbase can be scaled to an unlimited number of document types, and there is no limit to the number of attributes which can be assigned to each type. At the same time, such a system ensures continued high performance through an optimized attribute storage schema.

Adding Immediate Value to Business Processes

At the minimum, a document management system should deliver library services for basic document operations, such as check-in, check-out, browsing, and version control. The Documentum EDMS provides immediate value to business processes with a rich set of services that go beyond basic library operations to deliver format management, workflow, collaborative review, configuration management, and output management. A key Documentum differentiator is the transformation engine, which manages the conversion of documents from one format to another, and allows users to access any document, regardless of the applications they have on their desktop or the application in which the document was originally created. The system supports a wide variety of transformation filter products, so that customers can select the filter that is most appropriate for their own business needs.

Conclusion: Raising the Bar for Document Management

This article has discussed Documentum's key differentiators—the vital business capabilities which are entirely unique to the Documentum EDMS and which form a foundation for document management. These capabilities must be present to meet the requirements of the enterprise. As a result, Documentum has defined a new standard for enterprise document management—delivering true business value to the enterprise which is unmatched by other products.

No matter how they are described and marketed, LAN-based library services do not have the architectural foundation to scale to the enterprise. LAN-based library services are based on a relational implementation that treats every document as a record in a table. These systems have artificial limits on the number of attributes and do not support multiple types of documents. In addition, LAN-based library services do not address the needs of business processes, since they overlook the issues of workflow and virtual documents. Finally, the performance in these systems fails dramatically when the number of documents rises above a few thousand.

Relational document management systems are two-tier implementations which use a relational database to perform document management functions. Similar to LAN-based library services, relational document management systems treat documents as records in a database. Beyond the inherent performance problems of a two-tier architecture, these systems store documents as BLOBs.

Based on the new strategic relationship between Documentum and Informix, a whole new class of capabilities is now available to Informix users. By leveraging the power of the Informix database, in combination with the object model in Documentum, companies will be able to best utilize both structured and unstructured information throughout their organizations for competitive advantage.

About the Authors

Matt Shanahan is director of Product Marketing and Dick Hoffmann is director of Partner Development at Documentum.

About Documentum, Inc.

Documentum, Inc. develops, markets, and supports a family of object-oriented, client-server document management products that specifically address the challenges of managing intellectual capital effectively across large enterprises. Documentum is a recognized leader in the document management market. Headquartered in Pleasanton, California, Documentum sells the Documentum Enterprise Document Management System (EDMS) through a direct sales force, systems integrators, and affiliated distributors in the U.S., Canada, and Europe. Documentum has more than 180 customer sites in pharmaceutical, process, and discrete manufacturing and government applications around the world.

Documentum, Inc. is located at 5671 Gibralter Drive, Pleasanton, California, 94588; access Documentum's Web site at the following URL: http://www.documentum.com. To contact Documentum, call 510 463 6800.

26

INFORMIX DATABASE PERFORMANCE TUNING FOR DOCUMENT MANAGEMENT SYSTEMS

by Dan Hunsinger

Introduction

Of all the technological components of a typical imaging system—LANs, WANs, workstations, compression, decompression, optical devices, etc.—the database engine is probably the most important to optimize for performance. In the case of Bluebird Systems' imageABLE product, 36 relational database tables are used to manage everything—from facsimile requests, to which user is logged on and where, to image object locations on optical devices—and nearly all server transactions involve some sort of database access. This article will discuss the performance tuning of Informix databases for document management systems. This discussion will also introduce the imageABLE product as an example of a document management system.

Data Organization

INFORMIX-OnLine Dynamic Server is a very powerful relational database manager. Not only does it provide a standard SQL-compliant interface to data, but it also provides a way to intelligently organize the data for rapid access—while maintaining internal data integrity through any hardware or software failures.

dbspaces

A dbspace is a logical unit of physical database space which can be used to hold rows of data in relational tables. In Informix, a dbspaces consists of one or more "chunks" which are generally logical volumes within AIX. Logical volumes (through AIX) are assigned to physical space on actual physical devices.

This mapping scheme has several real-world advantages. First of all, it provides explicit control over what database tables go on what physical devices. In most complex imageABLE server transactions, several tables may be accessed at once. Spreading the information to separate physical devices allows for greater I/O overlap, refer to Figure 1.

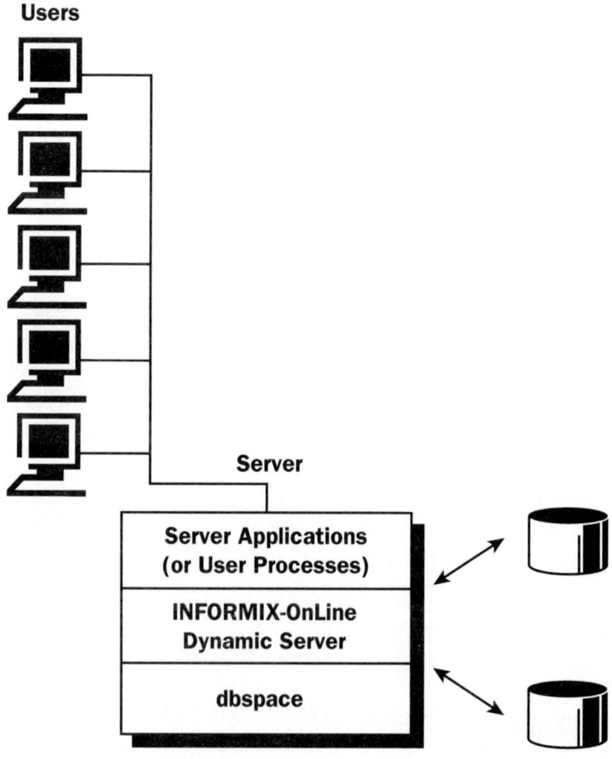

Figure 1: dbspace mapping schemes.

I/O tends to be a performance bottleneck for all relational database managers. Another advantage of the mapping scheme is that chunks can be added incrementally to dbspaces. Although it is best to plan for the total capacity of the system, it is not necessary to pre-allocate the mapping scheme on the first day of the system's operation. The current status of dbspaces and the assigned "chunks" can be monitored using *monitor*.

The imageABLE product is usually installed with nine standard dbspaces. Each of the usually large and/or frequently accessed tables are assigned their own dbspace to make sure that the space only contains rows from that table. Physically keeping the data together from the large tables means that the data is placed on fewer physical disk pages, which again tends to cut down on I/O.

Another good reason for a separate dbspace is to isolate the effect of many inserts and deletes. As with filesystems, frequent creation and deletion can fragment the physical space. If all tables are lumped together into the same physical space, the fragmentation could spill over to other tables. In this scenario, logically grouped (and accessed) data is physically spread apart and therefore tends to increase I/O rates. In the imageABLE system, the SAIMH and SAIMF tables are used to store facsimile, print, and general mail-routing information. When a facsimile request is made, entries are placed in these tables, and when the request is processed, the entries are deleted. The SAIMH and SAIMF tables are placed on their own dbspaces.

The ROOTDBS is a heavily used dbspace within each Informix installation. ROOTDBS is the default dbspace used by Informix. ROOTDBS is also considered the default dbspace where all tables are placed when a dbspace is not explicitly specified using the CREATE TABLE command. In imageABLE, administrators can create tables dynamically (through a Windows interface) for use as indexes for objects, such as images, documents, or COLD documents. By default, these keyword tables end up in the ROOTDBS and thus can create a performance bottleneck. For large production systems, it is usually best to move large keyword tables into their own dbspace, where the mechanism performs very well.

The Logs

Informix provides a sophisticated way to maintain internal data integrity and transaction recovery. As with any sophisticated feature, there are many ways to use it.

For simple backups, Informix provides a backup and restore utility that allows the entire database to be backed up to a tape device. A snapshot of an entire database is called a *level zero archive*. Additionally, there are two other archive levels available for incrementally backing up a database.

In between backups (or archives), Informix maintains running logs of all database transactions that impact data in the database. The purpose of the logs is to restore a database to the last successfully completed transaction—based on the last archive and the logs. If an up-to-the-minute backup is important, the log data can be continuously copied onto tape devices. For example, a company may not consider an up-to-the-minute backup important, since a day's worth of new documents can always be rescanned, in the event of a disk crash or some other disaster. In that case, the log files must be emptied, but can be emptied to ***/dev/null***.

Although the logging of database transactions provides a powerful mechanism for maintaining database consistency, such transactions can be resource intensive. As with other database data, the logical logs are mapped to a dbspace which, in turn, is eventually mapped to some physical location. The default location for the logs is the same ROOTDBS. For example, in an RS/6000 system with two or more physical drives, one disk can be severely over-taxed while other disks remain idle.

The other hard-learned lesson regarding log files is to determine their optimal size and to ensure that the log files are constantly emptied (to tape or ***/dev/null***). In simple terms, when the logs are full, the database stops. The size of the log space should be generally larger than the size required for the largest possible transaction. The database will only free log data that is stable—that is, data which has gracefully come to the end of a committed transaction. One potential problem occurs if one transaction generates enough database updates to fill the entire log space before completing. The database cannot release the log because the transaction is not complete, and it cannot allow the transaction to complete since it cannot be logged (and thus, it cannot ensure data consistency).

Memory Buffers

As mentioned earlier, the goal in managing a very large database is to minimize disk I/O as much as possible. INFORMIX-OnLine Dynamic Server has clever mechanisms for caching database pages in memory for both reading and writing. The current hit rates on the caches can be monitored using *monitor*.

Knowing the appropriate memory to set aside for database caching is highly application dependent. By setting the memory buffer size, it is possible to keep the cache hit rates above 95 percent—while not allowing for AIX (UNIX) paging. In the previously mentioned scenario, an RS/6000 system with 128 megabytes of memory can easily handle a load of approximately 20,000 pages per day. At peak usage, the cache hit rates are in the 97 to 98 percent range, there is no UNIX paging, and the CPU utilization never exceeds 20 percent, see Figure 2.

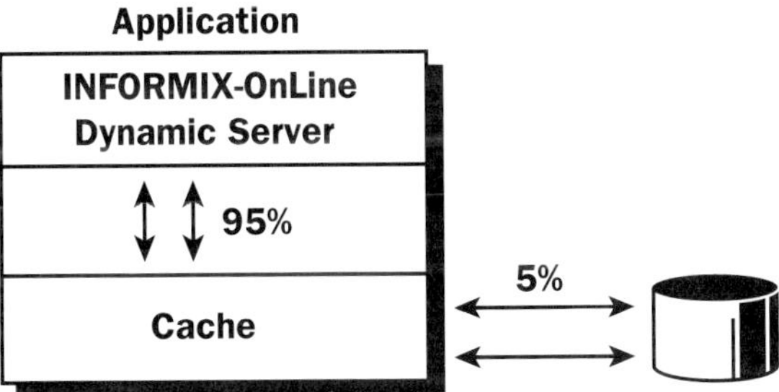

Figure 2: Highly optimized database caching improves performance.

The memory buffers are especially important for the imageABLE system, since some small, very frequently accessed tables are used for security validation. For example, the SAIACC table contains the relations between users, groups, and access levels. Since security is an issue on nearly all imageABLE server transactions, the entire table tends to stay in a memory cache to provide a very low overhead for security validation.

Indexes

Indexes are the method used by a relational database manager to allow extremely fast access to millions and millions of records in a table. In the imageABLE product, indexes on the database tables are created automatically during installation.

Statistics Update

Each time a query is run against the database, INFORMIX-OnLine Dynamic Server (OnLine Dynamic Server) takes a look at the current state of the indexes and tables, and chooses the best approach to the data. Sometimes, this involves using indexes. At other times, however, it requires scanning all records in a dbspace.

For performance reasons, OnLine Dynamic Server does not review the tables and indexes to determine their usability when executing a query. OnLine Dynamic Server keeps internal statistics about all tables and indexes which it uses in a form that can be quickly accessed during query optimization. A common mistake is to install a clean database (without rows, and with perfectly arranged indexes), and subsequently load in several hundred-thousand records. At about the 100,000 mark, OnLine Dynamic Server scans all the records in the dbspace, since it believes there is no data in the tables. Needless to say, performance can dramatically drop.

The **UPDATE STATISTICS** command looks at the current condition of all tables and indexes, and records the condition for use during query optimization. **UPDATE STATISTICS** records information, such as the number of physical pages used by each table, the selectivity of each index, the number of levels for each index's B+tree, and so on. In most cases, Informix's query optimizer is excellent when using valid data.

Clustering

Clustering is a method used by database managers to keep rows with the same or similar values in certain columns, physically close in storage. A good use for clustering is to physically group data which tends to be selected (read) together. This can sometimes mean that one physical dbspace read can fulfill an entire SELECT request—even when the SELECT returns more than one row. This method, in turn, tends to reduce the I/O requirements.

A good example of clustering usage within an imageABLE system is the *CONTR* field within the SAIVO table. If a folder, for example, contains 20 documents, then the *CONTR* field for the rows for each document has the same value. By clustering this field, the operation of seeing the folder contents (20 documents) can probably be resolved by one or two physical dbspaces page reads, and this reduces the I/O required for folder handling.

Keywords

The standard tables used by imageABLE for normal operation have been optimized for the best possible performance in most installations. However, when an imageABLE administrator creates a site-specific table for user indexes, it is necessary to create indexes that are appropriate for the way that users access the data. The choices for the indexes are the same as for any table: index or not on each column, unique or not, clustered, or a combination index.

Indexes are only useful when selecting from a table. Indexes are actually not useful when inserting and updating, as some database overhead is incurred to rearrange the B+tree for the index. Only place an index on a column which users frequently search. A very common mistake in setting up a new system is to either over-index a keyword category, or not index at all.

Concurrency

On a system with more than a few users, the ability to concurrently access the same or related data with little or no effect on other users is essential. The imageABLE product allows concurrent access to the database, since a separate AIX process is created for each client. For database-oriented server transactions, the server's ability to handle concurrency is a value-added pass through to the database manager. Note the following figure.

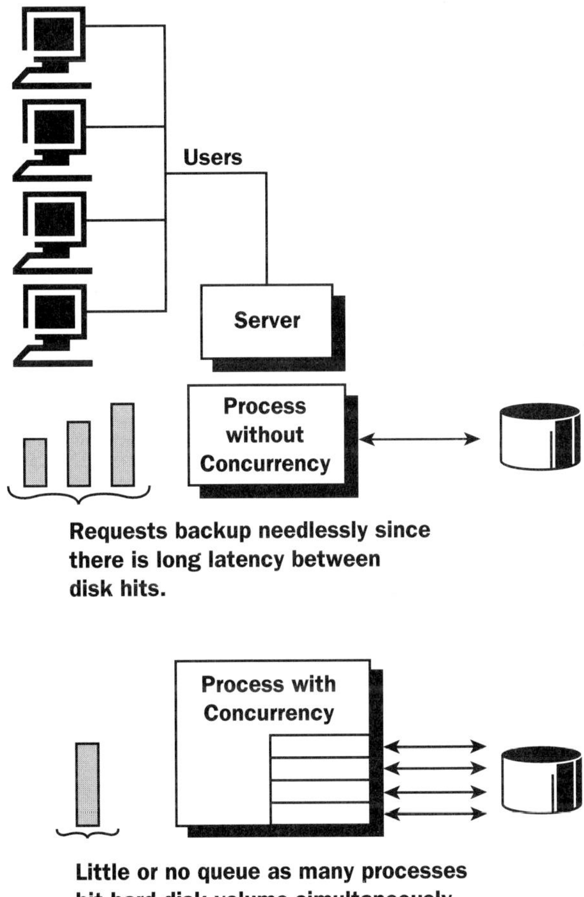

Figure 3: Concurrency takes advantage of disk latency.

Isolation Levels

The database isolation level is set from each client and determines how the pieces of the database will be locked for certain types of database transactions. INFORMIX-OnLine Dynamic Server implements four different isolation levels, ranging from DIRTY read to REPEATABLE read. In the lowest level (DIRTY), no lock held by another process can stop data from being read, and no new locks are generated by reading the database. In the highest level (REPEATABLE), no data can be read which has some other lock placed on it by another process, and the very act of reading the data (SELECT) can cause the data to be locked.

There are advantages and disadvantages to either extreme. With DIRTY read, a process is never stopped during a read by another process. On the other hand, the data read may not be fully committed and could potentially change. With REPEATABLE read, the data is always valid, but excessive locking can severely hurt concurrency.

In the imageABLE system, database information must be distributed concurrently to the clients. The SQL transaction is only open for a brief period while the data is read, and is closed before the data is sent to the client. In other words, due to the distributed architecture, data is assumed to be always "dirty." Thus, within the imageABLE system, setting the isolation to DIRTY read allows a high degree of concurrency. To further exploit this aspect of imageABLE and INFORMIX-OnLine Dynamic Server, the imageABLE 3.01 release allows an administrator to set the isolation level for all clients system-wide.

Lock Mode

Although the isolation level can help avoid database locks during reads (SELECTs), locks still occur, and should, during updates. In INFORMIX-OnLine Dynamic Server, locks allow processes to update shared data without creating an inconsistency. When a process must perform an update, it tries to obtain a lock on the data. If another process is also updating the same data, then the second process is temporarily blocked until the first one completes its transaction.

In INFORMIX-OnLine Dynamic Server, there are two lock modes which can be set table by table. Row-level locking obtains locks on individual rows. Row-level locking is useful since it explicitly locks the affected rows. However, it requires more overhead in processing lock requests. Page-level locking has much less overhead since the sheer number of locks is smaller. Yet, with page-level locking, data on the same physical data page is also locked, although the data itself may not be necessary to the transaction which generated the lock.

The default for the imageABLE system is page-level locking. Since imageABLE's update and insert transactions are quickly executed, this is usually sufficient. For row-level locking, a table's lock mode can be changed by simple ALTER TABLE commands.

Deadlock Detection and Retries

Although locks can be reduced by setting the database isolation and designing a product with as brief as possible transaction durations, deadlocks still occur. When locking conditions occur, most are resolveable. However, there are occasions when a database process cannot complete its transaction since it continues to wait for a lock to be freed. In this situation, there is no other choice but to roll back the transaction (thereby releasing all locks) and return an error to the application.

In such a case, the application making the database requests is the imageABLE server. The imageABLE server not only detects these temporary lock conditions, but also automatically retries the locks at the server level. This feature is available in release 3.01 of imageABLE. The administrator can specify a retry count and the number of seconds that the server should wait between retries.

Summary

An optimized database is a key for a successful imageABLE installation. INFORMIX-OnLine Dynamic Server provides a number of powerful ways to accomplish this. A number of successful large-scale installations have proven that elegant theories about data management can be easily applied to critical real-world situations.

About the Author

Dan Hunsinger is the system architect and senior manager of imageABLE Research and Development for Bluebird Systems. He is a contributing author in the field of imaging and electronic document management. He can be reached at danh@bluebird.com.

About Bluebird Systems

Bluebird Systems provides imaging products—including imageABLE—which support mission-critical and enterprise-wide systems and applications. The products comprise document imaging, workflow and COLD applications, which together provide a total document management solution. For additional information regarding imageABLE and other electronic document management products, please contact Bluebird Systems at 5900 La Place Court, Carlsbad, California 92008; telephone: 619 438 2220, or 800 669 2220 (in North America); and facsimile: 619 438 4560.

GUI Design in a Database Environment

=27 GUI Design Considerations

by Jeffrey Blake

Introduction

The realm of computer developers usually encompasses expertise in coding, architecture design, and the intricacies of hardware or software operating systems. However, few developers study ergonomics, color theory, or visual design principles; typically, these areas are considered the domain of visual designers.

When Microsoft™ Windows-based PCs became the standard for desktop publishing, many computer developers invested time in learning word processing and, in some cases, learned to use software specific to desktop publishing. This allowed developers, who were untrained as document designers, to unleash a flurry of home-grown desktop-published documents. The point of this discussion is that tools like desktop publishing packages and laser printers do not substitute for the study and mastery of good visual design techniques.

With the wide availability of Windows-based PCs and GUI development software, the phenomenon has resurfaced. There is a vast proliferation of full-featured, yet poorly conceived screen designs. Fortunately, many of the visual design principles used in desktop publishing can be applied to the design of GUI screens.

Visual Design Issues

Good design is essential to a successful interface. Too many screens are designed to accommodate all the functionality possible for a given set of tasks. However, providing functionality in its totality is not necessarily the best use of resources. Too often, a screen is cluttered with the minutiae of the application. A GUI designer must be careful to include all necessary information, while excluding information which is not essential. Where effective design principles are concerned, what is left out is just as important as what remains in an application.

Use of White Space

Designers often refer to areas void of clutter as white space. Using white space is an effective way to separate information by category or to minimize eyestrain in the viewing of text-heavy documents. Often used in the design of a printed page, white space can be incorporated in GUI design and contributes to the successful rendering of visual design concepts.

Colors

Colors are among the most misused components in the design of visual interfaces. Since GUI software typically offers a palette of thousands of colors, many developers feel compelled to overuse colors. Unfortunately, this misuse detracts from the overall design of GUI interfaces. Instead, color should be used for definite and specific reasons. For example, it's no coincidence that the color blue is selected to represent water and the color brown is used to indicate land in the design of maps.

Colors should be used judiciously and sparingly. When building an interface, it is best to select a specific color group. The Color Settings/Color Schemes from the Microsoft Windows control panel can be used to decide which colors are most effective in a grouping. It is best to select color groups which complement each other and provide information in a contextual sense.

After selecting a color group, choose a style for each selected color. The GUI designer should use each defined and specific set of colors consistently throughout the application. Consistency in the use of colors provides continuity for end users, and gives a compelling and professional look to applications.

3-D Visuals

Many GUIs in today's environments support some form of 3-D graphics. It is important to note that 3-D graphics are only 2-D graphics with effects which visually approximate the third dimension; thus, the key is to create the illusion of a third dimension. Renaissance artists, such as Leonardo da Vinci, produced the illusion of third-dimensional representations by effectively using light and shadow.

In terms of GUI design, the most common example of a 3-D visual is the 3-D box, used extensively in the Motif environment. By closely examining the 3-D box, in Figure 1, it is obvious that this graphics object is nothing more than a simple rectangle containing areas of light and shadow.

The light portions of the box are produced by the use of a light color, while the dark areas of the box are represented by a darker hue of the light color. To the user, this simple use of color produces a visual representation of the third dimension.

To create this illusion when building a GUI screen interface, use a simple paint program. Experiment with various color families to arrive at the optimal visual appearance of the interface. It is interesting to note that in many GUI enviornments, the use of gray as a base color is prevalent; it allows the color white to be used as a light variation, and the color black as a shadow. This prevalence is partly explained by the fact that early development platforms supported a limited number of colors, and the gray-white-black combination provided a good range of light to shadow.

Figure 1: 3-D box.

Charts

Many visual objects which are now common to the GUI environment are not much more than simple graphical ideas which are built one upon another. The example of a bar graph can be easily built out of a series of lines in various weights. A line weight is a number which signifies the thickness of a given line. For example, a line with a weight of 20 points appears much thicker than a line with a weight of four points.

To build a bar graph, begin by creating the X and Y axis using a lightweight line in a neutral color, such as black. For the bar in the bar graph, determine the maximum value and simply build a line with a dimension which is equal to the maximum value. In addition, create a line which represents the bar in a contrasting color, and use a line weight which is heavy enough to contrast to the smaller line weight used for the axis. If the graph requires a heavier bar, the use of the INFORMIX-NewEra ixBox can be used. Filling within the perimeter lines can be accomplished by simply creating an ixBox with a line weight so large that the perimeters seem to overlap. This method creates a box that appears to be completely filled with the line color. In addition, the developer can programatically control the size of the box dynamically, simply by changing the anchor value and reading a value from a database. This technique allows customized of bar graphs to change when data from the database changes.

The same idea can be used to build a barometer object, commonly used to show the progress of installations and similar operations, see Figure 2. First, create a 3-D rectangle with a paint or graphics package. Then, create an ixBox in INFORMIX-NewEra and increment the anchor value as the progress through the application increases.

Since INFORMIX-NewEra code is portable across Windows and Motif platforms (i.e., different screen resolutions), the issue of the portability of graphics objects remains. Obviously, the fact that the Windows and Motif platforms support different file formats is an important consideration, as well as the size and resolution of those graphic formats.

Figure 2: Barometer.

Bitmap Issues

When developing for more than one target platform, the GUI designer must be aware of all hardware which will be included in the deployment. Essential to the design process is a knowledge of the specifics related to the available graphics hardware.

The screen resolution determines the physical size of the display. A screen resolution of 640 by 480 results in less "real-estate" for the display of windows, controls, and images than a screen which has a screen resolution of 1040 by 720. Therefore, the constraints of hardware, such as screen resolutions, must be considered when designing visual interfaces.

The most effective approach is to design for the least common denominator. In other words, keep the screen metrics at the lowest possible resolution to accommodate the platform with the least robust characteristics. This is recommended because all platforms can accommodate a low-resolution image, however, a low-end screen cannot support graphics created for a high-resolution display.

Another significant issue involves color support. Again, high-end color adapters and monitors are capable of displaying millions of colors, while low-end hardware adapters support only 256 colors (or less). Even two similar hardware adapters and monitors can, at times, appear to display very different visual characteristics. The software drivers must also be examined in this environment to ensure consistency across platforms in a deployment. Using the design approach of the least common denominator can also be successful in such a situation.

Software

The right software and hardware products simplify the task of designing visual screens. In most cases, it is best to have more than one graphics-related software package with which to build and modify graphic images. Graphic images, or clip-art, can be easily obtained from either commercially available software packages or the Internet.

Optimal features of a graphics package include the following:

- The ability to cut and paste from other packages (irregular-shape cuts);

- The capability to produce color fills;

- The capability of handling multiple line widths;

- The ability to create text or import it from other packages;

- The ability to scale images (enlarge or reduce image size); and

- An extensive palette of colors for painting.

For most beginners, the Paintbrush program, included with Microsoft Windows software, provides most of the necessary features.

Programs with advanced features offer image alteration capabilities, such as the blurring or sharpening of an image's focus for special effects. Additionally, some packages provide color alteration modules with the following features:

- The manipulation of colors in scanned photographs;

- The conversion of monochrome (single color) images to color images;

- The conversion of color images to monochrome images; and

- The ability to make images "transparent" by varying degrees.

While software packages, such as Adobe™ PhotoShop™ and CorelPaint™, provide advanced features, there is usually a learning curve to overcome in learning advanced techniques. Despite such special effects, a simple design is often most effective.

Another useful software product is a graphics conversion tool. There are literally dozens of graphic file storage formats for the Windows platform alone; additionally, there are various Macintosh and UNIX formats. From time to time, images reside in a format that is unknown to your software. In such cases, it is necessary to convert the existing file format to a format recognized by a specific software package. This process can be greatly simplified by the use of a graphics conversion utility.

Graphics conversion utilities convert files from one format to another. In some cases, the utilities perform read and write in various disk formats. For example, conversion utilties can read a Macintosh disk and write the file to a DOS diskette format. One such example of a graphics conversion package is HiJack™ Pro for Windows.

Hardware

Arguably, the hardware devices most critical to graphics work include the graphics and video display units used by the computer itself. Many types of display units are available for Macintosh and PC platforms. Typically, image quality is defined by the number of pixels (picture elements on a screen) which can be accommodated by a display. This metric, known as screen resolution, measures the number of pixels across a screen by the number of pixels along a screen's height. The standard VGA (video graphics adapter) is defined as 640 by 480 pixels, while Super VGA is defined as 1040 by 720. The higher the resolution, the higher the quality of the image on the screen, and the higher the cost.

Scanners

Graphics work can be greatly enhanced by the use of a scanner. A scanner is a device which converts drawings, pictures, and photographs into computer files through the process of digitization. The original image is scanned by a laser or LED beam, and is reflected back by the beam; then, the image is converted into digital information. The digital information is finally converted into an image which can be saved in a format for use by a graphics software package.

The most popular scanners include the flat-bed scanner and the hand-held scanner. A flat-bed scanner is a desktop device; it usually features a flat-bed surface, where the image is placed for scanning by the laser. The hand-held scanner requires that a user physically move the scanner over an image. While not as convenient, hand-held scanners are, in most cases, less costly.

Video Capture

A video capture device is another useful tool for obtaining graphic images. A video capture board is a card which can be installed in the expansion slots of a computer system and accommodates an input from a VCR or video camera. With video capture capabilities, it is possible to play videos or shoot live video, capture those images on the computer, and subsequently, save the images to a graphics file.

Usability

An important concept in the design of visual interfaces is the notion of usability. The relationship between man and machines is known as ergonomics. Ergonomic principles are now applied to the study of visual interface design. The following are valid ergonomic concepts which can be directly applied to the INFORMIX-NewEra Window Painter.

The INFORMIX-NewEra ListBox

An INFORMIX-NewEra ListBox displays a list of elements in a box. This box can be "pulled down" with a mouse. The ListBox provides a list of available elements, and a control for scrolling up and down through the list.

An instance of poor usability can arise if the ListBox contains more than 30 rows for a single element list or if more than one element is displayed. Potentially, the user can spend too much time in scrolling through a list; ironically, the GUI designer may have created such a list with convenience in mind. At this point, the investigation of a different control mechanism is necessary, for example, a query-by-example field (due to the large number of potential rows available).

Another problem can occur when the GUI designer must accommodate a number of potential user-evoked events. The typical control of choice is a button; however, the screen is quickly cluttered when more than six buttons appear on the screen for similar choices. An adept designer can use a pull-down menu, adding an extra step for the user, yet resulting in a more pleasing and efficient-looking screen, refer to Figure 3.

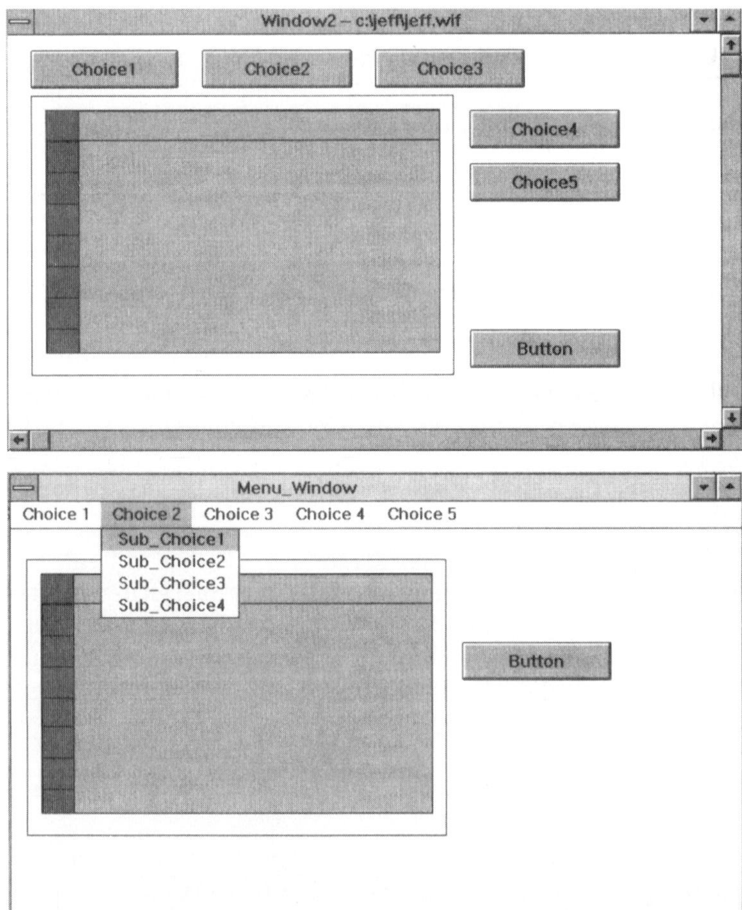

Figure 3: Example of before and after screens which contrast the button and menu styles.

Style Guide

Style guides can be used to standardize and document decisions regarding GUI design conventions. When distributed to a large group of in-house GUI designers, style guides help to ensure the uniformity and consistency of GUI interface design across many applications.

Conclusion

The GUI design concepts discussed in this article are intended as general guidelines. More information on GUI design is available in the sources listed in the following References section.

References

Journal of Human/Computer Interaction.

Mullet, K. and Sano, D. *Designing Visual Interfaces.* Mountain View, CA: Sunset Press, 1995.

Tuft, Edward. *The Visual Display of Quantitative Information.* Chesire, CN: Graphics Press, 1983.

Tuft, Edward. *Envisioning Information.* Chesire, CN: Graphics Press, 1990.

About the Author

Jeffery Blake is a systems engineer at Informix, Detroit, Michigan.

GOOD DESIGN CONCEPTS FOR INFORMIX APPLICATIONS

by Matthew Eichler

Introduction

This article describes elements of good software design. Examples and guidelines for software design are also provided in the context of this article.

Overview

Every software developer has an individual idea of what constitutes good design. "Good design" depends on your particular point of view:

Point of View	Good Design Is...
Users	Quick response time.
	Easy to learn, friendly interface (no manual required).
Programmers	Easy to read, well-docummented code (useful when taking over code).
	Modular design, discreet functionality.
	Re-usable components (it is not necessary to reinvent the wheel).
Project Managers	All functional requirements are met—the users are happy with the end result.
System Administrators	Easy to administer, needs little attention.
	Few hotline calls.

In the most general sense then, good design results in maintainable applications. It is useful to look at each aspect of bad design and examine how it impacts the maintability of an application:

Bad Design for...	Impact on Production System
Performance	System administrators must continually adjust the database schema, database server, and operating system in an attempt to improve performance.
Documentation and Readable Code	One programmer taking over for another wastes time in attempting to understand the inherited code.
Administration	System administrators waste time continually while tending to an application; this time could be better spent on mission-critical system projects.
Modules	The application is difficult and time-consuming to change—a seemingly simple change unexpectedly breaks other modules.
Re-usability	Programmers waste time by continually creating applications anew; no one took the required time to design with reuse in mind.

In all cases, valuable resources are wasted due to bad design. Many software process analysts have written about the impact of design defects on overall costs over time, note Figure 1.

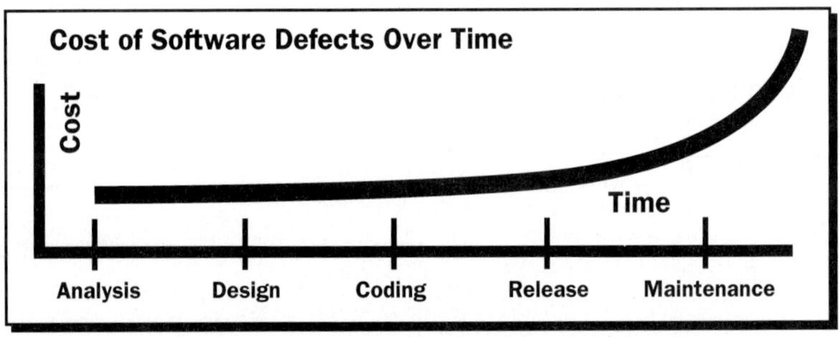

Figure 1: Cost of software defects over time.

The sooner that good design methods are used in the software process, the greater the cost benefits over time. Good design is nearly always a trade-off. What might be an excellent interface, widely accepted by users in the prototype phase, can be a disaster for performance once the application enters production. A fully-normalized database may be a good theoretical design, but is often difficult to maintain since normalization produces many database tables. Also, good design is measured differently by various business requirements; a telemarketing application might require few keystrokes and a plain character interface, while a decision support system for stockbrokers might require a graphical presentation mostly controlled by the mouse (the mouse would only slow the telemarketers).

Therefore, a software development team must continually define and document the meaning of good design based on the requirements of specific industries, users, and environments. This is a continual process which results in clear guidelines for developers and measurable results.

Eight Ways to Improve the Design of Informix Applications

Following are eight suggestions which can be used to improve the overall design of Informix applications.

Continually Review the Software Process

Establish a software process team to review and build standards, procedures, and tools for developers. The team should be comprised of representatives from all areas, including project management, analysis, programming, testing, and system administration.

The group should meet on a regular basis with clear agendas. Tackling good design can be an intimidating task to initiate, so it is best to take small steps first: master one issue at a time. For instance, the first goal might be to deliver a coding standards document in the first quarter of meetings. Then, a database design standards document might be the next deliverable.

Improve Analysis

Good design can only be obtained from good analysis techniques. Many software projects fail because the wrong problem was solved; this is a failure in analysis. The greatest cost benefits are gained by providing a thorough and accurate analysis of business problems. The software process team should develop guidelines for analysis procedures and standard analysis document formats. A standard analysis document would have required sections, regardless of the size of the project. Such sections include, for instance, a problem statement, a logical view of the proposed system (data flow diagram), cost/benefit analysis, and at least three alternative solutions. Also, establish review methods and metrics for analysis just as for the design and implementation phases of the software process.

Establish Coding Standards

A coding standards document can specify:

- Module, function, and in-line commenting formats;

- Naming conventions;

- How and when SQL statements are to be prepared;

- How and when to use referential integrity, stored procedures, and triggers;

- Report formats;

- User interface;

- How to use the scoping of variables and functions; and

- Error handling.

It is important to remember that coding standards evolve over time. Also, standards change as new tools are acquired; standards will be different for INFORMIX-SQL, INFORMIX-4GL, INFORMIX-ESQL/C, INFORMIX-HyperScript, and INFORMIX-NewEra.

Control Database Design

Teams that work with very large (multi-gigabyte) databases already know that database design should be managed separately from application design. The best solution is to hire one or more experienced Informix database administrators whose specialty is to advise on the building and maintenance of databases. For smaller companies, this luxury is not affordable. In such cases, a solution is to review the database design with outsiders who have several years of experience in building Informix databases.

Without separate database design reviews, programmers can easily fall into the trap of treating the database server as a black box and not design the databases with performance and maintainability in mind. Good database design methods should take into consideration the features available from today's Informix servers: stored procedures, triggers, referential integrity, constraints, fragmentation, and parallelism. Also, the software process team should develop tools for database version control, and link a particular version of the database with a corresponding version of the application.

Establish a Design Review Process

A good review process supplies invaluable feedback on a software project's progress to its developers. The software process team should provide guidelines for frequency and structure. Regardless of the review methods used, review processes should never be used as a means to criticize or denigrate the author of the reviewed product. A review should instead focus on pointing out potential problem areas, and allow the developer to decide how and when to fix the problems. Reviews can be at a high level (project reviews) or at a very detailed level (technical reviews). It is often useful to include outsiders to provide an objective view of the material. Types of reviews include the following: inspections, where every detail is considered; walkthroughs, where the material is presented with many details skipped; or unstructured reviews, where the material is freely discussed. Regardless of the method, thc team should have a Recorder document the list of issues unearthed by the review.

Establish Metrics

Metrics provide a quantifiable and identifiable way to measure the success or deficiencies of software design. The software process team can use metrics to determine how well their guidelines are working toward improving software design. Software metrics most often measure the number of defects, the part of the process in which the defects were discovered, and the time required to correct the defects. Provide simple tools (start with a small database and a single INFORMIX-4GL screen or an INFORMIX-NewEra window for entry) to allow developers and users to track defects; keep the tools in a single database for all projects. Metrics can extend to all phases: from missed requirements in the analysis phase to a conversion mistake in the deployment phase. Tracking defects should not be so time-consuming as to impact the developers' jobs, otherwise the results will be skewed.

Enable Reuse

Programmers should be educated and encouraged to develop functions and classes with reuse in mind. Libraries should be kept in a directory which is accessible to all developers and accompanied by simple tools (shell scripts or INFORMIX-ViewPoint forms, for instance) to query for information. Each function/class should be well-documented and published with regular updates. One of the charters of the software process team should be to manage libraries; reuse reviews should examine existing libraries for possible improvement and consider new reuse candidates. Existing libraries can become useless overnight as upgrades to new versions of tools occur, and business systems evolve. Reward and recognize programmers for the submission of good reuse functions and/or classes. Also, publish reuse guidelines.

Consider CASE

The Computer Assisted System Engineering (CASE) promise is to generate applications using models. Ideally, the development team evolves systems from a top-down approach; starting with high-level logical models of processes and data, then working down to a detailed design. CASE tools usually involve code generation to actually implement the system. The goal is for the team to not consider their business systems in terms of pages of source code and begin to think about systems as a set of component parts: building blocks which can be shared across the enterprise. Good CASE tools provide this approach by providing a central repository of components which projects and applications share. Some of the side benefits of CASE include the following: the ability to communicate views of systems to users with a level of detail which is easily understood; accurate requirements tracing; reuse; and automated documentation.

The first step towards CASE is obtaining a team consensus regarding methodology. Design parameters can include: Structured Analysis/Design, Object Orientation or both. Models to be considered can be based on those of Yourdon/Demarco, Gane/Sarson, or Rumbaugh. The decision will be based entirely on past experience, environment, and tools: structured for INFORMIX-4GL and INFORMIX-ESQL/C, object for INFORMIX-NewEra. Pushing developers up the steep learning curve requires much effort, so it is important to be in agreement on methodology. The next step is to carefully evaluate CASE tools and formulate a pilot project. Take time to look at the pros and cons of each package. There are Informix partners with integrated CASE products; check with your Informix salesperson for contacts. CASE was a buzzword for awhile and, as such, fathered many misconceptions. CASE is not a productivity tool; ramping up is a major and expensive undertaking. CASE is never "methodology independent." Tools always have some roots in a given methodology. Be aware that many graphical application builders and modeling tools are labeled as CASE; however, as independent products, they do not share a central repository. Thus, much of the benefits are lost. Look for integrated CASE tools which provide all required modeling tools and cover as many phases of development as possible in a single environment.

Examples of Standards which Help Improve Design

An Example of a Standard Analysis Document Format

The following example shows the summary view of an analysis document template with required and optional sections.

Section	**Required?**
Executive Summary • Condensed recap of points in narrative form	❏
Project Definition • Problem statement: Description of business problem to be addressed • Project scope/objectives: Requirements to be addressed	❏
Method of Study	❏
Business Requirements • User requirements; prioritized	❏
Current System • Description of current physical process: With references to source materials • Description of current logical process: Data flow diagrams	❏*
Proposed System • Description of proposed logical process: Data flow diagrams	❏*
Alternative Implementations • At least three alternatives are required, include pros and cons	❏
Recommendation	❏
High Level Acceptance Plan • User acceptance criteria: System external interfaces	❏
High Level Installation Plan • Constraints on installation, conversion, and installation tasks	
Cost Benefit Support	❏
Appendix • Sample source documents (forms, reports, and layouts) • Interview documentation	

* Unless re-engineering business processes, the logical DFDs of the current and proposed systems will be the same.

Examples which Make Code Easier to Maintain

Naming Conventions

Naming conventions in INFORMIX-4GL can assist the reader in immediately recognizing the type and scope of the variables. In this example, the standard for variable names is in lower case characters, with underscores for clarity:

Prefix	Type	Scope	Example
p_	scalar	local	DEFINE p_count INTEGER
m_		module (file)	DEFINE m_update DATE
g_		global	DEFINE g_company CHAR(30)
pa_	array	local	DEFINE pa_dates ARRAY[2] OF DATE
ma_		module (file)	DEFINE ma_timespans ARRAY[2] OF INTERVAL HOUR TO SECOND
ga_		global	DEFINE ga_names ARRAY[50] OF CHAR(30)
pr_	record	local	DEFINE pr_customer LIKE customer.*
mr_		module (file)	DEFINE mr_req_call LIKE req_call.*
gr_		global	DEFINE gr_serv_type LIKE serv_type.*
pre_	prepared statement	module (file)	PREPARE pre_upd_call FROM p_sqlstmt
curs_cursor			DECLARE curs_custcall CURSOR FOR pre_custcall

Naming conventions in INFORMIX-NewEra can assist the reader in recognizing immediately of which class the variable is an instance. Object-oriented languages often use a mix of upper and lower case letters for object names:

Prefix	Class		Example
vl	ixValue	VARIABLE	vlResult ixValue
ss	ixSQLStmt	VARIABLE	ssDeleteCust ixSQLStmt
sf	ixSuperField	VARIABLE	sfCustomerNum ixSuperField
st	ixSuperTable	VARIABLE	stCustomer ixSuperTable
tb	ixTextBox	VARIABLE	tbBlueBox ixTextBox
lb	ixListBox	VARIABLE	lbServiceTypes ixListBox
el	ixEditListBox	VARIABLE	elCallTypes ixEditListBox
wn	ixWindow	VARIABLE	wnCustEdit ixWindow

On the following page is an example of a standard review form. This form is intended for use in walk-through reviews.

Review Form

Producer:	Date:
Deliverable:	

Walkthrough Team

Reader:	Recorder:

Reviewers:

Findings: ☐ **Accept As Is**   ☐ **Accept with minor changes**   ☐ **Recommend Rewrite**

Issues: **Date Addressed:**

Figure 2: A standard review form.

A good way to structure walk-through reviews is to assign a person to read a standard review form aloud, and ask another person to record the issues which are brought up, so that the producer has a check list of items to work from.

Examples which Make the Production System Easier to Maintain, or which Improve Performance

Referential Integrity

Referential integrity guards the relationships between tables at the server, ensuring that updates to the database do not corrupt those connections. For instance, in a master-detail relationship, referential integrity can prevent the creation of a detail row without a master row, or prevents a master row from being deleted, if detail rows still exist.

Note the following tables:

```
CREATE TABLE customer
(
customer_num SERIAL NOT NULL,
    fname CHAR(15),
    lname CHAR(15),
    company CHAR(20),
    address1 CHAR(20),
    address2 CHAR(20),
    city CHAR(15),
    state CHAR(2),
    zipcode CHAR(5),
    phone CHAR(18),
  );
CREATE UNIQUE INDEX iu_customer01 ON customer(customer_num);
CREATE TABLE call_type
  (
    call_code CHAR(1),
    code_descr CHAR(30),
  );
CREATE UNIQUE INDEX iu_calltype01 ON call_type(call_code);

CREATE TABLE cust_calls
(
```

```
(
    customer_num integer,
                            (
      call_dtime DATETIME YEAR TO MINUTE,
    user_id CHAR(18)
        DEFAULT USER,
    call_code CHAR(1),
    call_descr CHAR(240),
    res_dtime DATETIME YEAR TO MINUTE,
    res_descr CHAR(240),
  );
CREATE UNIQUE INDEX iu_custcall01
ON cust_calls(customer_num, call_dtime);
Could be redesigned with referential integrity :
CREATE TABLE customer
  (
    customer_num SERIAL NOT NULL,
    fname CHAR(15),
    lname CHAR(15),
    company CHAR(15),
    address1 CHAR(20),
    address2 CHAR(20),
    city CHAR(15),
    state CHAR(2),
    zipcode CHAR(5),
    phone CHAR(18),
    PRIMARY KEY (customer_num) CONSTRAINT u_customer01
  );
CREATE TABLE call_type
  (
    call_code CHAR(1),
    code_descr CHAR(30),
    PRIMARY KEY (call_code) CONSTRAINT u_calltype01
  );
CREATE TABLE cust_calls
  (
    customer_num integer,
    call_dtime DATETIME YEAR TO MINUTE,
    user_id CHAR(18)
```

```
        DEFAULT USER,
    call_code CHAR(1),
    call_descr CHAR(240),
    res_dtime DATETIME YEAR TO MINUTE,
    res_descr CHAR(240),
    PRIMARY KEY (customer_num,call_dtime) CONSTRAINT u_custcall01
  );
ALTER TABLE cust_calls ADD CONSTRAINT
(FOREIGN KEY (customer_num)
    REFERENCES customer  CONSTRAINT r_custcall01);
ALTER TABLE cust_calls ADD CONSTRAINT
(FOREIGN KEY (call_code)
    REFERENCES call_type
    ON DELETE CASCADE CONSTRAINT r_custcall02);
```

Breaking Large Tables with Many Indexes into Smaller Tables

If a frequently accessed table has a row size greater than a page, has more than 20 columns or more than three indexes, it can benefit from re-design. Simply break the size up. A single large table can be split up into two or more smaller tables, based on how columns are grouped logically, how frequently column groups are accessed, and how columns are indexed. This re-design process requires a careful study of the way applications actually use the data in the table. The result is easier to manage than sets of data. This re-structuring can also result in a performance gain and the DBA has the opportunity to place the data in more than one dbspace. The following example is an invoice header table which is frequently queried by more than 15 users.

Studying the application and interviewing users determines that the table is queried by either invoice number, billing information, or shipping information:

```
CREATE TABLE inv_mast
    inv_num SERIAL PRIMARY KEY CONSTRAINT u_inv_mast01,
    ref_num INTEGER NOT NULL,
    ord_num INTEGER NOT NULL,
    ord_rev SMALLINT NOT NULL,
    contract_num INTEGER,
    amend_num SMALLINT,
    inv_date DATE NOT NULL,
    ref_date DATE NOT NULL,
    ord_date DATE NOT NULL,
```

```
print_date DATE,
inv_type CHAR(1) NOT NULL,
revenue_type CHAR(1) NOT NULL,
bill_cust_id INTEGER NOT NULL,
bill_cust_rev SMALLINT NOT NULL,
ship_cust_id INTEGER NOT NULL,
ship_cust_rev SMALLINT NOT NULL,
corp_cust_id INTEGER,
prospno CHAR(10),
b_contact CHAR(35),
b_title CHAR(20),
b_company CHAR(45),
b_addr1 CHAR(35),
b_addr2 CHAR(35),
b_addr3 CHAR(35),
b_city CHAR(35),
b_state CHAR(2),
b_zip CHAR(10),
b_country_code CHAR(3),
b_int_prefix CHAR(7),
b_phone CHAR(14),
b_fax CHAR(14),
b_notes VARCHAR(250,15),
s_contact CHAR(35),
s_title CHAR(20),
s_company CHAR(45),
s_addr1 CHAR(35),
s_addr2 CHAR(35),
s_addr3 CHAR(35),
s_city CHAR(35),
s_state CHAR(2),
s_zip CHAR(10),
s_country_code CHAR(3),
s_int_prefix CHAR(7),
s_phone CHAR(14),
s_fax CHAR(14),
s_notes VARCHAR(250,15),
mkt_segment CHAR(4) NOT NULL,
sls_chanl CHAR(4) NOT NULL,
```

```
    bus_type CHAR(4) NOT NULL,
    gov_contract_num CHAR(20),
    cust_po_num CHAR(20),
    resale_id CHAR(26),
    cr_terms CHAR(2) NOT NULL,
    taxable CHAR(1),
    fobflag CHAR(1) NOT NULL,
    ship_via CHAR(3),
    sa_contact CHAR(8),
    slsrep2 CHAR(10),
    sort_code SMALLINT,
    dept_code SMALLINT,
    sls_terr CHAR(10),
    pool_of_funds INTEGER,
    auth_num INTEGER,
    rma_num CHAR(6),
    global_mkt_flag CHAR(1) NOT NULL,
    notecodes CHAR(10),
    cr_reason CHAR(4),
    ord_tot MONEY(16,2) NOT NULL,
    tax_chg MONEY(8,2) NOT NULL,
    ship_chg MONEY(8,2) NOT NULL,
    spcl_fee MONEY(8,2) NOT NULL,
    usr_name CHAR(8) NOT NULL,
    date_stamp DATE NOT NULL,
    time_stamp CHAR(8) NOT NULL,
    cr_subcode CHAR(1),
    s_county CHAR(15)
  );
CREATE INDEX ix_inv_mast01 ON inv_mast (inv_date);
CREATE INDEX ix_inv_mast02 ON inv_mast (ref_num);
CREATE INDEX ix_inv_mast03 ON inv_mast (ship_cust_id,ship_cust_rev);
CREATE INDEX ix_inv_mast04 ON inv_mast (bill_cust_id,bill_cust_rev);
CREATE INDEX ix_inv_mast05 ON inv_mast (s_company,s_city);
CREATE INDEX ix_inv_mast06 ON inv_mast (b_contact,b_city);
CREATE INDEX ix_inv_mast07 ON inv_mast (b_company,b_city);
CREATE INDEX ix_inv_mast08 ON inv_mast (s_contact,s_city);
CREATE INDEX ix_inv_mast09 ON inv_mast (ord_num,ord_rev);
CREATE INDEX ix_inv_mast10 ON inv_mast (print_date);
```

```
CREATE INDEX ix_inv_mast11 ON inv_mast (cust_po_num);
CREATE INDEX ix_inv_mast12 ON inv_mast (sls_terr);
```

This table can be broken into three smaller tables with a one-to-one relationship. Most of the queries only access one of the three tables, so now the engine accesses smaller data pages. Notice that this is a trade-off in terms of disk space, since the primary key from the original table is now repeated three times:

```
CREATE TABLE inv_mast
    inv_num SERIAL PRIMARY KEY CONSTRAINT u_inv_mast01,
    ref_num INTEGER NOT NULL,
    ord_num INTEGER NOT NULL,
    ord_rev SMALLINT NOT NULL,
    contract_num INTEGER,
    amend_num SMALLINT,
    inv_date DATE NOT NULL,
    ref_date DATE NOT NULL,
    ord_date DATE NOT NULL,
    print_date DATE,
    inv_type CHAR(1) NOT NULL,
    revenue_type CHAR(1) NOT NULL,
    corp_cust_id INTEGER,
    prospno CHAR(10),
    mkt_segment CHAR(4) NOT NULL,
    sls_chanl CHAR(4) NOT NULL,
    bus_type CHAR(4) NOT NULL,
    gov_contract_num CHAR(20),
    cust_po_num CHAR(20),
    resale_id CHAR(26),
    cr_terms CHAR(2) NOT NULL,
    taxable CHAR(1),
    fobflag CHAR(1) NOT NULL,
    ship_via CHAR(3),
    sa_contact CHAR(8),
    slsrep2 CHAR(10),
    sort_code SMALLINT,
    dept_code SMALLINT,
    sls_terr CHAR(10),
    pool_of_funds INTEGER,
    auth_num INTEGER,
```

```
    rma_num CHAR(6),
    global_mkt_flag CHAR(1) NOT NULL,
    notecodes CHAR(10),
    cr_reason CHAR(4),
    ord_tot MONEY(16,2) NOT NULL,
    tax_chg MONEY(8,2) NOT NULL,
    ship_chg MONEY(8,2) NOT NULL,
    spcl_fee MONEY(8,2) NOT NULL,
    usr_name CHAR(8) NOT NULL,
    date_stamp DATE NOT NULL,
    time_stamp CHAR(8) NOT NULL,
    cr_subcode CHAR(1)
  );
CREATE INDEX ix_inv_mast01 ON inv_mast (inv_date);
CREATE INDEX ix_inv_mast02 ON inv_mast (ref_num);
CREATE INDEX ix_inv_mast03 ON inv_mast (ord_num,ord_rev);
CREATE INDEX ix_inv_mast04 ON inv_mast (print_date);
CREATE INDEX ix_inv_mast05 ON inv_mast (cust_po_num);
CREATE INDEX ix_inv_mast06 ON inv_mast (sls_terr);

CREATE TABLE inv_bill_mast
  (
    inv_num SERIAL PRIMARY KEY CONSTRAINT u_inv_blmast01,
    bill_cust_id INTEGER NOT NULL,
    bill_cust_rev SMALLINT NOT NULL,
    b_contact CHAR(35),
    b_title CHAR(20),
    b_company CHAR(45),
    b_addr1 CHAR(35),
    b_addr2 CHAR(35),
    b_addr3 CHAR(35),
    b_city CHAR(35),
    b_state CHAR(2),
    b_zip CHAR(10),
    b_country_code CHAR(3),
    b_int_prefix CHAR(7),
    b_phone CHAR(14),
    b_fax CHAR(14),
```

```
      b_notes VARCHAR(250,15)
  );
CREATE INDEX ix_inv_blmast01 ON inv_bill_mast
(bill_cust_id,bill_cust_rev);
CREATE INDEX ix_inv_blmast02 ON inv_bill_mast (b_contact,b_city);
CREATE INDEX ix_inv_blmast03 ON inv_bill_mast (b_company,b_city);
CREATE TABLE inv_ship_mast
  (
    inv_num SERIAL PRIMARY KEY CONSTRAINT u_inv_shmast01,
    ship_cust_id INTEGER NOT NULL,
    ship_cust_rev SMALLINT NOT NULL,
    s_contact CHAR(35),
    s_title CHAR(20),
    s_company CHAR(45),
    s_addr1 CHAR(35),
    s_addr2 CHAR(35),
    s_addr3 CHAR(35),
    s_city CHAR(35),
    s_state CHAR(2),
    s_zip CHAR(10),
    s_country_code CHAR(3),
    s_int_prefix CHAR(7),
    s_phone CHAR(14),
    s_fax CHAR(14),
    s_notes VARCHAR(250,15),
    s_county CHAR(15)
  );
CREATE INDEX ix_inv_shmast01 ON inv_ship_mast
(ship_cust_id,ship_cust_rev);
CREATE INDEX ix_inv_shmast02 ON inv_ship_mast (s_company,s_city);
CREATE INDEX ix_inv_shmast03 ON inv_ship_mast (s_contact,s_city);
```

Avoid the Use of Temporary Tables

A single SQL query with subqueries or joins might yield better performance than
selecting rows into a temporary table first, then joining or querying the temporary table.

```
SELECT char_code prod_code,
vcode1 prod_group
  FROM code_table
  WHERE virt_tabid = 21
  INTO TEMP prod_group_xref;
SELECT sale.prod_type,
        prod_group_xref.prod_group,
        year(sale.inv_date) sale_year,
        sum(sale.qty_shipped),
        sum(sale.item_tot)
  FROM sale,
        prod_group_xref
 WHERE sale.prod_code = prod_group_xref.prod_code
   AND sale.inv_date BETWEEN '07/01/1993' AND '07/31/1993'
   AND sale.revenue_type IN ( 'N','P','S' )
   AND sale.prod_type IN ( '022','024','042' )
   AND prod_group_xref.prod_group IN ( 'OL','SE' )
 GROUP BY 1,2,3
 ORDER BY prod_type, prod_group, sale_year;
```

> Following is the same query, without the use of a temporary table, which
> will probably run faster (depending on version, type, and configuration of engine
> used):

```
SELECT sale.prod_type,
        code_table.vcode1 prod_group,
        year(sale.inv_date) sale_year,
        sum(sale.qty_shipped),
        sum(sale.item_tot)
  FROM sale,
        code_table
 WHERE code_table.virt_tabid = 21
   AND sale.prod_code = code_table.char_code
   AND sale.inv_date BETWEEN '07/01/1993' AND '07/31/1993'
   AND sale.revenue_type IN ( 'N','P','S' )
   AND sale.prod_type IN ( '022','024','042' )
   AND code_table.vcode1 IN ( 'OL','SE' )
 GROUP BY 1,2,3
 ORDER BY prod_type, prod_group, sale_year;
```

A Reuse Example Using an INFORMIX-NewEra Class

The object-orientation of INFORMIX-NewEra makes it a natural language for reuse. The following shows a simple example of the redesign of an Exit Button class to ensure that exiting from the application is always handled in the same way. The class was designed to be used from the Window Painter: no visual attributes were changed, so a button can be pasted onto the window; then, an "**exitbtn**" can be typed into the "**classname**" property of the button:

exitbtn.4gh

```
INCLUDE SYSTEM "ixbutton.4gh"
CLASS exitButton DERIVED FROM ixButton
    FUNCTION exitButton  (
    container       ixVisualContainer           ,
    name            CHAR (*)          : NULL     ,
    enabled         BOOLEAN          : TRUE      ,
    shown           BOOLEAN          : TRUE      ,
    helpNum         INTEGER          : 0         ,
    geometry        ixGeometry       : NULL      ,
    appearance      ixAppearance     : NULL      ,
    tabIndex        SMALLINT         :
ixControl::defaultTabOrder,
    tabEnabled      BOOLEAN          : TRUE      ,
    title           CHAR(*)          : NULL      ,
    theDefault      BOOLEAN          : FALSE
  ) − constructor

END CLASS − exitButton
```

exitbtn.4gl

```
INCLUDE SYSTEM "ix4gl.4gh"
INCLUDE SYSTEM "ixbutton.4gh"
INCLUDE SYSTEM "ixwindow.4gh"


INCLUDE "exitbtn.4gh"


HANDLER exitButton::exitMsgBox() RETURNING VOID
    VARIABLE ok BOOLEAN
    VARIABLE p_quit SMALLINT
    VARIABLE thisWindow ixWindow = getWindow()
```

```
    LET p_quit = messagebox(title:NEW ixString("Exit Window"),
                               message:NEW ixString(
                                  "Do you really want to exit?"),
                               iconStyle:ixQueryIcon,
                                  buttonDefault:ixNoButton,
        IF ( p_quit = ixYesButton ) THEN
            LET ok = thisWindow.close()
        END IF


END HANDLER — exitButton::exitMsgBox


FUNCTION exitButton::exitButton (
                container       ixVisualContainer ,
                name            CHAR (*)           ,
                enabled         BOOLEAN            ,
                shown           BOOLEAN            ,
                helpNum         INTEGER            ,
                geometry        ixGeometry         ,
                appearance      ixAppearance       ,
                tabIndex        SMALLINT           ,
                tabEnabled      BOOLEAN            ,
                title           CHAR(*)            ,
                theDefault      BOOLEAN
           ) : ixButton (
                container       : container        ,
                name            : name             ,
                enabled         : enabled           ,
                shown           : shown             ,
                helpNum         : helpNum           ,
                geometry        : geometry          ,
                appearance      : appearance        ,
                tabIndex        : tabIndex          ,
                tabEnabled      : tabEnabled        ,
                title           : title             ,
                theDefault      : theDefault

           ) — constructor
        HANDLE SELF.activate WITH exitMsgBox
END FUNCTION — exitButton::exitButton
```

Conclusion

Good design leads to maintainable applications. Here are some guidelines:

- Establish a software process team to evolve standard practices that work towards improving software design.

- Improve the analysis process, as well as the design and implementation processes.

- Establish guidelines for coding.

- Separate database design from application design—apply quality controls to database schemas.

- Use reviews as checkpoints in the development process.

- Develop reusable modules and class libraries.

- Institute metrics to provide tangible measurements to help your team achieve its goals.

- Evaluate and implement tools, such as integrated CASE to support developers.

The following is a brief list of books on design:

Humphrey, Watts S. *Managing the Software Process.* Reading, MA: Addison Wesley Publishing, 1989.

Rumbaugh, James. *Object-Oriented Modeling and Design.* Englewood Cliffs, NJ: Prentice-Hall, 1991.

Yourdon, Edward. *The Decline and Fall of the American Programmer.* Englewood Cliffs, NJ: Prentice Hall, 1992.

Gause, Donald C. and Weinberg, Gerald M. *Exploring Requirements: Quality Before Design.* New York, NY: Dorset House Publishing, 1989.

About the Author

Matthew Eichler is a project manager in the Informix MIS Advanced Technology Group (ATG), Menlo Park, California.

Exploring the Functionality of INFORMIX-NewEra

by Lisa Braz and Carsten Schmitt

This article describes the design, features, and functionality available in release 3.0 of INFORMIX-NewEra. INFORMIX-NewEra provides a graphical development environment which can be used to quickly and easily create graphical database applications.

What Is INFORMIX-NewEra?

INFORMIX-NewEra consists of a suite of tools—the INFORMIX-NewEra development environment, language editor, debugger, class browser, and the Partition Wizard (for application partitioning). The INFORMIX-NewEra development environment is an easy-to-use environment for creating scalable, enterprisewide database management applications. It includes a graphical form painter and code generator (the Window Painter), an application development environment (the Application Builder), an object-oriented programming language, and a SuperView Editor. The SuperView Editor is used with the INFORMIX-NewEra development environment to create powerful data models. All of these tools are integrated into the INFORMIX-NewEra development environment.

Overview

This article introduces some key ideas about INFORMIX-NewEra and describes the types of applications you can create and the tasks you can perform by using INFORMIX-NewEra. For developers who work in graphical development environments, INFORMIX-NewEra provides all the necessary tools to create visual, enterprisewide, database management applications. INFORMIX-NewEra includes the Window Painter that generates INFORMIX-NewEra code automatically, the Application Builder for managing application files and supporting team development, and the powerful INFORMIX-NewEra programming language that allows for the customization of applications.

SuperView Editor

INFORMIX-NewEra includes a graphical SuperView Editor to build SuperView data models. A SuperView data model is a specialized view with a named set of relationships that models data in the database in a meaningful way. When used in conjunction with the Window Painter, SuperViews simplify the development and interface painting tasks.

The SuperView Editor can be used to perform other functions, such as to establish table relationships. SuperView data models specify the relationships between rows of data in the various tables that comprise the SuperView; create table and column aliases (unique table and column names); determine which columns to include, and the order in which they are to appear when building forms and reports; establish a default sort order for data; set input attributes and INCLUDE values; determine who can use the SuperView; and set locking modes and resource limits.

With display rules, SuperView data models can be used to control the appearance of data as printed or displayed on the screen. The elements that can be controlled include the font, style, case, size, color, alignment, and masks of displayed or printed data. When using SuperView-level display rules with INFORMIX-NewEra, select either pre-defined formats or define customized masks using INFORMIX-NewEra format strings.

A Graphical Window Painter

The windows, dialog boxes, and menus that comprise the visual interface of an application are created from the Window Painter. The Window Painter is a Multiple Document Interface (MDI) application. The Window Painter provides a canvas on which to paint the user interface to an application. Paint by using tools which are designed to implement the common components of a graphical user interface (GUI), such as radio buttons, text boxes, scroll lists, and so on. After painting the window, INFORMIX-NewEra generates the INFORMIX-NewEra code necessary to implement windows and dialog boxes.

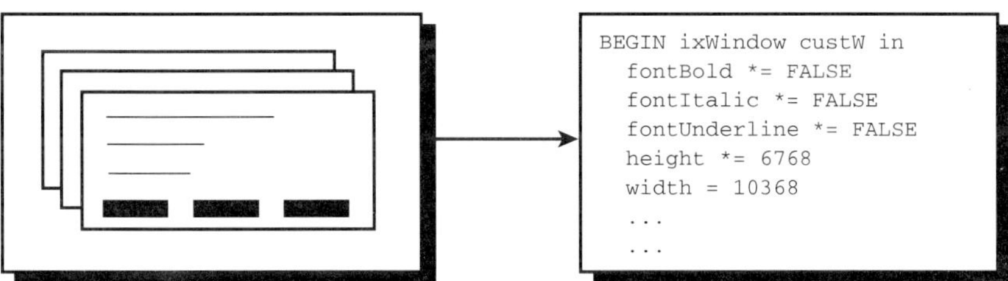

Figure 1: The Window Painter generates code.

An Application Builder

INFORMIX-NewEra helps to manage applications through the Application Builder. The programs which comprise an application can be grouped into a single project. These programs may contain INFORMIX-NewEra code generated by the Window Painter, INFORMIX-NewEra code that you have written, and C or C++ code. In addition, other third-party libraries or components can be included. The Application Builder can also compile, debug, and launch applications, although it is not necessary to perform these tasks in the Application Builder. The Application Builder also supports team development.

The Language of INFORMIX-NewEra

INFORMIX-NewEra is not only a development environment but also a powerful programming language that combines 4GL language with an object-oriented notation. The existing 4GL syntax can be used for program development, except for the user and screen statements (e.g., INPUT, DISPLAY, MENU, etc.) since the environment has changed from ASCII character terminals to a graphical user interface. Additionally, a complete OO-notation—which fullfills all criteria for successful OO development—extends the language. NewEra is based on classes which are used to instantiate objects. A set of standard classes is delivered with the development environment which can be extended by the developer. The class structure is oriented towards the theorems of Booch: it allows single inheritance, and the class members can be events (with handlers), constants, variables, or functions, whereby each member can be PUBLIC, PRIVATE, PROTECTED, or SHARED. Each class is defined in a header file (.4gh) and coded in a program file (.4gl). Following is an example of the class ixInteger:

```
CLASS ixInteger DERIVED FROM ixNumeric

PUBLIC VARIABLE value INTEGER


. . . .
PUBLIC FUNCTION isNull() RETURNING BOOLEAN
PUBLIC FUNCTION setNull() RETURNING VOID
FUNCTION ixInteger()


END CLASS
```

After instatiating an object of a class, class members can be used to manipulate the object. To access a member of a class, use the notation "class.member." Note the following example:

```
VARIABLE myInt ixInteger
LET myInt = NEW ixInteger()
IF (myInt.isNull()) THEN
     LET myInt.value=0
END IF
```

Within a class, members can be inherited from the parent class, overridden, or newly defined. This ensures the principles of encapsulation and polymorphism. The events declared for a class can be posted or called, and depending on this, return a value or do not return a value. The handler can be bound dynamically (at runtime) to its related event, which provides greater flexibility. Application partitioning can be accomplished easily through the Application Wizard, a component of the NewEra development environment.

The INFORMIX-NewEra Development Environment

INFORMIX-NewEra provides the environment and tools needed to develop graphical applications quickly and to manage applications. Use the following features to quickly create components of an application:

■   Use the SuperView Editor to establish a data model;

■   Use the Window Painter to create the application interface; and

■   Use the Application Builder to build, generate, and manage an application.

With INFORMIX-NewEra, it is possible to seamlessly integrate new portions as an application is extended.

Create SuperView Data Models

SuperView data models simplify the process of creating INFORMIX-NewEra applications by establishing views that capture the descriptions of database information and the relationships between them. Use the SuperView Editor to create the data models by following these steps:

1.   Select the tables to be included in the SuperView.
2.   Specify the relationships between rows of data in the various tables that comprise the SuperView.
3.   Specify the join columns between tables.
4.   Create aliases for tables and columns.
5.   Establish a default sort order.
6.   Modify the display rules.
7.   Set input attributes and INCLUDE values.
8.   Specify who can use the SuperView.

Paint the Graphical Interface of an Application

The INFORMIX-NewEra Window Painter can be used to easily design a database-oriented, graphical interface for an application. For example, instruct INFORMIX-NewEra to connect, query, update, and input to a database using point-and-click commands. After compiling the window, INFORMIX-NewEra code is generated.

Include a wide variety of window controls in an application, such as buttons, check boxes, edit boxes, scrolling lists, and menus. INFORMIX-NewEra also supports the OLE and OCX Microsoft standards.

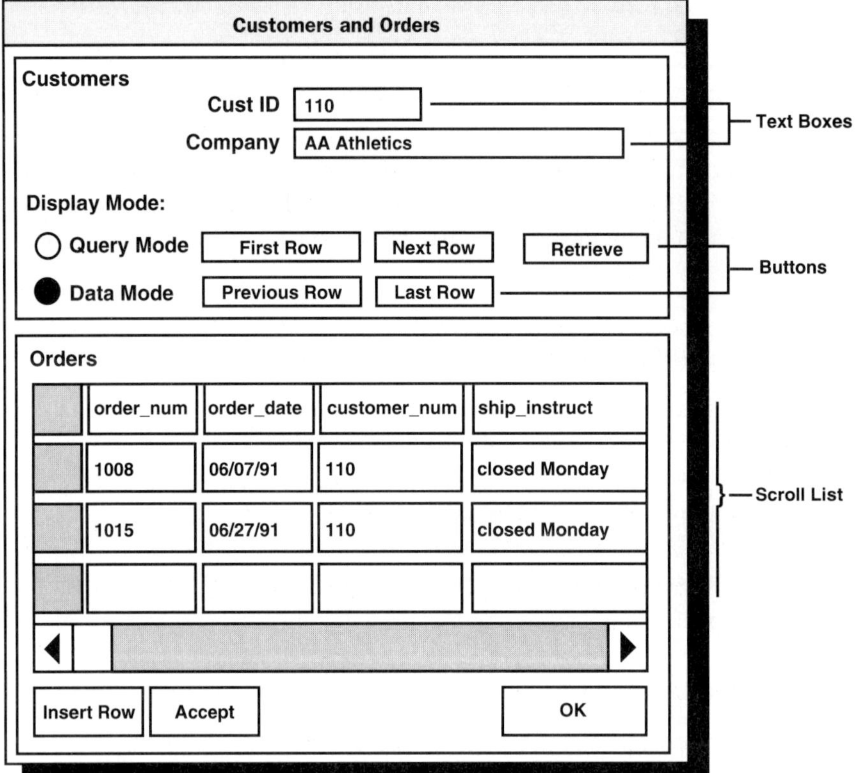

Figure 2: Adding controls to a window.

Develop User-Driven Applications

With INFORMIX-NewEra, end users determine how they want to use an application. The way an interface is painted, and the way that properties are set for the different parts of the interface, determines what happens when a user clicks a button or selects an item from a scrolling list. Following is the process for developing user-driven applications:

1. Paint the interface of an application in the Window Painter.

    Paint windows for the different parts of an application. A simple application may have only a few windows, whereas a large application can have hundreds of windows.

2. Specify the properties of the components painted in the window.

    The properties determine:

- The look of the components painted on the window.

- The way that the components can be edited by the user.

- The kind of validation which must be performed on any values specified by the user.

INFORMIX-NewEra provides default values for the properties; however, most developers will change some of the defaults. For example, the default properties of a button can be modified to include a descriptive title on the button.

3. Specify the behaviors of the components within the window.

For each component on the window, specify some code to be executed when the user interacts with the component (for example, when the user clicks a button).

4. Bring the parts of an application together in the Application Builder.

The Application Builder can be used to manage the files that comprise an application. From the Application Builder, generate, compile, debug, and execute program files.

5. Use the Debugger to quickly identify problems within code.

Use SuperTable to Interact with a Database

When painting windows, SuperTables can be used to easily retrieve, display, and edit data in a database. SuperTables obtain their data from the database schema or from SuperViews (which are created and managed with INFORMIX-NewEra). Figure 3 shows how SuperViews and SuperTables act as intermediaries between the database and user.

Two types of SuperTables are provided: grid form and free form. Use the grid form of the SuperTable when displaying multiple rows of data. The data appears in a table-like format, with rows and columns of data. Use the free form of the SuperTable when showing one row of data at a time. Free form SuperTables provide flexibility in the display of data; simply move the individual fields of the row (called SuperFields) anywhere in the window.

Figure 4 shows the two types of SuperTables.

Manage Multiple-Module Applications

The INFORMIX-NewEra Application Builder helps to manage large applications which are spread out over many files. In INFORMIX-NewEra, each application is considered a project. A project can consist of different components, whereby a conponent can be a program (consisting of multiple source files), or static and/or dynamic link libraries.

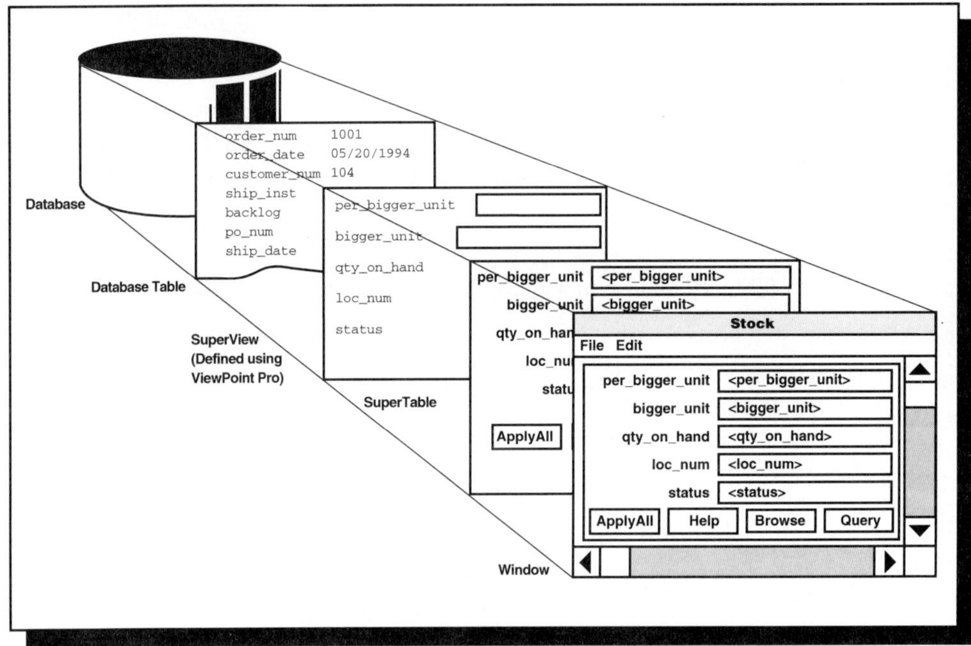

Figure 3: The SuperTable appears in the designed window.

A grid-form SuperTable can show multiple rows of data.

A free-form SuperTable shows only one row of data.

Figure 4: Grid form and free form SuperTables.

Using the Application Builder, specify a project. The Application Builder manages all the files pertaining to that project. The Application Builder provides an easy way to switch between projects when creating multiple applications. The repository used by the Application Builder supports private and shared workspaces which, in turn, enable team development.

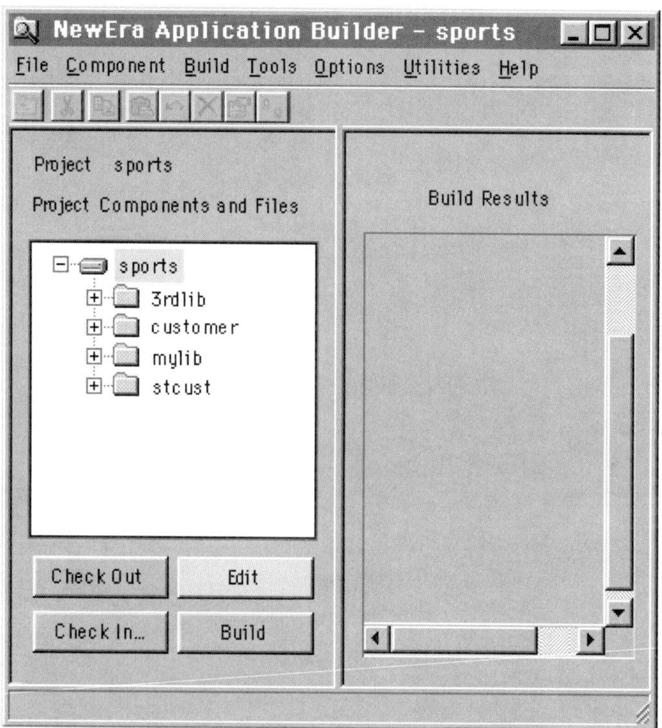

Figure 5: Use the Application Builder to manage application files.

Deploy Large Applications

INFORMIX-NewEra provides two compilers: one to compile C code, and another to compile either C++ or pseudo-machine code, called p-code. It is possible to switch between the compilers as necessary. The p-code compiler typically compiles and links faster than the C code compiler. Code generated by the C code compiler executes faster. Therefore, the p-code compiler should be used to create an application. After an application is complete, use the C code compiler so that the executable runs faster.

Application Partitioning

With application partitioning, an application can be divided into client and server partitions, whereby the client partition has a graphical user interface, and the server partition resides on a (bigger and faster) server and handles the business logic.

A good example where application partitioning can be used is in the generation of reports. To format a report, for example, the client must fetch data over the network from the server; however, this could slow the execution and the network. Therefore, it is more efficient to send the request to the server and continue to run the application while the report is generated on the server. Both client and server partitions are written in the NewEra language and are reusable, due to NewEra's class concept. The client resides on a Windows 95 or Windows NT machine, and the server resides on a Windows NT or a UNIX Motif workstation.

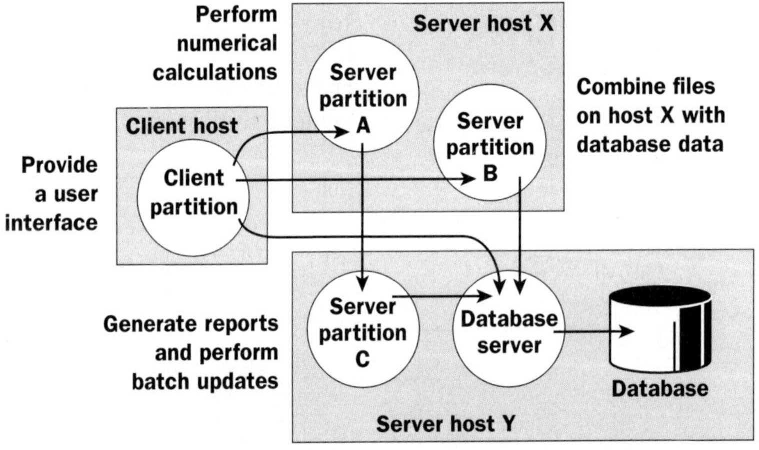

Figure 6: The Flexibility of Application Partitioning

Run Batch Programs

Run programs which do not require user input in batch mode. The program appears as an icon on the desktop while running. Programs to be run in batch mode include database update programs and reports. Note that for Windows clients, a workstation is busy while running batch jobs. Thus, it is preferable to schedule the running of batch programs during periods of low computer usage, such as overnight.

The INFORMIX-NewEra Architecture

INFORMIX-NewEra provides an architecture that allows developers to work smarter and faster. From allowing the creation of application modules in C or C^{++}, to allowing for the development of applications on different clients, INFORMIX-NewEra provides the flexibility and power to develop applications for an ever-changing business environment.

Develop Applications Quickly

The INFORMIX-NewEra development environment facilitates the development of a graphical database application. Several components of INFORMIX-NewEra improve productivity:

- The programming language fully supports object-oriented technology, allowing the reuse of code that is provided by Informix (the Standard Classes), as well as code created by developers;

- The Browser can be used to locate classes or to look up the details about classes, whether provided by NewEra third-party developers, or developers within your organization;

- SuperViews provide a high-level description of data that can be reused from application to application;

- SuperTables provide an easy, flexible way to view, input, and update data in a database;

- The Window Painter quickly paints an interface to an application rather than requiring the writing of the code that generates the interface; and

- The graphical development environment facilitates development work and project management work all within a single tool.

Create Scalable Applications

An application prototype can be created quickly by using the Window Painter. After achieving the look and structure for an application, expand or refine the application so that it meets all other business needs. If at a later time an application must be expanded to meet the needs of additional users, to run on different platforms, to perform more tasks, or to access different data, the application can be easily scaled to meet these additional requirements.

INFORMIX-NewEra is not a limiting factor in the growth potential of an application. With the design of INFORMIX-NewEra, it is possible to:

- Include as many modules as necessary in an application;

- Design and implement an application in a team environment;

- Acquire and release memory dynamically and automatically, thus allowing memory usage to be managed efficiently without error-prone manual programming; and

- Program in a number of languages other than INFORMIX-NewEra; for example, easily write some modules of an application in C or C++.

Prepare Portable Applications

INFORMIX-NewEra code will run on any future clients for which INFORMIX-NewEra is released. Any application developed in the Windows environment will deploy on a Motif client after simple recompilation. Note that you must use an Informix database while developing an application; when the application is deployed, however, it can access an ODBC-compliant database. Such open system techniques ensure that an application will be usable for years to come.

Extend Applications

By using the Standard Class Library provided with INFORMIX-NewEra, and any additional libraries purchased from other companies, the potential for an application is almost limitless. For example, the reuse of components from class libraries written by other companies allows developers to easily incorporate industry-specific or technology-specific functionality. Extend any class by creating derived classes, thus making the derived classes more specific for unique business requirements.

Work with SuperViews

The SuperViews created in the SuperView Editor can be used in INFORMIX-NewEra. A SuperView is a named set of relationships that models the data in a database in a meaningful way. For example, a SuperView might model a purchase order or a sales invoice by specifying the relationship between customers, orders, and invoice data in a database.

SuperViews allow a database administrator to specify the following for programmers in a group:

- Master/detail relationships;

- Format strings;

- Defaults; and

- Displayed titles for columns.

Harness the Power of Class Libraries

Informix provides over 40 classes which can be used within an application. These classes comprise the Standard Class Library. The Standard Class Library organizes these classes into five categories:

- VCL (Visual Class Library). These classes provide the graphical objects to create an interface to a program, such as buttons, menus, and check boxes.

- CCL (Connectivity Class Library). These classes provide the code necessary to access Informix databases, for example, to connect to a specific database on the server.

- FCL (File Class Library). These classes provide the code necessary to access non-database files. For example, use these classes to manipulate the message files.

- DCL (Data Class Library). These classes provide the means to manipulate program data. For example, use these classes to manipulate rows fetched from the database.

- ASCL (Application Server Class Library). These classes provide the means to communicate between a NewEra application on a Windows client host and another NewEra application on a UNIX or Windows NT host.

Create Additional Classes

By creating additional classes that are specific to an application, it is possible to build upon the classes provided by Informix. Create a class by building a derived class that is based on an existing class. The derived class inherits all the behavior of the base class; additionally, the derived class can be customized.

For example, Informix provides a base class for windows. By default, use this class when painting a window. However, a class can be derived which customizes the window in some way, perhaps by placing a company logo in a corner. Then, when a new window is created, use this class to include the logo on the window.

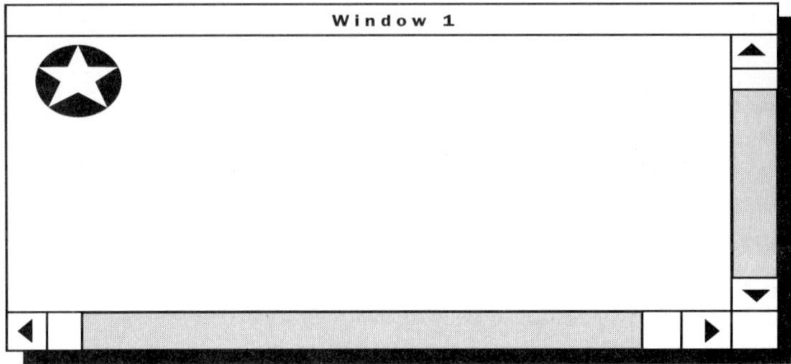

Figure 7: A logo appears automatically when using the derived class.

Access ODBC-Compliant Databases

INFORMIX-NewEra can be used to access data on Informix and non-Informix databases. INFORMIX-NewEra also allows you to run your application using databases that support ODBC by using the ODBC class library.

The Graphical Environment

INFORMIX-NewEra applications run in an end user's native environment. Users who are familiar with their environment are enabled to work quickly. The intuitive design of the graphical interface simplifies many of the common task that users perform, such as updating data in a database.

Easily Access and Manipulate Data in a Database

Several features of INFORMIX-NewEra allow end users to easily manipulate data in a database, for example:

■ End users can perform dynamic SQL queries, such as determining the database to access or the query to execute. They can even specify access to a non-Informix database as long as the application was designed to allow for this.

- End users can perform on-line transaction processing (OLTP) tasks, such as locking a row in a database table and quickly updating the information in the row.

- The graphical representation of a database (by way of a SuperTable based on a SuperView) helps users to manipulate data.

Use Context-Sensitive On-line Help

You can provide on-line help for each window of an INFORMIX-NewEra application. The end user displays the help message by pressing the designated Help key. The specified message for the window appears in a Help viewer. When planning to run an application in only the Windows environment, use the Windows help facility to prepare on-line help for end users.

Developers Who Are Currently Using INFORMIX-4GL

INFORMIX-NewEra is based on its predecessor, INFORMIX-4GL. INFORMIX-4GL code can be reused in INFORMIX-NewEra, with the exception of screen input or output statements, such as MENU and INPUT. When programming in INFORMIX-NewEra, developers will recognize many familiar 4GL statements, such as CASE and FUNCTION. INFORMIX-NewEra is an enhancement of the 4GL product with a more complete developer's environment, a graphical interface for end users, and the ability to use object-oriented technology and built-in class libraries.

Conclusion

The intent of this article has been to describe the design and features of release 3.0 of INFORMIX-NewEra.

About the Author

Lisa Braz is a writing manager at Informix, Palo Alto, California, and Carsten Schmitt is a senior Advanced Support engineer at Informix, Munich, Germany.

=30=

COMPARING AND CONTRASTING USER INTERACTION IN INFORMIX-4GL AND INFORMIX-NEWERA

by Jennifer Morgenthaler

Introduction

Most INFORMIX-4GL programmers are comfortable with the language of INFORMIX-4GL screen I/O. The MENU, DISPLAY FORM, INPUT, CONSTRUCT statements, and the rest of the INFORMIX-4GL I/O arsenal are familiar, straightforward elements of any screen-based INFORMIX-4GL application.

How does an INFORMIX-4GL programmer translate that knowledge into the graphical world through INFORMIX-NewEra? How do INFORMIX-NewEra graphical widgets compare in functionality and use to the old, familiar INFORMIX-4GL I/O statements? This article explores the topic of INFORMIX-4GL I/O versus INFORMIX-NewEra I/O, comparing and contrasting the INFORMIX-4GL legacy I/O statements with the INFORMIX-NewEra Visual Class Library (VCL).

General Differences

The key difference between I/O in INFORMIX-4GL (4GL) and INFORMIX-NewEra (NewEra) is that 4GL language is "procedural," compared to the "event-driven" nature of NewEra's architecture. In a procedural program, the programmer is in control. 4GL program flow begins at the top of the MAIN statement and continues through all function calls until it exits at the END MAIN statement. The end user can interact with the program only when the program is executing an I/O statement, such as MENU or INPUT.

In an event-driven program, however, the end user is in control. When an INFORMIX- NewEra program starts, visual widgets are displayed on the screen and program control is passed to the event loop. An incoming event, like a key press or mouse click, is dispatched to the appropriate event handler. Once the event handler code exits, control returns to the event loop. Therefore, only small snippets of code are executed at a time, and in an indeterminate order. The programmer cannot anticipate what will occur next, since it is entirely up to the end user.

Following is an example of the difference. An INFORMIX-4GL screen is presented to a user, with a menu and form displayed. The fields on the form are disabled until a menu command is selected, such as "Query." Programmatically, the MENU statement is in control, thus only the menu commands are "enabled." Once Query is selected, the code in the Query command clause executes, calling the CONSTRUCT statement. Once this CONSTRUCT statement takes control, the menu and any fields not in the CONSTRUCT field list are unavailable. When the CONSTRUCT statement exits, the menu is re-enabled, or the MENU statement also exits and the program continues to other tasks.

Recasting the above example into INFORMIX-NewEra, a window is presented to the user containing a menu, a SuperTable, and some buttons. All widgets are enabled, so the user can click in a field in the SuperTable and begin typing. What the SuperTable does with the data depends on what the user does next —click on the "Apply" button, or choose "Paste" off the menu, for example.

A second difference between INFORMIX-4GL and INFORMIX-NewEra is that INFORMIX-4GL provides functionality through statements, while INFORMIX-NewEra provides functionality through function calls. In addition, flexibility is also provided in INFORMIX-NewEra through event handlers which can be mapped to an event dynamically at runtime. This allows NewEra to be more flexible and extensible than 4GL, since changes to I/O behavior in 4GL require adding syntax to the language, whereas extending NewEra I/O means only adding a member variable or member function, or perhaps a new class, to the VCL. Furthermore, through subclassing, the programmer can accomplish this task.

There are also some differences between concepts which are directly mappable between INFORMIX-4GL and INFORMIX-NewEra. The windows, for example, operate somewhat differently between the two products. A 4GL programmer can only interact with a single window at a time. The INPUT statement, for example, addresses the current window, which is displayed on top of all other windows. The programmer can change the current window using the CURRENT WINDOW statement, but the end user can only interact with what the programmer selects as the current window.

In INFORMIX-NewEra, windows are real graphical objects which can be moved, resized, and selected independently. The programmer can address any window at a time, just by referencing it. In addition, the end user can interact with any window simply by clicking on the window or any element in it.

Database-Aware I/O Statements

The database-intensive functionality of the INPUT, INPUT ARRAY, and CON-STRUCT statements has been replaced by ixSuperTable and ixSuperField, two classes which are both visual and database-aware. In INFORMIX-4GL, the flow of data can be represented on the following page:

```
         SELECT                        DISPLAY
database ———> program variables ———-> screen


          INPUT                        INSERT
screen ———> program variables ———> database
```

In INFORMIX-NewEra, a SuperTable has its own internal storage, dynamically allocated, and its own display and entry fields in the form of SuperFields. Thus, the INFORMIX-NewEra flow of data is simpler:

```
         retrieve()
database ————-> supertable


         apply()
supertable ————> database
```

Freeform SuperTables replace the DISPLAY TO, INPUT, and CON-STRUCT statements, and gridform SuperTables replace the DISPLAY ARRAY and INPUT ARRAY statements. It is no longer neccessary to limit the number of rows displayed in a DISPLAY ARRAY statement, or buffer the rows, due to the static nature of INFORMIX-4GL arrays. SuperTables perform memory allocation dynamically with optional, configurable maximum rows.

Query-By-Example

INFORMIX-4GL supports query-by-example through the CONSTRUCT statement. The CONSTRUCT statement enables the fields in the field list in a special "query" mode, where datatype checking is relaxed to allow expressions like ">50" and picture strings, formats, include lists, and defaults are turned off. The user enters the query information and presses the ACCEPT key, and a fragment of a WHERE clause is generated.

In INFORMIX-NewEra, the end result is the same—a WHERE clause fragment is generated. However, the necessary steps are somewhat different. First, the SuperTable must be switched into "query" mode. This is accomplished by calling the setDisplayMode member function of ixSuperTable, and passing it the displayQuery flag. This relaxes the datatype checking, just as in INFORMIX-4GL, allowing the end user to type in the query information. There are two significant differences, however, in the support of query information entry.

INFORMIX-NewEra queries support wildcards for both the MATCHES and the LIKE clause. The user can type in either '*' or '?' to mean "match 0 or more characters." Additionally, the user can escape a wildcard character with "\." If the user is searching for anything containing the string "100%"—where the percent sign is part of the string and not a wildcard—he or she can type "100\%" in the field and the % will be treated as part of the search criteria.

In the first release of INFORMIX-NewEra, however, the WHERE clause fragment is generated with the LIKE keyword instead of MATCHES, allowing it to operate with non-Informix databases which support only the ANSI-standard keyword LIKE. In the first release, the "[]" set matching MATCHES is not supported in the default behavior, since the LIKE keyword is not aware of the [] set.

Help

INFORMIX-4GL supports help through help number attributes in most of the I/O statements, and through a HELP FILE and HELP KEY attributes set in the OPTIONS statement. When the user presses the help key in an I/O statement, the associated help number is referenced in the help file and its text is displayed on the screen.

In INFORMIX-NewEra, the help number attribute is a member variable of all visual objects. Thus, a button can have a help number, as can a SuperTable, menu, or window. The application itself also has a help number attribute. In addition, all visual objects have a displayHelp member function, which brings up the help viewer and displays the help text associated with that object. If the object doesn't have its help number set, the displayHelp function references the object's container, then the container's container, and so on, until a help number is found or the application is reached.

INFORMIX-NewEra supports both a 4GL-style help viewer, which uses Informix message files, and Windows help (through the Windows help system). The ixApp class has a member variable, helpStyle, which determines which viewer should be used, but the programmatic interface of help number, help file, and the displayHelp member function, is the same for both help styles.

There is no equivalent to the HELP KEY in INFORMIX-NewEra. The programmer must provide the interface to the help system, through a menu item, button, or keyPress event.

Functional Mappings

The following chart lists all the INFORMIX-4GL I/O statements and their INFORMIX-NewEra equivalents. For details on a class, member variable, or member function, see the Visual and Connectivity Class Reference. Of the INFORMIX-4GL statements discussed below, only DISPLAY remains in INFORMIX-NewEra. All other statements are no longer supported.

```
OPEN WINDOW NEW         ixWindow() + ixWindow::open()
CLEAR WINDOW            hide()
CURRENT WINDOW          no programmatic equivalent; programmer can access
                        all windows, and user can click on any window
CLOSE WINDOW            ixWindow::close()
```

```
OPEN FORM              ixWindow + other widgets (painted in Window Painter)
CLEAR FORM             no equivalent
CLOSE FORM             ixWindow::close()
```

```
CLEAR SCREEN           no equivalent
```

```
MENU                   ixMenu
COMMAND                ixMenu
KEY                    accelerator description; no direct equivalent
HELP                   helpNum statements activate handler
CONTINUE MENU RETURN    in the activate handler
EXIT MENU              no equivalent; procedural statement
NEXT OPTION            no equivalent; procedural statement
HIDE OPTION            disable()
```

DISPLAY TO fields	ixSuperTables; setCellValue()

DISPLAY ARRAY	ixSuperTables
ATTRIBUTE	setFont(), setColor()
ON KEY	cellKeyPress()
EXIT DISPLAY	no equivalent; procedural statement
INPUT	ixSuperTables; setDisplayMode(displayData)
CONSTRUCT	ixSuperTables; setDisplayMode(displayQuery)
BEFORE INPUT	no direct equivalent; could be beforeApply(), beforeRevert(), beforeRetrieve()
BEFORE FIELD	beforeCell(), beforeDataChanged(), or beforeQueryChanged()
AFTER FIELD	afterCell(), afterDataChanged(), or afterQueryChanged()
AFTER INPUT	no direct equivalent; could be afterApply(), afterRevert(), afterRetrieve()
ON KEY	cellKeyPress()
NEXT FIELD	focusCell()
CONTINUE INPUT	no equivalent; procedural statement
EXIT INPUT	no equivalent; procedural statement

INPUT ARRAY	ixSuperTables
BEFORE INPUT	no direct equivalent; could be beforeApply(), beforeRevert(), beforeRetrieve()
BEFORE ROW	
BEFORE FIELD	beforeCell(), beforeDataChanged(), or beforeQueryChanged()
AFTER FIELD	afterCell(), afterDataChange(), or afterQueryChanged()

AFTER ROW	
BEFORE INSERT	no direct equivalent; make calls before calling insert()
AFTER INSERT	no direct equivalent; make calls after calling insert()
BEFORE DELETE	no direct equivalent; make calls before calling delete()

AFTER DELETE	no direct equivalent; make calls after calling delete()
AFTER INPUT	no direct equivalent; could be afterApply(), afterRevert(), afterRetrieve()
ON KEY	cellKeyPress()
NEXT FIELD	focusCell()
CONTINUE INPUT	no equivalent; procedural statement
EXIT INPUT	no equivalent; procedural statement

CLEAR fields	ixSuperTables; setCellValue()
SCROLL	ixSuperTables; focusCell()
PROMPT	promptBox()
MESSAGE	messageBox()
ERROR	messageBox()
DISPLAY AT	ixLabel
DISPLAY DISPLAY	in separate Display Viewer modeless window

OPTIONS

MESSAGE LINE	no equivalent; message boxes are graphical windows
PROMPT LINE	no equivalent; prompt boxes are graphical windows
MENU LINE	no equivalent; menus are always at the top
COMMENT LINE	no equivalent; use modeless window with ixLabel
ERROR LINE	no equivalent; use messageBox()
FORM LINE	no equivalent; supertables are painted on the window
INPUT {WRAP|NOWRAP}	no equivalent; procedural statement
INSERT KEY	no equivalent; use buttons
DELETE KEY	no equivalent; use buttons
NEXT KEY	no equivalent; use buttons or scroll bar
PREVIOUS KEY	no equivalent; use buttons or scroll bar
ACCEPT KEY	no equivalent; use buttons
HELP KEY	no equivalent; use buttons, menu, or cellKeyPress()
HELP FILE	ixApp::helpFile
INPUT ATTRIBUTE	colors and fonts default through containership
DISPLAY ATTRIBUTE	colors and fonts default through containership
SQL INTERRUPT	ixSQLConnect supports SQL Cancel dialog box
FIELD ORDER	no equivalent; mouse means always unconstrained

Form Attributes

The following attributes are supported through member variables and member functions of the ixSuperField class.

```
AUTONEXT                autoNextOn, EVENT autoNext()
COLOR                   setColor(), setFont()
COMMENTS                use modeless window with ixLabel
DEFAULT                 setInitialDataValue(), setInitialQueryValue()
DISPLAY LIKE            supported through IDBA/Window Painter
DOWNSHIFT               setShiftPolicy( downShift )
FORMAT                  setFormat()
INCLUDE                 includeTable, useIncludes, EVENT includeFailed()
INVISIBLE               no equivalent
NOENTRY                 setDataState( readOnly )
PICTURE                 pictureString constructor parameter
PROGRAM                 blobEditor
REQUIRED                required, EVENT requiredFailed()
REVERSE                 setColor()
UPSHIFT                 setShiftPolicy( upShift )
VALIDATE LIKE           supported through IDBA/Window Painter
VERIFY                  verify, EVENT verifyFailed()
WORDWRAP                multiline fields are always wordwrapped
```

About the Author

Jennifer Morgenthaler is an R&D engineer at Informix, Palo Alto, California.

AN OVERVIEW OF THE VCL

by Eric McDermid

Introduction

This article is an introduction to INFORMIX-NewEra's Visual Class Library (VCL), which provides a core set of graphical components. From these components, modern and easy-to-use Graphical User Interfaces (GUIs) are built.

This article assumes no prior experience with GUI or object-oriented programming. It will be of special interest to developers migrating to INFORMIX-NewEra from INFORMIX-4GL, although such users should also refer to the article "Comparing and Contrasting User Interaction in INFORMIX-4GL and INFORMIX-NewEra," by Jennifer Morgenthaler.

Overview

INFORMIX-NewEra is generally backward-compatible with existing INFORMIX-4GL code, however, legacy INFORMIX-4GL user interface functionality was designed with character-based terminals in mind. While this functionality can be reproduced on GUI systems, it cannot take full advantage of the graphical platform. GUI platforms are based on a different set of assumptions, and require fundamentally different functionality.

INFORMIX-NewEra bundles this functionality into its Visual Class Library (VCL). The VCL provides a rich, extensible, and customizable set of components for developing platform-independent graphical database applications. Not only does the VCL provide standard GUI components such as text fields and push buttons, it also provides database-aware GUI components which can handle many common database functions, including QUERY and UPDATE, automatically.

The VCL Classes

The VCL classes are comprised of the following elements:

Windows

A window is the "canvas" on which the user interface is painted. An application might have many windows, each of which focus interaction on a particular task. Additionally, Windows supports many special behaviors. For instance, a "modal" window requires the user to complete one task before moving on to another. Alternately, "modeless" windows allow the user to move between tasks at will, or obtain more information about the task at hand. A user might increase the size of a window to obtain a larger workspace, or reduce the window to an icon to clear desktop space for another application. Windows are implemented by the ixWindow VCL class.

Frames

Frames are used to provide visual and logical groupings of other visual objects within a window. Frames can be used to point out important subtasks to the user, or as the basis for custom components to be used in applications throughout an enterprise. Frames are implemented by the ixFrame VCL class.

Labels

Labels are read-only text areas. They can be used as static labels to identify other components of the application interface, or to display dynamic information which the user cannot directly control. Labels are implemented by the ixLabel VCL class.

Lines and Boxes

Lines and boxes are typically used to add emphasis to other parts of a user interface. They are designed to make drawing simple. Lines and boxes are implemented by the ixLine and ixBox VCL classes, respectively.

Text Fields

Text fields are editable text areas, typically used to obtain textual input from the user. Textual input can be limited to a single line or to an arbitrary number of characters. Multi-line input is also allowed, in which case word-wrapping and scrollbars are handled automatically. Text fields are implemented by the ixTextBox VCL class.

Buttons

Buttons, as the name suggests, are much like their counterparts in the physical world. Users push buttons to make things happen. A button can be used to start a query, or to commit a set of changes. Buttons can identify themselves to the user by displaying either a text label or a graphical image. Buttons are implemented by the ixButton and ixPictureButton VCL classes.

Check Boxes

Check boxes are the GUI counterpart to toggle switches in the physical world. A check box can be either on (TRUE) or off (FALSE). Check boxes are often used to provide lists of options which the user can select, or to display the contents of a boolean variable. Check boxes are implemented by the ixCheckBox VCL class.

Radio Buttons

Radio buttons are much like check boxes, however, with one fundamental difference. Radio buttons are designed for lists of mutually exclusive options. Much like the car radio controls from which they take their name, only one radio button may be on (TRUE) at any given time. If the user "pushes" (turns on) one radio button, the previously selected radio button is automatically "unpushed" (turned off). Radio buttons are implemented by the ixRadioButton VCL class.

List Boxes

List boxes look much like text boxes, but are used to present lists to the user. Depending on the style of list box selected, the user might be allowed to select a single item, multiple items, or to specify a custom entry which isn't already in the list.

Additionally, list boxes can be configured to display all items at all times, or to save screen space by only displaying the current selection until the user asks for more selections. List boxes are implemented by the ixListBox and ixEditListBox VCL classes.

Menus

Dropdown menus are hallmarks of modern GUI interfaces, and are used to provide easy access to application functions without taking up a lot of screen space. Menus can be several levels deep, and can be associated with quick key combinations for users who cannot or do not wish to use a mouse. Menus are implemented by the ixMenu VCL class.

Database-Aware Components

One of the most distinguishing features of the VCL (and of INFORMIX-NewEra) is the amount of database functionality it provides automatically in database-aware components. Many common database application functions, which other programming tools (including INFORMIX-4GL) required the programmer to code by hand, are automatically provided by the VCL.

Additionally, the VCL allows programmers to override those built-in behaviors easily. Organizations with complex application logic or validation rules will find these features indispensable. Database-aware components are implemented by the ixSuperTable and ixSuperField VCL classes.

Since they are feature-rich, a separate article follows which discusses the ixSuperTable and ixSuperField components, entitled "An Overview of SuperTables."

OLE Controls

OLE sites and fields comply with Microsoft standards and enable the use of any OLE-enabled applications. DCX controls extend the functinality of INFORMIX-NewEra applications.

Conclusion

The INFORMIX-NewEra Visual Class Library (VCL) is both simple and powerful. It provides not only the fundamental building blocks of GUI applications, but also sophisticated data access components to make database applications easier to write and maintain.

Additionally, the VCL uses the backward compatibility of the INFORMIX-NewEra language to help preserve existing investments in INFORMIX-4GL. In most cases, existing application business logic can be preserved and presented to users in a more appealing and productive user interface.

Finally, the VCL offers room to grow, since developers can use VCL classes as foundations for their own customized user interface components. These new components can give corporate applications a common look and feel, make commonly needed functionality more maintainable, and offer less experienced developers an edge on the application logic which is central to the development organization. In addition, extensions to the VCL and other class libraries may even be marketable to other organizations with similar needs.

About the Author

Eric McDermid is a senior software development engineer at Informix, Palo Alto, California.

=32=

AN OVERVIEW OF SUPERTABLES

by Doug Fang

Introduction

SuperTables are database-aware Graphical User Interface (GUI) controls which are a part of the Visual Class Library (VCL) component of the INFORMIX-NewEra product. SuperTables are designed for the rapid development of database applications with intelligent default behaviors which can be easily extended and customized with application-specific business logic. This article will review the fundamental SuperTable concepts and briefly describe some of the key features.

Organization of SuperTables

SuperTables are composed of two kinds of VCL objects, ixSuperTable and ixSuperField. There is one ixSuperField object for each SuperTable column. SuperFields allow users to manipulate properties (e.g., foreground and background color) on a per column basis.

The ixSuperTable object can be thought of as a container for the ixSuperField objects. Properties affecting the SuperTable as a whole are manipulated through the ixSuperTable object.

In particular, the actual values for the rows retrieved from the database are associated with and manipulated through the ixSuperTable object. This set of rows, the dataSet, is populated when the user calls SuperTable's retrieve() method. The rows are individually stored as ixRow objects and the entire set of rows are manipulated through an ixRowArray object. SuperTables also contain another set of rows, the querySet, for storing the current QBE query. When the SuperTable's displayMode is displayData, the contents of the dataSet are visually displayed. Similarly, when the SuperTable's displayMode is displayQuery, the contents of the querySet are visually displayed. Alternating between modes is accomplished by calling the setDisplayMode() SuperTable method, either to displayQuery or displayData.

Visually, SuperTables can appear in two different forms: freeForm and gridForm. In freeForm, only one row is displayed at a time and each SuperField can be geometrically positioned independently in a window. In this form, SuperFields appear much like a TextBox. In gridForm, multiple rows are displayed at once in grid fashion.

SuperTable Features

SuperTables provide a number of powerful features which free the INFORMIX-NewEra programmer from re-coding the same functionality, as follows:

- Automatic data validation;

- Automatic built-in database behavior;

- Row-level locking;

- Retrieval, insert, update, and delete operations;

- Stale data check;

- Access to multiple heterogeneous databases; and

- SuperTables customizability.

Data Validation

SuperTables provide data validation at many different levels. At the cell level, each traversal between cells in a SuperTable triggers a Conversion check, a Verify check, and an Include check. In addition to this standard validation, the programmer can create validation checks through the before or afterDataChanged() events or the before or afterCell() events. At the row level, there is a Verify check and a dataRowCheck() event which is generated each time a row is modified. The NewEra programmer can choose to ignore, customize, or default each or all of these checks through event handlers.

Built-In Database Operations

SuperTables have methods to retrieve, insert, update, and delete rows from a database. But more interestingly, SuperTables support Optimistic and Pessimistic lock modes for maximizing concurrency. Pessimistic locking assumes that data is likely to become stale during edits, if not locked. A lock is placed on the current row as soon as it is modified and the row is applied to the database as soon as the user traverses to another row. Optimistic locking assumes that rows can be downloaded to a client and edited without much chance of their becoming stale during editing. When the editing of the rows in the dataSet is finally completed for each row, the apply() method locks the row (checking for stale data) and applies the change to the database. Whenever a row is locked, the current values of the row in the database are checked against their current values in the SuperTable and, if there is any inconsistency, the staleData event is raised.

Access to Multiple Heterogeneous Databases

SuperTables are implemented using the Connectivity Class Library (CCL) component of INFORMIX-NewEra. The two class implementations within the CCL allow Open Database Connectivity (ODBC) connections and native-Informix connections. The same INFORMIX-NewEra application written against an Informix engine will work against an ODBC-compliant dataSource with the same schema. In addition, multiple connections are supported within the same application. Hence, one SuperTable can retrieve or update data from one dataSource and another SuperTable can retrieve or update against an entirely different dataSource all within the same application.

Conclusion

INFORMIX-NewEra programmers can customize SuperTable behavior in three ways, depending on the degree of sophistication and customization needs. For simple customizations, all that the INFORMIX-NewEra programmer needs do is set the appropriate SuperTable properties in the form of constructor parameters or public member variables (e.g., no locking, pessimistic locking, or optimistic locking). For more advanced, finer grain customizations, the programmer can strategically select one or more of the rich set of SuperTables events and override their default behavior. Finally, the programmer can choose to create an individual subclass of SuperTable, and either override or add SuperTable methods and variables to the new subclass.

About the Author

Doug Fang is a new contributor to Tech Notes; he lives in San Francisco, California.